TRANSPORT POLICY
AND THE ENVIRONMENT

TRANSPORT POLICY AND THE ENVIRONMENT

Edited by David Banister

E & FN SPON
An imprint of Routledge
London and New York

First published 1998
by E & FN Spon, an imprint of Routledge
11 New Fetter Lane, London EC4P 4EE

Simultaneously published in the USA and Canada
by Routledge
29 West 35th Street, New York, NY 10001

Typeset in Times 10/12pt by
Cambrian Typesetters, Frimley, Surrey
Printed and bound in Great Britain by
TJ International, Padstow, Cornwall

This book was commissioned and edited by Alexandrine Press, Oxford

British Library Cataloguing in Publication Data
A catalogue record for this book is available
from the British Library

ISBN 0 419 23140 4

CONTENTS

THE CONTRIBUTORS

Melinda Accutt is a Lecturer in Department of Economics, University of Lancaster.

Margaret Anderson is Senior Lecturer in Environmental Planning at Wye College, University of London.

David Banister is Professor of Transport Planning, University College London. He was Director of the ESRC Transport and the Environment Programme.

Ian Black is a Senior Lecturer in the Centre for Logistics and Transportation, Cranfield University.

Lindsay Brook is Research Director at Social and Community Planning Research and Co-Director of SCPR's *British Social Attitudes* series.

James Cooper was Director of the Centre for Logistics and Transportation, Cranfield University. He died on the 7th August 1996 and this book is dedicated to him.

Carey Curtis is a Research Associate at the School of Planning, Oxford Brookes University.

John Dodgson is a Senior Consultant at National Economic Research Associates (NERA).

Tony Fowkes is a Senior Lecturer in Transport Economics at the University of Leeds.

Andrew Gillespie is a Professor at the Centre for Urban and Regional Development Studies, University of Newcastle upon Tyne.

Phil Goodwin is Professor of Transport Policy and Director of the ESRC Transport Studies Unit, University College London.

Wyn Grant is Professor of Politics at the University of Warwick.

Peter Headicar is Reader in Transport Planning at the School of Planning, Oxford Brookes University.

Patsy Healey is Professor of Planning at the Centre for Research on European Urban Environments, Department of Town and Country Planning, University of Newcastle upon Tyne.

John Henneberry is Senior Lecturer in the Department of Town and Regional Planning at the University of Sheffield.

Paul Lawless is Professor of Urban Policy at Sheffield Hallam University.

Alan McKinnon is Professor in the School of Management, Heriot-Watt University, Edinburgh.

Tony May is Professor of Transport Engineering at the University of Leeds.

Julia Meaton is Senior Lecturer in the Department of Geographical and Environmental Sciences, University of Huddersfield.

Chris Nash is Professor of Transport Economics at the University of Leeds.

John Peirson is Director of the Kent Energy Economics Group at the University of Kent.

Melvyn Peters is a Senior Lecturer in the Centre for Logistics and Transportation, Cranfield University.

Clive Potter is Lecturer in Environmental Management in the Environment Department at Wye College, University of London.

Phil Rees is Professor of Population Geography at the University of Leeds.

Kevin Robins is in the Centre for Urban and Regional Development Studies, University of Newcastle upon Tyne.

Alan Rogers is Senior Lecturer in Rural Planning at Wye College, University of London.

Yim Ling Siu graduated with distinction in Geography from the University of Leeds.

Robert Sugden is the Leverhulme Research Professor of Economics at the University of East Anglia.

Bridget Taylor is a Research Officer in the ESRC Centre for the Study of Elections and Social Trends at Nuffield College.

Riki Thérivel is a Sustainability Consultant with CAG Consultants. She is also a Visiting Professor at Oxford Brookes University, School of Planning.

Peter Townroe is Visiting Professor of Urban and Regional Studies at Sheffield Hallam University.

Roger Vickerman is Professor and Director of the Centre for European, Regional and Transport Economics, University of Kent.

ACKNOWLEDGEMENTS

The chapters in this book report on the research resulting from the UK Economic and Social Research Council's Transport and the Environment Research Programme (1992-1996). We would like to thank the ESRC for funding this research programme.

The views in each of the chapters reflect solely those of the authors.

The authors of the following chapters would like to acknowledge the input and assistance of other individuals, organizations and agencies:

Chapter 1: The work by Chris Newton on car ownership modelling and Richard Kneller on freight emissions modelling.

Chapter 3: Elizabeth Wilson, John Glasson, Bob Bixby and Donna Heaney for their assistance with the research project leading to the findings reported.

Chapter 4: Gordon Stokes for discussion on transport policy.

Chapter 6: Support from the Norwegian Road Administration, Luneburg City Council, Rees Jeffreys Road Fund, South Yorkshire Passenger Transport Executive, Department of Transport, Oxford City Council, Oxfordshire County Council, City of Oxford Motor Services, Thames Transit, York City Council, and the RAC Foundation for Motoring and the Environment. Feedback from the Standing Committee on Trunk Road Appraisal, the Royal Commission on Environmental Pollution, and the European Conference of Ministers of Transport.

Chapter 7: The research assistance of Philip Newman. The joint work of Michael Wegener and Klaus Spiekermann and for their permission to reproduce the maps in figures 7.6 and 7.7.

Chapter 8: David Maddison for valuable discussions on the external costs of transport, to Emile Quinet and Werner Rothengatter for comments on earlier versions of the chapter and to Alan Carruth and Andy Dickerson for helpful advice.

Chapter 12: Ranald Richardson, John Hentley and Jenny Grundy for contributions to the research on which this chapter is based, and to Andy Wanely, Malcolm Black, John Smith and Mrs Phill, of Burnside Community School, Wallsend, Kenton School, Gosforth High School and Heaton Manor School respectively for their help in administering the travel diaries.

Chapter 13: The Planning and Transport Officers of Ashford Borough Council, Ashford Chamber of Commerce and Industry, ProGraphics Design, Biddenden for their assistance.

Chapter 14: Ian Bateman, Alistair Munro, Bruce Rhodes, Chris Starmer and Kerry Turner for their collaboration in the research, and Daniel Kahneman, George Loewenstein, Graham Loomes and Richard Thaler for subsequent discussions.

Chapter 15: Support from the South Yorkshire Passenger Transport Executive and the Department of the Environment; the collaboration of Adax Antwi, Steve Crocker, Gordon Dabinett, Karl Dalgleish, Russ Haywood, Tony Gore, Andrea Kirkpatrick, and Geoff Vigar; and the advice received from Fred Robinson, Chris Law, Tom Worsley, and Phil Heywood.

Dedication

Jim Cooper died in August 1996. All the contributors to this book and fellow researchers in the Transport and the Environment programme would like to recognize Jim's many contributions to transport research, in particular the development of work on freight and logistics. We also remember him as a colleague and as an enthusiast for life. This book is dedicated to him.

INTRODUCTION:
TRANSPORT POLICY
AND THE ENVIRONMENT

David Banister

The transport sector (1996) is responsible for over 25 per cent of world primary energy use and 22 per cent of CO_2 emissions from fossil fuel use. It forms the most rapidly growing sector with energy use in 1996 at about 70 EJ (EJ = exajoule. Joule is a measure of energy [kg m^2 s^{-2}] and exa is 10^{18}). Without action, this figure will double to 140 EJ in 2025. Industrialized countries will contribute the majority of this figure until 2025. After that date, the majority of transport related emissions will come from those countries that are currently developing rapidly or that have economies in transition. Transport activity increases with rising economic activity, disposable income, access to motorized transport, and falling real vehicle and fuel costs. All these determinants of travel have been favourable over the last twenty years, hence the huge increase in travel, particularly by road and more recently by air.

Projections of transport greenhouse gas emissions follow the historic trends as CO_2 emissions are directly related to energy use in the transport sector. The assumptions made are that the relationships between transport fuel consumption and variables such as gross domestic product (GDP), fuel prices and vehicle energy efficiency will remain stable, at least until 2025 (Grübler et al., 1993). International comparisons reveal a strong correlation between transport energy use and GDP (GDP elasticity of 0.89 and $R^2 = 0.93$) (Blevis et al., 1996). But this relationship can vary by a factor of two at any given level of GDP. The growth of transport with income and time is faster for middle income countries than for very low income countries. By 2020 it is likely that if current GDP growth trends continue and the relationship with transport is stable, developing countries will have a third of the worlds car fleet, as compared with the current level of 14 per cent (Button and Ngoe, 1992). More recent research (e.g. Acutt and Dodgson, 1998) suggests that the relationship between energy use and economic factors is not stable and that car ownership and use may saturate at lower per capita levels than those found in the USA and Canada. In addition, technological innovation may result in greater levels of mobility being achieved with lower levels of energy input. There are also strong political and economic arguments for breaking the historic links between transport demand, energy use and economic factors as has happened in the energy sector (Banister, 1996; Peake, 1994).

However, transport also plays a crucial role in industrial and commercial organization, in the economic prosperity of countries and regions, and in allowing people to develop their own lifestyles. For many people, the availability of high quality transport allows them to improve their economic situation and quality of life. For others, the lack of transport or an inability to use it remains a constraint on their activities. Transport also allows firms to compete in national and international markets. Although transport is not a major component of total production costs (in most industries), it is sufficient to influence the competitive position of different producers. It also allows flexibility in production and distribution and, in conjunction with new logistics, has permitted the supply chains of firms to be reorganized more efficiently. Some would go further and suggest that transport is no longer the servant of mankind, but its master as it has shaped modern society (Tengström, 1992). Despite the many advantages brought about by the car and other transport, there are also serious negative consequences for society as a whole (table I.1).

In this introductory chapter we present some of the major environmental costs of transport, together with a commentary on the major debates. It is intended that the chapter acts as both the context and an appetiser to the fifteen chapters which follow. It is the only contribution to this book which is not based on substantive research results, as it is the review. The perspective taken is deliberately wide-ranging with the intention to make the reader think about the implications of transport on the environment and the role that policy should take in ameliorating these impacts.

THE ENVIRONMENTAL COSTS OF TRANSPORT

The interpretation of the environmental costs of transport taken in this book is a broad one (table I.1), but it can been grouped under four main headings – pollution, resources, environment and development. Decisions taken to improve benefits along one dimension may be likely to increase costs along another dimension or in another sector. The complexity of decision making in environmental policy cannot be underestimated, but difficult choices must now be faced by all governments. More detailed discussions on the elements of the environment, the role of transport, and policy measures can be found in Banister and Button (1993), Maddison *et al.* (1996) and Whitelegg (1993). In this section we summarise the main contributors to the environmental costs of transport, together with the scale and nature of that contribution (table I.1).

Table I.1. The environmental costs of transport.

1. POLLUTANTS	*Transport's Share*	*Impact*
Carbon dioxide	22%	Global warming
Nitrogen oxides	60%	Acid rain
Sulphur dioxide	4%	Acid rain, bronchitis
Carbon monoxide	80–90%	Morbidity, fertility
Benzene	80%	Carcinogenic
Lead	50%	Mental development
Hydrocarbons	50%	Toxic trace substances
Particulates	27%	Inflammation, cardiovascular Diseases
2. RESOURCES	*Consumption*	
Oil	54%	Depletion of natural resources
Land take		4.2 ha of land per km of 3-lane motorway – the road system uses 1.3% of the total EU land area
Ecology		Landscape and SSSIs destroyed
Ecosystems		Water quality, flood hazards, river systems modified
Accidents	In UK: 3900 deaths 45000 serious injuries	Pain, suffering, grief
3. ENVIRONMENT		
Noise		Stress, concentration, health
Vibration		Historic buildings
Community severance		Dividing communities
Visual impact and aesthetics		Changes in physical appearance
Conservation and townscape		Preservation
4. DEVELOPMENT		
Regional development		Location of industry
Local economic impacts		Income levels, employment, social impact
Congestion		Delay, use of resources
Urban sprawl		Traffic generation, induced development
Construction effects		Blight, property prices, compensation

Source: Based on Banister (1993) and Whitelegg (1993)

Pollution

• *Carbon Dioxide* is emitted from the combustion of fossil fuels and it is a major contributing factor to the increased greenhouse effect and global warming. High levels of CO_2 in the atmosphere will allow the retention of heat by the earth, and this in turn will raise average temperatures by up to 2°C in 2025.

Transport's contribution to the burning of fossil fuel is about 22 per cent and increasing. The amount of CO_2 emitted is directly related to energy use – at present there is no technological solution. The only way to reduce CO_2 emissions is to use less fuel or to switch to renewable energy sources. The second problem is that to achieve stabilization targets on a global level, the developed countries must make a substantial cut in their levels of emissions so that the developing countries can raise their levels.

• *Nitrogen Oxide* emissions when combined with other air pollutants can lead to respiratory difficulties and reduced lung function, particularly in urban areas. Volatile organic compounds and NO_x are the principal precursors of ground level ozone formation, the major constituent of smog. It is formed in the lower atmosphere by a photochemical reaction promoted by heat and sunlight. It also causes damage to crops and trees, leading to annual crop losses of several billion dollars in the US alone (USEPA, 1994). At the transboundary level, NO_x emissions converted to nitric acid and combined with SO_2 forms acid rain which has a severe impact on lakes, soils and forests. Transport accounts for about half the NO_x emissions and its share is rising as stationary sources produce less pollution.

• *Sulphur Dioxide* causes respiratory illness, in particular bronchitis, and as noted above is a contributor to acid rain. Transport contributes about 5 per cent of total SO_2 emissions, but in some countries this figure is much higher (up to 17 per cent) where diesel fuel is mainly used.

• *Carbon Monoxide* is an odourless and almost colourless gas, but is very toxic as it interferes with the absorption of oxygen. This in turn leads to increased morbidity and can affect fertility and general levels of health. It is particularly dangerous in urban areas where 'cocktails' of pollutants result in photochemical smog and surface ozone. Most of the CO comes for the transport sector, principally from the incomplete combustion of fuel.

• *Benzene* is a volatile organic compound, which is classified as a 'probable' carcinogen and may cause leukaemia in those with high levels of exposure.

• *Lead* has a long history of association with human health, particularly with the development of children but also with adult male hypertension and heart attacks. Road transport emissions have fallen substantially over the last ten years with the widespread introduction of lead-free petrol. In the USA, lead additives in fuel have been eliminated (US Department of Transportation, Bureau of Transportation Statistics, 1996). In many cases drivers feel that they are not contributing to environmental pollution because they use lead-free petrol. As can be seen here, the truth is very different.

• *Hydrocarbons* result from the incomplete combustion of fossil fuels and may again contribute to a variety of complaints including lung disease and irritation to eyes and throat.

- *Particulates*, particularly those very small particles under 10 microns diameter (PM_{10}) from diesel, are the focus of current concern. It has been estimated that up to 10,000 people die prematurely from PM_{10} emissions in the UK alone if results from six US cities are extrapolated to the UK (Bown, 1994). It should also be noted that transport is not the only source of pollution from PM_{10} and that the level of detailed knowledge of the science of particulates is not well known, but it does contribute to smog.

Resources

- *Oil* is the essential input to much of transport. In 1992 the UK transport sector used more than 43 million tonnes of petroleum products, 54 per cent of the UK total. This level has risen in both absolute and relative terms over the last thirty years. In the OECD countries, road transport in 1987 used 682 million tonnes of oil equivalent (47 per cent of the total). This level has risen from 446 million tonnes of oil equivalent in 1970 (+53 per cent).

- *Land Take*. Transport infrastructure occupies substantial areas of land – about 20% of the surface of urban areas in the UK and this increases in low density cities which are dependent on the car. In addition to the transport routes, substantial requirements are also needed for car parking and for terminals or interchanges. The total area occupied by Heathrow, Gatwick and Stansted airports is about 3000 ha, equivalent to the area occupied by 720 km of 3 lane motorway (RCEP, 1994). In the USA, public roads occupy 25,000 square miles of land, an area equal to the size of West Virginia. This figure increases to 29,000 square miles if off street parking, garages and driveways are included (DeLucchi *et al.*, 1994).

- *Ecology*. Road traffic is responsible for the majority of wildlife causalities caused by transport, and new roads disrupt natural habitats. A number of road schemes have affected sites of special scientific interest (SSSIs) which cover 8 per cent of the UK. National parks and areas of outstanding natural beauty (AONB) cover some 20 per cent of the UK and these are under increasing pressure for development with associated transport infrastructure. Solid waste from transport results from the disposal of vehicles and tyres, together with materials from construction. Although about three quarters of each car (by weight) is recycled (Holt, 1993), about 3.5 million tonnes from scrapped cars end up in landfill sites in the US (1994).

- *Ecosystems*. The economic and cultural value of biodiversity has been agreed at the 1992 Rio Summit, but roads and other transport infrastructures affect habitats and species. In addition, water and river systems can be affected so that there are impacts on quality of water. Arguments are taking place about whether habitat should be seen as unique or whether the developer should be required to recreate a new area of habitat of comparable size and containing a sufficient diversity of species. But slight changes in the local habitat can result in the migration or loss of species.

• *Accidents*. Transport is an inherently dangerous activity and nearly 40 per cent of the accidental deaths in Britain were transport related – in 1993 there were 3,820 people killed in road accidents and a further 45,000 serious injuries. Despite these figures, the trends are downwards with deaths from road accidents halving over the last thirty years. The overall figures in the UK are better than those in Europe, but comparisons are less favourable in the case of pedestrian deaths, particularly among children. Many countries (including the UK) have introduced targets to reduce deaths and injuries from road accidents to two thirds of the 1981–85 level by 2000.

Environment

• *Noise* is often cited as a nuisance in urban areas, but it is the peak or unexpected noise that creates problems. The OECD (1991) estimate that about 130 million people in OECD countries are exposed to unacceptable noise levels over 65dB(A) and 400 million are exposed to levels over 55 dB(A). Not all noise is transport related, but transport has been a major contributor to the growth. In some 'quiet' countries (e.g. parts of Scandinavia) only 5 per cent of residents are exposed, whilst up to 30 per cent of residents are exposed in 'noisy' countries. Prolonged exposure to noise can result in anxiety, depression and insomnia.

• *Vibration* is caused by all moving vehicles and road freight vehicles pose a particular problem in historic urban areas. It has health effects on those living adjacent to roads through sleep disruption and increased levels of stress and anxiety.

• *Community Severance* divides and causes the fragmentation of communities. Transport infrastructure, particularly in urban areas, is a major cause of severance and social division. It adversely affects the quality of life, activities on the street and the amount of social interaction within communities.

• *Visual Impact and Aesthetics*. These problems stem both from the infrastructure and the vehicles using it. Visual intrusion relates to the blocking out of light or view by transport, while aesthetics are concerned about the actual design of the transport facilities. Both concepts embrace the entire life-cycle concept and should cover new, existing and redundant facilities.

• *Conservation and Townscape*. Many roads and other transport routes pass close to historic and other buildings. Carbon and other particulate material soils buildings and can damage their fabric, especially if acid particles are deposited.

Development

• *Regional Development* objectives need to be balanced against economic and environmental priorities. The location of industry, new housing and other facilities are all transport dependent. Much of the justification for infrastructure investment has not only been to maximize economic growth, but also to enhance regional competitiveness. Yet the environmental costs of this location strategy do not seem to form even a minimal part of the decision.

• *Local Economic Impacts* are also important as access to jobs and employment means that income levels can be maintained or increased, and this in turn strengthens the social cohesion. The social impacts of infrastructure, together with its effect on labour markets are important determinants at the local level of social and economic well-being. However, there are also environmental costs which need to be included in those decisions.

• *Congestion* is an issue that is extending beyond just the traditional urban area to all types of transport, particularly where there is a terminal or interchange. Strictly speaking, even though traffic congestion is an externality in an economic sense, it really involves a lack of internal efficiency in the operation of transport systems. Congestion results in the loss of time and in environmental costs caused by increased pollution, noise and fuel use. Under congested conditions, the average private cost paid by the driver for the last kilometre is less than the marginal social cost imposed on other road users.

• *Urban Sprawl* has resulted from good quality transport infrastructure and cheap transport. Transport has been seen as a principal permissive factor in the development of suburban housing and in redirecting development pressures away from the city centre. Edge city developments and the growth of retail, business and leisure centres at motorway intersections and along bypasses, all bear witness to the powerful effect that transport can have on location decisions.

• *Construction Effects* are both immediate and longer term. Construction creates a substantial demand for materials and for the transport of waste. It also affects properties through blighting and creates difficulties in selling or moving as routes are often safeguarded for a substantial time prior to actual construction. Compensation for blighting and loss of quality is often not seen as sufficient by the recipient.

One current issue is whether the market can or should assign monetary values to these environmental costs. These costs are external to the price paid and are generally referred to as externalities as they are imposed upon society as a whole. The argument used by economists is that if these costs are not paid by the user, then there is little incentive to make efficient decisions (Maddison *et al.*, 1996). Those choices which entail a high environmental cost should be priced much higher than those that have a lower environmental cost.

Table I.2. Estimates of the External Costs of Transport in OECD Countries.

Cost Item	Road	Other Modes	All Transport
Noise	0.10	0.01	0.3
Local pollution	0.40		0.4
Global pollution			1.0–10.0
Accidents	2.00		1.5–2.0
Travel time	6.80	0.07	8.5

Based on Button (1990) and Quinet (1994)
Notes: The total pollution range depends on the assumed damage costs associated with global climate change. Figures are given as a percentage of GNP.

These costs are substantial. National estimates of the external costs of transport-related activities have been estimated for OECD countries (table I.2) in the range 0.3–1.0 % of GDP or 4.78 pence per vehicle kilometre for the costs of air pollution under urban driving conditions (1993).

ENVIRONMENTAL POLICY IN TRANSPORT

Many of the environmental costs of transport are non-linear in their effects (e.g. health effects and congestion), and the crucial issue becomes, not how to measure but how to avoid reaching critical levels where the environmental costs become too high (e.g. lethal doses of pollution and gridlock). The measurement difficulties are substantial and placing values (or money costs) on environmental factors tends to be subjective (Button, 1994).

The challenge for environmental policy in transport is to improve as many elements of this complex interrelated list of environmental costs (table I.1) without increasing those elsewhere, or at least being aware of them and making an informed choice. It should also be remembered that transport is only one (albeit important) part of the economy and so the environmental choices in the transport sector need to be balanced against other priorities. In addition, many of the issues listed here are not national (e.g. NO_x emissions). They relate to the global use of resources and the effects are manifest in other countries.

To achieve sustainable development at least five different sets of objectives need to be addressed. The main concern here has been with the *environmental objectives*. The second objective of sustainable development is to maintain competitiveness through *economic growth and development objectives*. Where possible, the environmental and development objectives should be working in the same direction – this is the 'win-win' situation, and many transport investment decisions have tried to achieve these benefits. For example, bypass schemes have been justified both on the economic benefits from reduced travel times and opening up new areas for development. They may also bring environmental benefits to town centres, but may damage ecosystems and consume open space along the new route. The debate must be over whether the economic benefits are outweighed by the net environmental costs or whether there are both economic and environmental benefits. In addition to these two fundamental objectives, the concerns over sustainability open up three new objectives. The *equity objectives* are concerned about the distribution of costs and benefits with society, both socially and spatially. These intragenerational effects are contrasted with the *intergenerational objectives* (futurity), highlighted by the most often quoted definition of sustainable development, namely 'development that meets the needs of the present without compromising the ability of future generations to meet their own needs' (WCED, 1987). The final objective is *participation* in its widest form. Too often in the past, decisions have been made without the support of the affected parties. To achieve the objectives stated for sustainable development, we have to carry out our daily activities in different ways, using resources more efficiently. Similarly, industry and the new post-industrial economy needs to be more sustainable in its activities. This requires clear policy directions through pricing, regulation and control, but the scale of change necessary to achieve sustainability objectives also requires political support from all affected parties. Unless this support is forthcoming, little progress will be made.

Underlying much of the debate over the environment and sustainability is the crucial link between the environment and competitiveness. Much of the literature talks about the balance between these two dimensions. We would argue that the most productive way actually to achieve sustainability objectives is through these two dimensions operating in the same direction – the 'win-win' situation. Porter and Linde (1995) have argued that the 'struggle between ecology and the economy grows out of a static view of environmental regulation, in which technology, products, processes and customer needs are all fixed' (p. 97). In the static world, firms have made cost minimizing choices. Environmental regulation raises costs and reduces market share of domestic companies on global markets. They go on to develop a dynamic paradigm, based on innovation and the capacity to improve competitiveness through shifting the constraints. Properly designed environmental standards can trigger innovation, which may more than offset the costs of compliance. We would go further and suggest that environmental incentives should be used to promote greater efficiency and innovation. A positive promotion of environmental incentives is one way to achieve sustainability objectives and gain public support through the demonstration effects of policy actions.

Transport policy makers have always accepted that transport imposes environmental costs. However the scale of the problem is now much greater, both in terms of the scale of the problem and its nature. There is much more transport today than there has been in the past and that trend is likely to increase, particularly with the emerging economies of Central and Eastern Europe and those of the Pacific Rim. In the longer term the greatest growth is likely to be in China and India. In addition, the rapid growth in air transport has added a further new element of travel. But it is the continuous growth in car ownership and use which forms the most important factor in assessing the environmental costs of transport. It is clear that the simple growth in transport poses environmental degradation, but there are also substantial qualitative factors (table I.1). For many years transport policy has been primarily concerned with the local problems of transport, principally congestion, accidents and noise. The debate in the last twenty years has become more sophisticated and complex as the broader impacts of transport have embraced both the global and the international effects.

Concern over the damaging effects of 'acid rain' on forests and water life grew in the 1970s and 1980s. The importance of NO_x and other gaseous emissions from cars was recognized as a major contributing factor. Concern also emerged in the 1980s over high level ozone depletion and its impact on the long-term incidence of skin cancer. Transport's role was relatively small, as it was confined to CFCs in air conditioning units. In the 1990s global warming has become the key issue with its impact on raising average temperatures and the consequences for climate change and sea level rises. The new agenda requires the collective action of national governments and international agencies in limiting the growth of CO_2 emissions.

The scientific evidence is powerful, but the essential catalyst for change has been public concern over environmental issues. In part, this interest is a reflection of increased affluence and being able to afford to take action on environmental issues. More fundamentally, there is a growing concern over the long term future of the planet and a commitment to sustainability. Transport has become one of the key elements in that debate, and one that is beginning to attract a disproportionate amount of attention. Transport contributes at all levels to the environmental degradation (local, global and transboundary), it has a high profile, it is perceived as being a major intruder, and it also interacts with other activities which can be seen as being environmentally harmful (e.g. tourism).

Transport is also seen as an area where governments can and have intervened through fiscal measures, regulation and the planning system. The EU has now taken a strong lead arguing that the price of transport, particularly road transport, should be substantially raised (CEC, 1996). EU intervention is justified on four criteria: cross-border externalities, the effects on the Internal Market, the possibilities of economies of scale (through joint research and EU standards), and policy spill-overs. The EU is proposing that common rules are introduced for annual road taxes, duties on fuel, user charges in road haulage, emission levels, add on technologies and other measures that can and should be introduced on a Europe-wide basis. They have taken the bold step to promote fair and efficient pricing across all modes of transport, but initially concentrating on road transport.

However, the fundamental role that transport plays in modern societies and economies is clearly recognized, and the dilemmas, choices and inconsistencies in many policy actions are also recognized. Many of the environmental costs imposed by transport are the consequences of policy decisions made for other reasons (e.g. regional development). Action to improve the environmental quality should also rest with governments, but governments will only act if there is a direct benefit and/or if there is sufficient public support and/or if there is some international agreement. This is the irony of the debate. It is reflected in the inconsistencies in peoples actions, and the inability of governments to take effective action.

People are aware of the environmental costs of transport and are supportive of actions by governments to improve environmental quality, provided that it results in no change in their lifestyles and they can continue their use of the car, and provided that it costs no more. This is a problem with no solution. It accounts for the general resistance against higher prices in transport so that some of the environmental externalities can be internalized (Johansson, 1987). It accounts for the belief that technological solutions will solve the problem through more efficient engines, alternative fuels (e.g. electricity or hydrogen) and add on technologies (e.g. catalytic converters). It accounts for the focus on positive planning policies to reduce journey lengths through higher densities and concentration of development in larger settlements. It accounts for the use of public awareness campaigns and raising the social consciousness to gain public support for actions that are often politically unpopular. In short, even if we could establish clear links between health quality and amount of motorized travel, this might not be a necessary condition to change radically policy direction. There will always be strong reasons to continue to keep the external costs of transport as externalities and resist the strong environmental case for internalizing them.

Environmental policy and transport must look to solutions which both allow movement and reduce the external costs of that movement. Decisions have been taken by both firms and households which have resulted in an increased dependence on the car and high levels of mobility, often at a relatively low price. Many people in developing countries aspire to similar levels of mobility and car ownership. These patterns of activity, and the distribution of facilities and land use patterns all mean that change is not easy. In addition, many trends in transport energy intensity are deteriorating, and this again results in additional environmental costs.

• As car ownership levels rise, car occupancy levels fall. This means that energy intensity of travel increases.

• As car ownership rises, the use of bicycles, motorcycles and public transport falls. This again means increased energy intensity.

• High income countries tend to have more efficient cars, but auxiliary equipment (particularly air conditioning) tends to reduce those gains.

• Similarly, higher safety standards mean that vehicles are heavier and use more fuel

• Many test cycles do not include cold starts, which can result in excess fuel consumption as high as 50 per cent (Hausberger *et al.*, 1994). Catalytic converters do not work when engines are at low temperatures.

• Poor road quality may also increase fuel consumption, estimated at 50 per cent in Russia (Marchenko, 1993).

• Many developing countries make extensive use of 'light trucks' (including minibuses), which have higher fuel consumption (+36 per cent) than cars (Greene and Duleep, 1993). Ironically, many high income households are now also buying 'off road vehicles' as second cars and 'person carriers' with high fuel consumption figures.

• Journey lengths have increased substantially as patterns of travel have become more car dependent. This again has contributed to increased levels of fuel consumption.

• Similar trends can be observed in the freight sector with the increased role of road freight, larger vehicles, longer distances and a general increase in transport intensity. This reflects the radical changes which have taken place in the structure of production with new supply chains and extensive use of logistics systems to reduce costs.

The signs are all in the wrong direction, even in those countries which have followed explicitly environmental strategies. To make progress, action needs to be taken in all four basic groups of policy measures listed below (Blevis *et al.*, 1996).

• Reducing energy intensity through vehicle downsizing, lower power to weight ratios, more efficient vehicle technology, changes in vehicle use (load factors, driving style), improvements in infrastructure – the technological options, fiscal incentives and pricing.

• Controlling emissions of carbon monoxide, VOCs, NO_x, N_2O and methane – use of technology and regulation.

• Switching to alternative energy sources with lower full-fuel-cycle greenhouse gas emissions, including renewable energy – use of technology and fiscal incentives.

• Reducing the use of motorized vehicles through switching to non-motorized transport modes, public transport, substitution of transport (telecommunications), shortening trip lengths, using linked trips and reductions in car use – regulation and pricing, together with behavioural change.

The option of non action is not available as the environmental costs of transport are increasing daily. Any analysis of the trends illustrates that the current dependence on the car is unsustainable and that likely future patterns of activities will substantially increase the demand for road and air transport. Action is being taken and difficult decisions have to be made about the most appropriate short term and long term changes that are required. It will involve new initiatives in all four of the policy measures group (Blevis *et al.*, 1996), and it will involve decisions at all levels. Some actions are most appropriate at the international level (e.g. agreements on targets), some at the European level (e.g. regulations on emissions levels), some at the national level (e.g. fiscal incentives and pricing of fuel), and some at the local level (e.g. location strategies and behavioural change). In all cases, public and political support must be central to any agreement. This is where there is still a chasm between statements of support for environmental policies in principle and real implementation of actions.

There are two basic reasons for this impasse. One is that we have not yet achieved a sufficiently robust research base to be able to test the effectiveness and impacts of particular policy actions. The data and models are not available, at least until now. One of the main objectives of this book is to present a series of economic and social research projects that have addressed some of these issues, so that a greater understanding of the complexity of the relationships between transport and the environment can be achieved. The second reason is that transport is a central part of everyone's daily activities and that real change is likely to be painful. Levels of public support are not yet sufficiently high for radical change, and new responses are developed so that existing patterns of travel can be maintained, albeit in a modified form. This means that the environmental benefits may be there, but in a different form or of a smaller scale than expected. This is where social research has a particularly strong input to make.

Until our understanding of the social and economic consequences of reducing the environmental costs of transport is at least as well developed as the technical arguments, little real progress will be made to achieving substantial change. Successful policy intervention requires both strong public support and a clear understanding of the consequences. This is why it is essential to present the results of the current research which is being undertaken so that the debate can be progressed further. The conclusion may be reached that major interventions in the transport sector are too difficult and too costly to introduce, and that one of the main consequences of the current travel and activity patterns at the end of the millennium is that they will always be unsustainable. In that case we may have to agree that technological improvement is the main way forward, and that other interventions will only help at the margin and not achieve the challenging targets on reducing emissions levels and resource consumption in the transport sector.

THIS BOOK

The introduction has attempted to outline the main issues in the debate over transport policy and the environment. It has not entered into the detailed discussion of the policy options or the implications of following particular strategies – that is left to the individual chapters in the book. The second purpose of the introduction is to place the research findings in the wider context of the international debate of transport and the environment.

The research reported in the book formed the output of the UK Economic and Social Research Council's major programme on Transport and the Environment (1992–1996). This is the first programme of substantive research carried out on these issues which incorporates the new agenda of global issues, air pollution, development, policy effectiveness and reducing the need to travel. It also forms the largest programme in the UK of social and economic research on Transport and the Environment. It has been carried out in parallel with the influential Royal Commission's report on Transport and the Environment (RCEP, 1994). As such it provides theoretical and empirical evidence to reinforce (and contradict) some of the main recommendations of that report.

Several of the contributions challenge existing convention on the effectiveness of regulation and pricing strategies in reducing the environmental cost of transport in both the passenger and freight sectors. The models developed have been designed to test policy alternatives at all levels. The empirical results paint a clear picture of the difficulty of effective policy implementation. This may be a defining moment in the debate over transport and the environment. There is a clear understanding of the nature of the problem as outlined above and the scale of the environmental costs produced by transport. There is also agreement over the range of options that are available (RCEP, 1994; Blevis *et al.*, 1996) and even over the scale of change required to achieve internationally and nationally set targets. These are two essential prerequisites for policy implementation. Yet the essential third ingredient is still missing. There is not sufficient public or political support for the implementation of the options. In addition, some of the recent research (including that presented here) is now beginning to question the effectiveness of some of the options which have until now been seen as essential to the achievement of sustainability objectives (Banister, 1997). As our understanding increases and the research evidence grows, the true scale of the changes necessary and the complexity of the behavioural responses is becoming apparent. There are no simple solutions.

REFERENCES

Acutt, M. and Dodgson, J. (1998) Transport and global warming: Modelling the impacts of alternative policies. Chapter 1 in this book.

Banister, D. (1993) Policy responses in the UK, in Banister, D. and Button, K. (eds.) *Transport, the Environment and Sustainable Development*. London: E & F N Spon, pp 53-78.

Banister, D. (1996) Energy, quality of life and the environment. *Transport Reviews*, **16**(1), pp. 23–35.

Banister, D. (1997) Reducing the need to travel, *Environment and Planning* B, **24**(2), pp. 437–449.

Banister, D. and Button, K. (eds.) (1993) *Transport, the Environment and Sustainable Development*. London: E & F N Spon.

Blevis, D., Orfeuil, J-P. and Pischinger, R. (1996) Mitigation options in the transportation sector, in *Climate Change 1995: Impacts, Adaptations and Mitigation of Climate Change: Scientific-Technical Analysis* (Contribution of Working Group II to the 2nd Assessment Report of the IPCC) Cambridge: Cambridge University Press, pp. 679–712.

Bown, W. (1994) Dying from too much dust. *New Scientist*, **141**(1916), pp. 12–13.

Button, K. (1990) Environmental externalities and transport policy. *Oxford Review of Economic Policy*, **6**(2), pp. 61–75.

Button, K. (1994) Overview of internalising the social costs of transport, in *Internalising the Social Costs of Transport*. Paris : OECD, pp. 7–30.

Button, K and Ngoe, N (1992) Vehicle Ownership and Use Forecasting in Low Income Countries. Transport and Road Research Laboratory, CR 278.

California Environmental Protection Agency (1994) Health Risk Assessment of Diesel Exhausts. Preliminary draft. CEPA, Office of Health Hazard Assessment.

Commission for the European Communities (CEC) (1996) *Towards Fair and Efficient Pricing in Transport: Policy Options for Internalising the External Costs of Transport in the European Union*. EC DGVII, Com(95)691. Brussels: CEC.

DeLucchi, M. A., McCubbin, D., Kim, J., Hsu, S.-L. and Murphy, J. (1994) The Annualised Social Cost of Motor Vehicle Use – Based on 1990-1991 Data. Institution of Transportation Studies, University of California, Davis, CA.

Greene, D. L. and Duleep, K. G. (1993) Costs and benefits of automobile fuel economy improvement: A partial analysis. *Transportation Research*, **27A** (3), pp. 217–235.

Grübler, A., Messner, S., Schrattenholzer, L. and Schäfler, A. (1993) Emission reduction at the global level. *Energy*, **18**(5), pp. 539–581.

Hausberger, S. *et al.* (1994) KEMIS-A Computer Program for the Simulation of On-Road Emissions Based on the Characteristic Driving Behaviour. Institute for Internal Combustion Engines and Thermodynamics, Technical University, Graz, Austria.

Holt, D. J. (1993) Recycling and the automobile. *Automotive Engineering*, **101**(10).

Johansson, P.-O. (1987) *The Economic Theory and Measurement of Environmental Externalities*. Cambridge: Cambridge University Press.

Maddison, D., Pearce, D., Johansson, O., Calthrop, E., Litman, T. and Verhoef, E. (1996) *The True Cost of Road Transport*, Blueprint 5. London: Earthscan.

Marchenko, D. (1993) Bad roads result in 150 billion losses. *Financial News*, 7 May, Moscow, Russia.

OECD (1991) *The State of the Environment*. Paris: OECD.

Peake, S. (1994) *Transport in Transition: Lessons from the History of Energy*. London: Earthscan.

Porter, M. C. and Linde, van der C. (1995) Towards a new concept of the environment competitiveness relationship. *Journal of Economic Perspectives*, **9**(4), pp. 97–118.

Quinet, E (1994) The Social costs of transport: Evaluation and links with internalisation policies, in *Internalising the Social Costs of Transport*. Paris: OECD, pp. 31–76.

RCEP (Royal Commission on Environmental Pollution) (1994) Transport and the Environment, 18th Report. (Chairman Sir John Houghton) Cm 2674. London: HMSO.

Tengström, E. (1992) *The Use of the Automobile: Its Implications for Man, Society and the Environment*. Stockholm: Swedish Transport Research Board.

US Department of Transportation, Bureau of Transportation Statistics (1996) *Transportation and the Environment*. Washington DC: US Department of Transportation.

USEPA (1994) National Air Quality and Emissions Trends Report 1900–1993. EPA - 454/R-94-026. Washington DC.

Whitelegg, J. (1993) *Transport for a Sustainable Future: the Case for Europe*. London: Belhaven.

WCED (World Commission on Environment and Development) (1987) *Our Common Future*. (Chairman Gro Harlem Brundtland) Oxford : Oxford University Press.

PART 1: *National Aspects*

The research reported in this book can be conveniently divided into three scales – national; regional; and local – and this is the structure imposed. At the national level, Melinda Acutt and John Dodgson report on their comprehensive modelling of greenhouse gas emissions (principally CO_2) on the car, public transport and freight sectors. Their model estimates emission levels based on fuel consumption calculations for each mode per passenger kilometre, and then predict the impacts of fuel price increases on car ownership, traffic and emissions. The models take account of changes in the stock, the age of the vehicle, the numbers of diesel vehicles, and the impacts of catalytic converters and cold-starts. The key variable in the analysis of the car sector is the fuel price levels and this also affects the modal split. Public transport demand relates to the growth in GDP, real fares and the real price of petrol. The results from the models are then tested with different assumptions on the growth in real fuel prices. The conclusions reached suggest that the current emissions levels of CO_2 between the different modes of transport are not as great as might be expected – public transport CO_2 levels are 11–63 per cent lower than car emission levels per passenger km. Prices have limited effects on travel, but the introduction of catalytic converters will have a dramatic effect on non greenhouse gas emissions. The cautious conclusion reached is that the global impact may be low in relation to the more localized and immediate external costs such as the effects of global warming is long term and widespread. The current debate is much more concerned with the local emissions effects.

This conclusion is supported by the chapter from Tony Fowkes and his colleagues at Leeds University. Their research has taken the National Travel Survey data (1985/86 and 1991/93) to assess changing patterns of demand from the different types of settlement and for different groups within the population. A category analysis approach has been used to examine changes in trip distance over time, location and by social group. It is concluded that overall changes in demography will not have a very great effect on traffic levels as a whole. But it is important when assessing the impacts of particular policies. A wider range of scenarios are tested here including: halting population movement out of cities; stopping any new road building; halving public transport fares; introducing road pricing in London or the conurbations; and increasing petrol prices by two or three times (to 2006). It is only this last option that has any significant effects on travel demand at the national level, but even here the exact nature of the effect depends on the elasticity assumption, with increasing elasticity as the level of prices increases. Over the six year period (1985/86 to 1991/93) travel distance has increased by 21%. About half of this increase can be explained by the increase in car availability. The remainder is due to people travelling further to carry out their activities. The fastest growth has been in the use of cars as passengers by non-car available people, particularly children.

One of the problems contributing to the growth in traffic, particularly by car, is the absence of appropriate Strategic Environmental Assessment (SEA) methods. In her chapter, Riki Therivel comments on the use of Environmental Impact Assessment (EIA) in transport, but suggests that this is piecemeal with a high level of variability in its quality. It is difficult to carry out a comprehensive SEA – the identification, assessment or mitigation of environmental effects of policies, plans or programmes – as appraisal methods differ, decision making structures differ and financing structures differ. Hence decisions tend to be piecemeal rather than comprehensive – what the French call "saucissonage". This chapter is critical about the current UK practice and explores the means by which SEA regulations and guidelines could be introduced, with examples taken of good practice from North America and elsewhere. The key elements of a comprehensive SEA would include scoping analysis, the development of indicators, mitigation measures, public participation and monitoring of impacts over time. The EC is introducing new guidelines, but current evidence of successful SEA applications seems to be limited to a few isolated cases in Europe and enlightened UK local authorities.

Part of the explanation for the slow progress on SEA is the limited use of public participation both to raise the level of debate and to create awareness and public acceptability. Public attitudes to environmentally based transport policy options forms the substance of the contribution from Bridget Taylor and Lindsay Brook. This chapter is based on information taken from successive British Social Attitudes Survey. They identify three major policy concerns on transport and the environment.

- The impact of traffic congestion and pollution on towns and cities, and the health implications;
- The environmental effects on major road building;
- The long term effects of unrestricted car use on the global environment.

The direction and strength of public opinion towards each of these issues and a series of other related questions is investigated through scales, correlation and multivariate analysis. There seems to have been a rise in environmental concerns (to 1993) and then a decline, coinciding perhaps with economic recession. Levels of public concern about traffic problems have been increasing, particularly recently and particularly in urban areas. Positive responses are made to positive policies (e.g. public transport investment and priority to green modes), yet there is little support for restraint measures, particularly pricing or restrictions on car use. These attitudes are consistent over time, and the inconsistency between concerns and action is also apparent. The most effective strategy is seen as doubling petrol prices, but this is one of the least popular options. The authors conclude that in the short term, people are materialistic and self interested, but in the longer term enlightened self interest may become more important. This new optimism is related to a clear recognition by some that we are over-dependent on the car, and this realization is related to levels of educational attainment.

The same dominance of the lorry with respect to freight transport is apparent. Alan McKinnon identifies four key changes that have resulted in significant increases in tonne-km and vehicle-km of road freight. Changes in logistics and patterns of trading links lead to high tonne-km. In addition the scheduling of production flow and management techniques influence the volume of freight. Surveys and simulations were carried out on the sensitivity of road freight costs to environmental taxes. The traditional arguments suggest very low price elasticities, but this view has been questioned by recent evidence which suggests that elasticities could be higher as there are several traffic reduction options available to firms. The empirical and simulation studies reported here confirm the low price elasticities. It is concluded that the greening of firms logistical operations requires a radical change in management culture and a reordering of strategic policies. This is unlikely, so the transport intensity of freight is likely to remain high and may even increase further, even if environmental taxes are substantially raised.

CHAPTER 1

TRANSPORT AND GLOBAL WARMING: MODELLING THE IMPACTS OF ALTERNATIVE POLICIES

M. Z. Acutt and J. S. Dodgson

Global warming is the name given to the expected increase in average surface temperatures of the Earth as a result of increased concentrations in the atmosphere of anthropogenic (i.e. man-made) greenhouse gases. These gases consist of carbon dioxide, nitrous oxide, methane, ozone and chlorofluorocarbons (CFCs). Concentrations of greenhouse gases have been rising since the Industrial Revolution. Increased concentrations reduce outward infrared longwave radiation and therefore, via complex lagged effects on climate and sea temperature changes, increase surface temperatures. Complex physical climate modelling using general circulation models has concentrated on predicting the effect on average temperatures of a doubling of carbon-dioxide equivalent trace gases over pre-industrial revolution levels. Estimates of this lie in a range from +1.5 degC to +4.5 degC, with a best-guess central estimate of +2.5 degC. This is now expected by the year 2100, and would represent a more rapid change in the Earth's climate than has been experienced at any time during the last 10,000 years (Houghton, 1996).

The problem of global warming is naturally of considerable international concern. In June 1992 the British government, along with around 150 other countries, signed the Framework Convention on Climate Change in Rio. In January 1994 the government published its proposals for meeting its Rio commitments in *Climate Change: the UK Programme* document. This set out the government's plans to meet its target of returning UK emissions of carbon dioxide and the other greenhouse gases to their 1990 levels by the year 2000. The government document proposed to save 10 million tonnes of carbon against the projected forecast for 2000, and to reduce nitrogen oxides by 25 per cent from their 1990 level, volatile organic compounds (VOCs) by 35 per cent, and carbon monoxide by 50 per cent.

A recent lecture to the Royal Society by Sir John Houghton (1996) summarizes the current view of the scientific community on global warming. The first report of the Intergovernmental Panel on Climate Change (IPCC) in 1990 had concluded that there was insufficient evidence that global warming could yet be observed above the natural variability of climate. However by its 1995 Assessment the IPCC felt able to conclude: 'The balance of evidence suggests a discernible human influence on climate.'

The transport sector is a significant contributor to greenhouse gases. In the UK energy used by transport accounted for one-third of total energy demand in 1994. Moreover this proportion has been rising as transport energy demand has been growing faster than other demands: total energy demand in terms of oil equivalents rose by 12 per cent between 1984 and 1994, whereas transport demand grew by 34 per cent, nearly three times as fast.

Since transport is largely powered by oil fuels, total carbon emissions from the sector grew by a similar rate to energy consumption. Actions to reduce carbon emissions from the sector must therefore be targeted, directly or indirectly, at the use of oil fuels. On the other hand, while transport is an important contributor to other greenhouse gases, particularly nitrogen oxides (NO_x), hydrocarbons (VOCs), and carbon monoxide (CO), their emissions are not directly proportional to fuel use and can be curbed by other policies, in particular 'end-of-pipe' measures such as the fitting of three-way catalytic converters to petrol-engined vehicles.

Figure 1.1 shows the splits of vehicle-km and of carbon emissions from the four main types of road vehicle category in 1994. Cars accounted for 67 per cent of these carbon emissions (but for 83 per cent of vehicle-km), large goods vehicles for 21 per cent of carbon emissions (but 7 per cent of vehicle-km), light vans for 9 per cent of carbon emissions (and 9 per cent of vehicle-km), and buses and coaches for 2 per cent of carbon emissions (and 3 per cent of vehicle-km).

In this chapter we first discuss the models we developed in this project to forecast greenhouse gas emissions from the transport sector under alternative policy scenarios. The main such models are the car model, the public transport model, and the road freight model. Next we consider our estimates of greenhouse gas emissions per passenger-km from different transport modes. The following section shows how the model can be used to predict the impact on car ownership, traffic and emission levels of different motor fuel price regimes. In the final section we discuss issues for future research and policy analysis.

MODELLING FUEL CONSUMPTION AND EMISSIONS

The Car Model

We aimed to model the car fleet in such a way as to take into account the way in which older vehicles with particular emission characteristics are replaced by

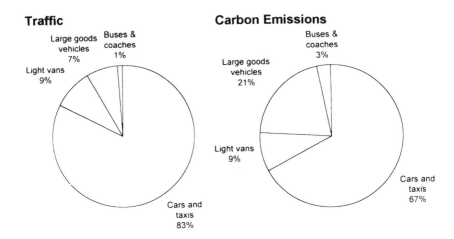

Figure 1.1. Contributions of the main types of road vehicle to traffic and to carbon emissions in 1994.

newer vehicles with (hopefully) better emission characteristics. To do this the car stock is broken down into nine engine size categories (<700 cc; 701–1000 cc; 1001–1200 cc; 1201–1500 cc; 1501–1800 cc; 1801–2000 cc; 2001–2500 cc; 2501–3000 cc; and over 3000 cc) and sixteen annual vintages of vehicle.

Figure 1.2 shows the basic structure of the car fleet model. In the base year, 1991, total car fuel consumption is the product and sum of three matrices. These matrices are: the car stock; annual km per vehicle; and fuel consumption per km. In practice km and fuel consumption are also broken down into three types of road, namely roads in built-up areas (corresponding to urban fuel consumption), roads except motorways in non-built-up areas (corresponding to an average speed of 90 km/h), and motorways (corresponding to an average speed of 120 km/h).

The base year car stock matrix is obtained from Driver and Vehicle Licensing Agency (DVLA) data on the number of vehicles of car body type licensed in 1991, by engine size and year of first registration. The annual km are derived from National Travel Survey data on annual km driven by vehicles of different ages and engine sizes: these data were 'smoothed' by estimating a statistical relationship between annual km and the age and engine size of the vehicle. As might be expected annual km are higher for newer cars than for older vehicles, while annual km are higher for larger vehicles than for smaller ones (a quadratic relationship fits better than a linear one). Average fuel consumption statistics for the 1991 fleet were derived from the test figures in the Department of Transport's *New Car Fuel Consumption* leaflet. Figures for earlier vintages were derived from a series of new car consumption statistics which we calculated

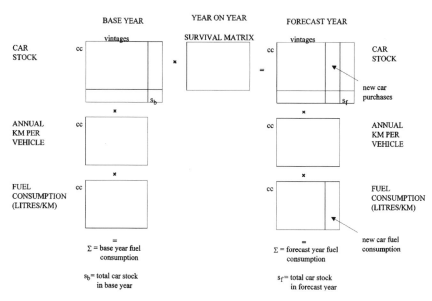

Figure 1.2. Car model.

from analyses of earlier years official fuel consumption statistics undertaken by Rice (1985) and Sorrell (1992).

The numbers of cars in the base year are then multiplied by year-on-year survival rates. These were derived from DVLA tables which show the numbers of cars licensed in a particular year in each engine size category, by year of first registration. By tracing a particular cohort of vehicles, e.g. those first registered in 1981, through tables for successive years it is possible to calculate year-on-year survival rates for each class of vehicle in the original stock matrix. These rates were averaged from a number of years of data to give our year-on-year survival matrix.

Multiplying the original stock by the survivor matrix then gives the numbers of vehicles in each category extant in the following, forecast, year. The total of these survivors is then subtracted from a forecast of total car ownership to give the required total of new car purchases in the forecast year. The model splits these new cars purchased between the engine size categories either on the basis of a default equal to the 1991 split or on the basis of a split specified by the user. This car stock forecasting procedure is then continued year-by-year to the year 2025.

Annual km per vehicle vary in the model with the fuel price, GDP, and a set of public transport fares using a constant elasticity formulation. We used National Road Traffic Forecast (NRTF) fuel price and GDP elasticity values of -0.15 and +0.20 respectively, while the cross-elasticities between public transport fares and car travel were derived as part of the present study (see Acutt and Dodgson, 1996 for a detailed explanation). The elasticity of car travel with respect to the petrol price of -0.15 appears consistent with evidence on the short-run value of this magnitude surveyed in Goodwin (1992).

Forecasts of future new car fuel consumption are based on a regression analysis of an index of past average fuel consumption, expressed as a function of lagged real petrol prices and a time trend. The version of this equation used in the model is:

$$\log fc = 4.6530 - 0.0113 \text{ time} - 0.2696 \log pp_{-1} - 0.2116 \log pp_{-4} -$$
$$0.1060 \log pp_{-7} \tag{1.1}$$

where fc = fuel consumption in litres per 100 km
  time = an annual time trend
  pp_{-1} = price of petrol lagged one year
  pp_{-4} = price of petrol lagged four years
  pp_{-7} = price of petrol lagged seven years

Since there is a one-to-one relationship between fuel burned and carbon dioxide emitted, carbon emissions can be found by multiplying the estimate of total fuel consumed by the appropriate emission coefficient. This, and all other emission coefficients in the models, are derived from an inventory of greenhouse gas emission coefficients in Britain compiled at the Warren Spring Laboratory (see Eggleston, 1992).

Other greenhouse gas emissions (of nitrogen oxides, volatile organic compounds, and carbon monoxide) are based on emission coefficients per car kilometre. Emission coefficients for new vehicles fall considerably because of the mandatory introduction of three-way catalytic converters (CATS) on most new petrol cars from 1993. Consequently, overall emissions of these other greenhouse gases drop as these new vehicles make up an increasing proportion of the total fleet and of total vehicle-kilometres. We allow for the 'cold-start' problem (that CATS do not light-up until the engine is warm) by presuming that CATS are not effective for the first 2 miles of all journeys: the appropriate proportion of all car journeys which are under 2 miles was derived from the 1989/91 National Travel Survey.

An increasing proportion of new cars in Britain are powered by diesel engines rather than petrol engines. In 1991 only 3.7 per cent of the car stock was powered by diesel, but 8 per cent of new cars were diesel. By 1993 5.9 per cent of the car stock was diesel, but in 1994 22 per cent of new cars were diesel. Our model allows for diesel cars by using different emission coefficients for that part of total vehicle-km in any year estimated to be diesel-powered. We have projected the future proportion of new cars which are diesel as 20 per cent as a base case. Increasingly questions are being asked about the environmental advantages of diesel fuel, and we do not believe that the UK government will encourage further diesel/petrol substitution. Indeed the slight duty differential in favour of diesel fuel compared with unleaded petrol was eliminated in the December 1994 Budget.

The Public Transport Sectors

Public transport demand is disaggregated into six sectors, largely on the basis of the availability of long series of annual data in this form. The six sectors are: British Rail (BR) InterCity; BR Network South East; BR Regional Railways; the London Underground; London buses; and other local buses. Data on passenger-km were regressed on GDP, real fare indices and the real price of petrol. Results of this exercise were then combined with elasticity estimates from previous studies of British public transport demand to derive forecasting equations for the six public transport modes. These forecasting equations also incorporate cross-elasticities of demand between real petrol prices and the demand for each of the public transport modes. Details of the methods and resulting forecasts can be found in Acutt and Dodgson (1994b).

The cross-elasticities, and the related set of cross-elasticities between public transport fares and the demand for car travel which are incorporated in the car model (see above), form the cross-modal link between the public transport model and the car model. It is difficult to derive estimates of cross-elasticities by normal means of statistical estimation, so the cross-elasticities are simulated via the relationship between cross-elasticities, and the product of own-price elasticity, modal traffic shares, and the diversion factors which show the proportion of any extra traffic on one mode which is diverted from the other. This yields the following equation (see Acutt and Dodgson, 1996; Dodgson, 1985):

$$e_{oj} = (e_{jj})(q_j/q_o)(dq_o/dq_j) \tag{1.2}$$

where

e_{oj}	=	cross-price elasticity between car travel and the fare on public transport mode j
e_{jj}	=	own-price elasticity on public transport mode j
q_j/q_o	=	modal share (traffic by public transport mode j divided by traffic by car)
(dq_o/dq_j)	=	'diversion factor' (proportion of any increase in travel on public transport mode j resulting from a fare reduction which is diverted from car)

We derived the diversion factors from a survey of transport experts. Together with own-price elasticity estimates, and mode shares from the 1989/91 National Travel Survey, we could then derive our two sets of six cross-modal elasticities.

The public transport models can then be used to predict public transport demand on each of the six modes as a function of GDP, the real fare level on the mode, and the real price of petrol. The London modes also allow for cross-effects between demand and the fares on other London modes. Our public transport demand forecasts are then combined with estimates of public transport emissions derived in our study.

The Freight Sector

In order to forecast emissions from the road goods sector we disaggregated the heavy goods vehicle fleet into six categories of truck (four classes of rigid, plus artics under and over 33 tonnes gross vehicle weight). Data from the Department of Transport's annual *Continuing Survey of Road Goods Transport* (CSRGT) were used to derive the proportions of total tonnage carried by different vehicles (Department of Transport, 1994). On the basis of past trends we presumed that the proportion carried in artics over 33 tonnes will continue to rise, but at a decreasing rate. We also projected trends in average load per vehicle for the six different vehicle classes to the end of the century.

Total tonne-km were forecast on the basis that the elasticity of tonne-km with relation to GDP will continue to equal the value of unity which applied in the 1980s and which is presumed in the 1989 National Road Traffic Forecasts. However, we also tested the sensitivity of the forecasts to a steady decline in this elasticity value to a value of 0.7 by the end of the century. This is based on the view of industry experts that the industrial reorganization (largely as a result of the construction of the motorway network and the concentration of distribution depots) which has increased average length of haul will start to slow down.

Fuel consumption forecasts were initially based on a presumption that average fuel consumption per vehicle-km would not improve. This was based on annual figures for the previous five years from the CSRGT which showed no improvement. However, this was viewed by the industry, and others, as too pessimistic, and consequently the figures were revised to allow for modest improvements in the fuel efficiency of most classes of HGV. Carbon dioxide forecasts were derived by combining the DERV fuel consumption forecasts with the carbon emission coefficient for DERV.

Other greenhouse gas emissions from goods vehicles are based on survival rates for goods vehicles (over and under 16 tonnes gross vehicle weight) derived from annual data on registrations in each year by age and type of vehicle supplied by the Department of Transport. These figures permit calculation of survival rates on a year-by-year basis, and are used to allow for the effects of new emission standards for new goods vehicles being introduced in October 1993 ('stage 1') and October 1996 ('stage 2'). Thus the freight forecasts allow for the impact of the absorption of new, lower-emission, vehicles into the fleet as older vintage vehicles are scrapped.

Goods vehicle emission forecasts were produced up to the end of the century, with longer-term forecasts (in which the vehicle fleet composition and load factors are assumed unchanged at their year 2000 levels) up to 2025. All the forecasts are provided on the basis of both the 'low' and 'high' GDP projections in the rebased 1989 NRTF. Detailed forecasts are not presented in the present paper, but can be found in Dodgson and Kneller (1995).

EMISSIONS OF GREENHOUSE GASES PER PASSENGER-KM BY MODE OF TRANSPORT

Table 1.1 shows our estimates of greenhouse gas emission rates by mode of transport. The car estimates are presented both for the 1993 car fleet, and for the year 2000 fleet: differences in the emissions other than carbon dioxide reflect the effects of the introduction of catalytic converters. Considering the carbon dioxide figures across modes, the 1993 car is the heaviest emitter. This emission level is forecast to drop by 5 per cent by the year 2000 as a result of more fuel efficient technology but the car remains the heaviest polluter. The bus has the next highest emission level, being only 11 per cent lower than the 1993 car. British Rail InterCity has higher emissions when diesel powered compared to electric, and of the two electricity estimates, gas generation gives significantly lower emissions levels than coal. British Rail Network South East has the highest emissions when coal-generated electricity is used, with gas-generated electricity and diesel producing similar emission levels. London Underground is electrically powered, and again gas-generation leads to lower levels of emissions. Overall the public transport modes result in between 11 and 63 per cent lower carbon dioxide emission rates per passenger-km than the 1993 car.

Considering NO_x emissions, the bus has the highest level. Diesel power

Table 1.1. Emissions per passenger-km (grams) by various modes in Great Britain.

Mode	CO_2 as carbon	NO_x	VOC	CO
Car(1993)	33.3	1.34	0.98	10.28
Car(2000)	31.7	0.57	0.52	5.57
Bus	29.7	1.75	0.66	0.8
InterCity(diesel)	22.9	1.35	0.35	0.52
InterCity(electric–coal)	19.5	0.30	0.005	0.017
InterCity(electric–gas)	12.2	0.21	0.001	0.002
NSE(diesel)	17.2	1.02	0.26	0.39
NSE(electric–coal)	28.6	0.44	0.007	0.025
NSE(electric–gas)	18.0	0.31	0.002	0.003
LU(electric–coal)	23.4	0.36	0.006	0.020
LU(electric–gas)	14.7	0.25	0.001	0.002

Note: NSE = British Rail Network South East services.
         LU = London Underground services.

produces the highest rates of NO_x emissions and so the British Rail diesel-powered estimates are higher than the year 2000 car figure as a result of the introduction of catalytic converters. The electrically-powered rail services show a similar pattern to the CO_2 emission levels, with higher figures resulting from coal-generated power as compared to gas.

The highest emission rate for VOCs is from the 1993 car. The bus and year 2000 car are the next highest emitters with 33 and 45 per cent lower emissions than the 1993 car. Slightly lower emissions result from diesel-powered rail services. However, significant reductions result from the use of electric power for rail services, cutting VOC emissions by over 99 per cent compared to diesel traction.

Carbon monoxide emission rates exhibit a similar pattern to VOC rates, although the car is significantly higher than all the public transport modes. The 1993 car emits 10.28 g per passenger-km compared to 0.8 g from the bus – the highest public transport emitter – and the year 2000 car still emits 5.57 g. The diesel-powered rail services result in slightly lower emission rates than the bus: but again the electrically-powered rail services result in significantly lower rates than all the other alternatives.

We have seen that regulatory policies such as the mandatory fitting of CATS to all new vehicles can have a major effect in reducing non-carbon emissions from the fleet as new cars make up an increasingly large proportion of the vehicle stock and (particularly because newer vehicles are driven longer distances each year than older vehicles) of total annual vehicle-km. This is shown by the contrast between the emissions of the 1993 and year 2000 car fleets in table 1.1.

Controlling fuel consumption and therefore CO_2 is likely to be more difficult. There have been improvements in the fuel efficiency of vehicles of a particular size, partly due to past increases in fuel prices and partly due to underlying technological advance. The switch to diesel also offered savings in fuel consumption, but increased concern is now being expressed about the health effects of other emissions from diesel engines. However, rising incomes have also increased the demand for larger cars with more features and consequently higher fuel consumption. (A particularly striking example of this is the new demand for 4–wheel drive vehicles for travel which largely takes place in urban or suburban areas.) Figure 1.3 shows the distribution of new cars by engine size in 1984 and 1994.

POLICY SCENARIOS

The British government rejected European Commission proposals to introduce a general carbon tax to deal with the problem of global warming. The Commission's proposed tax would not be a pure carbon tax since it would also tax nuclear power. In addition, it would grant short-term exemption to certain heavy industries which are particularly fuel-intensive in order to preserve their

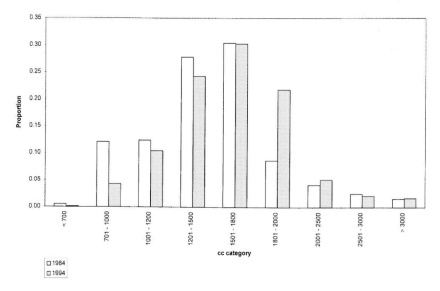

Figure 1.3.   Proportion of new cars by engine size.

international competitiveness. Nevertheless, it would have the advantage that the fossil fuels with the greater carbon content (particularly coal) would be taxed more heavily than those with the lower carbon content (particularly natural gas). This would encourage fuel-switching as well as fuel saving.

Instead the government adopted a two-pronged fiscal approach to reducing carbon emissions. First, Value Added Tax (VAT) was to be extended to domestic fuel, which had previously been zero-rated, at 8 per cent in April 1994, and was to be increased to the standard rate of $17\frac{1}{2}$ per cent in April 1995. However, the move was very unpopular. A compensation package for pensioners and others on low incomes was proposed, but the government failed to pass the increase through Parliament in its November 1994 Budget. Consequently, VAT on domestic fuel remains at 8 per cent.

The second prong of the fiscal measures to deal with global warming was increases in motor fuel duty. In early 1993 duty on unleaded fuel stood at 23.4 pence a litre. VAT was also levied at the standard rate. This meant that duty plus VAT accounted for some 65 per cent of the typical pump price of 47 pence a litre. In the March 1993 Budget the Chancellor of the Exchequer announced that the duty would be increased by at least 3 per cent a year every year to combat global warming. In the November 1993 Budget this was increased to a commitment to raise duties by at least 5 per cent a year. In November 1994 this pledge was reaffirmed, and duties on unleaded were actually increased by 7.5 per cent to 30.44 pence a litre. After the VAT increase on domestic fuel had been defeated in Parliament, an emergency mini-Budget imposed a further 0.88 pence

(2.9 per cent) on petrol –1.03p including VAT – together with increased duties on alcohol and tobacco, to cover the anticipated shortfall in revenue.

The Chancellor of the Exchequer reiterated this commitment in his November 1995 Budget. Duty on petrol and diesel was to be increased by $3\frac{1}{2}$ pence a litre from 28 November. (In addition duty on super-unleaded was to rise by a further 3.9p a litre in May 1986 because of increased environmental concern about this particular fuel.)

In Scenario 1 we allow for the government's commitment to increase real fuel duty by at least 5 per cent per annum. The petrol price series used allows for actual real fuel price changes and duty increases up to early 1996. Further duty increases are then imposed on the average of the 'low' and 'high' forecasts of the net price of motor fuel contained in the Department of Trade and Industry's 1995 energy use forecasts published in Energy Paper 65 (DTI, 1995). The 'low' forecast assumed constancy in real net prices, while the 'high' forecast allows for a modest increase.

Scenario 2 consists of the doubling of real motor fuel prices between 1994 and 2005 recommended by the Royal Commission on Environmental Pollution in their 1994 report on Transport and the Environment (Royal Commission on Environmental Pollution, 1994). We model this by calculating the annual percentage growth rate to secure the required doubling between 1994 and 2005: thereafter real fuel prices are held constant in this scenario.

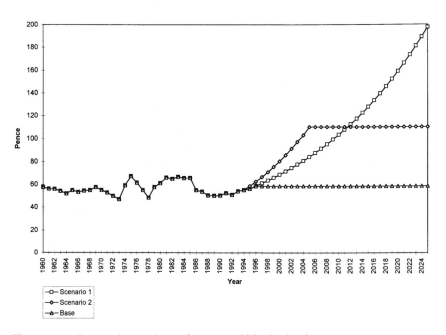

Figure 1.4.   Petrol price trends and forecasts, 1995 price levels.

Figure 1.4 shows these forecasts of fuel prices in pence per litre at 1995 price levels, together with a base case in which prices are held at their early 1996 level. The fuel price forecasts can also be compared with actual prices between 1960 and 1995 to show the effects of the energy price shocks which occurred in the mid-1970s and the early-1980s.

We have combined these fuel price projections with forecasts of GDP and car ownership. While many organizations produce short-term macro-economic forecasts (for example up to the year 2000) longer-term ones are less common. The forecast we have used is based on that of the Organisation for Economic Co-operation and Development (OECD) up to the year 2000. In their June 1995 *Economic Outlook* the OECD projected UK growth in real GDP at 3.4 per cent in 1995, 3.0 per cent in 1996, and 2.8 per cent a year between 1997 and 2000 (OECD, 1995, pp.12, 71). We have then presumed an annual growth rate of 2.5 per cent per annum between 2000 and 2025. This growth rate is also close to the average of the 'low' and 'high' growth rates used in the government's National Road Traffic Forecasts for the years beyond the end of this century.

Our car ownership forecasts are derived using a car ownership model developed by Chris Newton (Newton 1995). This model replaced the traditional logistic curve of car ownership per head with a Gompertz relationship. This has the property that although the function is curved, there is also an almost linear section between zero ownership and the saturation level: this is consistent with the evidence in the UK, where the rate of growth of car ownership has been slow to decline as ownership has increased. The curve takes the form:

$$C_t = S_t \, e^{-e^{cph}} \qquad\qquad (1.3)$$

where C_t = cars per head

S_t = saturation level of car ownership (estimated, from the point at which growth of C_t becomes zero, at 0.61)

cph   = a linear function of factors affecting car ownership, estimated by transforming equation (1.3)

cph was estimated, using co-integration techniques, as a function of the log of GDP per head, the log of the real price of petrol, the log of new car prices, the log of bus fares, the log of rail fares, and a time trend, using annual data from 1950 to 1993. From this model the estimated elasticity of car ownership per head falls as ownership increases: for 1990 the estimated income elasticity is +0.60, car price elasticity –0.06, petrol price elasticity –0.007, bus fare elasticity +0.09, and rail fare elasticity +0.03.

We combined our forecasts of petrol prices under alternative scenarios with our long-term GDP forecast, and with assumptions that real car prices and bus and rail fares remain constant, to forecast car ownership per head. Total car ownership was then predicted from the Office of Population Censuses and Surveys 1992 population projections for Great Britain (OPCS, 1995).

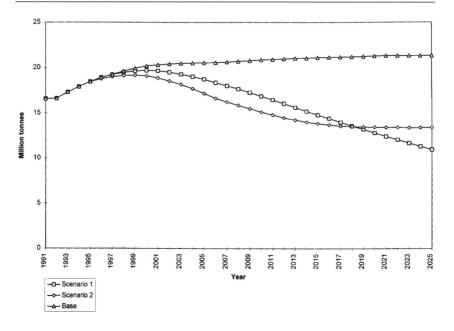

Figure 1.5.   Forecasts of carbon emissions from cars.

The GDP, car ownership, and petrol price projections were then fed into our car model to derive forecasts of carbon emissions, NO_x, carbon monoxide and volatile organic compounds (VOCs) up to the year 2025. Figure 1.5 shows carbon emissions. This shows that emissions from cars are projected to continue to rise, although at a decelerating rate, if petrol prices are held constant in real terms at their early 1996 levels. Carbon emissions will also initially continue to rise quite sharply even with real petrol price increases. However they would peak in the year 2000 with the government's petrol tax policy, and in 1999 with the sharper increase advocated by the Royal Commission. Our model predicts that car carbon emissions would return to their 1995 level by 2002 under the Royal Commission's proposed increases, and by 2006 under the government's strategy. Carbon emissions would return to their 1991 levels by 2006 under the Royal Commission scenario and by 2011 under the 5 per cent per annum duty increase scenario. Since we have assumed that under Scenario 1 duties are increased indefinitely, whereas under Scenario 2 prices are held constant after 2005, the petrol price and carbon emission curves eventually cross. Those for prices cross in 2012: because of the lagged impacts of prices on car fuel economy, those for carbon emissions cross in 2018.

Figure 1.6 shows NO_x emissions from cars, and illustrates the dramatic effect of the fitting of catalytic converters. Up to 2006/2007 the effect of the increased

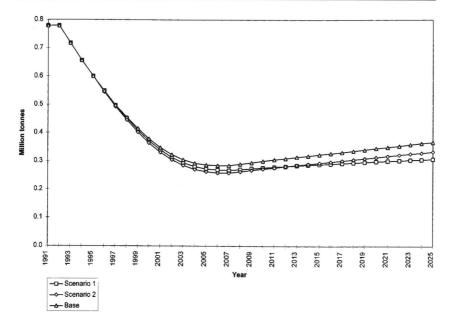

Figure 1.6.   Forecasts of NO$_x$ emissions from cars.

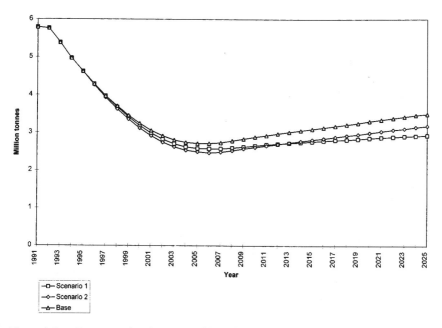

Figure 1.7.   Forecasts of carbon monoxide emissions from cars.

proportion of the fleet fitted with CATS outweighs the effects of increased road traffic. Beyond this date most vehicles will be fitted, and so further increases in road traffic will lead to some growth in NO_x emissions (though by this date the 'cold start' problem may have been resolved or reduced through technological 'fixes' such as pre-warming).

Figure 1.7 shows carbon monoxide projections, while figure 1.8 shows volatile organic compounds. Again CATS have a dramatic effect, though one that is rather less marked in the case of VOCs than in those of these other two pollutants.

Since we have used a car ownership model in which car ownership is sensitive to the price of petrol as well as to GDP, it is worth noting that some of the above changes in emissions under the alternative scenarios will be due to changes in the forecast numbers of cars. However, given the elasticities implied by the estimated parameters these effects are relatively small. For the year 2000 the total car fleet is forecast to be 17,893 vehicles (0.07 per cent) lower than the base forecast under Scenario 1, and 35,337 vehicles (0.15 per cent) lower than the base forecast under Scenario 2. For the year 2005 the total car fleet is forecast to be 36,499 vehicles (0.14 per cent) lower than the base forecast under Scenario 1, and 63,746 vehicles (0.25 per cent) lower than the base under Scenario 2.

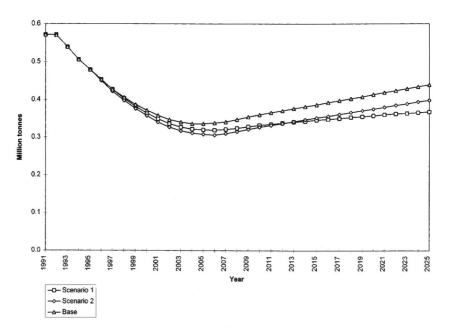

Figure 1.8.   Forecasts of volatile organic compound emissions from cars.

Other studies have considered the impacts of changes in the splits of new car purchases between different engine size categories (Acutt 1996), and of major reductions in public transport prices (Acutt and Dodgson, 1996). Because cross-elasticities of demand are low, even major changes in public transport fares would have relatively modest impacts on car emissions. In practice such reductions would be outweighed by the increased emissions resulting from the expansion of public transport service provision necessary to handle the increased demand for public transport services generated by such fare reductions.

FUTURE DIRECTIONS

The models discussed here have been developed further in a joint project with the Institute for Transport Studies at the University of Leeds to develop a model of road vehicle fuel consumption for the Department of Transport. This project has developed a Vehicle Market Model with 1994 as the base year. This model disaggregated the car fleet by fuel type (petrol and diesel) and distinguishes between private and company car ownership. A sub-model develops a model for predicting the split of new cars into different engine size bands and fuel and ownership types using a logit model. The theory of the structure of second-hand car prices has been used to develop an economic model of car scrappage. There are separate sub-models for heavy goods vehicles, smaller goods vehicles, and different types of buses and coaches. One of us has also been involved in a project to advise the Department of the Environment on modelling carbon emissions from all modes of transport.

The approach set out here has basically looked at the projected growth in the demand for transport and has not considered the role of supply-side restrictions, particularly increased highway congestion. Early runs of the model were based on car ownership forecasts in the National Road Traffic Forecasts. These forecasts are based on the presumption that road capacity will expand to accommodate increased traffic levels. Although we have now developed our own car ownership forecasting model this, and our annual-km forecasting method, are not supply-restrained: moreover the car ownership forecasts are not dissimilar from the NRTF ones under equivalent GDP and fuel price projections (though they do have the advantage that car ownership can also be seen to depend on car prices and public transport fares). Even though we suspect that more capacity can be squeezed out of the road network, a major future challenge is to develop national traffic forecasts which involve interaction between demand growth and capacity restrictions, where the latter include both congestion and user charge factors.

A major issue in determining the future split of cars and other vehicles into different types is the (supply-side) decisions of vehicle manufacturers. These decisions include not only the types of model to produce, but also the way in which different models are to be priced. A recent econometric study of the US automobile market has shown how complex these decisions are, as competing manufacturers determine the mark-ups on their different models in the light of competition from other models and the complex set of cross-elasticities of demand between different cars (Berry *et al.*, 1995). These pricing decisions will in turn react with consumer preferences for different features to determine the configuration and emission characteristics of the future vehicle stock.

At the other end of the vehicle's life is the scrappage decision. Vehicles are retired as their residual value falls below the cost (and inconvenience) of maintenance and repair. These residual values will be determined in the second-hand car market, where second-hand car prices will be determined in part by the prices of new cars and by tax and operating cost regimes. One policy option, much discussed in the United States, is that of accelerated scrappage through bounties (or 'cash for clunkers') to retire those older vehicles with less desirable environmental features (see Hahn (1995) for a recent empirical study).

A final, much more general issue, particularly in the light of suggestions that the external costs of transport emissions in terms of their impact on global warming may be low in relation to their localized and immediate external costs, is the overall costs and benefits of a policy to restrict greenhouse gas emissions from transport – especially where the main impacts of these policies are on carbon dioxide, which has no other external impact. Dodgson (1996) discusses some of these issues, including that of the relative weight to be given to present and future costs and benefits via the discount rate.

REFERENCES

Acutt, M. Z.(1996) Modelling greenhouse gas emissions from cars in Great Britain. *Transportation Planning and Technology*, **19**, pp. 191–206.

Acutt, M. Z., and Dodgson, J. S. (1994a) A Price–Sensitive Model for Forecasting Car Emissions. Paper presented to the Annual Conference of the Universities Transport Study Group, University of Leeds.

Acutt, M. Z., and Dodgson, J. S. (1994b) Multi-modal national traffic forecasts, in *Transportation Planning Methods*: Volume 1 (Proceedings of Seminar G, PTRC 22nd European Transport Forum). London: PTRC.

Acutt, M. Z., and Dodgson, J. S. (1996) Cross-elasticities of demand for travel. *Transport Policy*, **2**, pp. 271–277.

Acutt, M. Z., and Dodgson, J. S. (1996) The impact of economic policy instruments on greenhouse gas emissions from the transport sector, in Hensher, D. A., and King, J. (eds.) *World Transport Research: Proceedings of the 7th World Conference on Transportation Research*. Amsterdam:Elsevier.

Berry, S., Levinshon, J., and Pakes, A. (1995) Automobile prices in market equilibrium. *Econometrica*, **63**, pp. 841–890.

Department of Trade and Industry (1995) *Energy Projections for the UK: Energy Use and Energy Related Emissions of Carbon Dioxide in the UK 1995–2020*. Energy Paper 65. London: HMSO.

Department of Transport (1989) *National Road Traffic Forecasts (Great Britain) 1989*. London: HMSO.

Department of Transport (1994) *The Transport of Goods by Road in Great Britain 1993: Annual Report of the Continuing Survey of Road Goods Transport*. London: HMSO.

Dodgson, J. S. (1985) Benefits of changes in urban public transport subsidies in the major Australian cities. *Economic Record*, **62**, pp. 224–235.

Dodgson, J. S. (1996) Issues in evaluating the long-term global impacts of transport policy. *International Journal of Pollution and the Environment*, forthcoming.

Dodgson, J S, and Kneller, R A (1995) Goods Vehicle Fuel Consumption and Emission Forecasts. Department of Economics and Accounting, University of Liverpool.

Eggleston, H S (1992) *Pollution in the Atmosphere: Future Emissions from the UK*. Stevenage: Warren Spring Laboratory.

Goodwin, P (1992) A review of new demand elasticities with special reference to short and long run effects of price changes. *Journal of Transport Economics and Policy*, **26**, pp. 155–169.

Hahn, R W (1995) An economic analysis of scrappage. *RAND Journal of Economics*, **26**, pp. 222–242.

HM Government (1994) *Climate Change: the UK Programme*. London: HMSO.

Houghton, Sir John (1996) Global Warming: A Scientific Update. Technology Lecture to the Royal Society. London.

Newton, C R (1995) Forecasting Car Ownership. ESRC Transport and Global Warming Working Paper. Liverpool Research Papers in Economics, Finance and Accounting, University of Liverpool.

Office of Population Censuses and Surveys (1995) *National Population Projections: 1992 – based*. London: HMSO.

Organisation for Economic Co-peration and Development (1995) OECD *Economic Outlook* 57. Paris: OECD.

Rice, P (1985) A review of GB vehicle fuel efficiency and price–induced energy conservation, 1973–1984. *Traffic Engineering and Control*, **26**, pp. 425–433.

Royal Commission on Environmental Pollution (1994) *Transport and the Environment*, 18th Report. Cm. 2674. London: HMSO.

Sorrell, S. (1992) Fuel efficiency in the UK vehicle stock. *Energy Policy*, **19**, pp. 766–780.

CHAPTER 2

FORECASTING ROAD TRAFFIC GROWTH: DEMOGRAPHIC CHANGE AND ALTERNATIVE POLICY SCENARIOS

A. S. Fowkes, A. D. May, C. A. Nash and Y. L. Siu and P. H. Rees

The transport sector is a major cause of local, regional and global externalities. Increasing transport volumes on existing infrastructure result in rising noise and local air pollution; whilst new infrastructure involves property demolition and visual intrusion. The transport sector is a significant contributor to the problem of acid rain, and provides the fastest growing source of greenhouse gases in Britain and world wide. Whilst there are ways of mitigating some of these effects without influencing the rate of traffic growth, in other cases only a slowing of the rate of road traffic growth will help.

The official forecasts of road traffic growth suggest that traffic will roughly double by the year 2025 (DoT, 1989). However, these forecasts are very crude; they take no account of demographic change (for instance, that increasing proportions of new car owners will be female, elderly and living in cities), and with the exception of petrol prices do not allow for the effects of any policy instruments. Our major aim has been to examine the implications for traffic growth of these issues. In addition we, and others have undertaken many studies of demand elasticities and of specific measures such as road pricing. A second aim was to integrate the results of these studies into a revised transport demand forecasting framework, in order to reach some conclusions on the issue of the extent to which alternative future transport policy scenarios could change the rate of road traffic growth.

The layout of this chapter is as follows: in the next section, we outline the methodological approach we used. Following that, we consider the results first of the population forecasting exercise, then of the analysis of trip making using the National Travel Survey and finally of the tests of alternative policy scenarios.

Finally we comment on our future research plans before summarising our conclusions.

METHODOLOGY

The project involved essentially four steps:

(a) Analysis of 1985/6 National Travel Survey data to provide base year trip rates and mileages for population groups defined in terms of socioeconomic characteristics, location and car availability. (At the time of starting the project, this was the most recent NTS data set available from the ESRC data archive, and repeated delays in the availability of more recent NTS data sets meant that, in the end, we were forced to rely on cross-tabulations kindly supplied by the Department of Transport rather than analysis of raw data for more recent surveys). Alternative breakdowns of the population were examined to find one which explained a large amount of the variation between groups without requiring excessive detail or leading to too small a sample size in individual cells. Whilst a number of previous studies have examined the effects, for instance, of population density or ageing in isolation, we were keen to avoid problems of multi-collinearity with other variables by considering all the most important factors affecting trip-making behaviour simultaneously.

(b) Production of population forecasts by the same categories for the year 2006. In principle, this should have been an easy task, since our starting point was obviously the OPCS projections for that year. Indeed it was their availability which led us to concentrate our modelling on 2006 as being the most distant 'year for which suitably disaggregated projections were available. However, it turned out that there is relatively little to link our NTS categories with official population forecasts. Only two variables were common to both NTS and population data sets – age and sex. In terms of geographic classification we have used the settlement type classification of the NTS which recognizes the sizes of the settlements in which members of the interviewed sample lived. Our task was therefore to develop a method to maximize the use of the information contained in the projections of the administrative area populations in producing projections of settlement type populations. The aim was to transform the projected populations for official sub-national units (126 areas, mainly of administrative character) into projections for settlement type. Predictions of car available people by person type were achieved using logistic growth curves with standard DOT saturation levels.

(c) Projection forward of base year trip rates in order to obtain forecasts of transport demand by mode and settlement type for the year 2006. The first stage of this was to compare trip rates for 1985/6 with those for 1991/3, having satisfied ourselves that these surveys referred to similar stages of the economic cycle. We found that even within our categories there was a big increase in miles travelled

over this period, and that it varied enormously by person type. Because of worries that sampling errors were throwing up some extreme values, we applied a smoothing procedure before using trends over this period to predict forward to 2006. Obviously this procedure implicitly assumed that growth in incomes, relative prices and qualities of modes of transport and other relevant variables not explicitly modelled continued broadly unchanged over the period from 1986 to 2006. Hence our forecasts for 2006 represent a base case against which to compare alternative policies rather than a forecast of what we actually believe is likely to happen.

(d) Applying the results of other studies to calculate elasticities or other parameters by which these forecasts could be adjusted to allow for the effects of other policies in the year 2006. Evidence on elasticities was collected from a variety of sources, the most valuable being the survey by Goodwin (1992), as well as our own previous work in Fowkes, Sherwood and Nash (1993). A particular issue arose regarding the assumption to be made about the way in which elasticities vary with the absolute level of the variable in question. A review of the theoretical and empirical evidence suggested that generally elasticities would increase as the variable in question increased but that the effect would be less than proportional. Following the evidence of some stated preference work we did in connection with the London road pricing studies (HFA, Accent, ITS, 1993), we adopted a functional form in which elasticities rose at half the speed of the variable in question. Since completing this work we have seen the results of a further important stated preference study of higher fuel prices (Terzis *et al.*, 1995) which chose to follow a constant elasticity function, but commented that a semilog function (in which the elasticity rose in proportion to the value of the variable) also gave a good fit. We take this as further evidence that the truth lies somewhere between the two, as in our model. It was however suggested to us that there is likely to be a counter effect of growing incomes reducing price elasticities as money becomes less important relative to other factors. We know of no evidence on such an effect but as a sensitivity test estimated the results assuming that price elasticities fall, other things being equal, in proportion to income growth.

We categorized policies in which we were interested as follows:

A. Infrastructure

Highway construction can be carried out at different rates, with consequences for the level of road congestion. This was examined by incorporating the results of the work of Christie (1995), which implied a mean reduction of around 7.5 per cent in private transport by 2006 as a result of a decision not to invest in new highways, compared with a continuation of existing policies. Public transport investment, such as Manchester Metrolink, tends to be location specific and so not well suited to our model. These were not therefore tested directly, although obviously it would be possible to adjust our forecasts to allow for the impact of such schemes.

B. Management

Traffic management could be used as a means of traffic growth restraint. We felt that the implications for traffic growth are similar to those of road congestion under (A) above. Policies to favour fuel efficient vehicles would obviously affect the level of pollution from any given level of mileage, but would also lessen the effect of fuel price rises as drivers switch to more fuel efficient vehicles.

C. Information

Real time information could be given to drivers and public transport users, or more general public awareness campaigns could be undertaken. It was not felt that our model would be able to handle this, except by adjusting the output taking into account the results of other studies.

D. Pricing

D1. Road Pricing. Various schemes of road pricing might be introduced by 2006 and have a restraining effect on road traffic growth; these were allowed for by using the results of such studies, and in particular the London road pricing studies (MVA, 1995) to adjust our predictions by settlement type, on the basis of the 'high' price assumptions. Motorway tolls were not allowed for, as we have not produced forecasts of travel by type of road.

D2. Fuel Duty. The UK government is already committed to raising petrol taxes by 5 per cent p.a. in real terms until the end of the century; evidence on elasticities was used to adjust our forecasts for increases in fuel prices. Goodwin (1992) found that the evidence pointed to a long term elasticity of traffic with respect to petrol prices of around -0.3. Following Fowkes *et al.* (1992), we took our base values for London as -0.1 for commuting and business and -0.3 for leisure. The evidence pointed to higher figures elsewhere, and we adopted figures 50 per cent above these. Given our assumed functional form (discussed above), these elasticities would effectively double for a 200 per cent increase in petrol prices.

D3. Public Transport Fares. The UK government's policies regarding bus deregulation and rail privatization carry with them real limitations on what national and local government can do to subsidise the general level of fares, but we considered what would happen if large reductions in fares were implemented, again using evidence on elasticities and cross elasticities of demand. Cross elasticities of demand are believed to vary with circumstances; the cross elasticity of demand for car travel with respect to public transport fares is believed to be low, and generally smaller where the existing car mode share is high and vice versa. The evidence pointed to base cross price elasticities ranging from 0.08 for London down to 0.05 elsewhere.

E. Land Use

The planning mechanism could be used to concentrate residential development more heavily in existing built up areas, to counteract the drift to more rural areas. We were able to examine the size of the transport effects involved from shifts between our four area types, by assuming that those shifting would take on the average travel behaviour of those of similar characteristics and car availability already living there.

Full details of the assumptions involved in our policy tests, as well as detailed results, are contained in Fowkes *et al.* (1995).

ANALYSIS OF TRIP-MAKING BEHAVIOUR

Our analysis of 1985/6 trip rates and mileages showed no real surprises. Elderly persons travel far less than younger people, as do those not in full time employment. Other things being equal, males travel much further than females. For all groups, car availability is closely correlated with distance travelled. When we further broke these categories down by area type, we found that those living in rural areas make somewhat fewer trips, but travel much further, than those living in urban areas. A complete account is given in Nash *et al.* (1995).

The next step was to examine the trend in miles travelled by person type between 1985/86 and 1991/93 (Fowkes *et al.*, 1995). We found an average growth of around 21 per cent. Of this, rather less than half was accounted for by people switching to being car available from non- car available. We were somewhat surprised that non-car available people have increased their miles travelled by 18.5 per cent, whereas car available people have increased by only 7.2 per cent; the majority of this growth was as car passenger, particularly amongst children. After using regression analysis to smooth this growth between person types, we projected it forward to 2006. The result was an increase in private travel mileage of 65 per cent between 1992 and 2006 on the basis of existing trends. Unless car occupancy rates rise significantly, this implies a considerably larger increase than the official road traffic forecasts.

POPULATION FORECASTS

The population projections to 2006 are outlined in table 2.1 according to four NTS area types (i.e. 'London', 'Other Conurbation', 'Other Urban Areas', and

'Rural Areas') and in terms of four groups of age/sex structure (i.e. population aged 15 or under, population between ages 16 and 29, 30 and 59, and population aged 60 or over). It should be noted that our definition of 'rural' includes small towns of under 25000. In sum, from 1989 to 2006, the average percentage change of the population projections in the four broad NTS area types are: 'London' +1.76 per cent, 'Other Conurbation' -2.96 per cent, 'Other Urban Areas' +5.43 per cent and 'Rural Areas' +8.51 per cent. Also, three significant trends are found. First, there is a significant decline in population of ages 16-29 for all the NTS area types although a general increase is found for other age groups. Second, there is a substantial difference in the change in population aged 60 or over from 1989 to 2006 between the four broad NTS area types. For 'London', female population aged 60 or over declines significantly (-16.97 per cent) even compared to the elderly male population (-6.45 per cent). For other conurbation areas, it is noticeable that the elderly male population increases by 2.16 per cent while the females population declines by 2.96 per cent. For 'other urban' and 'rural' areas, the elderly projected population increases by approximately 9.7 per cent (15 per cent for males and 7 per cent for females). Third, there is a significant increase of population ages 15 and under in 'London' (16.40 per cent), and 'rural areas' (11.63 per cent).

Some of these changes may sound quite large. However, when applied to the category analysis model of trip mileages, the net impact was very small. A more complete account of the methodology plus some crude calculations of the likely impact of demographic change on total transport demand are contained in Siu *et al.* (1994) and Siu *et al.* (1995). Overall, population growth was estimated to raise tranport demand by around 4.7 per cent. The shift in population to less densely populated locations would add around 0.45 per cent to that growth. This would be slightly offset by a tendency for population to be concentrated amongst less mobile groups, but the net effect would only be around to depress transport demand by around 0.07 per cent.

Of course, it is possible – and indeed likely – that we have underestimated the scale of these effects because of the crude breakdown into categories we were forced to adopt. For instance, it may be that within built-up areas of a given size, population is shifting to less dense locations, and that amongst elderly people the very elderly are accounting for an increasing proportion. Even a dataset of the size of NTS did not provide sufficient sample size for such more detailed issues to be investigated simultaneously with all the other factors affecting trip making behaviour. Nevertheless, we believe that our analysis does justify the conclusion that overall changes in demographics will not have a very great effect on traffic levels as a whole. We still believe that such a breakdown may prove important when examining the impact on travel behaviour of alternative policies, although fully taking this into account would require more detailed information on the responses of the different groups to policy measures than was available to this project.

Table 2.1 Trends of projected population changes by age/sex for the four NTS area types, 1989 to 2006.

NTS Area Types	Age/Sex Groups	1989-1991 (in per cent)	1991-1996 (in per cent)	1996-2001 (in per cent)	2001-2006 (in per cent)	1989-2006 (in per cent)
London	Persons < 16	2.16	8.38	4.42	0.67	16.40
	Males 16-29	-0.97	-8.85	-5.96	2.44	-13.05
	Males 30-59	1.47	5.18	4.34	-0.01	11.34
	Males 60 & over	-1.73	-4.34	-2.52	2.09	-6.45
	Females 16-29	-1.47	-10.80	-6.60	2.11	-16.19
	Females 30-59	1.72	5.81	4.30	0.17	12.45
	Females 60 & over	-2.93	-7.49	-5.84	-1.80	-16.97
	Total Population	*0.26*	*0.31*	*0.58*	*0.61*	*1.76*
Other Conurbation	Persons < 16	0.70	3.68	0.09	-2.98	1.39
	Males 16-29	-4.18	-13.88	-8.35	-0.01	-24.38
	Males 30-59	1.44	4.99	2.60	-0.76	8.44
	Males 60 & over	-0.36	-1.23	-0.18	3.99	2.16
	Females 16-29	-4.34	-14.42	-8.68	0.25	-25.04
	Females 30-59	1.44	5.31	2.95	-0.60	9.32
	Females 60 & over	-1.45	-4.28	-3.82	0.05	-9.21
	Total Population	*-0.49*	*-0.99*	*-0.94*	*-0.57*	*-2.96*

Table 2.1 Continued.

NTS Area Types	Age/Sex Groups (in per cent)	1989-1991 (in per cent)	1991-1996 (in per cent)	1996-2001 (in per cent)	2001-2006 (in per cent)	1989-2006 (in per cent)
Other Urban Areas	Persons <16	1.40	5.22	2.60	-1.51	7.82
	Males 16-29	-2.61	-10.35	-7.01	1.64	-17.48
	Males 30-59	2.09	7.59	5.29	1.26	17.09
	Males 60 & over	0.66	2.78	3.57	7.25	14.92
	Females 16-29	-2.77	-10.74	-7.50	-0.16	-19.85
	Females 30-59	2.16	7.36	5.16	-0.69	14.54
	Females 60 & over	0.77	0.94	1.14	2.79	5.74
	Total Population	0.64	2.03	1.74	0.91	5.43
Rural Areas	Persons <16	1.22	5.16	2.71	2.11	11.63
	Males 16-29	-2.10	-9.54	-6.64	1.70	-15.91
	Males 30-59	1.86	7.97	5.75	2.43	19.13
	Males 60 & over	-0.19	3.11	3.87	8.06	15.50
	Females 16-29	-2.52	-10.16	-7.29	12.43	-8.72
	Females 30-59	2.37	7.75	5.62	0.65	17.25
	Females 60 & over	0.96	1.40	1.55	1.60	5.63
	Total Population	0.63	2.39	2.08	3.17	8.51

Future Policy Scenarios

The results of a series of policy tests for future levels of private transport are reported in table 2.2. These tests are:

1. halting the drift of population from conurbations to rural areas;
2. failing to build new or expanded roads to increase capacity so that congestion substantially worsens;
3. halving public transport fares;
4. introducing road pricing either (a) in London or (b) in all conurbations;
5. (a) doubling or (b) tripling petrol prices.

It will be seen that even if it were possible completely to halt the drift of population from conurbations to rural areas, the impact on growth of private travel would be very small. Similarly both reducing public transport fares and implementing road pricing in conurbations have little effect on overall national levels of private mode travel, although obviously these policies may have other benefits; halved public transport fares provide a significant increase in mobility particularly for the non car available and road pricing has its major effect on the most congested city centres. Of these tests, only those concerning petrol prices really have a substantial effect on road traffic at a national level, and only tripling petrol prices totally suppresses growth over this period. It should be noted that this result comes about as a result of using our best estimate of the long run petrol price elasticity, so we are assuming full adjustment to the higher price. Also we assume a particular functional form in which the elasticity increases as the level of price increases, although not as fast as with the popular semilog form. There is some justification for the form we use, but more research on this would be welcome. Finally, we have not allowed explicitly for the impact of reduced traffic levels compared with the base on levels of congestion. Obviously reduced congestion could attract back some of the traffic priced off by the higher petrol prices, but this tendency would be offset by any reduction in road investment associated with the lower rate of traffic growth; to some extent such an effect may already be picked up by the petrol price elasticity in any case.

Future Research Plans

We believe that this work has demonstrated the need, for policy analysis, of a much more detailed strategic multi-modal transport model which can break the population down by location and demography and is policy sensitive. To some extent this may come out of the current Department of Transport review of the National Road Traffic Forecasts, but that is likely to continue to focus solely on private transport. We are, therefore developing such a model. This model will build on the results of this project but will update them using the more recent

Table 2.2.   Summary of tests: private transport effects (private transport in billions of passenger miles per annum).

Private (billion miles per annum)	London	Conurbation	Urban	Rural	Total	Percentage Change on 1992
1992	26.3	33.6	127.1	116.7	303.7	
2006 base	32.3	58.0	208.4	201.7	500.5	+64.8%
1. 2006 with adjusted population	33.1	61.7	207.6	195.3	497.7	+63.9%
2. 2006 congested	30.0	58.2	192.6	188.5	463.3	+52.5%
3. 2006 with halved N	31.0	56.6	203.2	196.7	487.5	+60.5%
fares M	31.3	56.9	204.5	197.9	490.6	+61.5%
4. (a) 2006 with road pricing in London	30.1	58.0	208.4	201.7	498.7	+64.2 %
4. (b) 2006 with road pricing in London & the other conurbations	30.1	54.6	208.4	201.7	494.9	+62.9%
5. (a) 2006 with N doubled M	25.9	42.0	150.0	145.5	363.4	+19.7%
petrol prices	27.4	45.5	162.7	157.7	393.3	+29.5%
5. (b) 2006 with N tripled M	20.8	30.3	107.7	104.7	263.6	-13.2%
petrol prices	23.3	35.7	127.3	123.6	310.0	+2.1%

Notes
N denotes our normal elasticity assumptions
M denotes elasticities reduced in proportion to income growth(see section on methodology above for discussion of this point).

National Travel Survey data now available, and will model choices such as car ownership and mode choice in much greater detail than was possible in this project, in part restoring some of the work that was cut out of this project as a result of a budget reduction. At the same time, a priority for investigation must be the way in which the relevant elasticities change from short run to long run and as the absolute levels of the variables in question change.

CONCLUSIONS

In this project, we have developed a simple category analysis model that allows for the fact that travel behaviour differs significantly by person type and location.

We then developed population projections that were consistent with this model to allow for projections forward to the year 2006. Despite significant shifts in the structure and location of population between our base year (1985/86) and our forecast year of 2006, it did not appear that these would in aggregate lead to more than a very minor change in travel volumes.

It was found that the distance travelled for persons in a particular person type and location had risen by some 21 per cent between 1985/86 and 1991/93, and that less than half of this was accounted for by rising car availability; indeed the fastest growth was in the use of cars as passengers by non-car available people, particularly children.

A number of policy tests were conducted. A halt to the drift to more rural areas had a very minor effect, whilst a policy of halting road building to allow congestion to restrain traffic growth would not prevent substantial further traffic growth. A halving of public transport fares would only have a minor effect on road traffic growth (from this it seems reasonable to assume that the same is true of any feasible improvement in public transport services, since to achieve a quality improvement which would have the same impact on the generalized cost of public transport as a nationwide halving of fares would be a demanding target). Thus we are thrown back on the 'stick' rather than the 'carrot'. According to our model, a major increase in petrol prices could indeed achieve a considerable slowing down of private transport growth; if they were trebled in such a way that the long run effect of the increase was experienced by 2006 then this would be sufficient to prevent any traffic rise over the period between now and 2006. Of course, further increases would be necessary to prevent traffic growth after 2006. This result does depend critically on the relationship between short and long run elasticities and on the way in which elasticities change as absolute levels of the variables in question change. We believe that we have incorporated the best evidence available on these issues, but further research is needed.

REFERENCES

Christie, C. (1995) The effects of congestion on drivers' behaviour, in *Models and Applications*. Proceedings of Seminar F. London: PTRC, pp. 41–57.
DoT (1989) *National Road Traffic Forecasts (Great Britain) 1989*. London: HMSO.
Fowkes, A.S., May, A.D., Nash, C.A., Rees, P.H., Siu, Y.L. (1995) An Investigation into the Effects of Various Transport Policies on the Levels of Motorised Traffic in Great Britain in 2006. University of Leeds, Institute for Transport Studies Working Paper 446.
Fowkes, A.S., Sherwood, N. and Nash, C.A. (1993) Segmentation of the Travel Market in London: Estimates of Elasticities and Values of Time. University of Leeds, Institute for Transport Studies, Working Paper 345.
Goodwin, P.B. (1992) A review of new demand elasticities with special reference to short and long run effects of price changes. *Journal of Transport Economics and Policy*, **26**, pp. 155–169.

HFA, Accent, ITS (1993) *Review and Specification of Model Elasticities.* Report for DoT London Congestion Charging Project. London: HMSO.

MVA (1995) *The London Congestion Charging Research Programme, Principal Findings.* Prepared by the MVA Consultancy for the Government Office for London. London: HMSO.

Nash, C.A., Siu Y.L. Fowkes, A.S., May, A.D. and Rees, P.H. (1995) Alternative Strategies to Reduce Road Transport Growth. Paper presented to the 7th World Conference on Transport Research, Sydney, Australia.

Siu, Y.L., Rees, P.H., Fowkes, A.S., Nash, C.A., and May, A.D., (1995) Demographic Change and Future Transport Demand: An Analysis of the British Situation 1989-2006. University of Leeds, Institute of Transport Studies, Working Paper 432, (also School of Geography Working Paper 95/03).

Siu, Y.L., Fowkes, A.S., Nash C.A., May, AD., and Rees, P.H. (1994) Road Traffic Growth and the Environmental Effects of Alternative Transport Strategies. Paper presented to the VSB Advanced Studies Institute Conference on Transport, Environmental and Traffic Safety: The Role of Policies and Technology, held in Amsterdam, The Netherlands.

Terzis, G., Dix, M., Bates, J. and Dawe, G. (1995). Effects and elasticities of higher fuel prices, in *Transport Policy and Its Implementation*, Proceedings of Seminar C. London: PTRC, pp. 247–259.

Chapter 3

Strategic Environmental Assessment in the Transport Sector

Riki Thérivel

The application of environmental impact assessment (EIA) to policies, plans and programmes has been discussed virtually as long as its application at the level of individual projects. Such so-called 'strategic environmental assessment' (SEA) is seen as a way of overcoming some of the limitations of project EIA, and of helping to put the concept of sustainable development into practice.

The transport sector is particularly in need of effective environmental appraisal. EIA of transport projects has been carried out for years, but has been beset by an inability to adequately address cumulative impacts, generated traffic, modal alternatives, global-level impacts, and a range of other strategic-level issues which can only be effectively considered at decision-making stages which precede the planning of individual projects. A number of organizations, most notably the UK's Standing Advisory Committee on Trunk Road Assessment (1992) have suggested that the application of SEA to transport policies, plans and programmes could be one way of overcoming these problems.

Nevertheless, transport-related SEAs are beginning to be carried out in countries such as Poland and the Slovak Republic as well as the more traditional environmental leaders such as the Netherlands and the United States. Early experience with these SEAs and those from other sectors shows that SEA does not have to be an enormously complex exercise, and that it can lead to improvements in transport planning, including more transparency and public acceptance. This is particularly important at a time when many transport projects, particularly road projects, are being met with considerable public resistance. However, the use of SEA in the transport sector is still limited by such issues as the lack of comparability in existing appraisal techniques for different transport modes, decision-making structures which are poorly adapted to multi-modal transport planning, and the technical complexity of the subject.

This chapter considers how SEA has been carried out in the transport sector in the first half of the 1990s, as well as its potential applications in the second half. It first reviews what SEA is and why it is particularly needed in the transport sector. It continues with an overview of existing SEA regulations and guidelines, and SEAs that have been carried out to date worldwide. It then discusses possible SEA methodologies for the transport sector in greater detail, focusing particularly on those that might be applicable at more strategic levels of decision-making or at a national level, where fewer SEAs have been carried out to date. Examples of existing SEAs are presented to illustrate these methodologies. The chapter concludes with a review of issues which need to be resolved to make SEA a truly useful and effective tool to improve decision-making in the transport sector.

Definitions and Concepts

Strategic environmental assessment can be defined as the process of identifying, assessing and mitigating the environmental effects of a policy, plan or programme (PPP) and its alternatives, preparing a written report on the findings, consulting the public regarding the findings, and taking the findings and public comments into account during PPP decision-making. In turn, a policy can be defined as an inspiration and guidance for action, a plan as a set of coordinated and timed objectives for implementing the policy, and a programme as a group of projects in a particular area. Examples of transport policies include rail privatisation, the imposition of road pricing or carbon taxes, and broad decisions regarding transport modes. Plans include traffic management and parking plans for specific areas. Programmes could include strategies for the construction and maintenance of roads, rail and other infrastructure. As these definitions imply, policies influence plans, which in turn influence programmes and projects. Similarly, the SEA for a policy can set the context for SEAs of subsequent plans and programmes, and finally project EIAs,[1] and national-level SEAs can influence in turn regional/provincial and local-level SEAs, in a form of 'tiering'.

The aim of SEA is to minimize the PPP's negative environmental impacts, foster public participation in decision-making, and ultimately improve the decision-making process for the PPP. SEA, especially at the programme level, is strongly rooted in the techniques and approaches used for project EIA. However, evolving SEA practice indicates that many of these techniques are not appropriate at the policy and plan level, and that SEA is cheapest/easiest to do and also most effective if it is integrated throughout the PPP-making process, rather than applied as a separate procedure once the PPP has been finalized (as is often done in project EIA). Figure 3.1 illustrates this integration of environmental information in decision-making.

SEA is particularly needed in the transport sector, due to the extent of the transport sector's environmental impacts, and to limitations in existing environmental assessment practice in the transport sector. For instance, an analysis of sixty UK environmental impact statements for roads prepared between 1988 and

Strategic decision-making process	Environmental[a] information: input to the strategic decision-making process[b]
Determine strategic objectives	Determine environmental objectives
Identify issues of concern and determine indicators	Determine baseline environmental conditions, identify environmental issues of concern, and determine environmental indicators
Determine alternative ways in which the objectives can be achieved	Include environmentally superior alternatives(s)
Evaluate and compare alternatives	Predict environmental impacts of alternatives
Select and fine-tune selected alternative	Identify ways of mitigating the environmental impacts of the selected alternative
Formal decision[c]	SEA report and formal consultation
Implementation programme	Establish environmental guidelines for implementation and monitoring

Notes

a Some SEAs focus on sustainability rather than environmental issues: this involves expanding the objectives, indicators, issues of concern etc. to also include economic and social factors.

b Note that each of these stages can/should include input by the public and other relevant authorities.

c There may well not be a formal decision stage. This has proven to be a major hurdle to, for instance, the establishment of a Europe-wide SEA Directive. However it is a problem only when SEA is seen only as an add-on to the decision-making process, rather than a more integrated SEA-and-decision-making model.

Figure 3.1. SEA process: links to decision-making

1993 found that most of them did not even discuss the issues that they were legally required to consider (see table 3.1), much less more strategic issues. This situation has very much improved since the Department of Transport published its *Design Manual for Roads and Bridges* (DoT, 1993), but some basic weaknesses of project EIA remain.

First, transport schemes are particularly prone to what the French call '*saucissonage*': cutting the road (or rail)-sausage into little pieces, each of which is analysed separately without considering the sausage as a whole. Thus a long road will be cut into shorter sections to facilitate analysis, a byproduct of which is that the subsequent EIAs for small road sections can each state that its particular section of road has insignificant environmental impacts. An example of this was highlighted in 1992 by Friends of the Earth (*The Observer*, 29 November), who showed that the UK government's road construction programme included several individual schemes that, together, would form most of a second ring road

Table 3.1 EIA requirements (as given in EC Directive 85/337) addressed by sixty UK road environmental impact statements (EIS), 1988-1993: average score[a].

Site description	1.4		
Project description	1.4		

	Baseline study	*Impact prediction*	*Impact mitigation*
Human beings	1.1	1.1	0.8
Flora	1.0	0.8[b]	0.7[c]
Fauna	0.8	0.9[b]	0.7[c]
Soil	0.5	0.2	0.1
Water	0.6	0.4	0.4
Air	0.4	0.6[b]	0.2
Climat	0.1	0.2	0.1
Landscape	1.2	0.8	1.3
Impact interactions	0.4	0.8	0.3
Material assets	0.4	0.8	0.3
Cultural assets	0.9	0.7	0.4

Notes

a 0 = no information in the EIS
   1 = a sub-standard analysis with significant omissions
   2 = an adequate analysis with only minor inadequacies, or which explains why the topic is not discussed
   3 = a high-quality and competent analysis

b mostly mentioned as having no significant impact when issues of concern were identified

c mostly linked to landscape mitigation measures

around London: the EISs for these schemes would only have addressed the local impacts of each proposed road, not the national-level implications of having a second ring road (e.g. possible additional freight traffic between the continent and areas west of London, or changes in travel patterns on the existing M25 ring road). This '*saucissonage*' also means that project EIAs rarely consider cumulative impacts such as the progressive degradation of natural habitats (Treweek *et al.*, 1993) or the cumulative air and noise pollution caused by multiple transport projects.[2] *The Design Manual for Roads and Bridges* does note that assessment may need to cover the combined or cumulative impacts of several schemes 'in some cases', and highlights advantages, in terms of choice of alignment and design, of considering related schemes together. However it also notes that 'Since schemes in the Overseeing Department's programmes have been initiated and progressed with different timescales the adoption of such an approach may not be feasible in practice'.

Project EIAs rarely discuss the new traffic and development projects that are generated as a result of a new transport project. For instance, construction of a motorway is often followed by proposals for new towns and retail developments near its junctions. Similarly, traffic on new roads generally exceeds that displaced from existing roads because roads themselves generate traffic: where there is a road, people will travel on it. By addressing entire projects, cumulative impacts, and generated traffic and developments, SEA can help to improve the effectiveness of project EIA.

However, SEA can also go beyond good practice EIA to address strategic and sustainability issues at the appropriate decision-making level. By the time most transport EIAs are prepared, decisions taken at a more strategic level will have eliminated the possibility of a modal change, or of using traffic management rather than building new infrastructure. The existing structure of government departments and legislation (where, for instance, one government ministry may be responsible for road construction, another for public transport, and perhaps another for land use planning) reinforces this difficulty. Yet it is a modal shift which, over time, is most likely to reduce the environmental impacts of the transport sector. SEA would ensure that environmental factors are considered appropriately when these strategic-level decisions are made, leading to more sustainable development.

SEA could consider the impacts of actions that have an environmental effect, but not in the form of projects. An example of this is the privatization of the UK's rail sector, which is clearly having an environmental impact through changes in management and user behaviour, but not primarily in the form of new projects.

SEA can also address people's concerns about wider transport issues. Recent examples of this concern occurred during the construction of the Newbury bypass and the M3 motorway at Twyford Down, where local residents and other groups were not only worried about the environment at those specific sites, but also about the perceived inevitable predominance of cars, bureaucratic style of decision-making, and lack of forum for their concerns. The cost of this concern came in terms of the need for increased site security, as well as potential political repercussions. By considering these issues and making the decision-making process more transparent, SEA can help to incorporate these views at the correct level of decision-making, avoiding later problems.

Existing SEA Regulations, Guidelines and Practice

SEA systems are becoming increasingly established around the world. Table 3.2 summarizes existing SEA regulations and guidelines related to the transport sector and land use planning. Still other countries apply SEA on an *ad hoc* basis or to other sectors. As can be seen, SEA regulations and guidelines are (with the conspicuous exception of the United States) very recent, and practical experience with SEA is still developing rapidly. Table 3.3 gives examples of SEAs prepared to date for the transport sector. It is interesting to note that the presence of SEA regulations itself does not lead to SEA practice, nor does the lack of regulations hinder practice. For instance, no SEAs have been carried out in the Czech Republic to date despite relevant regulations, whilst more than 100 have been carried out in the UK (mostly for development plans) in response to guidance. Plan and policy SEAs are also carried out less frequently than SEAs of programmes or multiple projects.

SEA Methodology for the Transport Sector

As can be seen from table 3.2, only a limited number of regulations and guidelines have emerged to date which relate to the transport sector, and many of these apply to a restricted range of policies, plans and/or programmes. However, existing experience with SEA does suggest good practice SEA procedures. Here only a broad outline is provided, based on the steps shown in figure 3.1, and focusing on national-level SEA and SEA of policies and plans. Examples from a range of existing transport SEAs are given, both to illustrate specific methodologies and to show the links between the SEA stages. The reader is referred to DHV Environment and Infrastructure (1994), English Nature (1996), Sadler and Verheem (1996), and Therivel and Partidario (1996) for a more detailed discussion of SEA methodology. Techniques for the environmental appraisal of the transport sector have been discussed and/or analysed by, for example, Birdlife *et al.* (1995, 1996), Buchan (1990), Marcial Echenique and Partners (1995), MVA Consultancy *et al.* (1994), RSPB/WWF (1995), SACTRA (1992), and Steer Davies Gleave (1996).

Probably the most crucial aspect of SEA is that it should be a process which accompanies the PPP-making process, and not an add-on near the end of PPP-making. SEA is most likely to improve decision-making if it is carried out in parallel with the decision-making process. In turn, such an integrated SEA model implies that SEA would generally:

• be carried out by the authority responsible for preparing the PPP, perhaps with input from consultants, rather than carried out primarily externally;
• focus primarily on the formulation of overall PPP objectives, alternatives, and mitigation measures, rather than on detailed baseline descriptions and impact predictions;
• consider the public's views and those of other interested groups from the outset, rather than consulting them near the end of the decision-making process; and
• as a side effect incrementally educate and change the outlook of decision-makers who may traditionally have focused almost exclusively on financial and engineering factors.

Determining environmental objectives. A clear statement of the PPP's objectives, including environmental objectives, is important for several reasons: it sets

Table 3.2. SEA regulations and guidelines related to the transport sector (based on Partidario, 1996).

Country	SEA applies to:*	Regulations	Guidelines
Canada (federal)	Cabinet proposals	Cabinet directive, 1990	Guidance by Federal Environmental Assessment and Review Office, 1993
Czech Republic	'Development programmes, conceptions and proposals for legal acts'	Czechoslovak Federal Act 17/1992 EIA/SEA Act 1992	Guidelines by Czech Institute of Applied Ecology, 1996
Denmark	Government proposals (e.g. bills)	Administrative order, 1993	Guidance by Ministry of the Environment, 1994
European Commission	If Directive is approved: plans and programmes directly above project level, including transport projects	Possible SEA Directive being discussed	–
Netherlands	1. Land development plans and structure schemes, national physical plans fixing the locations of projects 2. Cabinet proposals	1. Environmental Protection (General Provisions) Act 1987	2. Internal guidelines for an environmental test ('e-test') published by the Directorate for General Policy Affairs, 1992
New Zealand	Ojectives, policies, rules, plans	Resource Management Act 1992, sec. 32	Guidance by the Ministry of Environment
Poland	1. Land use plans 2&3. Specified strategic actions	1. Land Use Act 1995 2. Executive order 1995 3. Draft SEA legislation	

Table 3.2. Continued.

Country	SEA applies to:*	Regulations	Guidelines
Slovak Republic	Transport policies, selected territorial plans, 'Generally binding legal directives'	EIA Act 127/1994	Guidance by Ministry of Environment, 1995
United Kingdom	1. Local authority development plans 2. Government policies	—	Guidance by Department of the Environment: 1. 'Environmental Appraisal of Development Plans: A Good Practice Guide' 2. 'Policy Appraisal and the Environment'
United States (federal)	'Major federal actions significantly affecting the quality of the human environment'	National Environmental Policy Act 1969	Guidelines by Council on Environmental Quality
United States (California)	'The whole of an action which has the potential for resulting in a physical change either directly or ultimately'	California Environmental Quality Act 1970	State CEQA Guidelines (as amended in 1995)

Note: * only those related to transport and land use planning are listed here

Table 3.3. Examples of transport SEAs carried out worldwide (ECMT, 1996; Verheyen and Nagels, 1996).

	Policy/Plan*	Programme/Multi-project
International		High speed rail (HSR) network (EC) HSR routes Antwerp-Rotterdam (Belgium, Netherlands) Thematic study HSR project Paris-London-Brussels-Köln-Amsterdam Channel Tunnel
National	Transport 2005 (Denmark) Second transport structure plan (Netherlands) Road and traffic plan 1998-2008 (Norway) Fifteen-year multimodal national transport plan (Spain) National transport policy (Slovenia) National road management plan (Sweden) National transport policy (Poland)	Main road network development plan (Finland) HSR programme assessment (Italy) Express motorway network (Hungary) National motorway network (Poland)
Regional	Road planning in the South region of Sweden (Sweden)	Iron Rhine rail cargo: multimodal comparisons (Belgium) Northern corridor (France) Intermodal proposals for the A7-A9 route (France) Nordrhein-Westfalen road programme (Germany) Betuwelijn cargo rail line (Netherlands) Amsterdam-Utrecht corridor study (Netherlands)

Table 3.3. *Continued.*

	Policy/Plan*	Programme/Multi-project
Local	Greater Hull transportation strategy (UK) San Diego 1994 regional transportation plan (US) Shasta County regional transportation plan (US) El Dorado County regional transportation plan (US) San Joaquin Council of Governments regional transportation plan (US)	Dublin transport initiative (Ireland) Trans-Pennine transport study (UK) Setting Forth (UK) Santa Clara County congestion management programme (US)

Note: *The distinction between policy/plan and programme/multi-project is not always clear, and divisions in this table are indicative only.

a positive and consistent direction for the formulation and implementation of the PPP, avoids irrelevancies and the need for crisis management, and allows environmental, social and economic issues to be appropriately integrated into the decision-making process (Ferrary, 1996; Heatley, 1996). The primary objective of most transport PPPs will be economic and/or social, for instance reduction of transport costs or improvements in accessibility. However, transport objectives will also include environmental elements such as the need to meet commitments or regulations regarding air pollution emissions, or protection of the natural environment. Some of these objectives will be binding constraints (e.g. EC limits on air pollution emissions), whilst others will be more indicative. Generally objectives are established by politicians or bureaucrats, but they can also be determined through public fora or groups of experts. Figure 3.2 gives examples of transport PPPs' objectives.

Determining baseline environmental conditions, identifying issues of concern, and selecting environmental indicators. In project EIA, baseline environmental conditions will normally be determined through literature reviews and field surveys. In most SEAs, instead, the area involved will be so large that detailed field surveys will be impossible. Nevertheless, it is important to know enough about the baseline conditions in the area to allow issues of concern to be identified. This can be done through literature reviews (e.g. state of the environment reports and previous project EISs), aerial photography, use of geographical information systems, and field surveys of representative locations. However, even then appropriate information may not be available, especially at the policy and international level. For instance the SEA for the European high speed rail network (CEC, 1993) concluded that 'it has not been possible to quantify the impact on agriculture, landscapes and sensitive sites . . . because sufficiently detailed data are lacking on a European scale'.

The process of 'scoping'– determining appropriate spatial and temporal limits for the SEA, environmental components which it will address, and methodologies for doing so – is a crucial part of the SEA. Without effective scoping, the SEA can easily consider issues that are not relevant, become unmanageably complex, and be less useful for decision-making. The baseline environmental information will help to indicate issues of concern on which the SEA will focus. These could include air pollution levels that are near or above regulatory standards, habitats that are rapidly declining, or areas that are particularly affected by noise. Scoping is generally carried out in discussions between the various interest groups involved, and sometimes with public participation: it can involve the use of mapping, checklists, scenario development, workshops and Delphi techniques.

One result of scoping will be a list of indicators by which environmental conditions and the attainment of the PPP objectives can be 'measured'. Indicators can be selected on the basis of expert knowledge or the views of the

---

HIGH-SPEED RAIL LINK ANTWERP-ROTTERDAM (Mens en Ruimte, 1996)

Primary objective:
   to provide environmentally friendly solutions for transboundary mobility

Environmental objectives:
   safeguarding of open spaces in Flanders
   avoidance of 'silence areas' in the Netherlands
   accordance with the environmental and spatial objectives of the
   National Environmental Plan and national policy document for future
   spatial development in the Netherlands
   protection of nature areas in Flanders and the Netherlands

TRANSPORT STRATEGY FOR THE GREATER EDINBURGH AREA
(Scottish Office, 1994)

Primary objectives:
   enhancing accessibility to and from Scotland north of the Firth of Forth
   protecting the environment of Edinburgh
   ensuring any new crossing of the Forth is environmentally acceptable

Environmental objectives:

global issues:
   minimize emissions of greenhouse gases
   minimize emissions of other air pollutants
   minimize consumption of non-renewable resources

natural resources:
   minimize impacts on high quality landscapes
   minimize impacts on areas of nature conservation interest
   minimize impacts on historic and cultural resources
   minimize impacts on open countryside and agricultural resources

local environmental quality:
   minimize concentrations of CO
   minimize increases and maximise reductions in traffic noise

development plan policy:
   implementation of the adopted development plan strategies should not
   be hindered

Figure 3.2. Examples of transport PPPs' objectives.

people affected by the PPP. Much has been written about indicators (e.g. in
OECD, 1994; DoE, 1996), and many lists of indicators exist, although none has
been officially agreed for the transport sector. Different indicators will be

appropriate for the different levels of PPPs and scales of area studied. As shown in figure 3.3, the indicators can be global/national, regional, or local: the French example uses a relatively large number of indicators, which are divided into national (more objective and quantifiable, shown here) and regional (more qualitative and anthropocentric, not shown). The EC example uses a more restricted number of indicators, focused primarily at the international level. Indicators can also consider wider sustainability issues such as equity and quality of life. Environmental targets can be set, for instance to reduce congestion by $x\%$ or reduce CO_2 emissions by $y\%$ (Sheate, 1992); these targets can be linked to carrying capacities.

INTERMODAL TRANSPORT PROGRAMMES IN NORTHERN FRANCE: NATIONAL LEVEL
(MdE, 1994)

1. *Air:* annual emissions of
   greenhouse gases (in tonne-equivalents of CO_2)
   generators of acid rain (anhydrides)
   possible carcinogens (e.g. heavy metals, diesel particles)
   oxidants or irritants (HC and anhydrides)

2. *Water:* annual emissions of
   possible carcinogens (eg. heavy metals)
   generators of acid rain (anhydrides)
   radioactive wastes (in tonne-equivalents of radium, and m^3 of wastes
   with high, medium and low radioactivity)

3. *Renewable energy:* annual consumption of primary materials (in tonne-
   equivalents of petrol)

4. *Land use:* no. hectares of land taken by projects

5. *Noise:* no. hectares subject to noise greater than 40dB(A), 55dB(A), and
   65dB(A)

TRANS-EUROPEAN RAIL NETWORK (CEC, 1993)

land use (in 1000 ha)
primary energy consumption (in PJ)
emissions of CO, NO_x, HC, SO_2 and particulates (all in kt), and CO_2
(in 1000 kt)
acid equivalents (in 1000 kt)
CO equivalents (in 1000 kt)
'unsafety' (in no. of fatalities)

Figure 3.3. Examples of environmental indicators used in transport SEAs

Including environmentally superior alternative(s). Alternative ways of achieving the PPP's objectives then need to be identified. This list should include not only the 'do nothing' alternative, but also alternatives which achieve the objectives at minimum environmental cost. At the policy level, alternatives could include financial investments to reduce the demand for transport or to promote public transport. At the plan level, the siting of housing or transport infrastructure could be optimised to minimize the need to travel, or to encourage travel by foot or bicycle. Figure 3.4 shows the alternatives considered in two transport SEAs.

Predicting the magnitude and significance of the different alternatives' environmental impacts. The magnitude of impacts which the various alternatives have on the environmental components/indicators identified earlier should then be predicted. Impact prediction techniques must consider different spatial

---

TRANSPORT STRATEGY FOR THE GREATER EDINBURGH AREA
(Scottish Office, 1994)

In addition to the baseline situation in 1990 and the 'do nothing' alternative, the SEA evaluated five alternatives, each composed of a different combination of individual transport-related measures (e.g. new road projects, rail improvements, traffic management, congestion charging), representing 'themes':

A. No new Forth road bridge, significant rail improvements across the Forth, and low-cost road and public transport improvements.
B. New bridge, rail improvements and a busway
C. No new bridge, improvements to public transport in and around Edinburgh
D. New bridge plus road links
E. New bridge plus regional structure plan proposals, including a light rail system

22-YEAR TRANSPORTATION PLAN FOR THE SAN DIEGO REGION (SDAG, 1994)

1. Preferred alternative: major expansion of the rail transit system, and a relatively modest increase in the expressway system.
2. 'Quality of life' alternative: greater expansion of the rail transit system and lower highway capacities in the additional transit corridors.
3. 'Cost-constrained' alternative: new transport facilities limited to those which could be built and operated by existing funding sources
4. 'No build – federal' alternative: new facilities limited to federally funded projects which received environmental approvals
5. 'No build – state' alternative (the environmentally preferred alternative): new facilities limited to federally funded projects currently under construction or approved.

Figure 3.4. Examples of alternatives considered in transport SEAs.

dimensions of impact (e.g. national, local), different temporal dimensions (long-term, short-term, irreversible), different types of impacts (e.g. on noise, air pollution, employment), and the cumulative impacts of a range of actions. A PPP may affect some sectors of the community differently from others, so distributional impacts may need to be considered. The methodology must be robust and based on reasonable assumptions.

Some SEA-specific impact prediction models already exist for the transport sector, primarily at the programme/network level: these generally use projected traffic flows to predict such impacts as air pollution or noise. Because the characteristics of trains are more uniform than those of road vehicles, impact prediction methodologies are particularly well developed for the rail sector. GIS techniques are also likely to become a major tool for impact prediction in the future: 'the combination of GIS with transport models would enable energy use, climate change and acidification issues to be analysed and proxy measures for air quality to be developed' (ECMT, 1996). However, it is likely to take several years before GIS is widely used in SEA, due to the current dearth of relevant environmental data in most countries. Models have also been developed which predict changes to access and employment, and costs to operators and users, likely to result from improvements to the traffic network and changes in travel cost. On the other hand, impact prediction techniques applicable to individual transport projects or to programmes are often inappropriate at more strategic levels of decision-making. Although such models exist and are used in SEAs, they often require detailed information which is not yet available on a large scale, are based on assumptions which may not hold true beyond the project level, and do not take account of the prevailing political and social situation. Furthermore many strategic decisions will not need the detailed information which results from these models.

A typical way of presenting impact predictions in SEA is in a matrix such as that shown in figure 3.5, but graphs and verbal descriptions are also often used. Matrices are a particularly popular way of comparing different PPP alternatives. Generally, existing models do not deal well with such issues as the distribution of impacts, cumulative impacts, cross-border impacts, and generated impacts. Nor are there models to appraise the impacts of transport PPPs on other types of PPPs (eg. agriculture, energy). The second example in figure 3.5 shows a relatively rare case where the generated impacts of a transport plan have been considered.

The significance of impacts (which must consider the politico-economic context within which the methodology is used[3]) can be appraised using a variety of techniques, including goals achievement matrices, planning balance sheets, and extended versions of cost-benefit assessment techniques. These models often include some form of impact weighting to reflect the greater perceived importance of some impacts, or the greater sensitivity of some environmental components. These weightings can be determined by experts or by the people affected by the PPP.

Identifying ways of mitigating the environmental impacts of the selected alternative. Once an alternative has been selected, any negative impacts of that alternative should then be minimized, and positive impacts maximized. This will partly already have been done during the design of the PPP. However, further mitigation measures can involve guidelines/criteria for the siting and design of subsequent projects (including constraints on types of projects or on

---

TRANSPORT STRATEGY FOR THE GREATER EDINBURGH AREA
(Scottish Office,1994)

	1990	do min.	A	B	C	D	E
Daily CO_2 emissions (% of 1990)	100	125	126	130	119	131	123
Daily CO emissions (% of 1990)	100	33	33	33	29	33.5	30
Impact on high quality landscapes	n/a	–	1.6 km in AGLV*, 0.6 km adjacent to AGLV	0.6 km adjacent to AGLV	1.8 km adjacent to AGLV	1.6 km in AGLV	0.6 km adjacent to AGLV

* area of great landscape value

22-YEAR TRANSPORTATION PLAN FOR THE SAN DIEGO REGION
(SDAG, 1994)

From the chapter on growth inducement: 'Overall, the plan is designed to serve the planned growth for the region . . . Policies in the land use and pedestrian element and the transportation element encourage higher density residential uses, employment centers, and mixed-use development adjacent to transit centers and transit corridors . . . Siting the highest density uses near transit facilities would encourage more efficient use of mass transit and could reduce some vehicle miles travelled . . .

(Route) SR-125 is located in the outlying areas of the urbanized part of San Diego County. Development in these areas could result in longer commute lengths and increased vehicle miles traveled. This could have an adverse impact on air quality and energy consumption. However, these new highway segments would also relieve congestion on existing roads, which would reduce energy consumption and emissions of air pollutants.'

Figure 3.5. Impact prediction methods used in transport SEAs.

TRANS-EUROPEAN RAIL NETWORK (CEC, 1993)

Landscape: 'For landscapes of high cultural-historical value . . . this impact may be too severe. In such a case the best solution is the safeguarding of these landscapes from the (rail) line. Crucial to this approach is the definition and identification of valuable landscapes . . . The visual impact on landscapes can also be reduced by clustering transport infrastructure.'

22-YEAR TRANSPORTATION PLAN FOR THE SAN DIEGO REGION
(SDAG, 1994)

Land use: 'General Plans and Community Plans should be updated to reflect current status of future improvements to regional arterials, freeways and expressways, or corridors . . . These measures will help to inform the public of future conditions in purchasing, holding, or developing land and reduce the potential for incompatible development.'

Biological resources: 'Project-level environmental assessments on individual projects proposed in the (plan) would include specific mitigation measures to reduce identified significant impacts to biological resources . . . Planning for new highways must be integrated with habitat conservation planning to ensure that core preserve area habitat values would not be compromised.'

Figure 3.6. Examples of impact mitigation proposed in transport SEAs.

the locations where projects can be sited), criteria for approving lower-level plans and programmes, links to the PPPs of other sectors (e.g. land use, housing), beneficial 'shadow' PPPs or projects which aim to replace environmental losses, and public awareness campaigns. Mitigation measures must be effective and realistic (given the economic and political climate). Ideally, they should also be phased so that their implementation can be easily monitored. Figure 3.6 gives examples of some mitigation measures discussed in existing transport SEAs.

SEA report, formal consultation, and decision-making. One of the main purposes of SEA is to make the decision-making system more transparent. As was indicated earlier, consultation with relevant other government organizations, non-government organizations (NGOs), experts and the public should be carried out throughout the SEA: when determining the PPP's objectives, alternatives to be analysed, environmental indicators and issues of concern, the perceived importance of impacts, and mitigation measures. However, a formal round of public consultation may take place after the results of the SEA process have been written up in an SEA report. For instance, for the high-speed rail line from Antwerp to Rotterdam, after the SEA was prepared, information sessions were organized in all communes along the route, information stands were set up at city halls, brochures were distributed, and press articles and radio broadcasts informed residents about the rail line and the SEA; 23,000 written reactions were received in response (Mens en Ruimte, 1996).

SEA reports vary widely in length and approach. For instance, the publically-available report ('executive summary') for the trans-European rail network is a glossy, 34-page leaflet, whilst that for the San Diego regional transport plan is a more technical report of 241 pages. Arguably, a shorter summary report may be of greater use for public consultation and decision-making, whilst technical appendices could contain background information.

The PPP decision-making process will almost invariably be a nebulous, political process which involves a balancing of environmental, social and economic factors. Problems may arise where financial and environmental decisions are made by different groups, or where different transport modes are planned by

---

TRANS-EUROPEAN RAIL NETWORK (Dom, 1996)

'Apart from the international survey conducted by the consultants, no NGOs were involved in the official procedure, nor was a formal public consultation process conducted. Even through environmental protection groups have expressed their concerns regarding the environmental implications of the network, no clear strategy to address these conclusions has been developed. As far as can be established, the SEA has had no significant influence in the decision-making process on the network, except for demonstrating that (high-speed rail) is – for most aspects – a more environmentally friendly mode . . . One of the major problems in assessing the role of the SEA in the decision-making process is that no trade-off analysis was ever made between environmental effects, socioeconomic effects, and investment implications.'

HIGH-SPEED RAIL LINK ANTWERP-ROTTERDAM (Mens en Ruimte, 1996)

'The results of the study . . . are directional but not binding. The final selection on the line location... will have to take account of the assessment results and the results of the consultation and public participation procedures . . . other political agreements, such as the financing of the line . . . (influence decision-making more than do environmental considerations) . . . however, the lowest-cost alternative also proved to be the one with the lowest environmental impact. Thus, no conflict between construction costs and environmental choice arises.'

Figure 3.7. Examples of public consultation and decision-making in transport SEAs.

different bodies. This may be partly overcome through regular meetings, a clear division of roles, and an agreement about the role which SEA should play in decision-making. Figure 3.7 shows two examples of how public participation was conducted and decisions were made for transport SEAs.

Establishing environmental guidelines and monitoring. The implementation stages of the PPP – establishment and application of environmental guidelines and a monitoring programme – are crucial to effective SEA. Without them, it is difficult to know whether the PPP is being implemented correctly, whether its environmental impacts are as predicted, and whether any problems are arising which need to be remedied. Unfortunately, very few (if any) SEA monitoring programmes exist in the transport sector to date. This may be remedied in the future with increasing use of GIS and regularly-updated environmental databases.

ISSUES AND CONCLUSIONS

The use of SEA has grown rapidly since the early 1990s, partly in response to the evolution of a Europe-wide SEA Directive, but also because SEA is increasingly seen as a good practice technique which can help to improve the PPP, increase transparency, and reduce conflict. This is particularly needed in the transport sector, which is very complex (multi-modal, multi-scale, multi-actor), inextricably linked to virtually every other economic sector, not prone to straightforward technical solutions, and emotive, and which has severe environmental impacts. SEA for the transport sector will continue to grow, and will increasingly affect transport planning. However, a number of factors presently limit the effectiveness of SEA (and sustainable transport planning generally), and need to be addressed in the late 1990s.

First, different authorities are often responsible for different transport modes and scales, and use different criteria for appraising and choosing transport projects. This makes it difficult to identify and implement solutions that involve switching modes or more efficiently linking modes.

Second, transport planning is generally carried out in conjunction with land use planning at a local level, but less so at a national scale. National-level transport PPPs and projects may thus be decided on without being set in a national-level planning or sustainability context, making it difficult to achieve local-level sustainability aims.

The current trend towards the privatisation of parts of the transport sector, notably rail, is likely to significantly reduce the potential for both strategic transport planning and SEA. Privatization generally results in a splintering of decision-making (reducing the possibility for integrated, strategic planning), competition for the profitable segments of the transport sector (e.g. the routes between major cities) and a corresponding decay in the less profitable (and often more equity-promoting) segments, and increased emphasis on financial aspects to the detriment of environmental considerations. SEA needs to be used when decisions regarding privatization are made, as well as on tenders for privatised services (Cullingford, 1996).

Transport planning has traditionally been based on very sophisticated transport models which work well for single modes and restricted areas. The current trend in SEA is to try to expand these models, at virtually the same level of specificity, to much larger areas, several modes and/or a greater number of environmental factors. The resulting models are enormously complex and expensive, whilst often based on questionable assumptions; they result in information which may be too detailed for a strategic-level decision, and with a high level of uncertainty. Especially at the policy and plan level, there is a need to use simpler, cheaper, and more descriptive assessment techniques such as simple matrices and expert judgement; these techiques may lead to less precise results, but these are at a level of detail appropriate for strategic decisions, are often no less robust or more uncertain than those of complex models, and are easier to understand by the decision-maker and the public.

Finally, transport PPPs are only as effective as their implementation on the ground. Implementation of sustainable transport PPPs will increasingly involve changes in user behaviour rather than new infrastructure or technology. In turn, user behaviour will not change unless people understand the reasons for, and agree with, the need to change. As such, ignoring the public during transport-related decision-making may well make the resulting PPP ineffective. Transport SEA in the late 1990s needs to incorporate public participation as an integral factor, not as a late, legislatively-mandated add-on.

NOTES

1. In practice, the terms policy, plan and programme are often used interchangeably. It is the concept of tiering that is important here, rather than distinctions between the tiers.
2. These cumulative impacts do not only mean that air pollution caused by one road needs to be added to that caused by other nearby roads. In some cases this pollution may grow synergistically, as is the case when smog forms through the interaction of other pollutants, causing new pollution that is worse than the sum of the original pollutants. Different types of pollutants can also have cumulative impacts: maps drawn by ASH Consultants show a progressive decline in 'tranquil areas', i.e. areas that are both quiet and visually unspoilt.
3. In at least one case, different impact weighting systems were used for two countries affected by a rail line.

REFERENCES

BirdLife International *et al.* (1995) *The Impact of Trans-European Networks on Nature Conservation: A Pilot Project.* Sandy, Beds.: RSPB.

BirdLife International *et al.* (1996) *Strategic Environmental Assessment and Corridor Analysis of Trans-European Transport Networks: A Position Paper.* Sandy, Beds.: RSPB.

Buchan, K. (1990) *Wheels of Fortune: Strategies for Transport Integration in the South East of England.* London: South East Economic Development Strategy.

Commission of the European Communities (CEC) (1993) *The European High Speed Train Network: Environmental Impact Assessment, Executive Summary,* DGVII. Brussels: CEC.

Cullingford, R. (1996) Strategic Environmental Assessment in the UK's Rail Sector. MSc dissertation, Oxford Brookes University, Oxford.

Department of the Environment (DoE) (1996) *Indicators of Sustainable Development for the UK.* London: HMSO.

Department of Transport (DoT) (1993) *Design Manual for Roads and Bridges,* Vol. 11, *Environmental Assessment.* London: HMSO.

DHV Environment and Infrastructure (1994) *SEA Existing Methodologies.* Report for European Commission DGXI. Brussels: CEC.

Dom, A. (1996) SEA of the trans-European transport networks, in Therivel and Partidario (eds.) *op. cit.,* pp. 73–85.

English Nature (1996) *Strategic Environmental Assessment and Nature Conservation.* Peterborough: English Nature.

European Conference of Ministers of Transport (ECMT) (1996) *Strategic Environmental Assessment in the Transport Sector.* Report by Mens en Ruimte. Brussels.

Ferrary, C. (1996) *European Experience in Strategic Environmental Assessment.* London: Entec.

Heatley, A. (1996) A Study of Strategic Environmental Assessment of Multi-modal Transport Policies, Plans and Programmes. MSc dissertation, Oxford Brookes University, Oxford.

Marcial Echenique and Partners (1995) *Methodology for Transport Impact Assessment.* Report for European Commission DGVII. Brussels: CEC.

Mens en Ruimte (1996) *Case Studies of Strategic Environmental Assessment.* Report for European Commission DGXI. Brussels: CEC.

Ministere de l'Environnement (MdE) (1994) *Le corridor nord: Evaluation environnementale des programmes intermodaux de transport.* Lille Cedex: Association Amenagement-Environnement.

MVA Consultancy, Oscar Faber TPA and Institute for Transport Studies, University of Leeds (1994) *Common Appraisal Framework for Urban Transport Projects.* London: HMSO.

OECD (1994) *Environmental Indicators: Core Set.* Paris: OECD.

Partidario, M. (1996) SEA regulations and guidelines worldwide, in Thérivel and Partidario (eds.) *op. cit.,* pp. 15–44.

Royal Society for the Protection of Birds/Worldwide Fund for Nature (RSPB/WWF) (1995) *Feasibility Study for Common Appraisal of Transport Options in the Newport and South Wales Area.* Sandy, Beds.: RSPB.

Sadler, B. and R. Verheem (1996) *Strategic Environmental Assessment: Status, Challenges and Future Directions.* Report 53, The Hague: Ministry of Housing, Spatial Planning and the Environment of the Netherlands.

San Diego Association of Governments (SDAG) (1994) *Final Environmental Impact Report for the 1994 Regional Transportation Plan.* San Diego: San Diego Association of Governments

Scottish Office (1994) *Setting Forth: Environmental Appraisal of Alternative Strategies.* Edinburgh: Industry Department, Roads Directorate.

Sheate, W. (1992) Strategic environmental assessment in the transport sector. *Project Appraisal,***7**(3), pp. 170–174.

Standing Advisory Committee for Trunk Road Assessment (SACTRA) (1992) *Assessing the Environmental Impact of Road Schemes.* London: HMSO.

Steer Davies Gleave (1996) *State of the Art on SEA for Transport Infrastructure.* Report for European Commission DGVII. Brussels: CEC.

Therivel, R. and M.R. Partidario (eds.) (1996) *The Practice of Strategic Environmental Assessment.* London: Earthscan.

Treweek, J. , S. Thompson, N. Veitch and C. Japp (1993) Ecological assessment of proposed road developments: A review of environmental statements. *Journal of Environmental Planning and Management,* **36**(3), pp. 295–307.

Verheyen, R. and K. Nagels (1996) Methodology, Focalisation, Evaluation and Scope of Environmental Impact Assessment. Fourth Report: Strategic Environmental Assessment, Theory and Practice. Report 212 (draft), University of Antwerp.

CHAPTER 4

PUBLIC ATTITUDES TO TRANSPORT ISSUES: FINDINGS FROM THE BRITISH SOCIAL ATTITUDES SURVEYS

Bridget Taylor and Lindsay Brook

For transport policies to be sustainable they need both to be designed to be compatible with and contribute to sustainable development, and to be broadly acceptable to the general public. The premise that motivates our work is that those involved in formulating and implementing transport policy need to understand not only public attitudes to transport policy options and how these attitudes vary between subgroups, but also more fundamentally why different people have certain attitudes and where these attitudes come from. This understanding is necessary if policies are to be formulated and presented in such a way as to gain public support, and if policy-makers wish to try to change attitudes and thus travel behaviour.

During recent years transport issues have become much more prominent on the public agenda. They have gained considerable, if intermittent and selective, attention from the media. Three aspects in particular have come to the fore. One is the impact of traffic congestion and pollution on our towns and cities, and on our health and particularly that of our children. A second is the environmental impacts of major road-building schemes and the controversy about their effectiveness in relieving (or generating) congestion (SACTRA, 1994). The third is, of course, the long-term effect of the unrestricted use of cars on the global environment (Royal Commission on Environmental Pollution, 1994).

At the same time, but for different reasons, there have been controversies about the merits or otherwise of rail privatization and bus deregulation, and most recently the possiblity of privatization of the London Underground. This in turn has fuelled a developing – if still embryonic – debate about the proper role of public transport and how different transport modes – many now under diverse ownership and control – might be integrated. For example, in a recent report

(UK Round Table on Sustainable Development, 1997), the disadvantages for the travelling public of unrestricted car use have been highlighted.

Meanwhile, in terms of government transport policy, there have been a few notable developments recently. While many road widening and 'improvement' projects (as well as maintenance) continue, expenditure on new road building projects has been significantly reduced. These cut-backs may have been driven more by financial imperatives and by growing protest movements against major road-building schemes (and increasing public sympathy for the aims of the protesters) than by any government conversion to alternative thinking on transport policy. The policy of increasing duty on road fuel by 5 per cent per annum over the rate of inflation has been in effect for a few years and is set to continue, so that the price of fuel is increasing in relation to the RPI. The shift towards a package approach for funding local authorities' transport projects may facilitate funding for schemes such as park-and-ride projects, and allows groups of local authorities to work together on such projects. Overall government spending on transport (excluding the more controversial areas such as under-valuation of parts of the railway system which has been sold off) has been reduced with a small shift in the balance from roads to public transport, but the latter continues to attract the smaller share by far.

While the last government continued to oppose the setting of national targets for reducing road traffic, a private members' bill tabled by a Liberal Democrat MP, with provisions to empower councils to set local targets, received all-party support, albeit much watered-down. This was enacted just before the general election (May 1997) as the Traffic Reduction Act.

Earlier work, based mainly on results from the 1993 *British Social Attitudes* survey[1] (Taylor and Stokes, 1994), revealed high levels of public concern about traffic congestion and the environmental impact of traffic and the encroachment of large-scale road-building schemes on the countryside. Nonetheless, levels of support for broadly 'sustainable' transport policies were more limited. In other words, we found that concern about problems does not translate very directly into support for policies designed to mitigate their effects.

Now that we have readings on attitudes on transport issues from several more years of *British Social Attitudes* (BSA) surveys,[2] have levels of public awareness of and concern about transport issues risen in recent years, alongside the increasing prominence given to them in policy debates and in the media? Secondly, have levels of support for more sustainable policy options increased? We might reasonably hypothesize that, as the transport debate has developed, acceptance of more sustainable transport policies would have risen.

We can also look at the direction and strength of public opinion among various sub-groups. Are some groups in the population more concerned about, and more supportive of, certain policies than others, or is there little variation? What characteristics are variations in attitudes associated with? What are the likely sources of such differences in attitudes? Are people's views motivated mainly by self-interest, or is there a more altruistic or idealistic element behind some of the attitudes they hold?

THE DATA

From its inception in 1983, the BSA survey series has included a number of questions designed to measure levels of concern about the environment. Some of these asked specifically about the impact of road-building and road traffic. However, it was only in 1993 that a new set of questions was developed to tap public attitudes towards different policy options, and to link these with measures of environmental concern and with people's own travel behaviour and modes of transport. Most of these items have since been repeated, some every year, others less often. Clearly our time-span on most measures is limited, and so year-on-year shifts in opinion need to be interpreted with caution. Small changes could well be due to sampling and measurement error, or to random fluctuations. We also need to be alert to possible influences from extraneous factors, such as the prevailing economic climate. Nonetheless, as we shall see, some shifts are large enough and consistent enough to be interpreted with some confidence as providing evidence of real change. Thus we now have sufficient data to begin to talk about patterns of attitudes over time, and to distinguish real change from stability or fluctuation.

LEVELS OF ENVIRONMENTAL CONCERN

Evidence from successive BSA surveys and from many other sources leaves no room for doubt that concerns about environmental degradation in general, and the depredations of road traffic in particular, are widespread. But these concerns must be considered in a broader context. Support for core welfare provision (health, education and state pensions) consistently outstrips support for other government spending programmes – even law and order measures. Moreover, support for 'non-core' spending programmes is over the years rather more fickle, reflecting current concerns – such as rising unemployment in the early 1990s. And when made to *compete* as priorities for public funds with other major spending programmes, both roads and public transport feature barely at all.

Turning to spending on environmental protection measures, we find that the proportion favouring more (or much more) government expenditure rose from 34 per cent in 1985 to around 60 per cent in the early 1990s, but has since fallen sharply to 42 per cent in 1996 – a drop possibly attributable to the impact of the latest economic recession in changing people's priorities. This suggests that there has been a real increase in concern for the environment generally, but that this is vulnerable to be squeezed when times are hard and other priorities (such as jobs) feel more pressing.

A similar pattern over time is seen in response to a set of three questions asking respondents to trade off environmental protection against other priorities:

Table 4.1. Sacrifices to protect the environment.

Percentage agreeing/ agreeing strongly	1990	1991	1993	1994	1995	1996
Government should do more to protect environment, even if this means higher taxes	66	60	43	58	61	57
Industry should do more to protect environment, even if this means fewer jobs	75	64	51	65	61	67
People should do more to protect environment, even if this means higher prices	75	68	50	72	67	60

Majorities remain ready to put environmental protection above living standards, but these majorities were severely dented between 1991 and 1993 by the recession, and have not yet fully recovered[3].

Clearly concern about the environment generally, and about threats to the countryside, is widespread – but who will crusade for either? Recent BSA figures tend to confirm our conclusion of a decade ago, that 'concern is relatively passive' and that the small number of activists are typically – though by no means entirely – highly educationally qualified, middle class and many already members of 'environmental' organizations[4]. The environmental threat asked about was 'a new housing development in the countryside' (with hindsight, 'a major new road' might have been a more pertinent scenario). We found that *likelihood* to take action rose from 86 to 92 per cent between 1986 and 1994. But the proportions willing to take action that would *commit* them to a cause, and involve time and effort, remain much lower. Moreover, people (hardly surprisingly) are rather more likely to *say* they *might* do something about an environmental issue than they are to have *taken action*.

CONCERN ABOUT TRANSPORT ISSUES

Exhaust Fumes and Ill-Health

BSA trend data from the 1980s reveal growing concerns about the environmental dangers of road traffic. By the end of the decade, these had grown to such an extent that new measurements had to be devised effectively to capture the public mood. In 1993, we fielded a new series of parallel questions about six environmental hazards, one of them 'air pollution caused by cars'. Few people discounted its danger 'for them and their family' (Brook, 1994), rating it in between 'pesticides and chemicals used in farming' (thought slightly less dangerous), and 'air pollution caused by industry' (thought slightly more so). In 1993, 40 per cent of respondents rated exhaust pollution as 'extremely' or 'very' dangerous; in 1996 42 per cent did so.

On another measure, concern about an increase in ill health due to air pollution from cars in Britain's cities, rose significantly in recent years; the proportion rating a large increase in ill health as 'certain to happen' rose from 16 per cent in 1993 to 25 per cent in 1996, while the proportion rating it 'not very likely' or 'certain not to happen' fell from 20 per cent to 11 per cent.

Threats to the Countryside

It is useful to compare concern about traffic with concern about other environmental threats. We have a question, introduced in 1985, which asks respondents to name, from a list of seven hazards, which they see as the 'greatest' and the 'next greatest' threat to the countryside. Between 1985 and 1994, 'motorways and road building' rose from almost last to second place, and the proportion identifying this as a threat more than doubled over this period, from 21 to 43 per cent, just behind 'industrial pollution'. Much of this change occurred fairly recently, just between 1993 and 1994.

A modified version of this question, listing nine hazards, was introduced in 1995 and repeated in 1996. The proportion citing 'new roads and motorways' rose from 29 to 33 per cent over the one year, rising from joint third to second place behind 'land and air pollution', but ahead of both 'new housing' and 'industrial development'.

Traffic Congestion, Pollution and Noise

When asked in 1995 about how likely several environmental problems were to become serious, respondents named both traffic congestion and traffic noise as much more serious than either the greenhouse effect or oil and gas shortages.

Other measures, more directly addressing the problems of traffic congestion, pollution and noise, were introduced in 1993 and 1994, and repeated in 1995. Respondents were asked to rate the seriousness of each *for them* on a four-point scale. Substantial majorities saw each of the problems as 'serious' or 'very serious', with only very small minorities rating them 'not very serious' or 'not a problem at all'. The table 4.2 shows the proportions who see the problems as 'very serious'.

We note a number of points. First, the rise in proportions rating each problem as 'very serious' is large enough and/or consistent enough to suggest a real increase in public concern about traffic problems. Secondly, evidently traffic problems are seen (as yet) to be worse in urban areas and on motorways, than in

Table 4.2. Traffic congestion, pollution and noise.

Percentage saying 'very serious'	1993	1994	1995
Congestion on motorway	22	44	42
Congestion at popular places in the countryside	16	18	22
Increased traffic on country roads	11	18	21
Exhaust fumes from traffic in towns and cities	n/a	50	63
Traffic congestion in towns and cities	n/a	44	50
Noise from traffic in towns and cities	n/a	27	32

rural areas. Moreover, levels of concern about *rural* traffic problems have risen less than have levels of concern about *urban* traffic problems. Thirdly, urban traffic pollution both elicits the highest levels of concern (greater even than congestion) and shows the greatest increase. This may be partly attributable to media attention to health risks from pollution caused by vehicle exhausts, and partly because many more people live in cities and towns than in the country.

These items can be combined into a summary scale measure to facilitate comparison over time. The advantage of combining several individual items to form a scale is that this tends to cancel out some of the variations in response that may be due to extraneous factors such as question wording, order, context and so on. We have constructed a three-item scale for 1993, 1994 and 1995, and a six-item scale for 1994 and 1995. Each has a potential range of 1 to 10, where the higher the score the greater the level of concern. These summary measures demonstrate clearly how concern overall has risen in recent years; we will come back to these scales later when we come to assess attitudes towards policy options.

While most of our time-series are short, and the number of items small, we seem nonetheless to have sufficient evidence to say that public concern about traffic problems has been increasing, particularly in the most recent years and particularly about urban areas.

POLICY

Clearly there are widespread concerns about road traffic, especially over pollution and ill-health, and concerns have tended to increase over the last decade or so, though some were dented somewhat by the impact of the economic recession in the early 1990s. But what, if anything, do people think should be done about road traffic?

As we have already noted, there is a higher level of concern than there is support for policy measures intended to help alleviate the problems. While traffic problems are widely recognized, many of the policy options currently under

Table 4.3. Levels of concern.

'Concern scales' (means)	1993	1994	1995
Three-item	6.4	6.7	7.2
Six-item	n/a	7.1	7.7

discussion gain only limited support. The state of public opinion parallels, and indeed partly explains, the position of both government and opposition: both appear to recognize that the introduction of measures to restrict road travel is inevitable, but neither has (yet) changed its policy stance to any great extent. Of course, the current debate about transport is relatively new and the problems complex, and a government of any party would face the same dilemma.

As we shall see, support for 'cost-free' policy options is easy to find. Levels of support for different measures are varied. The pattern often conforms approximately to models such as 'people want others to limit their car use but not to reduce their own'. Nonetheless other factors also seem to be at work. Indeed, there appears to be a significant minority who are so concerned about environmental aspects of road transport (and some about congestion as well) that they are prepared to support policies which would place limitations on their own behaviour and incur considerable costs.

Support for Public Transport

The essence of public attitudes to transport policy is encapsulated in responses to two straightforward questions, introduced in 1996. Thus we find that while as many as 68 per cent think it very important to improve public transport in Britain, only 28 per cent think it very important to cut down the number of cars on the roads; a tiny 3 per cent feel able to say improving public transport is not important.

On a different measure, three-quarters say that over the next few years government should give priority to the needs of public transport users, compared with only 15 per cent putting the needs of motorists ahead. It is hard to believe that such overwhelming support for public transport respondents, with little change over recent years, think that car drivers still have 'too easy a time' of it in Britain's cities and towns.

These patterns of responses beg several key questions: why do people think it important to improve public transport if not to reduce car use; and at the same time eschew effective measures to reduce car use? And who will be using the newly improved public transport?

Two parallel questions show that public support for public transport has been growing over the last few years.

Table 4.4. Policy choices.

If government had to choose, should it improve . . .	1991 %	1993 %	1994 %	1996 %
. . . in towns and cities				
- roads	44	39	37	26
- public transport	55	59	62	72
. . . in country areas				
- roads	38	34	34	29
-public transport	61	64	65	68

Substantial majorities now favour improvement to public transport, over roads, in both rural and urban areas. Note particularly the recent and rapid rise in the priority accorded to public transport in towns and cities (in line with responses to the questions on 'traffic problems' reported above). We also find that opposition to closing even rail and bus services that do not pay for themselves enormously outweighs support for shutting them down, by about five to one. This suggests that transport is yet another area where most people see market forces alone as inappropriate (McKie and Brook, 1996).

But we need to put this growing enthusiasm for public transport in the perspective of priorities for other government spending programmes. When asked to choose, from a list of ten, which they think should be the government's first and second spending priorities, in 1996 77 per cent of respondents named health and 66 per cent named education, dwarfing all others. Public transport came in with a meagre 7 per cent, albeit up from 3 per cent in the 1980s, behind housing, industry, social security, and police and prisons, though now ahead of roads on just 3 per cent.

Opposition to New Roads

These figures largely mask a substantial shift over quite a long period against building more roads in rural areas programmes:

Table 4.5. Attitudes towards road building in rural areas.

Providing more roads in country areas. . .	1986 %	1987 %	1990 %	1996 %
. . . should be stopped altogether	10	10	13	15
should be discouraged	40	46	52	53
don't mind	29	27	24	23
should be encouraged	20	13	10	8

Still on the broad priorities for transport policy, we find (in 1995) the following order of priorities for more government spending within the area of transport:

Table 4.6. Expenditure priorities.

% supporting spending to ...	%
... improve facilities for pedestrians and cyclists	63
improve local rail services	55
improve local bus services	51
improve long distance rail services	46
improve existing roads	37
build more roads	20

Building more roads was the only area in which the proportion favouring less spending (33 per cent) outweighed that favouring more spending. Note also that even improving existing roads was given a much lower priority for more spending than either various forms of public transport or pedestrian and cycling facilities. We might speculate that, had these questions been asked even just five years earlier, the findings would have been quite different.

We find also that support for construction of more motorways to ease congestion has fallen from 40 per cent in 1991 to 25 per cent in 1996. And, suggestive that many people are listening to the so-called 'Great Debate' about transport, agreement with the argument that 'building more roads just encourages more traffic' has risen significantly from 47 per cent in 1993 (when the question was first asked) to 57 per cent in 1996. There is apparently majority support for expansion of public transport, including giving this priority for public funding over investment in roads, and indeed signs of growing opposition to road building. All this sounds like rather good news, but what of attitudes towards more specific measures aimed at restraining car use?

Restraint Measures: 'Sticks' and 'Carrots'

Few among the public take a completely *laissez-faire* attitude to car use. Yet barely half dispute unrestrained car use even at the price of environmental damage, although public opinion does seem to have been changing quite quickly in this respect in recent years (table 4.7).

And when presented with the statement: 'For the sake of the environment, car users should pay higher taxes', only one in five agree, down even from the quarter expressing this view in the early 1990s. Barely half agree. There is no evidence at all of any increase in support for this approach (table 4.8).

We turn next to look at attitudes to some more specific measures aimed at

Table 4.7. Attitudes to car use.

People should be allowed to use their cars as much as they like, even if it causes damage to the environment	1995 %	1991 %	1993 %	1994 %
Agree/agree strongly	19	17	17	17
Disagree/disagree strongly	43	40	48	51

Table 4.8. Attitudes to taxes.

For the sake of the environment, car users should pay higher taxes	1990 %	1991 %	1993 %	1994 %	1996 %
Agree/agree strongly	24	26	19	23	19
Disagree/disagree strongly	54	47	50	57	54

limiting car use and promoting other forms of transport. We have two sets of questions which aim to address these issues. We look first at questions which were introduced in 1993 and repeated in 1995 – some also in 1994 – but not in 1996. Here we are more interested in *relative* levels of support, between various policy measures and over time, than in *absolute* levels of support for particular measures. In table 4.9, the options are ordered according to level of popularity and a pattern is clearly seen. Pedestrianization, and measures to help public transport, gain the greatest support. Vehicle permits for city centre access are, perhaps surprisingly, endorsed by half the sample. But only around a quarter favours motorway tolls and urban road charges, and even fewer favour higher parking charges.

Table 4.9. 'Pro-sustainable transport' policy options.

Percentage strongly in favour/in favour	1993	1994	1995	Change 1993-1995
More pedestrianization	69	n/a	68	-1
Greater priority for cyclists and pedestrians	n/a	n/a	64	n/a
Greater priority for buses	60	61	61	+1
Improve public transport	49	55	58	+9
Introduce vehicle permits in city centres	49	n/a	49	-
Introduce motorway tolls	24	n/a	22	-2
Road-pricing in city centres	18	n/a	25	+7
Much higher parking charges	16	n/a	17	+1

Clearly the 'carrot' measures – support for public transport and pedestrianization – are widely acceptable; in contrast the 'stick' measures, which increase the price of motoring, gain little support. Furthermore, growth in support for 'sustainable' transport measures over the last couple of years has been limited. Certainly support for improvement in public transport has risen significantly, and (more surprisingly perhaps) support for urban road charges shows signs of rising, albeit from a very low base. But otherwise attitudes to various policy options have been remarkably static.

This stability is also seen in the structure of attitudes to policy options. Factor analyses of responses to the transport policy items asked in 1993, 1994 and 1995 consistently reveal the same structure of attitudes, whether we take those asked in all three years, or the more restricted set asked in just one or two years. We find that the items consistently divide into two groups: those about relatively popular measures aimed at supporting public transport, walking and cycling, and the relatively unpopular measures to restrict the use, and increase the costs, of car use.

These findings are of course in marked contrast with those recording the rise in concern about transport problems. This can be seen more clearly when we summarize the individual transport measures in a scale parallel to the 'concern' scale. The scale is constructed from nine[5] policy items asked in both 1993 and 1995 and has, like the 'concern' scale, a potential range of 1 to 10, with high scores representing support for sustainable transport measures. Here we compare it with the 3-item concern scale.

Table 4.10. Scales (mean scores).

	Concern*	Policy**	Correlation
1993	6.4	5.6	0.14
1994	6.7		
1995	7.2	5.7	0.23*

* 3-item scale; ** 9-item scale

While concern has risen steadily and significantly, overall policy attitudes on these measures have remained almost unchanged.

We can go a step further and construct two sub-scales: one using the three items about measures supporting pedestrianization and public transport, and a second, made up of the five items tapping attitudes to restricting car use. The higher the score, the more supportive is the respondent of 'sustainable' policy measures:

Table 4.11. Policy scales (means).

	Pro-public transport/ pedestrianization*	Anti-car**
1993	6.9	5.0
1995	7.0	5.1

* 3-item scale; ** 5-item scale

It is immediately apparent that pro-public transport and pedestrianization measures are much more popular than the anti-car measures. The table 4.11 also shows that on both policy scales there was virtually no change between 1993 and 1995. Widespread and growing concern about traffic problems is not being translated into support for more sustainable policies aimed at mitigating these problems.

The second set of questions about policy measures was introduced in 1996. Respondents were presented with a number of ways of raising money to improve public transport and asked how much they supported or opposed each. In table 4.12 the items have been re-ordered from the most to the least popular.

The most popular measure was halving spending on new roads, followed, perhaps surprisingly, by road pricing on motorways and urban roads. Doubling the cost of petrol over ten years and raising VAT gained much less support, and least popular of all (perhaps sensibly) was cutting spending on maintenance of existing roads. But although we have seen widespread support for improvement of public transport, none of the suggested means to pay for it gains much support.

The same respondents, in a separate question, were presented with a range of

Table 4.12. Policy measures for promoting public transport.

	% supporting/ supporting strongly	% opposing/ opposing strongly
Cutting in half spending on new roads	36	34
Charging £1 for every 50 miles motorists travel on motorways	30	47
Charging all motorists £2 each time they enter or drive through a city or town centre at peak times	30	51
Gradually doubling the cost of petrol over the next ten years	16	61
Increasing taxes like VAT that we all pay on goods and services	12	68
Cutting in half spending on maintenance of the roads we have already	6	72

Table 4.13. Policy measures to reduce car use.

	No difference %	Little less %	Quite a bit less/ give up %
Gradually doubling the cost of petrol over the next ten years*	38	30	30
Greatly improving the reliability of *local* public transport	44	26	28
Charging all motorists around £2 each time they enter or drive through a city or town centre at peak times*	45	19	35
Greatly improving *long distance* rail and coach services	52	24	23
Charging £1 for every 50 miles motorists travel on motorways*	56	21	22
Making parking penalties and restrictions much more severe	62	16	21
Special cycle lanes on local roads	74	12	13
A free school bus service for your children	67	8	22

Notes: * Those without access to a car were not asked these questions.
The question about a free school bus service was asked only of those with children aged 4–15 living in the household.

measures which 'might get people to cut down on the number of car journeys they make', and asked what effect, if any, each might have on their own car use. Three of the measures (marked with an asterisk) were identical in the two questions. In the table above, the measures are ordered from most to least 'effective'.

Of course we need to bear in mind that we are all rather bad predictors of our own behaviour in hypothetical situations. Nonetheless, the results are interesting if not altogether encouraging. Again we are interested in relative rather than absolute levels of responses. Most effective in reducing car use would seem to be doubling the price of petrol, which we have just seen to be rather unpopular. Seen as least effective are cycle lanes, and free school buses – a form of local public transport improvement – both of which we know to be popular. The picture looks rather mixed. Improving local and long distance public transport, for which we find widespread support, might be moderately effective in reducing car use. Urban road charges, which are rather unpopular, might induce a substantial minority to give up or reduce significantly their reliance on cars; motorway tolls appear likely to be less effective. Increased parking restrictions and charges appear to be both unpopular and unlikely to be very effective – but are being implemented widely.

WIDER POLICY AND LIFE-STYLE ISSUES

Clearly any substantial shift in transport policy to support public transport, cycling and walking at the expense of support for car users and roads, would over the longer term have a considerable impact on our way of life and require some changes in behaviour. In this section we attempt to explore two aspects of public attitudes to these wider lifestyle issues, as far as our data allow. We look first at people's attitudes to their own car use, and then at some rather miscellaneous evidence about attitudes to society's car use, and the way of organising our lives collectively which car use supports.

We have a few questions which tap people's attitudes to their car use, or what is sometimes referred to as 'car-dependence'. Table 4.13 suggests that it may be very hard to persuade motorists to cut down on their driving. Yet there are signs that the public is becoming readier to admit to over-dependence on cars (table 4.14).

Over the three years, the proportion acknowledging that some car trips are not strictly necessary showed a modest increase, while the proportion strongly agreeing almost doubled. There has been a small increase too in the proportion willing to disagree with the statement that 'driving one's own car is too convenient to give up for the sake of the environment', up from 24 per cent in 1993 to 29 per cent in 1996. But those endorsing the proposition (35 per cent) still outnumber those disagreeing with it. And around three out of five people with access to a car say they would find it 'really inconvenient . . . more or less every day of their lives' if they were denied the use of it.

On this and other evidence, it would be difficult to disagree with the conclusions in Cullinane (1992): 'The level of attachment of most people to their car is such that it will take some positive action from outside to force any real reduction in traffic, and that this positive action will have the most impact if it hits people's purses directly.'

Next we investigate how people view society's car use broadly, and whether

Table 4.14. Car dependence.

Many of the short journeys I now make by car I could just as easily walk	1993 %	1996 %
Agree strongly	13	24
Agree	37	35
Neither agree nor disagree	10	12
Disagree	24	19
Disagree strongly	10	7

Note: the base excludes those who reported that they never travel by car (12 per cent in 1993, 5 per cent in 1996)

or not they perceive any problems with our heavily car-based way of life. The items on recent BSA surveys are not ideal for this purpose, but some useful interpretations can be made. We look first at some items on attitudes to activities in countryside and then at a couple of items which tap perceptions of issues to do with land use planning.

In 1994 only one quarter of respondents agreed that protecting the countryside depends on limiting the number of visitors, albeit up from just 14 per cent in 1987. And virtually no-one identifies tourism as a threat to the countryside, even when presented on a list with other 'threats'. When asked (in 1994 and 1995) about six possible measures[6] to protect 'popular places in the countryside', majorities of respondents supported all of them – suggesting that countryside protection is recognized as a problem. The measure most widely supported was 'pay and protect' (51 per cent in 1995), and promoting alternative sites (again 51 per cent). We should note that both of these measures might be seen as accepting the current level of countryside activity, and aiming to repair the damage or divert activity elsewhere (that is, to 'manage' demand more effectively). Least popular were measures that involved *rationing* of some kind: closing down the site at certain times of year, issuing visitors' permits, and cutting down and closing car parks, and cutting advertising and promotion. All of these less popular measures are ones which might be seen as aiming to reduce the level of (car-borne) countryside activity.

Yet both pollution and road-building, for example, are widely seen as threats to the countryside. And over half (54 per cent) in 1994 thought the countryside is so popular now that there is no pleasure in visiting it. There is clear evidence from BSA and elsewhere that concern about damage to the countryside has been rising steadily over many years. Yet it appears that so far most people do not connect this with overuse by visitors to the countryside, and are not (yet) ready to accept the measures which are necessary to protect the countryside from the threats that concern them, many of which entail restrictions, particularly on car use, and costs.

We turn last in this section to two items which we can use to investigate public perceptions of issues about land use planning and the location of activities (which of course have travel and transport implications). One item addresses the issue of housing developments in country areas. We find that there was a modest shift in opinion in the latter half of the 1980s against building new housing in country areas: in 1986, 64 per cent of respondents said that this should be stopped or discouraged, compared with 70 per cent in 1990, but this figure has not risen since. However, it seems reasonable to speculate that this has more to do with concerns about the visual impact of new developments in the countryside, rather than with the implications of these developments for road traffic generation.

The second item concerns out-of-town developments. The proportion opposing the movement of shops and offices out of urban centres rose substantially

Table 4.15. Location choices.

Shops and offices should be encouraged to move out of town and city centres	1993 %	1995 %
Strongly agree/agree	26	21
Neither	25	17
Disagree/strongly disagree	44	55

over two years. This again provides evidence that some people have learnt from the debate on transport (table 4.15).

Using this somewhat patchy evidence, we can surmise that while many people identify and are concerned about some of the environmental damage caused by road traffic, most people do not to any great extent appear to make causal connections between individual car travel behaviour – particularly their own behaviour – and the need for restrictions on car use to ameliorate these problems. And where people do perhaps make connections between 'life-style choices' and environmental impacts (and people may be thinking in terms of aesthetic or social concerns rather than of road traffic), they may look more to the collective level, such as the use of planning controls, rather than the individual level where individual behaviour and choices – including their own – are a key mechanism for change.

And indeed, we might ask, why should they do otherwise? Government policy has changed only at the margins, and has not indicated clearly the need for a fundamental change in the way in which we all – individually and collectively – organize how we get to the things we need and want. Many, perhaps most, people may be awaiting a clear and confident lead from government, politicians, businesses, transport experts and so on, both in explaining the need for and in *implementing* more sustainable transport policies. Of course we are all as individuals responsible for the consequences of our own behaviour. But change needs to come from government and other powerful collectives, as well as from individuals for two equally important reasons. One is that change is needed at the strategic level in the structural framework of our transport, economic and planning system within which individuals make *constrained* choices about their travel behaviour. The second is that a rational and reasonable lead from those in positions of power will help individuals better understand why and how they can modify their own behaviour in ways which contribute to a more sustainable life-style.

WHO AND WHY?

Next we turn to the question of whether attitudes to transport issues are largely uniform, or whether they differ between sub-groups, and if so, how. We also investigate whether sub-group differences are stable or changing over time. These findings may give us some insight into *why* attitudes differ – what are their sources? Such insight is valuable to those who need to gain public support for policies, and who seek to change behaviour through changing attitudes.

There are several possible approaches that could be taken. One would be to select a range of 'concern' and policy items, and cross-tabulate them by a range of likely characteristics, to look for response differences between the various sub-groups (see Stokes and Taylor, 1995). A second approach is to use the composite scale measures and look at the mean scale scores for different subgroups. This is the approach adopted here. A third approach is to use multivariate analysis, which we shall come to later.

The 'Traffic Concern' Scale

Table 4.18 in the Appendix to this chapter shows mean scores on the six-item 'traffic concern' scale[7] for sub-groups of selected characteristics[8], for both 1994 and 1995. This scale is used because it is composed of a more comprehensive range of items than others we might have used. Its drawback is that it gives us only a one-year interval, so differences in the scores between the years should be interpreted with caution. As before, higher scores indicate greater concern.

The first point to note is that all groups show high levels of concern, with few big differences between groups. Secondly, we can see that concern rose in all groups between 1994 and 1995. The biggest variations appear when we look at travel behaviour[9] and car ownership/use. Differences between sub-groups were negligible in 1994, but in 1995 those who use public transport and those in non-car owning households appear to be particularly concerned about traffic problems. Supporters of the Labour Party and of the Liberal Democrats are appear slightly more concerned about traffic problems than Conservative Party supporters, but the differences are not large.

The Transport Policy Scale

Next we use the 9-item scale[10] on sustainable transport policies for 1993 and 1995 (see table 4.19 in the Appendix for the full tabulation of the mean scale scores).

Here it is on education that we find the greatest differences in attitudes. In 1993 degree-holders were markedly more supportive of these policies than those with lower educational qualifications, and by 1995 they were if anything even more distinctive, registering the highest level of support of any of the sub-groups examined. Differences by car ownership and travel behaviour are again notable. Those using public transport, and those using neither car nor public

Table 4.16. Support for sustainable transport policies by educational group (mean scores on 9-item policy scale).

	1993	1995	Change 1993-1995
Highest educational qualification			
Degree	6.4	6.7	+0.3
Other higher education	5.6	5.7	+0.1
A level	5.8	5.8	-
O level	5.5	5.6	+0.1
CSE	5.6	5.2	-0.4
None	5.4	5.5	+0.1
Travel behaviour			
Car driver	5.3	5.4	+0.1
Car passenger	5.4	5.8	+0.4
Driver & passenger	5.3	5.5	+0.2
Car & public transport user	6.0	6.1	+0.1
Public transport user only	6.4	6.1	-0.3
Neither car nor public transport user	6.4	6.2	-0.2
Household car ownership/use			
No car	6.2	6.2	-
One car	5.4	5.7	+0.3
More than one car	5.6	5.4	-0.2
All groups (mean)	7.1	7.7	+0.6

transport, are more supportive of these policies, particularly when compared with car drivers. Those in non-car owning households are also particularly supportive. Liberal Democrat supporters also appear to be keener on sustainable transport policies than supporters of the other main parties (table 4.16).

The pattern of attitudes we identified in different sub-groups in 1993, when the transport module was first fielded, remained substantially similar in 1995. Educational level, particularly having a degree, is an important influence on support for sustainable transport policies, perhaps becoming more important. Both car ownership and travel behaviour remain important factors. These two attributes are obviously correlated, which leads us to ask the question: do they each have an independent influence on attitudes or is one accounted for by the other?

To control for these and other possible inter-correlations of factors, we turn finally and briefly to multi-variate analysis[11]. This allows us to establish which characteristics significantly and independently influence policy attitudes, which are more important and which are less so. We repeated on the 1995 data analyses carried out on the 1993 data (Stokes and Taylor, 1994), to see whether anything had changed. We used linear regression which enables us to establish

the importance of relevant independent characteristics in accounting for individuals' attitudes to sustainable transport policy options as measured by the
scale. Some variables were tested and found not to be significant, and are
omitted from the table; these were gender, class and income in 1995, and age in

Table 4.17. Results of multi-variate analysis.

'Anti-car' policy scale: coefficients	1993	1995
Age		
18–24	-0.43*	
25–34	-0.51**	
35–44	-0.13	
45–54	-0.12	
55–64	-0.05	
(65+)		
Highest educational qualification		
Degree	1.33**	1.52**
Other higher education	0.51**	0.53**
A level	0.57**	0.59**
O level	0.28*	0.37**
CSE	0.37*	-0.06
(None)		
Party identification		
(Conservative)		
Labour	-0.09	0.11
Liberal Democrat	0.31*	0.31
None	-0.39*	-0.37*
Other parties, DK, NA	-0.44	-0.12
Number of household vehicles		
None	0.16	0.56**
One	-0.24*	0.32**
(More than one)		
Individual travel behaviour		
(Car driver)		
Car passenger	0.34*	0.54**
Driver & passenger	-0.13	0.20
Car & public transport user	0.77**	0.70**
Public transport user only	1.04**	0.43
Neither car nor public transport user	0.93**	0.73**
Proportion of variance explained (R square)	16%	16%
Sample size	1070	860

Notes: * indicates coefficients significant at the five per cent level
  ** indicates coefficients significant at the one per cent level

1993. Table 4.17 shows the beta coefficients which measure the relative importance of having each particular characteristic compared with the omitted characteristic for each set; so, for example, for age they show the effect of being in each group compared with being in the oldest age group. The larger the coefficient the bigger the influence. The significance of the coefficients is also indicated.

The results for the two years are broadly similar, showing that the major influences on policy attitudes have remained largely constant. These are, as identified for 1993 (Stokes and Taylor, 1994) educational level and both car ownership and travel behaviour. Clearly more highly-educated people are more supportive of sustainable transport policies, and degree-holders are particularly distinctive. This is the largest single factor influencing policy attitudes, and if anything its importance has increased over time.

The influence of household car ownership may also have grown in importance recently, with those in non-car owning households much more supportive of sustainable policies; and with those in single-car households more in favour than those in multiple-car households. Individual travel behaviour continues to have an important influence on attitudes, independent of car ownership, with car drivers remaining the least enthusiastic about new policy options.

Thus the earlier findings remain true for 1995. We have identified two sources of influence on policy attitudes: first, a fairly immediate, material self-interest represented by car ownership and travel behaviour; and second, idealism or – perhaps more accurately – a longer-term enlightened self-interest, associated with higher education.

CONCLUSIONS

Concern about traffic problems, especially in urban areas, has continued to rise to very high levels across all social groups. Change in support for more sustainable transport policies has, however, been much more patchy, with support for some measures having risen significantly, while on others there has been no change. And certainly support for new policies has not been increasing in line with rising concern, let alone catching up. The public debate and media attention to transport problems is clearly reflected in the public's anxiety about congestion, pollution and noise, but seems to have only limited impact in shifting attitudes in favour of more sustainable policy measures. So far this would seem to be rather bad news for policy-makers.

Why are the messages failing to get across? This may be due – in part at least – to a lack of understanding among the general public of the long-term implications of failing to confront Britain's road traffic problems and a lack of confidence to take difficult decisions. This in turn may stem from a lack of clarity and direction from politicians, policy-makers and transport experts.

Importantly, however, concern about environmental degradation is not strongly correlated with concern about traffic congestion. We find that people concerned about congestion are rather distinctive in their characteristics from those concerned about environmental impacts. Sustainable transport policies tend to win greater support among those concerned about environmental impacts of unrestricted road traffic than among those concerned about congestion. Degree-level education emerges as an important factor in support for these policies independent of other attributes such as income, with graduates being much more likely than the less well-educated to endorse more sustainable policy options.

These findings provide some grounds for suggesting that forms of public information about the environmental impacts of road traffic compared with other modes of travel, together with broader environmental education now provided in many schools, might help gain support for more sustainable policy measures. But this alone is unlikely to have a major (or quick) impact on travel behaviour.

Of course we should make a important proviso that the *British Social Attitudes* survey (like other surveys) asks respondents to judge policy options, such as road pricing, on which no-one – not the government, and not even the experts – has a good idea of the overall outcome, let alone how adopting it would affect each individual. Given these uncertainties, and setting them against the high level of public concern, we suggest that if the nature and impact of these types of measures were better understood and more widely discussed, the policies might be seen as less disruptive in their impact than many people may fear, and attract greater popular support than they currently do.

Differences in attitudes to transport policy between the supporters of the different political parties are relatively small, in sharp contrast to many other major areas of policy debate. Although national elections are unlikely ever to be won or lost on the basis of differences between the transport policies of the contenders, a party that can evolve a more sustainable and integrated transport policy which addresses public concerns may have much to gain.

In conclusion, we suggest that a clear, confident and rational lead from government, in shifting transport and associated policies (such as land use planning) to a more sustainable foundation is essential if we – as individuals and society – are to change to a more environmentally (and socially) sustainable way of life. While sticks as well as carrots are probably essential in order to induce the necessary changes in behaviour, it may well prove that for both individuals and those in power, the changes will not be as painful as some people clearly fear and that there will be valuable benefits to be gained.

APPENDIX

Table 4.18. Concern about road traffic (mean scores on six-item scale).

	1994	1995	Change 1994-1995
Sex			
Male	7.1	7.6	+0.5
Female	7.1	7.8	+0.7
Age			
18-24	7.0	7.5	+0.5
25-34	7.1	7.5	+0.4
35-44	7.1	7.7	+0.6
45-54	7.2	7.8	+0.6
55-64	7.1	7.7	+0.6
65+	7.0	7.8	+0.8
Highest educational qualification			
Degree	7.3	7.7	+0.4
Other higher education	7.0	7.6	+0.6
A level	7.0	7.6	+0.6
O level	7.1	7.7	+0.6
CSE	7.1	7.6	+0.5
None	7.1	7.8	+0.7
Travel behaviour			
Car driver	7.0	7.4	+0.4
Car passenger	7.1	7.8	+0.7
Driver & passenger	7.0	7.6	+0.6
Car & public transport user	7.1	8.0	+0.9
Public transport user only	7.2	8.1	+0.9
Neither car or pub. transport user	7.2	7.8	+0.6
Household car ownership/use			
No car	7.1	8.0	+0.9
One car	7.1	7.7	+0.6
More than one car	7.1	7.6	+0.5
Party identification			
Conservative	7.0	7.5	+0.5
Labour	7.3	7.8	+0.5
Liberal Democrat	7.1	7.8	+0.7
None	6.9	7.4	+0.5
All groups (mean)	7.1	7.7	+0.6

Table 4.19. Attitudes to sustainable transport policies (mean scores on nine-item policy scale).

	1993	1995	Change 1993-1995
Sex			
Male	5.6	5.7	+0.1
Female	5.6	5.7	+0.1
Age			
18-24	5.7	5.7	-
25-34	5.5	5.4	-0.1
35-44	5.6	5.8	+0.2
45-54	5.5	5.6	+0.1
55-64	5.7	5.7	-
65+	5.6	6.0	+0.4
Party identification			
Conservative	5.5	5.6	+0.1
Labour	5.6	5.8	+0.2
Liberal Democrat	6.0	6.0	-
None	5.2	5.3	+0.1
All groups (mean)	5.6	5.7	+0.1

NOTES

1. The development and fielding of the 1993 questionnaire module on transport issues was made possible by a grant from the ESRC (Ref. 1 119 251 021) under its Transport and the Environment Programme. The authors are grateful to the Council for its financial support.

2. Funding for later BSA questionnaire modules on attitudes to transport has come from the Countryside Commission and more recently from the Department of Transport. The authors thank them both.

3. Even larger majorities in 1996 endorsed the views that:
'Industry should be prevented from causing damage to the countryside, even if this sometimes leads to higher prices' (92 per cent)
and that
'The countryside should be protected from development, even if this sometimes leads to fewer jobs' (76 per cent)
but support was considerably lower in those years when inflation and unemployment respectively were on the increase.

4. Of course, activists are by their nature much more difficult than most survey respondents to track down and interview. So we readily admit that our sample of activists is unlikely to be typical of that group as a whole.

5. To the eight listed in Table 4.9, we have added a ninth:
'Car users are still given too easy a time in Britain's towns and cities'
 which is not an integral part of the battery of policy option questions.

6. The question ran:
'Beauty spots and other popular places in the countryside often get crowded.' Suppose

one of these was visited so much that enjoying its peace and quiet was being spoiled. To limit the number of visitors, are you in favour of or against . . .

. . . cutting down or closing car parks near the site?
. . . stopping anyone at all from visiting it at particular times of year?
. . . making visitors pay and using the extra money to help protect it?
. . . issuing free permits in advance so people will have to plan their visits?
. . . cutting down on advertising and promoting it?
. . . advertising and promoting *other* popular places in the countryside instead?

7. The six items used to construct the 'traffic concern' scale for 1995 and 1996 are:

- congestion on motorways
- increased traffic on country roads and lanes
- traffic congestion at popular places in the countryside
- traffic congestion in towns and cities
- exhaust fumes from traffic in towns and cities
- noise from traffic in towns and cities

Each was rated separately on a four-point scale: 'a very serious problem', 'a serious problem', 'not a very serious problem', 'not a problem at all'.

The first three of these items were asked in 1993, and form the 3-item scale for 1993, 1994 and 1995.

8. The variables chosen are gender, age (mainly in ten-year bands), highest educational qualification, party identification, travel behaviour and household car ownership/use.

9. To be classified as a car driver, the respondent would have to drive a car 'daily or nearly every day'; and to be classified as a public transport user, the respondent would have to use it weekly or more often. To be classified as a 'car and public transport user', the respondent would have to drive a car every day or nearly every day and use public transport at least once a week. This classification is used throughout the chapter.

10. The nine items used to construct the transport policy scale for 1993 and 1995 are:

- people should be allowed to use their cars as much as they want, even if it causes damage to the environment
- buses should be given more priority in towns and cities, even if this makes things more difficult for car drivers
- car drivers are still given too easy a time in Britain's towns and cities
- Britain should do more to improve its public transport system, even if its road system suffers
- drivers charged tolls on all motorways
- only vehicles with permits for essential business allowed in city centres in working hours
- motorists charged for driving in city centres in working hours
- much higher parking charges in towns and cities
- many more streets in cities and towns reserved for pedestrians only

The first four items were rated on a 5-point response scale, from 'strongly agree' to 'strongly disagree', with a mid-point. The last five items were rated on a 5-point response scale, from 'strongly in favour' to 'strongly against', with a mid-point. The second, fourth and ninth items were used to construct the 3-point 'pro-public transport' sub-scale, the other six were used for the 'anti-car policy' sub-scale, for 1993 and 1996.

11. Multi-category variables which may not be ordered, such as highest educational qualification, need to be coded as a series of 0/1 dummy variables to be used in regression.

One fewer dummy variable than the number of categories of each independent variable needs to be created, since the value of the omitted category is entirely determined by the other dummies. The omitted category serves as a reference category and is shown in parentheses in the tables.

REFERENCES

Brook, L. (1994) *Public Attitudes to Transport Policy Options: End of Award Report to the ESRC*. London: SCPR.

Countryside Recreation Network (1995) *A Drive in the Country? Examining the Problems of Recreational Travel and Working Towards Solutions*. Proceedings from a workshop held at Aston Business School, Birmingham, on 1 November 1994, Cardiff: CRN.

Cullinane, S. (1992) Attitudes towards the car in the UK: some implications for policies on congestion and the environment. *Transportation Research*, **24**(4), pp.291–301.

Curry, N. (1994), *Countryside Recreation, Access and Land Use Planning*. London: Spon.

Heath, A., Evans, G. & Martin, J. (1995) The measurement of core beliefs and values: the development of balanced socialist/*laissez-faire* and libertarian/authoritarian scales. *British Journal of Political Science*, no. 24, pp.115–32.

McKie, D. and Brook, L. (1996) A decade of changing attitudes, in Taylor, B. & Thomson, K. (eds.) *Understanding Change in Social Attitudes*. Aldershot: Dartmouth.

Royal Commission on Environmental Pollution (1994) *Transport and the Environment, The 18th Report*, Cmd.2674. London: HMSO.

Standing Advisory Committee on Trunk Road Assessment (1994) *Trunk Roads and the Generation of Traffic*. London: HMSO.

Stokes, G. and Taylor, B. (1994) Where next for transport policy? in Jowell, R. *et al.* (eds.) *British Social Attitudes: the 11th Report*. Aldershot: Dartmouth.

Stokes, G. and Taylor, B. (1995) Public Attitudes to Transport and the Environment: Results from the 1993 British Social Attitudes Survey. Paper presented at the UTSG Conference, Cranfield.

Taylor, B. and Stokes, G. (1996) Public Attitudes towards Sustainable Transport Policies. CREST Working Paper no. 43. Oxford and London: CREST.

UK Round Table on Sustainable Development (1997). *Making Connections*. London: UK Round Table.

Young, K. (1987) Interim report: the countryside, in Jowell, R., *et al.* (eds.) *British Social Attitudes: the 1987 Report*. Aldershot: Gower.

CHAPTER 5

LOGISTICAL RESTRUCTURING, FREIGHT TRAFFIC GROWTH AND THE ENVIRONMENT

Alan McKinnon

According to current road traffic forecasts, the amount of lorry traffic[1] on Britain's roads will increase by between 56 per cent and 115 per cent over the period 1994–2025 (Department of Transport, 1995*a*). This is based on three critical assumptions: that the annual rate of economic growth will average between 2 per cent and 3 per cent, that increases in road tonne-km and GDP will be perfectly correlated, and that the consolidation of loads will reduce the ratio of vehicle-km to tonne-km by roughly 30 per cent. The latter two assumptions are not based on an analysis of the causes of freight traffic growth, but instead rely on a combination of extrapolation and guesswork. Earlier research has indicated that the amount of lorry traffic is influenced much more by the restructuring of companies' production and distribution systems (hereafter called 'logistical' systems) than by changes in the physical mass of goods in the economy or in the allocation of freight between transport modes (McKinnon, 1989*a*, Fowkes *et al.*, 1993). The research reported in this chapter examined the effect of recent developments in logistics on firms' demand for road freight transport, in an effort to establish the true causes of lorry traffic growth and to assess the extent to which it might be constrained by environmental policy measures.

It is possible to differentiate four levels of logistical decision-making which can have an influence on the volume and pattern of freight movement (McKinnon and Woodburn, 1993). Decisions at these levels determine:

1. Logistic structures: i.e. numbers, locations and capacity of factories, warehouses and terminals.

2. Pattern of trading links: created by commercial decisions on sourcing, subcontracting and distribution, and manifest as a freight network linking a company's premises to those of its trading partners.

3. Scheduling of product flow: the programming of production and distribution operations translate trading relationships into discrete freight flows. Adherence to a just-in-time (JIT) regime, for example, usually requires frequent delivery of small orders.

4. Management of transport resources: within the framework defined by decisions at the previous three levels, transport managers still have discretion over the use of transport resources.

Decisions made at levels 1 and 2 influence the number of tonne-km of freight movement generated by a company's logistical system, while decisions at levels 3 and 4 translate the required volume of freight movement into road vehicle-km. The growth of lorry traffic is the result of a complex interaction between decisions made at these different levels. The research examined the relative contribution of these different types of logistical decision to traffic growth and assessed their sensitivity to increasing road transport costs. These costs are likely to rise in future years as the environmental costs of road freight transport are increasingly internalized in higher taxes. In measuring this price-elasticity of demand for road freight transport, one must take account both of logistical cost trade-offs and opportunities for firms to rationalize their use of existing freight capacity.

DATA SOURCES

The main source of UK data on road freight movement is the Continuing Survey of Roads Goods Transport (CSRGT) (Department of Transport, 1995*b*). More limited information about road freight operations in other European countries is available from Eurostat and ECMT. These official statistics provide a sound basis for observing freight trends, but offer little insight into the *process* of freight traffic growth. To explore the underlying causes of freight traffic growth, an original survey was conducted of a large and varied sample of manufacturers and retailers.

The manufacturers were drawn from sectors which, according to the CSRGT, had exhibited a high rate of road tonne-km growth over the past decade: food and drink, construction and building materials, chemicals and fertiliser, paper and publishing, transport equipment and other manufactured articles. Electrical and electronic equipment, non-electrical machinery and textiles/clothing/footwear were chosen to represent the residual 'other manufactured articles' category, which could not be subdivided. Postal questionnaires were sent to the eighty largest manufacturers (by sales revenue) in each of these sectors, listed in the Dunn and Bradstreet Directory. Eighty-eight of these firms returned satisfactorily completed questionnaires, of which forty-four also agreed to be interviewed. A further twenty-nine were interviewed, but did not complete a questionnaire. Altogether 117 manufacturers participated in the study, constituting a response rate of 18 per cent. It is estimated that these firms accounted for around 18–20 per cent of UK manufacturing output in 1993. The sixty largest retailers in the UK were also invited to participate in the study. Twenty-three of them agreed to be interviewed, yielding a response rate of 38 per cent. Collectively they held around 35 per cent of the UK retail market in 1993. In all cases interviews were semi-structured and held with one or more senior logistics/distribution executives in the companies.

Effect of Logistical Changes on Road Freight Demand

The surveys revealed evidence of a multitude of logistical changes, many of them specific to particular firms, sectors or product groups. It was, nevertheless, possible to identify several major underlying trends which were widely prevalent. These will be summarized within the four-level logistical decision-making framework:

Logistical Structure

The dominant trend at this level was the spatial concentration of economic activity, particularly of warehousing operations (table 5.1). Despite the Department of Transport's (DoT) claim in 1984 that the spatial concentration of industry was a 'spent force' (Department of Transport, 1984), centralizing pressures remain quite strong across all the sectors studied. The degree of centralization is also greater than reductions in factory and warehouse numbers would suggest as many firms are adopting 'focused' production and distribution strategies, concentrating the production of particular products and storage of particular categories inventory within their existing factory and warehouse systems.

One surprising finding of the study was that many of the firms that had

Table 5.1. Concentration of production and warehouse capacity, 1989-1994: percentage of firms (sample of manufacturers surveyed by interview).

Sector (no. of firms)	Number of Plants			Number of Warehouses		
	increase	no change	decrease	increase	no change	decrease
Food/drink(19)	5	84	11	0	63	37
Construction/materials (9)	0	56	21	11	44	44
Chemicals/pharmaceuticals(10)	10	70	20	0	50	50
Textiles/clothing/footwear (7)	0	71	29	0	86	14
Paper/publishing (9)	0	78	22	11	44	44
Electrical/electronic equip. (12)	0	92	8	0	58	42
Automotive products (6)	0	100	0	0	67	34
All Sectors (72)	*3*	*79*	*18*	*3*	*58*	*39*

centralized their operations over the previous five years claimed that this had little or no effect on their total road transport requirement. Detailed analysis of their operations revealed that there were three situations in which little extra traffic was generated:

1. Where a firm's factories or warehouses were already specialiszed by product and it was moving from a 'multi-focal' form of centralization to a 'single-focal' structure. The concentration of activity at a central location within the combined market area of all the products could actually reduce the average length of haul.

2. Where there was previously a large amount of inter-haulage between plants/ regional depots. Centralization eliminates the need for this cross-shipment.

3. Where firms retained localized break-bulk operations. By geographically separating the stockholding and break-bulk functions, firms were able to enjoy the benefits of inventory centralization while preserving the efficiency of the transport operation. This strategy allowed them to maintain a high degree of load consolidation on trunk movements and to confine the more transport-inten-sive local distribution operations to relatively small hinterlands around the break-bulk depots.

4. It is difficult, therefore, to generalize about the effects of centralization on freight traffic levels. There would be little point in trying to correlate factory and warehouse numbers with average length of haul and lorry-km at an aggregate level as the relationship between these variables is highly sensitive to the struc-ture of individual firms' logistical systems.

Pattern of Sourcing and Distribution

Three major developments have been observed at this level which are signifi-cantly affecting traffic levels:

1. *Expansion of market areas.* In some sectors, such as beer, soft drinks and milk, there has been a major switch from localized to nation-wide marketing and distribution. In some cases, firms are extending their own logistical operations to support this market growth; in others, they are gaining wider market exposure by channelling their products through retailers' distribution systems.

2. *The channelling of shop supplies through retailer-controlled distribution centres.* One of the most dramatic changes in the pattern of freight flow over the past 20 years has occurred in retail distribution as a result of multiple retailers sharply increasing the proportion of supplies channelled through their distribu-tion centres. This major switch from manufacturer-controlled to retailer-controlled distribution has rationalized the shop delivery system, reducing vehicle-kms per tonne supplied (McKinnon and Woodburn, 1994). Between 1985 and 1995, for instance, the average number of lorry deliveries required to

transport 1000 cases to Safeway stores has dropped from around five to under one (Freight Transport Association, 1995). Transport savings at this secondary distribution level (from distribution centre to shop) have been partly offset by a lengthening of supply lines upstream of the retailers' distribution centres (Paxton, 1994). Over the past few years, however, retailers have begun to rationalize primary distribution (from factory to distribution centre) and to co-ordinate it more closely with secondary distribution, primarily to improve vehicle utilization. No attempt has yet been made to assess the net effect of retailers' logistical activities on lorry traffic levels.

3. *Vertical disintegration of manufacturing.* Over the past 10–15 years, firms have been concentrating their resources on core activities and contracting out ancillary functions which can often be performed more cheaply and effectively by outside agencies. This is well illustrated in the computer industry, where much of the basic assembly of PCs is now entrusted to contractors. Statistical confirmation of this trend can be found in both the Census of Production and Input-Output Tables (Black *et al.*, 1995). The vertical disintegration of manufacturing operations has effectively added extra links to the supply chain. Processes that were previously undertaken in close proximity on the same production site now take place in different locations creating a demand for additional freight movement. In some cases, the sub-contracted operation is at the beginning or end of the core manufacturing activity and can thus be carried out 'in line' as products flow through the supply chain. Where it is an intermediate stage in the process that is externalized, products must be shuttled between the main assembly point and the contractor's plant.

Scheduling of Flow

In the postal questionnaire survey, senior distribution/logistics executives in eighty-seven large British manufacturing firms indicated what they considered to be the main factors causing an increase in their demand for road freight transport. The two most frequently mentioned causes were changes in customer service requirements, which in most cases would be motivated by a desire to reduce inventory levels, and the adoption of low inventory strategies by the manufacturers themselves. Around a third of the firms consulted in a supporting interview survey of manufacturers and retailers claimed that JIT was increasing the amount of lorry traffic to and/or from their premises, though in most cases the increase was thought to be marginal. Several firms in the electronics and automotive sectors, where the true JIT principle has been widely applied, have tried to minimize its impact on traffic levels by having nominated carriers consolidate inbound supplies either at a 'supply house' or by means of 'milk round' collection services. These practices have been examined in earlier studies (Charles and Richardson, 1993; Allen, 1994).

In the course of the survey, frequent reference was made to 'just-in-time', though many managers used the term loosely to describe simply a reduction in lead times and order sizes. This latter trend was evident in all the sectors examined, even among primary producers of low value bulk materials, such as cement, aggregates and chemicals. It was clear from the interviews that very few firms had tried to monitor the effects of tighter inventory control on traffic levels. Where the delivery of inbound supplies was the responsibility of the vendor, as was normally the case, the manufacturer requesting 'JIT' delivery often had limited awareness of its transport implications. Furthermore, the assertions that firms made about the consequences of 'JIT' for the transport operation could not be independently verified. Some logistics managers may have tried to play down these consequences as this is known to be a sensitive environmental issue.

The area in which JIT appears to be having the greatest impact is in retail distribution (where it has become known as 'quick response'). At this end of the supply chain, it is inducing a fundamental restructuring of retailers' and manufacturers' operations, with major repercussions for all four levels of logistical decision-making. This restructuring is reducing the impact of quick response (QR) on lorry traffic levels. Manufacturers in sectors such as food, drink, electrical appliances and detergents, are now placing greater emphasis on the mixing of product ranges in an effort to maintain the degree of load consolidation. This is increasing the flow of traffic between factories and via centralized distribution facilities. Retailers are helping to maintain the level of vehicle utilization within the new QR regime in three ways:

(*i*) by receiving a particular supplier's products at a single distribution centre and then cross-shipping them to other centres;

(*ii*) by using their returning delivery vehicles to make *ex works* collections;

(*iii*) by employing 'nominated carriers' to provide an upstream consolidation service.

Most of these measures are maintaining and, in some cases improving, vehicle utilization, but at the expense of adding extra links to the supply chain and increasing the total distance that products travel *en route* from factory to shop. Although this appears to be producing a net increase in road tonne-km, the traffic growth is much less than would be occurring if the distribution system were not being adapted to accommodate QR.

If JIT were having a pronounced effect on road freight operations, one would expect to see the average payload weight carried by lorries declining. Analysis of CSRGT data over the period 1984 to 1994 shows that, in the case of rigid vehicles, it has indeed been steadily diminishing (figure 5.1). As these vehicles are commonly used to deliver supplies of components to manufacturing premises, this could be evidence of a JIT effect. The average payload weight on articulated lorries has remained fairly stable since 1984. This does not necessarily mean that this class of vehicle has not been subject to a similar JIT effect. It is possible that JIT has been depressing consignment weights in some sectors but this has been offset by a greater consolidation of loads in others, such as retail distribution. The slight increase in average payload overall resulted from a net shift in the total freight tonnage from rigid to articulated vehicles. Claims that the adoption of JIT is greatly increasing road freight volumes are not, therefore, borne out by analysis of the available transport statistics.

Management of Transport Resources

Many of the trends observed at this level are depressing the ratio of vehicle-km to tonne-km and thus, *ceteris paribus*, reducing lorry traffic levels. The following measures are being widely applied: use of larger vehicles and compartmentalized vehicles able to carry composite loads, the introduction of computer-assisted vehicle routing and improved return loading. Increased backloading of vehicles is reflected in official statistics which show that between 1983 and 1993 the proportion of lorry-km run empty fell by 11 per cent. This favourable trend appears to have been the result of a lengthening of lorry journeys, an increase in the number of drops per trip, an expansion of load matching

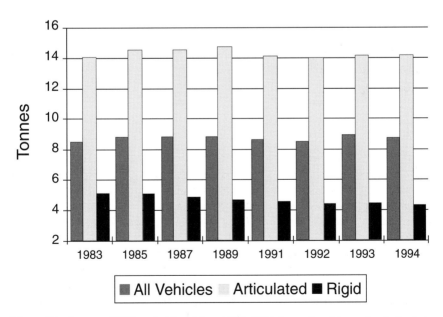

Figure 5.1. Average HGV payload weights, 1983–1994 (i.e. ratio of tonne-km to loaded-km). (*Source*: Department of Transport: CSRGT)

services, a growth in the reverse flow of packaging, and new return loading initiatives by retailers and manufacturers (McKinnon, 1996). Other rationalization measures, such as the switch to more space-efficient handling equipment, the 'flexing' of depot area boundaries and the carriage of third-party traffic in own-account/dedicated vehicles, are still relatively uncommon, though becoming more widespread. Major counteracting pressures have been the displacement of freight from rail to road, particularly among primary producers, and tightening 'health and safety' restrictions on the height of palletized loads. Overall, however, the study has revealed that there is considerable scope for further rationalization of road freight operations at this level in the decision-making hierarchy.

In summary, the research confirmed that changes in firms' demand for road freight transport are the result of a complex interaction between decisions made at these different levels. Traffic reduction measures at one level, such as the consolidation of loads in larger vehicles or improved vehicle routing, can easily be offset by traffic generating measures at another, such as inventory centralization or an increase in delivery frequency. The nature and strength of these conflicting pressures varies both within and between sectors, making generalization difficult. This would frustrate any attempt to input the results of an analysis of the causes of freight traffic growth at the micro-level into macro-level freight traffic forecasting models.

SENSITIVITY OF LORRY TRAFFIC GROWTH TO ENVIRONMENTAL TAXES

Recent research has suggested that taxes on road freight movement will have to rise substantially if environmental and social costs are to be fully internalized. The Royal Commission on Environmental Pollution (1994) estimated the external cost of road freight movement in the UK (arising from accidents, noise and air pollution) at between £1.6 bn and £3.6 bn per annum. A more recent study by the European Commission (1995) has valued these external costs at 33.2 ecus per 1000 tonne-km, equivalent to a total figure of £3.8 bn for the UK in 1994, slightly above than the RCEP's upper estimate. Full internalization of the environmental costs at the higher EC level would have entailed increasing British lorry taxes by roughly 110 per cent, which, in turn, would have inflated road freight transport costs by approximately 30 per cent. Estimates by Kageson (1993) of the costs of making European transport 'pay its true costs' are of a similar magnitude.

In an effort to assess the sensitivity of logistical systems to large transport cost increases, manufacturing firms participating in the postal questionnaire survey were asked how they would be likely to respond to a 50 per cent increase in road transport costs. (This survey was conducted prior to the publication of both the RCEP's and EC's external cost estimates.) Relatively small proportions of the firms consulted anticipated that this would force them to make less use of road transport by transferring freight to alternative modes, restructuring their logistics systems, reducing the geographical extent of their sourcing and marketing or cutting the level of customer service (McKinnon and Woodburn, 1996). There were, nevertheless, significant inter- and intra- sectoral variations in these responses, reflecting differences in product value density, geographical location and competitive position.

Computer simulation was used to model the effect of increasing road transport costs on logistical cost trade-offs for products of differing value density. A hypothetical company was created serving 300 customer locations around the UK. It could be a retail organization supplying its own network of branch stores or a manufacturer or wholesaler distributing products to external customers. The spatial distribution of customers reflected the distribution of population throughout the UK at district level, suggesting that the company was operating in a consumer market. The analysis was confined to one link in the supply chain extending from warehouse to customer. Different types of distribution system were tested, ranging from one in which all inventory was centralized at a single point to a decentralized system in which inventory was dispersed to twelve regional depots. The addition of depot locations followed the sequence derived theoretically by Stoker (1975) and given empirical confirmation by McKinnon (1989b). The final siting of depots was at points where distribution facilities are already clustered, such as Lutterworth and Warrington.

The modelling exercise attempted to establish the transport cost levels at which firms would have an economic incentive to restructure their logistical systems or move to a more consolidated pattern of delivery. Unlike in previous studies, an effort was made to examine the relationship between inventory centralization and the scheduling of freight flows (determined at levels 4 and 2 in the decision-making hierarchy). It is not possible in this chapter to summarize the results of all the scenarios tested or to discuss the long list of assumptions underpinning this analysis. The general conclusion, however, was that even in the case of products with a relatively low value density, transport costs would have to rise by over 100 per cent to make it economically beneficial to move to a more decentralized structure (table 5.2). This is equivalent to a six-fold increase in fuel taxes and well in excess of the increase required to internalize environmental costs according to the European Commission. It is likely too that the modelling exercise will have under-estimated this transport cost threshold as it failed to incorporate all the benefits that firms claim to derive from centralization and took no account of transitional restructuring costs.

Sensitivity analyses, involving changes in demand variability, level of stock cover, warehouse cost function, order lead time and delivery time-windows, indicated that the general results were fairly robust. No attempt was made to model possible changes in the modal split. It is likely, however, that only a relatively small proportion of road freight would be likely to transfer to other modes. It can be safely concluded that the overall demand for road freight transport would be

Table 5.2. Optimal numbers of warehouses at different levels of road transport cost and delivery frequency: hypothetical firm.

| Value density £/tonne | Typical product | Present level | | Level of Road Transport Costs | | | | | | | |
| | | | | +50% | | +100% | | +150% | | +200% | |
		W	D	W	D	W	D	W	D	W	D
50	Cement	3	3	3	3	3	3	7	10	7	10
100	Compound fertiliser	3	3	3	3	3	3	7	10	7	10
500	Paper	3	3	3	3	3	3	6	3	7	10
1000	Cakes	3	3	3	3	3	3	3	3	7	7
5000	Stainless steel sinks	2	2	2	2	2	2	3	3	3	3
10000	Clothing	1	1	2	2	2	2	2	2	2	2
20000	Personal computers	1	1	1	1	1	1	1	2	2	2

W = weekly delivery; D = daily delivery.

relatively insensitive to steep increases in transport costs, well in excess, for example, of those proposed by the RCEP (1994). This was confirmed, for example, by one major retailer of fast-moving consumer goods, which estimated that road haulage costs would have to increase four-fold to offset the inventory and warehousing benefits from reducing its number of distribution centres from three to two.

Superficially, the results of this analysis appear to indicate that the elasticity of demand for road transport would be very low. This would support most expert opinion which, as Bleijenberg (1996) observes, suggests that '*the price elasticity of transport is very low, around -0.1*' (i.e. a 1 per cent increase in freight transport costs would reduce the volume of freight movement by 0.1 per cent). Much of this opinion is based on the results of theoretical modelling work, such as that described above. Bleijenberg goes on, however, to cite the results of an empirical study undertaken for the World Bank by Oum *et al.* (1990) which found, to the authors' surprise, that the '*price sensitivity was considerably greater than generally assumed.*' The discrepancy between this empirical study and the results of the earlier modelling exercises may be attributable to the failure of the latter studies to take full account of the range of traffic-reduction options available to firms. The modelling work has tended to over-emphasize the importance of spatial structures, which are relatively fixed in the short term, and under-estimate the extent to which firms can modify other aspects of their distribution operations often at relatively short notice.

In the interview survey, however, many logistics executives claimed that their demand for road freight transport would be fairly insensitive even to quite large transport cost increases. This did not simply reflect their confidence in the stability of logistical cost trade-offs; it also related to the status of logistical activities within the business. In many firms, transport costs are accorded little importance. Many of the interviewees reported that senior management in their firms seldom gave much consideration to the transport implications both of higher-level strategic decisions and of operating practices in other functional areas, such as production and sales. Transport was commonly regarded as a basic service to be provided in accordance with the requirements of other departments. Much greater importance was attached to the maintenance of a competitive level of customer service than to the minimization of transport costs, especially as these costs represent on average only around 1–2 per cent of sales revenue and as the real cost of road haulage had been declining for several years. There is also a strong desire to reduce fixed costs by closing distribution facilities wherever possible. Contrary to the impression given in much of the literature, the main trigger for this centralization is not a reduction in transport costs, resulting, for example, from road development. Firms are influenced much more by the operational opportunities that transport improvements create, such as extending the daily delivery range of vehicles.

Encouraging evidence nevertheless emerged of firms trying to rationalize their road freight operations. Table 5.3 lists examples of rationalization measures that firms had either implemented or were contemplating. Although they are motivated primarily by a desire to improve economic efficiency, they can also yield worthwhile environmental benefits. For example, the reduction in empty running between 1983 and 1993, which was reported earlier, would, *ceteris paribus*, have reduced the nation's road haulage bill by approximately £600 million per annum and cut CO_2 emissions by 720,000 tonnes annually.

Many of the rationalization measures individually yield only marginal reductions in vehicle-km, though collectively can have a significant effect on total lorry traffic. Some are solely the responsibility of transport management; most, however, require agreement with other, usually more senior, branches of management and often with trading partners. The management of transport within a broader logistical framework has expanded the range of rationalization options, while the strengthening of logistics' position within the corporate hierarchy has increased the pressure on other functions to use transport more efficiently. The 'greening' of firms' logistical operations at a more fundamental level will, nevertheless, require a much more radical change in management culture and a re-ordering of strategic priorities.

While significant rationalization can be effected at the lowest level in the management structure, the main potential for reducing the 'transport-intensity' of firms' production and distribution operations lies at higher levels in the corporate hierarchy. This would involve restraining the underlying growth in freight tonne-kms as recommended by the RCEP. It proposed that the average rate of tonne-km growth be slowed from 20 per cent per decade, which it

Table 5.3. Effects of rationalization measures on lorry traffic.

	Measure	Reduction in Lorry- km	Relevant Levels of Logistical Decision-making
Return Loading			
Large supermarket chain	Use of returning shop delivery vehicles to make *ex works* collections	11 million	2,3,4
Load planning/routing			
Brewer	Use of computer software	8 per cent	4
Packaging / handling			
Computer printer manufacturer	Redesign of packaging	64000	2,4
Detergent manufacturer	Increasing pallet height from 1.7 to 2.1 metres	1.6 million	2,4
Mail order firm	Loose loading rather than bagging of parcels	6 per cent	4
Load Consolidation			
Footwear retailer	Use of drawbar units on longer hauls	55000 (6 per cent)	4
Two car manufacturers (spare parts)	Combining delivery operations	20 per cent	1,2,3,4
Manufacturer of batteries	Combining delivery operations with two manufacturers of personal care products	25 per cent	1,2,3,4
Brewer	Composite distribution of different products in same vehicle	20 per cent	2,3,4
Ordering system			
Confectionery manufacturer	Sales dept. abandoning monthly ordering cycle	10 per cent	2,3,4
Mail order firm	Adoption of nominated day delivery system	10 per cent	2,3,4

regarded as being environmentally-unsustainable, to 10 per cent per decade and suggested that this could be achieved by higher fuel prices modifying '*manufacturing and distribution patterns over a number of years by shortening the average length of trips*' (RCEP, 1994, p.179). Analysis of the logistical trade-offs and decision-making processes currently underpinning these patterns suggests that the RCEP seriously under-estimated the fiscal inducements that would be required to achieve this objective.

NOTE

1. In vehicles with a gross weight in excess of 3.5 tonnes.

REFERENCES

Allen, J. (1994) Just-in-time and the environment. *Comment*, No. 3, Exel Logistics, Bedford.

Bleijenberg, A. (1996) *Freight Transport in Europe: In Search of a Sustainable Course.* Delft: Centre for Energy Conservation and Environmental Technology.

Black, I. *et al.* (1995) Modelling the Links between Economic Activity and Goods Vehicle Movements. CCLT Research Report no.2, Cranfield University.

Charles, D. and Richardson, R. (1993) *The Convergence of Transport and Communications.* London: CEST.

Department of Transport (1984) *National Road Traffic Forecasts, 1984.* London: HMSO.

Department of Transport (1995a) *Transport Statistics Great Britain,* 1995 edition. London: HMSO.

Department of Transport (1995b) *Transport of Goods by Road in Great Britain.* London: HMSO.

European Commission (1995) *Towards Fair and Efficient Pricing in Transport: Policy Options for Internalising the External Costs of Transport in the European Union.* Brussels: CEC.

Fowkes, A.S., Nash, C., Toner, J.P. and Tweddle,G. (1993) Disaggregated Approaches to Freight Analysis: A Feasibility Study. Working Paper 299, Institute for Transport Studies, University of Leeds, Leeds.

Freight Transport Association (1995) *Freight Matters 1/95: Time Sensitive Distribution.* Tunbridge Wells: FTA.

Institute of Grocery Distribution (1993) *Retailer Distribution Profiles '93.* Letchmore Heath: IGD.

Kageson, P. (1993) *Getting the Prices Right.* Brussels: European Federation for Transport and the Environment.

McKinnon, A.C. (1989a) The growth of road freight in the UK. *International Journal of Physical Distribution and Materials Management,* **19**(4).

McKinnon, A.C. (1989b) *Physical Distribution Systems.* London: Routledge.

McKinnon, A.C. and Woodburn, A. (1993) A logistical perspective on the growth of lorry traffic. *Traffic Engineering and Control,* **34**(10).

McKinnon, A.C. and Woodburn, A. (1994) The consolidation of retail deliveries: Its effect on CO_2 emissions. *Transport Policy,* **1**(2), pp.125–136.

McKinnon, A.C. (1996) The empty running and return loading of road goods vehicles. *Transport Logistics,* **1**(1).

McKinnon, A.C. and Woodburn, A. (1996) Logistical restructuring and road freight traffic growth: An empirical assessment. *Transportation,* **26**(2).

Oum, T.H, Waters II, W.G. and Yong, J.S. (1990) A Survey of Recent Estimates of Price Elasticities of Demand for Transport. Working Paper, World Bank, Washington..

Paxton, A. (1994) *The Food Miles Report: The Dangers of Long Distance Food Transport.* London: SAFE Alliance.

Royal Commission on Environmental Pollution (1994) *Eighteenth Report: Transport and the Environment.* London: HMSO.

Stoker, R.B. (1975) Incorporating market characteristics into physical distribution models. *European Journal of Operational Research,* **2**, pp. 232–245.

PART 2: *Regional Aspects*

The central set of chapters in this book have a regional focus, but also draw on experiences from Europe and the United States. Examples and alternative strategies towards transport and the environment provide contrasting choices which could be made. Phil Goodwin starts with the statement that there is broad agreement over policies to reduce the environmental impact of transport, but implementation is patchy, as some more controversial policies are not touched and others are applied inconsistently. There is also disagreement over the effects and effectiveness of policies with some having unintended outcomes. He argues for an improved basic understanding of the processes of individual and institutional responses to policy changes, and a reconsideration of the effectiveness of policies. Responses are usually more varied and complex than conventionally acknowledged and further work is required on our understanding of the conditions under which policies are most successful. These issues are illustrated with a range of policy vignettes (e.g. park and ride, road pricing, town centre pedestrianization) describing the expected and actual outcomes, and how solutions can be reached – always expect the unexpected.

The renewed interest in the links between transport and planning is continued with Roger Vickerman's contribution on transport and regional development. He reviews, develops and comments on the measurement of regional accessibility from a micro-economic foundation. The central theme of the chapter is an assessment of the impacts of traffic improvement in five European corridors. These corridors are analysed through the inter-regional distribution of the economic impacts of transport, based on economic potential and the network connectivity. This inter-regional analysis is supplemented by an examination of the production potential and trade flows, and an intra-regional impact analysis. All elements are then brought together in an appraisal framework. Two interesting points emerge from the empirical analysis. It seems that intra-regional variations in access to the local and regional networks are often the critical determinant for locations in peripheral regions. Transport as an instrument of social cohesion is often only seen as determining the inter-regional network, such as the Trans-European Networks (the TEN), not the local network. Most new major links (particularly the High Speed Rail Links) bring greater additional benefits to the already accessible locations rather than to the newly accessible locations. Accessibility is relative and the new infrastructure links favour existing locations.

The second contribution by Roger Vickerman, this time as a co author with John Peirson, develops a model to estimate the full social costs of each mode of transport. The resulting efficient prices are then used to predict the shifts in demand in London and on the inter-urban passenger road network. Empirical evidence has been collected for both the external and internal resource costs of transport, together with the appropriate elasticities. The predicted consequences of efficient prices are reflected in demand, costs, revenues and implied investment. The results are controversial as doubt is cast on the effectiveness of price based policies to reduce the levels of the external effects of road transport. They conclude that substantial shifts away from road transport does not occur with efficient prices as all forms of transport in urban areas (London) are substantially underpriced, particularly at the peak. Taxation of the large external costs of road transport would raise sufficient revenue to cover the deficits from increasing the prices for public transport operations. With respect to the inter-urban road network, there is an over supply of capacity at the aggregate level, and prices should only be increased where there is localized congestion.

As with the national level research, the road freight sector has an important role at the regional level. Jim Cooper and his colleagues at Cranfield University have systematically analysed the contributions of the supply chain (sourcing – inventory – transport) to the demand for transport. Their main aim is to consider what policy responses might be desirable if the supply chain is to contribute to sustainable transport. The role that logistics can and is playing in creating integrated supply chains is considerable, and this study has investigated six sectors and ten components of logistics strategies. In terms of their implications for transport and environmental pollution, two components substantially increase the transport costs - focused production (concentrating on a limited range of products) and pan European sourcing. The chapter then tries to explain the contribution of a range of factors to the increase in freight traffic. These include external factors (e.g. the growth in GDP), the restructuring of industry and the commodity mix (including relocation), transfer from rail, average haul length, the intensity of vehicle use, vehicle size and the transport cost operating structure. All these factors influence the organization and structure of the supply chain. The system is sensitive to change. It is suggested that if the costs of transport rise (through congestion and taxation), then new forms of supply chain will result.

The final regional perspective explores the well known Californian approach to air quality improvement, and concludes that recent policy initiatives have had relatively little impact. Wyn Grant demonstrates the much greater contributions made by the switch to new vehicles and reductions from stationary sources. In addition, Californians are almost exclusively concerned with the local air pollution emissions and the adverse health effects. Little attention or recognition is given to the global warming debate. A range of recent policy initiatives are investigated. These include – the electric vehicle programme which was a catalyst for research and development, but has resulted in a post-ponement of the programme to achieve the 2 per cent target for zero emission vehicles in 1998; the limited success of various regulations to reduce trip rates at workplaces by car; the clamp down on the gross emitter, or the 'cash for clunk-ers' programme; and the use of reformulated gasoline. The Californians have always been enthusiastic about technological solutions, particularly if it requires little change in travel patterns and costs no more. The centrality of the car is unassailable. It is difficult, if not impossible, to introduce effective curbs on its use in a democracy. Perhaps there are clear lessons to be learnt in Europe?

CHAPTER 6

UNINTENDED EFFECTS OF TRANSPORT POLICIES

P. B. Goodwin

By about 1992 arguments based on congestion, local environmental quality, and strategic environmental sustainability, had converged to the extent that urban transport policy *in principle* now nearly everywhere proposes a reasonably well-defined approach, which usually consists of:

- containment or reduction of the total volume of traffic;
- improved and expanded public transport systems;
- better provision for pedestrians and cyclists;
- pedestrianization, and traffic calming, to reduce the dominance of vehicle traffic;
- traffic restraint and traffic management, aimed at reduced flows and increased reliability rather than maximizing the throughput of vehicles;
- the control of land-use changes and new development in such a way as to reduce journey length and car use wherever possible;
- interest in (but not commitment to) charging people directly for the congestion and environmental damage they cause using the roads.

It was remarkable that broadly speaking the same list of policies was advanced by those whose starting point was the need to find an economically efficient answer to the waste of economic resources caused by excessive traffic, and by those whose starting point was the need to address environmental problems of local pollution and global change. Influencing overall demand levels and providing less congesting ways of providing for movement were seen as having both economic and environmental advantages. This opened the possibility of agreement between interests which would otherwise be (and in some other sectors are) antagonistic.

However, while there is a very rapid implementation of various parts of this package, there is also a tendency for implementation to be patchy, confined to one or two areas of policy only, while some areas remain untouched, and others seem still to be entirely inconsistent.

OBJECTIVES OF THE STUDY

The problem of implementation appeared to be partly because there was not yet a generally agreed body of experience about what the effects of these policies really are, and there was also a continuing undercurrent of concern that the intended effects may be damped or reversed by unintended effects due to complex system-wide or individual or institutional responses designed to avoid the planned changes. Hence the question 'what could go wrong?' was seen as a way of helping to improve the definition of the policies, and the alertness of planners in monitoring and adapting them. This question formed the core research.

Thus the project sought to improve basic understanding of the process of individual and institutional response to policies; to use this understanding to assess the direct and indirect responses of travel behaviour; to reconsider the effectiveness of these policies in the light of more complex patterns of response; and to suggest conditions under which the policies are most successful, and how they might be improved.

METHODS

The research methodology depends on longitudinal monitoring of changes in attitudes and behaviour over time, with 'before-and-after' studies as the most important, though not only, tool. This was backed up by reanalysis of secondary sources from other locations, statistical analysis of aggregate and disaggregate data, analytical interpretation of policy processes, and theoretical consideration of travel choices and adaptation using modified economic and other frameworks.

Factual information for the main case studies is shown in the table 6.1 below. The timetables for the other monitoring, general and theoretical work are not specified in the table as they were continuous throughout the project. The opportunity has also been taken in this chapter to report results from other studies, which are listed in the bibliography.

RESULTS

The following boxes (figures 6.1 to 6.8) summarize some of the main results of the study and associated other research, starting with relatively well-defined questions related to specific policy instruments, and moving to more subtle and complex forms of potential unintended effects. ·

Table 6.1. Survey timetable, funding and approach for main case studies.

	Lüneburg	Oxford	Sheffield	Trondheim	York
Co-funding	Rees Jeffreys, Lüneburg city council	Rees Jeffreys, plus data from council	Exchange data for D.Phil project with PTE and DoT, plus access to earlier panel surveys	Data from Norwegian Road Admin, Rees Jeffreys, and collab with SINTEF	Rees Jeffreys plus data from council
1992 4	before diary			after stated preference	
1993 1					
1993 2	on street				
1993 3			interviews		
1993 4	on street				
1994 1		car park			car park
1994 2			interim report		
1994 3	after diary	main report		main report	main report
1994 4					
1995 1	on street				
1995 2	main report				
1995 3	integrated report	integrated report	semi-final interviews		integrated report
1995 4					
Main policy focus and methodology	Pedest & other centre improvements 2-wave panel, on-street attitudes, discussions with policy actors	Traffic restraint, park-and-ride. New car park surveys, access to historic data, discussions	New rail system, after subsidy and deregulation. Qualitative interviews plus access to panel travel diaries since 1981	Road tolls. Repeated stated preference experiment (access to 1990 before survey)	Traffic restraint, park-and-ride. New car park surveys plus access to historic data, discussions

Hypothesis. The intended effects are (*a*) to reduce traffic in central areas by transferring the final stage of a car journey to public transport; (*b*) to attract more people to the town centre overall . . . An unintended effect may be to increase car use for the non-central area part of the journey, by increasing the parking opportunities for people who previously travelled by public transport.

Methodology. New surveys of park-and-ride users in Oxford and York, together with comparative analysis of available studies from Chester, Bristol, Maidstone, Norwich, Nottingham, Shrewsbury and Sheffield. Questions related to (*a*) what users did before the park-and-ride opened, and (*b*) what they would do if it was not available.

Conclusions. A range from 42 per cent to 81 per cent of users had previously driven all the way into the town centre, and from 2 per cent to 12 per cent had previously gone elsewhere – the intended effects. But from 5 per cent to 40 per cent had previously travelled all the way by public transport – the unintended group. When asked what they would do otherwise, 33 per cent to 78 per cent said they would use car and park in the centre, and 1 per cent to 21 per cent said they would not continue to come. 9 per cent to 35 per cent said they would travel all the way by public transport. Both methods are uncertain, but there is a consistent prima facie case that park-and-ride may attract a significant minority of its users away from public transport services outside the town centre.

Proposed Solutions. It would help (*a*) not to locate park-and-ride sites too close to the town centre; (*b*) to make improvements to the attractiveness of public transport services outside the town centre, including bus priority measures on trunk roads leading to the town; (*c*) reduce central area parking provision.

Figure 6.1. Unintended effects of park-and-ride. (Main references: Parkhurst, 1994, 1996*a*, 1996*b*).

Hypothesis. Pedestrianization is intended to improve the environmental quality of the town centre and thereby make it more attractive. An unintended effect might be to reduce the volume of retail trade by making it more difficult for people to do their shopping by car.

Methodology. Literature reviews focusing on Germany and Britain; pedestrian counts, on-street surveys in twenty towns notably Belfast, Dresden, Schwerin, Reading; analysis of retailing indicators including turnover, rateable value, rents, empty shops; historical data from Munich, Nurnberg; case study in Lüneburg.

Conclusions. The unintended effect is a very strong and recurrent perceived problem among retailers, but typically only temporary in the real world, due to problems of disruption of shopping patterns which can last for a year or two. In most cases well-implemented pedestrianization improved retailing success and was popular among shoppers and (after a time) retailers. The number of pedestrians has increased by 20-40 per cent in many cases. However, part of the increased volume of trade is absorbed in higher rents or local taxes, bringing benefits to other groups besides retailers. There are also problems at the margins of the pedestrianized area, and potential loss of political momentum if implementation is slow or complicated.

Proposed Solution. Pedestrianization of large areas, using traditional street patterns, high design standards, and relatively speedy implementation, is most successful. While political consensus is crucial, this is not necessarily helped by slow and cautious progress. Initial resistance of retailers seems inevitable, but should not be too influential since it usually later turns to support.

Figure 6.2. Unintended commercial effects of town centre pedestrianization. (Main references: Hass-Klau,1994; Hass-Klau *et al.*, 1994, 1996)

Hypothesis. Restricting development of new supermarkets in out-of-town locations and encouraging them in town centres is intended to reduce the dominance of car use for this sort of shopping. However, it is not clear whether this will be effective, and may increase the pressure for more car parking in town centres.

Methodology. Literature review, surveys of shoppers in Oxfordshire and Swindon, GIS modelling using 'Transcad', interviews with thirty-five retailers providing home delivery services.

Conclusions. Certain types of bulk food shopping are now typically done once a week, with a strong preference for the nearest supermarket so that over two-thirds of such trips are less than 2 miles, even for large non-central stores. Car use is overwhelmingly favoured by car-available shoppers – including town centre locations. This has resulted in inconsistency between policies seeking to reduce car use and policies seeking to revive town centres (PPG13 and PPG6). The results suggest that development control will not be a strong lever in this particular context. However, there has been a recent spontaneous development of home delivery services, largely as a market response rather than as a result of planning intervention, directed partly at avoiding the hassle and difficulty of bulk shopping, including congestion and carrying goods. The scale is still small, but rapidly growing. Surveys and model results suggest that home delivery services can significantly reduce vehicle mileage while increasing (rather than restricting) the convenience of the shopper.

Proposed Solution. It is not suggested that the direction of development control should be radically changed or abandoned, but its effects in relation to food shopping are likely to be modest at least in the short run. Meanwhile, delivery services should be encouraged, especially using locations or technology which enables goods to be chosen without a car trip. Such services could be developed in parallel with strengthening the role of smaller local shops, perhaps as part of a network of collection and delivery facilities.

Figure 6.3. Unintended effects of development control for supermarket location. (Main references: Cairns, 1995, 1996*a*, *b*, *c*)

DISCUSSION – CONCEPTUAL FRAMEWORK, THEORY AND MODELS

The approach developed during the project was based on the proposition that constructs such as utility maximization and achieved equilibrium are of limited use in providing insights into counter-intentional responses. Rather, it is helpful to conceive individuals engaged in a continual process of adaptation, where the *search for higher utility* is the key to response, rather than the achievement of maximum utility. The difference is not only formal, since the former refers to a process that (by definition) takes place over time whereas the latter is a state that (by implication) is timeless. Another, non-trivial, difference is that observation of behaviour at any arbitrary point of time cannot be assumed to have settled down as a response to prevailing conditions.

One consequence of this approach is that it both explains the existence of such empirical findings as longer-term elasticities being higher than shorter term ones, and also requires that those findings are used in any sensible forecasting procedure. Another consequence is that evaluation (for example by discounted net present value of consumer benefit or cash flows) is demonstrably affected.

Hypothesis. Intended effects are to reduce traffic in the bypassed streets, and increase speed of travel on the improved road. Unintended effects may be to induce extra traffic overall, thus reducing the relief to alternative routes and reducing the size or duration of the speed improvement.

Methodology. Literature review, inference from elasticities, comparison of traffic growth rates, before-and-after studies of road schemes, comparison of forecasts and outcomes.

Conclusions. Inference from empirical research on demand elasticities, value of time, and time budgets, suggests that a 10 per cent speed increase would lead to a 5-10 per cent increase in the volume of traffic. Observed traffic about a year after construction averaged about 10 per cent more than forecast on improved sections, but over 16 per cent more than forecast on 'relieved' alternative routes, not all the errors being due to induced traffic. Specific improved roads show estimated induced traffic of up to about 40 per cent, the larger figures being in congested urban conditions: in some cases traffic even increased, rather than reduced, on the alternative routes. Induced traffic was greater in the long run (up to ten years) than the short run. A rule of thumb for an average UK road scheme is 10 per cent induced traffic in the short run and 20 per cent in the longer run. Results were very variable, sensitive to the policy context in studied areas, and large enough to have a significant effect on the economic evaluation of projects. Induced traffic reinforces (but is not the main cause of) the unfeasibility of matching road capacity to unrestricted traffic growth in urban areas.

Proposed Solutions. A strategic approach to try to match road capacity to demand has now been abandoned, not primarily due to the problem of induced traffic, and the results support this. On those occasions where new bypasses are still built, it is suggested that they can be of lower capacity than traditionally assumed, and must in any case be accompanied by simultaneous traffic restriction measures in the bypassed area, with demand management on the improved road.

Figure 6.4. Unintended effects of road construction, especially bypasses. (Main references: SACTRA, 1994; Goodwin, 1996*a,b*)

Hypothesis. Moderating the growth in traffic requires stick-and-carrot measures which both reduce the attractiveness of car travel and increase the attractiveness of alternatives. An unintended effect may be that the 'sticks' bear particularly heavily on rural areas, especially low income groups who depend on car use, and for whom improved alternatives are unrealistic or non-existent.

Methodology. Analysis of household travel data for rural areas, covering incidence and structure of trips, and interactions between income and location effects.

Conclusions. Most traffic in rural areas is not generated by residents, but by visitors or those passing through. For residents, there are higher levels of car ownership and use, but much of this appears to be an income effect rather than deriving from location constraints: it is true that low income rural residents have higher car use than low income urban residents, but this is a very small proportion of the total amount of traffic. However, about 5 per cent of rural residents, being the poorest groups, are adversely affected by car travel costs, and have significantly reduced possibilities of adapting to them than their urban counterparts.

Proposed Solutions. A relatively slow rise in car travel costs is easier to adapt to, partly by location of homes and activities and partly by the evolution of better alternatives. Smart card systems would make it feasible to enable poor rural residents to have access to somewhat cheaper petrol (by cross-subsidy) if desired, though large discounts would be impractical.

Figure 6.5. Restrictions of mobility of rural residents. (Main references: Stokes, 1995, 1996)

Hypothesis. Individuals and households seek independence from the constraints of time and space by acquiring and using cars. However, this may in the longer run be self-defeating, if it reduces the opportunities and choices open to them.

Methodology. In depth qualitative interviews, analysis of panel surveys of households in Europe and United States, desk study of alternatives to car use, attitude surveys, literature reviews.

Conclusions. Prolonged car use results in greater dependence by users, whose knowledge and interest in alternatives declines, and a car-based life-style develops. At the social level, land-use patterns and declining levels of service of public transport reinforce this process. A result is that over time cars become converted from 'luxury' to 'necessity'. Around 50 per cent to 80 per cent of car owners perceive themselves to be dependent on car use for their life style, but it is a much smaller proportion of trips (around 10 per cent to 30 per cent) which can be unambiguously described as car dependent. A similar proportion are marginal, in the sense that the trip is unnecessary or very easily done by an alternative mode (e.g. the increasing numbers of very short trips by car). Up to a third of car users report they would like to drive less, if circumstances allowed. Extrapolation of current trends suggests that in future there will be more car trips, and fewer of them will have decent alternatives, so car dependence absolutely and relatively will increase. Thus would result in unacceptable travelling conditions, and defeat part of the objectives of increasing car ownership.

Proposed Solution. It is suggested that targeted policies can be aimed successfully at reducing or diverting those car trips which, at present, are the least dependent. In the longer run, it is necessary to intervene in the cycle by which first alternatives to car use are rejected, then information about them is rejected, and finally they disappear though lack of support.

Figure 6.6. Unintended effects of seeking independence through car ownership. (Main reference: Goodwin *et al.*, 1995)

Hypothesis. Road pricing, especially in congested urban areas, is intended to reduce traffic levels to the point where advantages to the traveller are not outweighed by congestion and environmental costs imposed on everybody else. Unintended effects may be (*a*) that continual professional focus on this issue diverts attention from more realistic or practical second-best policies, and (*b*) that financial pressures distort the policy to less environmentally-friendly objectives.

Methodology. Policy analysis of evolution of the argument about road pricing; review of experience in cities that have implemented some version of tolls or price control.

Conclusions. The main real world experience of road pricing has been of repeated, very substantial studies, invariably demonstrating that road pricing would produce substantial benefits of reduced congestion, economic advantage and environmental improvement, but not implemented. What has been implemented mostly are a few toll systems where the funds produced are (in part at least) used for provision of extra road capacity.

Proposed Solution. It is suggested that underemphasis on the use of road pricing revenues has been the main weakness of the policy debate, since it is this that determines whether road pricing reinforces, or undermines, other transport policies, and whether it will be politically popular or unpopular. The revenues should in large part be used to pay for higher quality of alternatives to car use, including better public transport and higher design standards for pedestrianization etc. In any case, transport authorities need a twin strategy (one with and one without road pricing, the former expected to be superior but the latter often easier) so that progress does not completely depend on resolution of this particularly difficult political question.

Figure 6.7. Road pricing – diversions and distortions (Main reference: Goodwin,1995)

Hypothesis. Analytical techniques including a wider range of behavioural responses, and all modes of transport (including public transport and walking) are necessary to assess the full effects of environmentally friendly policies. An unintended effect may be to emphasise modelling at the expense of understanding and implementation, or to focus on the wrong improvements.

Methodology. Consideration of the role of forecasts in policy development, and conceptualization of a modelling framework that would be able to capture the most important findings of the other case studies.

Conclusions. While the range of behavioural adaptations is undoubtedly important (and much wider than those captured in traditional models), it is suggested that equilibrium models are not capable of providing the most necessary understandings, because the key questions are the process, mechanisms and timescale of adaptation. Non-equilibrium dynamic models are necessary that can address questions like how long will it take to have an effect, and which order should policies be implemented in. Equilibrium models (however complex) are likely to have important systematic errors which affect the evaluation of alternative policies, and divert attention from more important policy questions to less important ones (and even on those, give biased advice).

Proposed Solution. A framework of evolutionary models (both aggregate and disaggregate) is proposed, using longitudinal data such as time series and panels, where the focus is on process rather than end-state.

Figure 6.8. Better models and forecasting procedures (Main references: Dargay and Goodwin,1994; Dargay and Vythoulkas, 1996)

Omission of dynamic effects, when they exist, unfairly predisposes to certain sorts of policies in preference to others. This arises because over time people have the opportunity to soften the effects of policies which in the short run make them worse off, and take greater benefit from policies which make them better off – this always being the direction of adaptation before taking account of external costs and social interaction.

However, this conclusion is only useful if it is possible to identify the characteristics and pathways of the adaptive processes of interest.

Figures 6.9 to 6.11, due mainly to Dargay and Vythoulkas (1996) and Parkhurst (1996), offer an outline of what such an approach would mean in practice, related to the specific case of park-and-ride services: in principle the same could be applied to each of the case studies. Thus figure 6.9 operates at the completely general level, distinguishing responses which are those of the 'target' (i.e. intended behaviour by a particular group) and those which relate to a different affected group or different area of activity. Figure 6.10 then depicts the interactive effects of activities, policies, and the context in which they are implemented. And Figure 6.11 attempts to track this through in terms of behavioural responses to park-and-ride policies.

Two strong conclusions which come from the research are that the effects of policies are likely to be *broader* and *longer* than has been assumed, and that

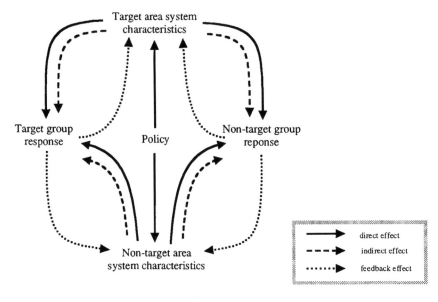

Figure 6.9 The various responses to policy measures.

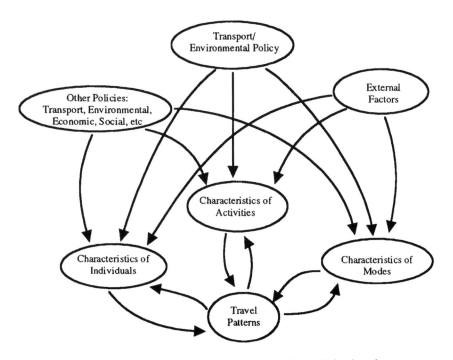

Figure 6.10 The interaction between the various factors affecting behavioural response.

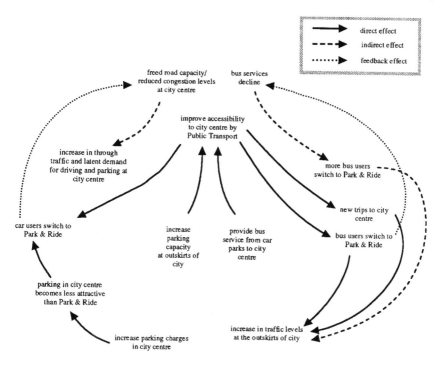

Figure 6.11 Behavioural responses to park and ride policies.

therefore there are new requirements for data structures, forms of survey, content of monitoring programmes, methods of analysis, and where appropriate models for forecasting and evaluation.

The *breadth* arises from a systemic approach: patterns of movement form a complex interacting system. Inadequate public transport affects the impact of park-and-ride. Induced traffic from road construction influences the financial viability of public transport. Traffic restraint determines the achievement of congestion relief from a bypass. The quality of pedestrianization affects the political acceptability of traffic restraint. The structure of relative prices influences the response to pedestrianization. Reductions in traffic due to one policy will be offset by increases due to the absence of another policy. And so on.

The *length* arises because each of these effects takes place in real time, and proceeds with the pace and complex pathways that individuals and households and institutions are able to adapt their behaviour – for some purposes, very swiftly indeed, and for others constrained by existing homes and jobs and family commitments and imperfect information and human motivation for action or inaction, and land-use patterns and the general inertia of bureaucracy or democracy.

These effects influence the reliability of forecasts and the partiality of appraisal – both formal economic assessment and descriptive environmental assessment. The suggestion is not only that the complexity increases the uncertainty of policy assessment (although it does, and therefore puts greater emphasis on the need for continual monitoring and adaptation of policy in preference to a concentration on 'end-state' design years or postulated equilibrium). It is also that there are inherent biases arising from ignoring system-wide processes, sequence of implementation, and the pathways of response, with the likelihood then of wrongly being steered away from good policies, or accepting bad ones.

It is not necessarily the case that the use of a formal forecasting model is always an essential precursor to successful policy – there are examples of successful policies with no models, and unsuccessful ones with very substantial modelling exercises. Nevertheless, it is helpful to consider the sorts of features that a model would have to have to give guidance on policy which captures the sorts of interactions which emerge from the research, and for this purpose a notional 'perfect model' is described, which in principle would address all the findings of the research. It becomes clear that it has to be explicitly dynamic in order to distinguish the different paces of response to different types of policy, and it has to take a very much broader range of choice and behaviour, even in response to quite small scale policy initiatives, than is currently established practice.

The research has not produced such a model. But it does perhaps give some insight into the 'forecasting deficit' that must inherently arise when such factors are ignored in policy assessment, and therefore both assists and in a sense justifies the greater role that seems likely to be accorded to political and professional judgement in the next stage of policy development. What does seem robust is that the *insight* from such an approach, whether formally captured in a model or not, is a necessary part of the preparation for transport planners who do not want to be caught unawares by unexpected effects of their policies: it is necessary always to expect the unexpected.

DISCUSSION – SUCCESS AND FAILURE IN TRANSPORT POLICY

It should be emphasized that just because behavioural responses are complicated and may be not what was hoped, this does *not* mean that all such policies are a waste of time.

One instructive comparison is that between the experience of two of the great transport policy developments of our time – pedestrianization and traffic calming on the one hand, and road pricing on the other. In debate, these are sometimes counterposed as two alternative methods of solving problems of congestion and environmental damage, one essentially by regulation, the other by the market. It is intriguing also that champions of the two have tended to use different vocabularies and methods to argue their case – pedestrianization largely using the conventions of the town planner, with limited use of models, road pricing using the conventions of the economist and often very elaborate and expensive modelling exercises.

The real world experiences of the two approaches are radically different.

Pedestrianization and Traffic Calming (Hass-Klau, 1996)

It seems that pedestrianization may be counted – with some caveats – as a success story in achieving one of its two main objectives, the creation of a safe, pleasant street environment that when implemented well can be so attractive as to bring other benefits, especially commercial success and political popularity, in its wake.

But success in the other main objective, to reinforce a general transport strategy encouraging walking and discouraging vehicle use, is much less clear. Five main problems have been noted.

1. The need for high quality design standards in general, and public transport access to and within the town centre in particular, are necessary conditions.

2. There is a very delicate balance between too tough a policy on exceptions (which causes resistance and operational difficulties) and too relaxed a policy (which undermines the need to retain a pedestrian 'feel' to the street space).

3. There is the problem of the margins of the pedestrianized area: while forecasts of 'traffic chaos' have often been exaggerated, nevertheless the underlying question of the effect of pedestrianizing an area on the rest of the town is a real one, especially when considering competition for a limited overall amount of trade.

4. Experience of commercially successful pedestrianization in other towns never seems to predispose traders to expect success in their own town – their political resistance, for a period, seems to be a virtually inevitable part of the pedestrianization process.

5. (And linked with the previous point) There are transitional difficulties during the early days of implementation, likely to last in the order of one to three years. At the other extreme, we observe that the longest established major pedestrianized centres have been building a base for up to about twenty years, and some are still showing signs of continuing response.

Traffic calming in Germany, the Netherlands and other countries has been implemented with a wide range of declared objectives, including a general strategy of reducing the dominance of vehicle traffic and changing the 'balance of power' in streets in favour of residents, pedestrians, and cyclists. In Britain it has tended to be more narrowly focused on increasing safety by reducing speed, though recently there is interest in wider objectives.

Considered as an addition to the toolbox of detailed traffic engineering measures to tackle very local problems, there are indications of reasonable levels of success. Speeds are typically reduced, say by around 10 mph, and accidents can be reduced by up to 50 per cent. Depending on the measures used, a large proportion of through traffic can be removed from residential streets, and there are now reasonably well-established devices and design principles to assist discrimination between different classes of vehicles (e.g. buses, cars, lorries), and to influence the design of bus stops, pedestrian crossings, and boundaries between different sorts of area.

Concerning wider impacts, there is some evidence that area-wide traffic calming can have a small impact on local trade: in most towns where any data are available, businesses in the traffic calmed areas did slightly better than in the control areas. However, during the period of construction itself there can be significant traffic disruption: since 'after' surveys were mostly carried out soon after implementation of traffic calming measures the short term effects of disruption and the longer term effects of a more pleasant area have not usually been distinguished. The most important result may be that in the two areas where traffic calming has been carried out comprehensively, Buxtehude and Borgentreich, there has been a high number of businesses with increase in turnover and a low number of businesses with a decline in turnover. This is a somewhat similar pattern to that found with the more ambitious pedestrianization schemes, and may suggest that pedestrian-friendly traffic calming needs to be quite ambitious to have a positive effect.

It was realized early on that by traffic calming one street the problems of accidents, speeds and volume of traffic were liable to be transferred to the neighbouring streets. Although schemes are now designed more carefully and there are more area-wide traffic calming schemes, there remains a perceived problem that traffic calming is still moving traffic around without tackling the main issue of reducing overall traffic levels. Residents interviewed in York commented that as a result of traffic calming on residential roads in the city, traffic had now diverted onto smaller, less suitable roads than it was previously using, which themselves had previously had very low traffic flows. Other criticisms have been made that traffic calming, especially in Britain, has been implemented on too limited a scale, and with too small budgets, to expect any substantial influence. The concept has been devalued by being perceived as little more than a combination of unpleasant speed-bumps and poorly cared for planters of shrubs. It is also known that poorly designed schemes can cause great difficulties for buses and emergency services.

It may be that in the long term the use of odd devices to slow traffic down in locations where it is damaging and threatening will be seen as a temporary expedient. However, at present it is often the only procedure available, and it has usefully prompted a re-examination of such issues as the relative priority in traffic flow of cars and buses, and the relative claims for space of pavement and carriageway.

Thus in summary, neither pedestrianization nor traffic calming are completely free of problems, but the nature of those problems is increasingly well-understood by reference to real-world experience.

Road Pricing

By contrast, the main real world experience of road pricing is of its continual *non*-implementation. Discussion of the analytical framework and presumptions that have dominated official appraisal of road pricing options suggest that non-implementation may not simply be a matter of fear of the unknown, but may be directly connected to a misdirection of attention, away from aspects which (even in theory) are inherent to the nature of road pricing and which must determine its real world success. Thus the analysis of road pricing proceeds from the experience of interaction derived from more successful policies, and seeks to apply a similarly interactive approach in theory (in the absence of successful practice). The question therefore is rather different: what would road pricing need to become successful in the real world? It is suggested that road pricing is neither a necessary nor a sufficient condition for successful transport policy, but it does create the most favourable conditions for success.

It is not strictly necessary because it is possible to achieve the changes by sufficiently determined application of a broad package of other policies – but they would need to be more extreme and costly without road pricing than they would be with. It is not strictly sufficient because even if the most elaborate and far reaching scheme were to be implemented, its own success would depend largely on the application of a broad package of other improvements and constraints. It is notable that broadly the same policies are favoured under both scenarios, but they are likely to differ in intensity and detail, since the pattern of demands and traffic flows which evolve in the absence of road pricing are unlikely to be economically optimum, and therefore should not be taken at their face value as constraints on the plans adopted.

Thus without road pricing, one relies more on proved techniques and tried-and-tested traffic management methods, as compared with the uncertain outcome of untried new road pricing technology. On the other hand, all those tried-and-tested tools are working uphill: if the basic financial signals are unfavourable, it will be very much more difficult to achieve comparable effects, and traffic growth continually undermines the policies' successes.

The policy conclusion of this discussion is that transport authorities need, in effect, to have a twin strategy, simultaneously working up a strategic approach that combines road pricing with the best package of complementary measures, and another version that builds the best package but without road pricing. One can be confident in this case that the option with road pricing will nearly always give better calculated returns, on paper, than the one without. But unless road pricing is seen as part of such a package, the conclusion is that it would never reach the point of real implementation anyway.

Process and Politics of Implementation

There are three main general observations that may be made from the experience in the specific cities studied in the project (especially, but not only, Oxford, York and Lüneburg).

1. It is apparent that there has been an increasing recognition over the period that a 'balanced transport policy' must involve a wide range of different policy instruments – parking, priority, development control, pedestrianization, public transport – but a considerable difficulty exists in delivering all of those elements in a consistent way. In retrospect, one can see that the policies have been in the making for many years, even decades, but the *sequence* of implementation of each element does not derive from deliberate forward planning: rather, it is dominated by the constraints of available funds, political acceptability, institutional pressures locally and nationally, and a professional and political learning process. Planners have felt that much of the task has been an uphill battle against considerable difficulty, and the level of political determination has been decisive in overcoming opposition.

2. There is a problem in defining 'success'. Measured against the general growth in car ownership, maintaining traffic levels and congestion may be described as a substantial achievement. On the other hand, those congestion levels are widely felt to be too high. It is not clear that in the absence of restraint traffic growth would, or could, actually have been very much greater. The question is how to identify 'what would have happened otherwise?' Although undoubtedly useful for the process of forming realistic targets, it is of course always possible to describe a worse alternative than the actuality, but then a policy can suddenly be made to appear more or less successful not by changing anything in the real world, but by redefining the unobservable alternative. This seems unhelpful both in encouraging consensus around the possibilities of making life better (as distinct from 'less worse'), and in providing measurable indicators to monitor achievements or failures.

3. There is an important implication in the observation of relatively high or stable levels of congestion even following substantial policy initiatives. This is that favourable responses by some individuals, e.g., to use public transport, or walk, or use park-and-ride, etc., release road space which is then available for other people to use by car. The *subsequent responses* by other individuals are just as important for the overall success of a policy, as the initial responses by those targeted.

Although specific conditions will be difficult in every city, a general expectation might be of a three-stage process.

The first stage consists of political preparation, consensus-building, and planning. This can take as long as the political process allows – even decades, for some British towns – and may last until some external event (e.g. an election with a change in power, or a crisis of pollution or security) results in a degree of political determination and courage. The implementation of some *other* policy, such as a ring road or a park-and-ride scheme, can create the conditions for timing of the political process, but seems to be less necessary as a technical precondition than is sometimes assumed.

The second phase, of early implementation, does bring some benefits very swiftly, and if schemes are well designed and the implementation well managed, can increase political support, but there are also short term problems and some loud voices against.

In the third phase, the principle commands much broader support, and becomes a well-rooted part of the perception of the town, but there are continuing pressures for change and development, including extending the boundaries, adjusting the exceptions, seeking improvements to public transport or, alternatively, greater levels of parking. This phase is where it becomes apparent that each policy is increasingly dependent on other transport and planning policies for continuing success.

GENERAL CONCLUSION

A related theme appears, to some degree, in all of the case-studies. This is the inherent inadequacy of any policy to achieve even quite narrow objectives without interacting with other policies.

• Parking policy is undermined if cross-city centre journeys are too easy and large amounts of private parking remain uncontrolled.
• Park-and-ride policies are undermined by too cheap central parking, too expensive bus services or by ignoring transport policy beyond the urban boundary.
• Access restrictions applied without overall car restraint may shift the traffic problem to the suburbs.
• Public transport priority is undermined by road construction, lack of enforcement, or inadequate funding.
• Bypassing is easily undermined without the imposition of significant car restraint in the urban area, *i.e.* closing roads to through-movement.

It seems likely that the successful development of sustainable transport policies is increasingly bound to force onto the agenda the need for *integrated transport policies* – not necessarily in the historical sense which emphasized coordinated ownership of different modes, but with a new emphasis which comes from the specific context of the unavoidable necessity for demand management.

REFERENCES

Cairns, S. (1995) Travel for food shopping: The fourth solution. *Traffic Engineering and Control*, July/August.

Cairns, S. (1996a) Delivering alternatives: Successes and failures of home delivery services for food shopping. *Transport Policy*, **3**(4).

Cairns, S. (1996b) A Geographical Investigation of Travel for Food Shopping. D Phil Thesis, University of Oxford.

Cairns, S. (1996) The Real Effects of Environmentally Friendly Transport Policies (Consultative Draft), Report 96/16, chapters 7.2–7.4. Transport Studies Unit, University College London.

Dargay, J. M.. and Goodwin, P.B. (1995) Evaluation of consumer surplus with dynamic demand changes. *Journal of Transport Economics and Policy*, **26**(2), pp.179–193.

Dargay, J.M. and Vythoulkas, P. (1996) The Real Effects of Environmentally Friendly Transport Policies (Consultative Draft), Report 96/16, chapter 9. Transport Studies Unit, University College London.

Goodwin, P. B. (1995) Road pricing or transport planning? in Johansson and Mattson (eds.) *Road Pricing: Theory, Empirical Assessment and Policy.* Amsterdam: Kluwer.

Goodwin, P.B. *et al.* (ed.) (1995) *Car Dependence.* London: RAC Foundation for Motoring and the Environment.

Goodwin P. B. (1996a) Extra Traffic Induced by Road Construction: Empirical Evidence, Economic Effects and Policy Implications. Round Table 104, European Conference of Ministers of Transport, Paris.

Goodwin, P.B. (1996b) The Real Effects of Environmentally Friendly Transport Policies (Consultative Draft), Report 96/16, chapter 8. Transport Studies Unit, University College London.

Hass-Klau, C. (1993) Impact of pedestrianisation and traffic calming on retailing: A review of the evidence from Germany and the UK. *Transport Policy*, **1**(1).

Hass-Klau, C., Downland, C. and Stokes, G. (1994) Lüneburg: the Making of a Car-Free Town Centre. Paper presented to Environmental and Transport Planning Conference, Brighton.

Hass-Klau, C., Downland, C. and Stokes, G. (1996) The Real Effects of Environmentally Friendly Transport Policies (Consultative Draft), Report 96/16, chapter 3. Transport Studies Unit, University College London.

Parkhurst, G.P.(1994) Park-and-ride: Could it lead to an increase in car traffic? *Transport Policy*, **2**(1), pp. 15–23.

Parkhurst, G.P. (1996a) The Economic and Modal-split Impacts of Short-Range Park-and-ride Schemes: Evidence from Nine UK Cities. Report 96/29, ESRC Transport Studies Unit, University College London.

Parkhurst, G.P. (1996b) The Real Effects of Environmentally Friendly Transport Policies (Consultative Draft), Report 96/16, chapter 6. Transport Studies Unit, University College London.

SACTRA (1994) *Trunk Roads and the Generation of Traffic.* London: HMSO.

Stokes, G.(1995) Rural transport policy in the 1990s. *Transport Policy*, **3** (3).

Stokes, G. (1996) The Real Effects of Environmentally Friendly Transport Policies (Consultative Draft), Report 96/16, chapter 7.5–7.6. Transport Studies Unit, University College London.

CHAPTER 7

TRANSPORT PROVISION AND REGIONAL DEVELOPMENT IN EUROPE
Towards a Framework for Appraisal

Roger Vickerman

There has been a great upsurge of interest in the role of infrastructure, particularly transport infrastructure, in the process of economic development. This has occurred both in the economics literature and in policy analysis. Several reasons can explain this interest. Transport infrastructure is traditionally provided by the public sector and in most Western European (and indeed other advanced) countries the pressure on public budgets had led to a trend downturn in capital expenditure over the period from the mid 1960s. By the late 1980s economists were beginning to question the extent to which this was counter-productive given the role of infrastructure, as a public good, in enhancing the productivity of private capital (Aschauer, 1989, 1990). Better infrastructure would therefore enhance the competitiveness of industry using that infrastructure. In addition, it was increasingly being shown that, at a regional level, the provision of infrastructure could clearly be related to the level of economic development (Biehl, 1986, 1991; Munnell, 1990, 1992). Thus there was a case for using infrastructure as a policy instrument in promoting the convergence of regional growth paths. These arguments clearly come together at a policy level in the European Union in the 1993 White Paper on *Growth, Competitiveness and Employment* (European Commission, 1993) where infrastructure, in the form of trans European networks, is used to promote the twin objectives of competitiveness and cohesion.

The arguments put forward most strongly by Aschauer have been heavily criticized on both economic and econometric grounds (e.g. Gramlich, 1994). The economic arguments are principally that the causality cannot be shown, the association of more infrastructure with higher levels of economic activity is a reflection of the demand for such infrastructure and the greater ability to pay for it (whether publicly or privately). The danger of promoting more public investment in infrastructure is that this will crowd out private investment. Where infrastructure is seen to raise a regional rate of growth this may be primarily because of the multiplier effect of the construction, the infrastructure itself does nothing for indigenous firms and remains a burden on the public sector.

These are essentially macroeconomic, aggregate, arguments. The microeconomics of how the provision of additional or better infrastructure affects the performance of firms in a region or the relative competitiveness of 'exporters' and 'importers' has not been so fully explored. There is one strand of literature which has touched on this, though again mainly at an aggregate level, that on accessibility. The argument here is that improvements in infrastructure improve accessibility when measured in time or costs and that it is accessibility which is a key determinant of regional economic performance. This mainly geographical approach goes back to the work of Clark *et al.* (1969) and has been most fully developed by Keeble *et al.* (1982, 1988). The usual approach is to measure a region's accessibility to all its potential markets (hence the use of the term economic potential) in terms of their income levels deflated by a measure of the cost of access. Adjustments can be made for natural and political boundaries and for the quality of the infrastructure. Changes in infrastructure can be simulated through examining the effect of changing access costs on individual links. This gives the impression of smooth, continuous changes in accessibility through space implying that the benefits of improvements in infrastructure will be concentrated more in more central regions than in peripheral regions such that infrastructure can never promote cohesion, except where it involves overcoming some physical barrier (e.g. a fixed link to an island or a mountain tunnel).

The research reported in this chapter aimed to explore the gap between these two broad traditional approaches, essentially to provide a better microeconomic foundation to the definition and measurement of accessibility such that this could be integrated into more aggregative, production function studies of both competitiveness and cohesiveness. The principal hypothesis was that a disaggregation of measures of the impact of infrastructure on both spatial and sectoral dimensions would generate a more sensitive and effective tool. The achievement of this would also have the added benefit that it could provide a basis for better evaluation of infrastructure, where the regional benefits (and costs) are frequently cited but rarely satisfactorily demonstrated.

Against this background and principal hypothesis, four principal objectives can be identified:

• to develop a methodology for assessing the inter-regional distribution of the economic impacts of new transport infrastructure;
• to relate regional production potential to accessibility-based measures of

potential, assess the implications for trade-flows and assess the sectoral impact of new transport infrastructure through its effects on location and production decisions in different sectors;
• to examine the intra-regional effects of such infrastructure by treating space as continuous;
• to develop an appraisal framework for transport infrastructure which allows specifically for these wider regional impacts.

INTER-REGIONAL DISTRIBUTION OF ECONOMIC IMPACTS OF TRANSPORT

Traditionally the effects of new transport infrastructure have been assessed through measuring the implicit reduction in transport costs between regions. The assumption is made that these reductions are symmetrical between regions and these impacts are measured on the basis of simplified networks which attribute all the impact to a zonal centroid (with some allowance for intra-regional traffic). The problem with this approach is that it assumes a continuity in the supply of transport both within and between regions which tends to produce relative smooth transitions of economic potential.

It has been recognized therefore that it was necessary to achieve a degree of spatial disaggregation. The literature on accessibility (see Newman and Vickerman, 1993; Vickerman 1995b, for a review) suggested the adoption of a corridor approach which recognized that transport provision is concentrated between major centres and secondly through a recognition of intra-regional variations. The corridor approach is relatively simple and a set of five different case-study corridors in Europe was identified for detailed examination of the way transport improvements affected economic performance along the corridors.

The Impacts of Transport Improvements in Five Corridors

A set of contrasting corridors was required to explore the differing regional dimensions of transport development. This required regions in differing economic and geographical situations, but also with differing strategic needs: core and peripheral regions, regions with strategic core-periphery links, and regions with differing economic structures.

The five corridors selected were:

• Lille-Aachen
• Northern England/Southern Scotland
• Bordeaux–Santander
• Nîmes-Tarragona
• Southern Spain

For each of these corridors the following information was assembled to assess the balance of infrastructure provision to regional needs:

(i) a set of accessibility indicators based on existing economic potential, on existing network connectivity and change allowing for new infrastructure planned to 2010, and on mode sensitive measures which allow for specific changes in infrastructure provision and on a spatially disaggregated measure (see Newman and Vickerman, 1993, 1994; Vickerman, 1995b, for details and discussion of these indicators);

(ii) existing regional economic and social structure based on as disaggregate sectoral data as possible for output and employment at NUTS2 regional level. This is rather aggregate in some of the corridors but consistent information is not available at NUTS3 for most of the corridors;

(iii) existing traffic and trade flows, disaggregated where possible by sector and by origin-destination – typically this involves aggregate traffic flows by detailed origin and destination and sectorally disaggregated trade flows identifying 'imports', 'exports', and intra-regional movements;

(iv) current regional policy (both EU and national level policies) and other specific regional information from the regions concerned, including both 'high level' infrastructure plans, such as trans-European networks, and their relationship to national and regional infrastructure.

A set of accessibility calculations were made for the corridors as a base point using both current (variously 1990 or 1993) levels of infrastructure provision and infrastructure as planned for 2005-2010. Four basic approaches to accessibility measurement were used:

• economic potential, following the work of Keeble et al. (1982, 1988);
• an aggregated mode-specific measure, weighted according to modal split, following the theoretical justification given by Rietveld (1989), as developed by Simmonds (1992), but with penalties introduced to reflect the existence of national borders;
• a best-mode dependent measure, allowing for joint usage of modes (i.e. based on a subjective assessment of the best mode or modes to use for any particular origin-destination pair), as developed by Lutter et al. (1992);
• a network connection dependent measure, as developed in the ICON index by MCRIT (CEDRE, 1993)

These are defined in more detail in the Appendix and see Newman and Vickerman (1994) and Vickerman (1995b) for further discussion. The aggregated mode-specific measure was used for most of the comparisons, but with reference to the others to ascertain whether these suggested rather different possible outcomes.

This enabled a set of interim conclusions to be drawn about the possible advantages of particular indicators and the likely improvements needed to help explain and evaluate the role of transport provision in each of these corridors, which we shall consider briefly in turn.

Lille-Aachen

This is a region which is geographically central in the EU, but essentially a transit region and with important border effects straddling four countries, France, Germany, the Netherlands and Belgium itself (figure 7.1). It is mainly characterized by small to medium sized cities but lies between major conurbations, experiencing industrial restructuring or decline. The region experiences high levels of congestion on a transport system which is largely road based, especially for international traffic, but is likely to face restructuring from new high-speed rail connections which will benefit the ends of the corridors but by-pass the central part.

Before allowing for the effects of borders, the main urban centres in this corridor display very consistent levels of accessibility. Lille has the highest value, but all the other centres had over 90 per cent of the Lille value, except for Tournai (87 per cent) and Maastricht (86 per cent). The introduction of border effects has a dramatic effect on this. The accessibility value for Lille itself is reduced to some 36 per cent of its basic (without border effects) level, that for Aachen is similarly reduced, though rises slightly relative to that of Lille (94 per cent). These two cities are within the large economies of France and Germany, respectively, and benefit from that, even if they are cut-off to some extent from natural hinterlands across borders. The Belgian cities suffer much more if border effects are imposed, having values between 60 per cent and 70 per cent of that of Lille, but the greatest impact is on the value for Maastricht, virtually cut off from its own national market, which has an accessibility value only 57 per cent of that for Lille. Of course, this rather mechanistic distance-based measure does not allow for the competitive advantages which cities such as Maastricht have been able to exploit from their position on borders.

Changes in accessibility were explored for various developments of the PBKAL rail system. This would only serve Lille directly for all destinations, but Liège and Aachen could also benefit. The basic high-speed links London-Paris-Brussels produced improvements in accessibility to all cities, though the additions to the network produced only marginal improvements on the base case. The biggest impact was again felt by the city with the best initial accessibility, Lille. Further benefits for cities such as Mons, Charleroi or Namur will depend on their connectivity to the new network.

Northern England/Southern Scotland

This is also an old industrial region, but less central, on the edge of the European core. The corridor, which is actually twin transport corridors to the east and west

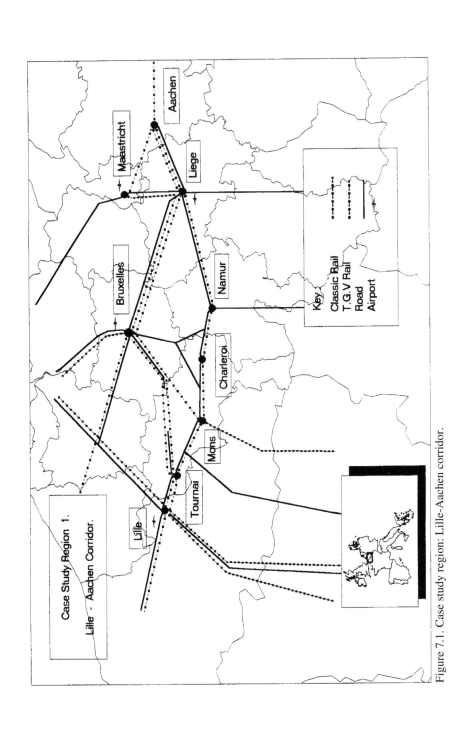

Figure 7.1. Case study region: Lille-Aachen corridor.

of the Pennines from Sheffield/Manchester to Edinburgh/Glasgow, is treated as a single corridor region which has a good basic infrastructure (figure 7.2). This has not been upgraded as much as in other comparable regions of Europe and, given its location, is less of a transit corridor. Access to airports is more important for this region than in others, but an emphasis has been placed on the need to develop better rail based links, especially for freight transport given the opportunities created by the Channel Tunnel.

This case study involves a region which is entirely within a single member state and for which internal accessibility is more important than external accessibility. Nevertheless, since it includes some of the core manufacturing areas of the UK, accessibility to export markets is critical and, therefore, both external and internal accessibilities need to be included. This is particularly relevant to the UK case because of the improvements to accessibility associated with the completion of the Channel Tunnel. The popular hypothesis that the northern region is disadvantaged by location relative to markets in the European core, and that this disadvantage will be compounded by Channel Tunnel effects, led to a comparative analysis being carried out for London and Birmingham as part of the accessibility calculations.

Manchester has a clear advantage over other locations in the case study region. This is not surprising given its good air accessibility, its location relative to major destinations, inside and outside the UK, and its own size. Within the case study region, of the cities considered, only Middlesbrough, however, fails to achieve an accessibility index at least 80 per cent of that of Manchester. All of the other centres are both on major corridors and form transport nodes in their own right. Potential is more discriminating. The same rank order is maintained, with the exception of Newcastle which, as a smaller centre, does not score as highly as Leeds, Edinburgh or Glasgow. The suggestion that all of the centres in the case study region are disadvantaged relative to London and Birmingham is borne out by the indicators. Birmingham has an accessibility index 7 per cent greater than Manchester and London 22 per cent greater. The figures for potential identify a much greater difference, for Birmingham by 53 per cent and London has a figure five times that of Manchester.

Three alternative scenarios were tested on this base case:

1. The addition of the Channel Tunnel with the high-speed rail network of the PBKAL complete. This increases the accessibilities of all the cities but in proportion to the base values, thus increasing the distinction between the more southerly and more northerly centres and those on and off main routes.

2. The addition of domestic high-speed rail in the UK along the main north-south corridors (the East Coast and West Coast routes) with similar speeds to those of TGV. This improves the relative accessibilities of the case study cities to London, though not by a large margin. That for Manchester rises from 81.8 per cent of the London figure to 82.4 per cent, Leeds from 72.3 per cent to

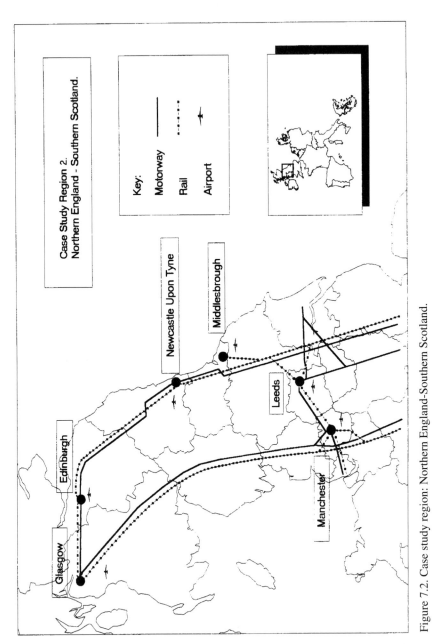

Case Study Region 2.
Northern England - Southern Scotland.

Key:
Motorway
Rail
Airport

Glasgow

Edinburgh

Newcastle Upon Tyne

Middlesbrough

Leeds

Manchester

Figure 7.2. Case study region: Northern England-Southern Scotland.

74.2 per cent and Glasgow 66.1 per cent to 69.1 per cent. This scenario would of course accentuate the role of accessibility to London and relatively worsen the intra-regional accessibility off the main north-south corridors, e.g. Manchester to Leeds or Newcastle, Leeds to Glasgow.

3. The retention of conventional rail, but improvement of air links on all relevant routes such that all links over 200 km had a direct air alternative to rail. Generally this would produce smaller improvements in accessibility than the development of a genuine high-speed rail network. The exceptions to this are Leeds, and even more so Middlesbrough, which are smaller cities, have poor current air services, and in the latter case lie off the main rail route. This suggests that for smaller regional centres, the development of air routes may offer a better option than expensive new infrastructure of the type necessary for high-speed rail.

The broad conclusion from this is that improved rail does offer some gains, but the improvements in accessibility are not great relative to the likely costs. There is little change in either accessibility levels relative to London or in the ranking of the case study cities. Given the domination of the core European destinations, this gain in accessibility, such as it is, is achieved at the expense of intra-regional improvements in accessibility. Since it is unlikely that all centres could be connected directly this may lead to substantial intra-regional shifts.

The ICON indicator shows generally good accessibility with Manchester, Leeds, Glasgow and Edinburgh all having an aggregate access to networks of less than 0.5 h. Middlesbrough and Newcastle are slightly less well connected (0.5 to 1 h). This reflects the generally well developed networks of all modes available. The rather minimal change resulting from new transport developments is confirmed by inspecting the recalculation of the ICON indicator for the network planned for 2010. This makes very little change to the contours of access.

Interestingly the Keeble and Lutter studies produce slightly different classifications of this case study region, and in particular certain parts of it, in terms of the degree of centrality implied by accessibility. Glasgow and Edinburgh are classified as being in peripheral regions by Keeble (mainly as a result of the use of Level I regions). The Manchester and Leeds areas fall into Keeble's core region, and Newcastle and Middlesbrough are classified intermediate. The Lutter *et al.* study classifies Manchester and Leeds, but also Glasgow and Edinburgh, as inner central. Newcastle and Middlesbrough are inner peripheral. This is largely accounted for by the quality of air communications, combined with the access to other important UK centres for Manchester and Leeds. This might suggest the region should be classified as part of the central urban region of the Community, but the generally lower level of economic performance justifies its treatment rather differently. The higher level of accessibility enjoyed is mainly the result of past economic performance, plus the greater reliance on air transport necessitated by the UK's island status.

This presents one of the problems of a time/distance based measure of accessibility which may accentuate the apparent accessibility of centres dependent on air transport, ignoring the extra cost which reliance on this mode may impose. Even more difficult to assess for this region, is the extent to which the anticipated journey times, used as the basis for accessibility calculations, can be achieved in practice given the capacity constraints on all of the relevant networks. Natural growth in traffic within this region will lead to serious problems of delay which, if not tackled, will reduce effective accessibility, and, more seriously, the perceived accessibility of transport users.

Bordeaux-Santander

This case study deals with the Atlantic Coast corridor into the Iberian peninsula, a corridor of emerging importance in its European context (figure 7.3). The existing infrastructure is relatively poor and has the added problem of a major barrier within the corridor (the Pyrenees, compounded by a change of rail gauge), but links into a major industrial area of Northern Spain. This is a strategic corridor, linking an intermediate region on the edge of the core with one on the inner edge of the periphery, which is likely to be affected by high speed rail links in both directions. The French TGV-Atlantique is proposed to be extended from Tours towards Bordeaux and there are plans for further development of the AVE high speed network in Spain. It has therefore, the potential both to benefit from new transport, and to suffer from an increasing transit effect due to inadequate intra-regional and intra-corridor integration.

Base accessibilities were calculated both including and excluding border effects. Not surprisingly the dominant centre is Bordeaux, given its location relative to major European centres. However, the substantial concentration of population in N.E. Spain means that Bilbao has the highest potential figure (over 150 per cent of the Bordeaux figure), when own population is taken into account. Although border effects reduce the absolute level of accessibility by about 50 per cent, the relative accessibility levels remain roughly the same, between 60 and 80 per cent of the Bordeaux figure, except for Bilbao which falls from 88 per cent of the Bordeaux figure to 82 per cent.

The possible improvements considered were the completion of the French TGV-Atlantique as far as Bordeaux, the improvement of a core rail network in Pais Vasco to standard track gauge and with 200 km/h maximum speeds linking Bilbao, Irun, Vitoria and Pamplona (with a connection to the proposed Madrid-Barcelona high-speed line at Zaragoza), and the improvement of the Madrid-Burgos road link. The results are as expected. The completion of the French TGV link creates an improvement for Bordeaux and Bayonne, but the incompatibility of track gauge limits the impact on the Spanish cities. If border effects are allowed for there is an even more marked improvement for the French cities, but some of the benefit does spill over into Spain when the border effect penalty is removed. If

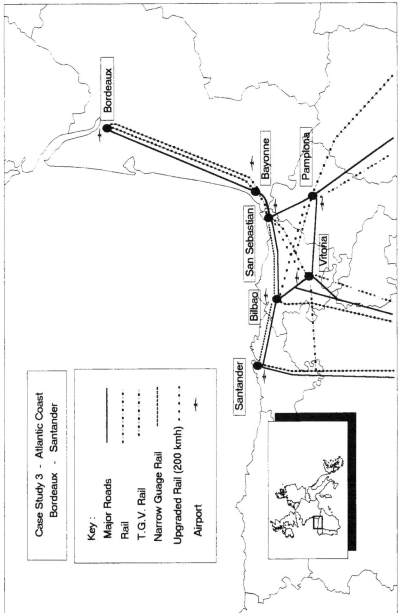

Figure 7.3.Case study region: Bordeaux-Santander.

the Spanish rail improvements are added to the French TGV, accessibility improves more widely across the study region. The French centres gain a further boost, especially in the case without border effects, the most marked effect in Spain is at Pamplona, the city with the worst accessibility in the base case. In contrast, the improvement of road accessibility to Madrid has little or no effect on accessibility. The distance and journey times make this an unattractive proposition for business travel even with improvements, since it cannot compete with air.

The main conclusion here seems to be that some improvements to external accessibility can be gained from the French high-speed rail improvements, although these will tend to benefit the already more accessible French cities more than the Spanish. For the latter to benefit would require major improvements to the intra-regional network to allow better connection and through working. The removal of border barriers is an important part of this.

The ICON indicator shows that accessibility to networks is quite good for most of the coastal region with the Bordeaux, Bayonne, and San Sebastian-Bilbao areas having levels of access to networks of less than half an hour. Most of the rest of the case study region has times of less than one hour except for some inland regions and the Landes of Aquitaine. Inland parts of Pais Vasco have rather poorer accessibility, and accessibility is extremely poor in Cantabria (worse than 1.5 hours), with the exception of the immediate area around Santander. Comparing the expected 2010 network with that of 1995 shows major improvements along the line of the principal rail corridor from Bordeaux to the Spanish frontier, which has improving effects on the current 'shadow' areas off the main corridor. Within the Spanish part of the region the major impacts are on the inland areas close to the French frontier, and again particularly the Pamplona area. The Santander area benefits relatively little from these improvements. By 2010 the ICON indicator suggests that the whole of the case study region, except for parts of Cantabria, would be within the 1h band of access to transport networks, with an almost continuous corridor within 0.5h from Bordeaux to Bilbao and inland to Vitoria.

The region is classified as peripheral by both the Keeble and Lutter *et al.* indicators. The Keeble indicator allocates the French region to the inner periphery and the Spanish ones to the outer periphery. The Lutter *et al.* indicator distinguishes more clearly between the Bordeaux region and the three predominantly urban Spanish regions, which have reasonably good accessibility for their location and are classified as inner peripheral, and the southern part of Aquitaine which is more clearly outer peripheral. This reflects the way in which accessibility clearly varies along a corridor.

Nîmes-Tarragona

This region parallels the previous one and is concerned with the Mediterranean Coast corridor from France into Iberia. This is a corridor with greater development potential than the corresponding Atlantic coast corridor. Not only is it part of a core-periphery corridor, but is also part of an important intermediate development zone, that of the western Mediterranean between Barcelona and Venice (figure 7.4). Within the corridor, industrial restructuring is underway and there are important effects along the corridor between different locations from the proposed development of high speed rail links.

As might be expected, this region displays a rather different pattern of accessibility measures from the Atlantic Coast corridor discussed above. The size and importance of Barcelona dominates the region, despite the better access by land modes to more of the French towns. Border effects are also more significant in this region, both in absolute and relative impact. The removal of borders improves accessibility values of the Spanish cities by around 250 per cent, but those of the French cities by only around 60 per cent to 80 per cent. Thus, with border effects in place, Montpellier dominates Barcelona with an accessibility value some 12 per cent greater, but following removal of border effects its accessibility value is calculated as only 85 per cent of that of Barcelona. Interestingly the accessibility values of the other Catalan cities, Tarragona and Girona, improve proportionately less than that of Barcelona with the removal of borders. Those of Beziers and Perpignan fall dramatically from over 90 per cent of the Barcelona value to 65 per cent. Potential values are consistently dominated by Barcelona and the other Catalan cities, given the greater concentration of population.

The improvement scenarios tested for this region were, first, the Madrid-Barcelona high-speed rail link, then the high-speed rail link from Barcelona to the French frontier and linking to the TGV-Méditerranée, and finally road improvements in Spain were introduced as an alternative to the rail improvements.

Once again TGV extensions improve accessibility for all towns, whether connected directly or not, but with the biggest improvements for those directly connected. In this case study, the high-speed rail link proposals were developed in both directions, rather than just toward the European core. The critical link was, however, that towards the core, which has a greater impact on accessibility for both Catalan and French cities than the Madrid-Barcelona link. This is especially true for the case without border effects in which, for example, Barcelona's accessibility rose by about 4 per cent with the Madrid high-speed link, but a further 30 per cent with the French link in place. The corresponding figures for Montpellier were 3 per cent and a further 11 per cent. In the case with border effects in place, the impact of the Madrid-Barcelona link on Barcelona's accessibility is not sufficiently strong to raise its accessibility to that of Montpellier, but the completion of the Barcelona-Montpellier link raises that of Barcelona by 18 per cent and of Montpellier by only 8 per cent, enough to raise Barcelona's accessibility to above that of Montpellier. There may here be some evidence of the less desirable impacts of a corridor effect on the French part of the region, the benefits accruing to Barcelona.

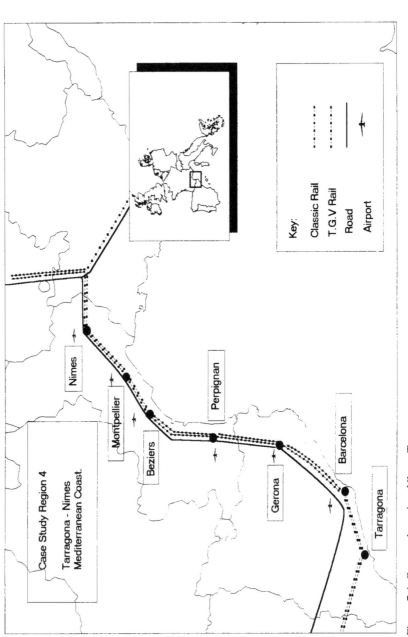

Figure 7.4. Case study region: Nîmes-Tarragona.

These examples confirm clearly that it is where links go as much as their existence which has an important effect on accessibility. The alternative road improvements had virtually no impact on accessibilities. Again the distances are too great for road to compete effectively with rail and air for the main business destinations. The impact on freight transport would be likely to be more substantial, however.

The ICON indicator reveals good accessibility to networks along the coastal belt and the main inland corridors leading to Toulouse and Zaragoza. There is a clear break at the frontier, associated with the Pyrenees. However, a substantial part of this corridor has access times of less than one hour to the main transport networks.

This entire case study region is classified as inner peripheral by the Keeble index. The Lutter *et al.* index classifies it much less consistently. Barcelona is clearly identified as belonging to the inner central group on the basis of its good communications to other core cities. The coastal regions immediately to the east and west of Barcelona, including Gerona and Tarragona, benefit from Barcelona's position and are classified as inner central, but the inland provinces of Cataluña are intermediate. In Languedoc-Roussillon, the Perpignan and Montpellier areas are also intermediate and the area around Nîmes is inner peripheral. The inland areas of the region and the coastal area around Narbonne and Beziers are classified as outer peripheral.

Both of these case studies demonstrate clearly the potentially clustering effect of high speed rail developments. The greatest benefits are likely to be enjoyed by the existing main centres and it is the links towards the core regions which have the main impacts within the regions. We have not, of course, additionally tested the relative accessibility of the centres within these regions relative to those in core regions, but other research suggests that these would indeed gain even more in terms of these basic accessibility measures from improvements in intermediate periphery corridors (see Vickerman *et al.*, 1995; Spiekermann and Wegener, 1996, for evidence).

Southern Spain

This is a purely peripheral corridor of lagging economic development and with poor infrastructure. It presents an interesting case study, however, because it has in part benefited from an early decision to impose new infrastructure in the form of the AVE high speed rail link between Madrid and Seville (figure 7.5). The region, however, lacks the right connecting infrastructure to spread the benefits into all parts of the corridor, and thus serves as a good example of the way transport can promote uneven development within a region.

As would be expected, accessibility varies much more substantially between the study cities in this case study region than in the preceding ones. Compared with Seville, which has the largest potential, accessibility measures in the base

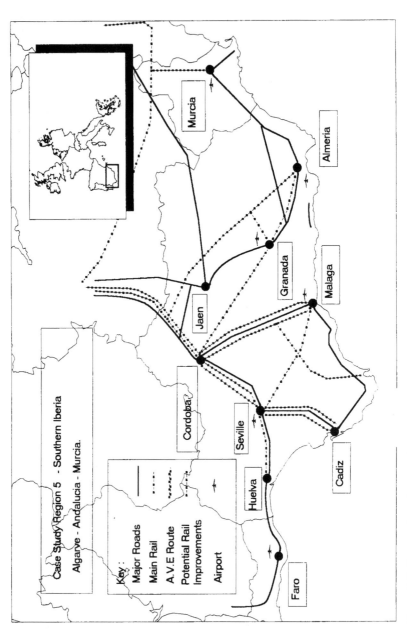

Figure 7.5. Case study region: Southern.

case vary from 112 per cent in Malaga to 18 per cent in Huelva, only 94 km distant. The suspected poor accessibility in the eastern part of Andalucia, especially in inland areas, is confirmed. Almeria has an accessibility measure 46 per cent of that of Seville, Granada only 22 per cent, although the larger population of Granada gives it a potential value 87 per cent of that of Almeria. The value for Murcia, in the extreme east of the case study region, 36 per cent of the accessibility value for Seville, would be greater if account had been taken of the possibility of using the better air facilities available at Alicante.

The improvements tested for this region were: the AVE high-speed rail link Seville-Cordoba-Madrid, opened in 1992, and the proposed onward extension to Barcelona (and thence to join the French network); the completion of improvements of road links to Madrid; improvement of regional rail links, with two possible networks centred on Seville and Cordoba based on speeds of 150 km/h. As in the previous two case studies, the concentration on business travel means that road improvements over these distances have only marginal effects on the accessibility index. Much greater benefits are gained from TGV improvements, but these are highly concentrated in this case on Seville (+18 per cent) and Cordoba (+60 per cent), the cities with stations on the high-speed rail route, and to a lesser extent at Cadiz (+14 per cent) and Malaga (+8 per cent) which can gain direct access through these two points. Huelva gains a massive 50 per cent increase in accessibility from a very low initial base.

The regional rail improvements have no real impact on Seville or Cordoba (except that improvements centred on the latter marginally reduce the accessibility of the former). Bigger impacts are felt in Malaga (+2 per cent), Cadiz (+7 per cent) and Huelva (+17 per cent). Generally the bigger impacts are gained from connections based on Seville than on Cordoba, given the shorter distances involved to connect to the high speed route. However, these improvements are relatively small given the need still to interconnect at Seville with the high-speed route. There are no impacts from any of these changes on the situation of Faro across the border in Portugal. These improvements do not suggest a reduction in the spread of accessibility measures across this region. Improvements to the regional network are important, but demonstrate that for a peripheral region, it is peripherality which dominates.

The ICON indicator confirms the impression that only the Seville region has good connections to transport networks (less than 0.5 hours). The coastal region between Cadiz and Malaga has an intermediate accessibility of 1 to 1.5 hours average access. Most of Algarve is poor (times of between 1.5 and 2 h), with similar values for the Almeria area, and substantial parts of the mountainous regions of eastern Andalucia have access times in excess of 2 hours. Adding the effect of all plans to 2010 suggests substantial improvements in the general level of accessibility in this case study region particularly in the coastal regions of Andalucia and in the corridor between Seville and Cordoba. Some improvements are also noted in the corridor leading north out of Algarve towards

Lisboa. However, substantial parts of the case study region will continue to have accessibility times to networks in excess of 1.5 h. Only the immediate Seville and Malaga areas have levels of accessibility consistent with core regions of less than 0.5 h.

These regions are classified as outer peripheral by the Keeble index. The Lutter *et al.* index identifies Algarve and the Seville province of Andalucia as inner peripheral, on the basis of the better communications provided by good air links largely associated with the tourist industry, and this helps the Malaga province even more which is classed as intermediate.

PRODUCTION POTENTIAL, ACCESSIBILITY AND TRADE FLOWS

The case studies above are all based on the use of relatively traditional accessibility measures, albeit extended in various ways, and calculated on the situation for personal business travel. This can give misleading implications on the actual economic impacts on a region of proposed alternative improvements to transport. Traditional measures of accessibility imply two rather difficult assumptions, that a given improvement in one mode of transport has the same effect on all region-pairs and that the effects are symmetrical between regions (Vickerman, 1995*b*). The main difficulties with these assumptions are that:

1.   Regions may specialize in different products which use different modes of transport or for which transport costs have a different degree of significance in total costs or value-added.

2.   The degree of scale economies achieved in any one sector may differ between regions, thus even with an improvement in accessibility a less-accessible region may be at a disadvantage because it cannot achieve the level of scale economies of another region.

In an ideal situation we would relate sectorally disaggregated inter-regional flows to a measure of inter-regional transport costs, allowing for the relative importance of transport in the value-added of that sector. Unfortunately such a degree of disaggregation does not exist in available data and if it did the incidence of zero or near-zero flows would make interpretation extremely difficult. The objective was addressed therefore by using the five case-study corridors and assembling as much information as possible from both transport and trade data for the regions within each corridor in order to examine the way in which these relate to each other.

For each NUTS-2 region within each corridor we have aimed to construct a partial, sectorally disaggregated, trade-flow matrix, by origin and destination. Our primary concern has been to identify the importance of intra-regional and transit traffic relative to genuine trade flows for each region; the importance of traffic moving along each corridor (i.e. how far the corridor presents a sensible and integrated concept for understanding transport planning and its implications); the relationship of these transport related issues to regional economic structures, and the relevance of current transport infrastructure plans to each region's needs along each corridor. Within the case study regions selected, extremely rich data were available for Spain, rather less good data for France and much poorer for the UK and Belgium.

In some respects these trade-flow matrices are somewhat disappointing – they do not yield as much insight into the structure of the relationship between transport and trade as had been hoped. What they do confirm is that a very high proportion of freight traffic, particularly road freight traffic, is intra-regional. For the Spanish regions this figure was between 63 per cent and 92 per cent. The patterns of in- and outflows (imports and exports of a region) were also largely balancing, large inflows were associated with large outflows along each corridor. Sectors which create large in- or outflows tend to be those with a large share of intra-regional traffic. Work is continuing to link these sets of data.

This leaves open the question as to whether new transport infrastructure has distorting effects on different sectors in such a way as it can change the competitiveness of a region and thus provide a bias in favour of one region over another along the corridor in question. It has, however, been possible to show how a further disaggregation of regions by space can produce uneven effects of new infrastructure within the region as shown in the following section.

INTRA-REGIONAL IMPACTS OF NEW TRANSPORT INFRASTRUCTURE

The analysis above has been largely based on indicators constructed at a regional level, typically NUTS-2 or NUTS-3. These ascribe a level of accessibility to a whole region, calculated for a node, thus resulting in a discontinuous accessibility measure at each regional boundary. These are usually smoothed to present an apparently continuous accessibility surface. One of the main issues which has emerged in terms of modal competition is the connectivity of each modal network, and the degree of connectivity between such networks. This requires a more precise, continuous view of space than that which most region based indicators can provide. To allow for these intra-regional variations, especially of connecting networks, a raster method based on 10 km squares was used in conjunction with software developed at IRPUD, Dortmund by Spiekermann and Wegener (1994, 1995) (see Vickerman et al., 1995; Spiekermann and Wegener, 1996, for detailed discussions). This spatial disaggregation has been achieved initially for the key high-speed rail network in Europe, but the method can easily be applied to further networks. Here accessibility is calculated along the proposed networks between the identifiable stations served, each raster square is then linked to the nearest such station assuming a much lower speed and imposing a time penalty for connection.

Recalculation of accessibility on this continuous accessibility basis highlights

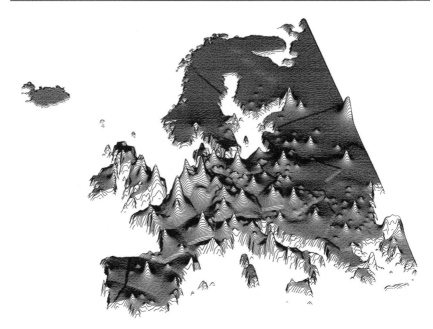

Figure 7.6. Accessibility surface by high speed rail, 1993. (*Source*: Vickerman *et al.*, 1995)

substantial intra-regional variations in accessibility, especially between nodes connected to high speed networks and those not, as well as between central and peripheral nodes (figure 7.6). Introducing improved transport in the form of the full proposed high speed rail network for 2010 shows improvements in accessibility for all connected regions, and also leads to some of the greatest relative improvements in accessibility for nodes in peripheral regions (figure 7.7). However, nodes not so connected face declining relative accessibility, as do regions effectively by-passed by the new networks (including those through which new lines pass but have no station). Figure 7.7 also illustrates that within the benefiting metropolitan regions there are key differences between core cities, suburban areas and edge of city locations, with the latter benefiting in many cases from the development of secondary station sites.

AN APPRAISAL FRAMEWORK – ACCESSIBILITY AS CHOICE

The original objective of this project identified the need to produce a measure of infrastructure which reflects the needs of both regional production and trade and which must distinguish between the requirement for infrastructure within a region and that outside. It has become increasingly clear that the aim of moving towards a single definition of indicator is essentially unrealistic. Disaggregation

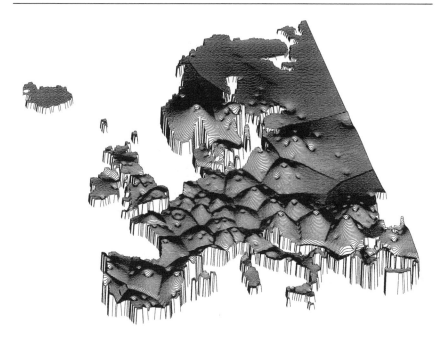

Figure 7.7. Relative change in accessibility surface by high speed rail, 1993–2010. (*Source*: Vickerman *et al.*, 1995)

by space and, to a lesser extent than expected, by sector, showed the advantages of each individual approach, but more importantly highlighted the diversity of accessibility as a concept. No one indicator adequately captures, for example, on one hand the needs of a bulk product geared predominantly to intra-regional demands and, on the other, the business or financial services sector. More important would be to understand the relationship between these indicators as part of any appraisal framework.

What has become clear is that good accessibility can be experienced by some sectors in some locations whilst close by others experience poor accessibility. Cities in peripheral locations with airports, for example, appear to experience much better accessibility than others in more central locations reliant on conventional rail or road. But this accessibility will be much more localized in the peripheral regions, will depend on those activities for which air is an acceptable mode of transport and may be structured to a certain limited number of occasions in the day. The tendency to measure accessibility as the sum of distances or times to destinations often overlooks frequency which may be a key determinant of the level of accessibility perceived. Furthermore, the cheap carriage of bulk goods by sea may not appear good in terms of an accessibility index, but may be an important contributor to the competitiveness of a maritime peripheral region.

This suggests that for evaluation purposes it is not sufficient just to measure accessibility indicators. We need to make an assessment of the welfare implications of these indicators, and the basis of any welfare assessment is that of choice (Vickerman, 1996). Choice here involves being able to evaluate not just quality of service, but implies a positive evaluation to a range of different services being available. This is similar to the concept of an option value being placed on alternatives which a consumer normally does not reveal preferred, but still values. For the purposes of evaluation we shall need to assess the relative weight to apply, for example, to adding to potential travellers' choice sets by building a high speed rail line, or adding more destinations with direct flights from a local airport, or improving the frequency of flights to the current most popular destination. The key factor here is that increasing the range of easily accessible destinations may open new markets, which reflects the usual evidence of the volume of newly generated traffic on newly created routes.

Choice, in this context, also has another dimension since choice is also likely to imply competition which will have the effect of making routes more competitive. One of the problems faced by peripheral regions is that they tend to be subject to the monopoly control of a single operator as well as a single mode for most transport. Competition, between both operators and modes, may result in lower costs to the user which can be reflected in fairly standard indicators. What is more difficult to incorporate is the change in competition which will occur as a result of an improvement, such as in infrastructure.

The construction of a bridge or tunnel or high speed railway line, for example, may be expected to lead to a reduction in the capacity offered by alternative modes such that prices adjust in a manner related to the marginal costs of providing the new infrastructure. Although this is likely to happen in the long run as a result of either more rapid depreciation of assets or bankruptcy, it does not necessarily happen in the short run. The relative fixity of costs and low marginal costs means that capacity may frequently increase on routes with new infrastructure with consequent downward pressure on prices. This may lead to a rapid short-run expansion in the markets such as the 25 per cent or more increase in newly generated traffic observed on new TGV lines and in the case of the Channel Tunnel. The effects of this short run increase may be to lead to an upward shift in the trend of traffic growth on that route, some of which may be diverted from other routes, but much of which may be genuinely new traffic. In other cases, where for example both the old and new modes are operated by a government agency, there is an immediate adjustment of capacity which does not provide the opportunity for the step change in the growth rate.

This discussion suggests that the form of any indicator used needs to be able to reflect a more complex choice structure than just the traditional destination/mode/route structure. The key point, however, seems to be the identification of missing choices in a choice set which act as a constraint on accessibility.

Conclusions

The key results from this research so far fall into four main themes:

Initial Accessibility shows Marked Variation along Corridors, especially taking into account access to Networks, Border Effects etc.

Allowing for access to networks and border effects measures of accessibility values can fall,even for locations with good accessibility, to only around one-third of their values assuming ubiquitous transport across all regions. This occurs even in generally well connected, central regions such as those of the Lille-Aachen corridor, but in the most peripheral regions it is notable that it is not just that the level of accessibility falls relative to central areas, but the variation between different locations along the corridor (especially for those locations off the main networks) rise substantially. This confirms the view that often it is intra-regional variations and access to local and regional networks which may be as critical for locations in peripheral regions as their actual peripherality. This is an important point in the consideration of transport as an instrument of cohesion in regional development.

We have concentrated here on the greater detail permitted by examination of corridors in detail. The measures of accessibility for each corridor are not strictly comparable, but the use of a set of key destination zones outside the corridor does provide a broad indicator of the relative levels of accessibility experienced in each corridor. The purpose was not the production of an indicator of levels of accessibility in different regions, but rather how accessibility would change in different regions as a result of different changes in transport provision.

Planned Improvements to Transport Networks may change these Initial Values differentially but typically reinforce Good Accessibility

The key point about most new transport infrastructure, such as that of the trans-European networks and especially that for high-speed rail, is that it aims to improve the quality of service to those markets which are most likely to be able to generate revenues which can justify the investment. Making assumptions about the locations of access points or stations reveals an increasing differentiation of points along a corridor. This may be within an overall improvement of the absolute levels of accessibility of that corridor but the biggest absolute increases are enjoyed by those locations with the highest starting values. Relative gains are shown to be greater in the more peripheral metropolitan areas when based just on time costs, but this has ignored so far the level of service likely to be enjoyed. Intermediate stops on high-speed networks may also suffer relatively poorer levels of service when frequency is taken into account, we have not completed a refinement to allow for variations in level of service, but the implications are clear from a simple extrapolation of our results so far. This will reinforce intra-regional as well as along-corridor variations in accessibility and thus the likely effects on a region's economy.

Different Sectors have Different Needs for Transport in Terms of both Mode and Destination such that New Transport Infrastructure has Differential Effects on Sectors within a Region

Whilst it is recognized that road transport dominates in the carriage of both passengers and freight, typically 75 per cent or more of freight volumes, in inter-regional freight, and in the carriage of bulk freight, rail becomes much more significant. In Spain for example 70 per cent of rail freight hauls were over distances of 150 km and over half of these were longer than 500 km. Whilst the carriage of materials accounts for about half of all road freight volumes with a very rapid rate of growth it has only around a 15 per cent share of international traffic - this reflects the way that the bulk of road freight by volume is very local in its nature and only affects the region of origin. New inter-regional infrastructure thus typically has limited impacts on the majority of a region's enterprises, or their competitiveness.

These results confirm the view that we have to take a more eclectic approach to the measurement of accessibility as an indicator of the services provided by transport infrastructure. It has to reflect sectoral needs, it has to reflect local variations in access to networks and it has to reflect the position of a region within a wider network (as measured here by position within a corridor). Accessibility is essentially a relative concept, once certain minimum absolute levels of provision are reached, but accessibility is only an indicator of transport provision, it requires further understanding of the way that accessibility is used to further the interests of a region's enterprises to achieve an understanding of the economic impact. We have not solved this issue, but we have put a lot of the building blocks of a solution into a clearer perspective and further analysis of the data assembled will clarify this further.

Evaluating Changes in Accessibility in a Region requires Further Evaluation of Changes in the Set of Transport Choices available, the Appropriate Set depending on the Activities in the Region

The set of choices available will be closely related to the competitive structure of transport provision as well as to modes and routes. This implies a more complex structuring of the choice set in order to identify links between activities and the elements of transport choice. The main problem left here is how to model the process of competitive response to new transport provision since the speed of this may have important implications for the long run changes. This is the main factor requiring much further research. Changing technology in transport and changing technology in the ways that activities use transport will have important impacts on the perceived choice sets. The concern raised by the case studies here is that new technologies will impact in different ways in different types of region. Changes adopted in central regions may have spillover effects in more peripheral regions, the concern is that the effect is to reduce choices in peripheral regions where the new technologies may be less appropriate. This interaction between regions is a continuing concern.

This chapter has concentrated on identifying the issues which are essential in moving towards a workable evaluation framework. What has been achieved is some clear evidence of the variations in the concepts and relevance of accessibility in differing regions, and a firmer basis for defining such indicators in terms of microeconomic concepts of choice. There remains much to be done in refining operational measures, but, until that is achieved, great care will have to be exercised in the formulation of policy which has generally assumed that new infrastructure will improve accessibility, and that improvements in accessibility will generate increases in welfare.

APPENDIX: ACCESSIBILITY MODEL SPECIFICATIONS

Economic Potential

Economic potential is based on the summation, for each region, of the values of all regions' incomes, adjusted by a measure of intervening distance

$$P_i = \Sigma_j \frac{y_j}{d_{ij}^2}$$

where y_j is the income of region j and d_{ij} is the measure of the intervening distance from i to j.

Potential ascribes income levels to regional centroids and uses a distance based deterrence function which assumes a degree of continuity in transport costs. This produces a deceptively uniform reduction in potential as we move away from the centre. Potential measures capture fairly well the achieved levels of GDP per capita in peripheral regions, but they do not capture the variety of regional experiences in the intervening space.

Aggregate Mode Specific Accessibility

Following the theoretical justification provided by Rietveld (1989), Simmonds (1992) developed the potential model to allow for an aggregation of different modes. This method has been used in CERTE and TecnEcon (1994). The model can be developed for business travel using an appropriate set of destinations for each origin, or for freight using appropriate markets and/or goods characteristics.

The index uses a modal share model for each link to define a composite time for that link, which is combined with a measure of the importance of that destination to give an aggregate measure of accessibility for each origin. Modal share depends on the mode's speed and a measure of average access and wait times for the mode.

The model is calibrated on the basis of a negative exponential model, the usual approach to passenger mode and destination choice models using time as the deterrence effect.

$$P_{ijm} = \frac{\exp(-\lambda_{ij})}{\sum_m \exp(-\lambda_{ij} t_{ijm})} \tag{1}$$

where λ_{ij} is allowed to vary with distance to ensure that modal time advantages relate to distance as given by:

$$\lambda_{ij} = \Lambda \left(\frac{\Delta^\rho}{d_{ij}}\right) \tag{2}$$

A modal share weighted average of the times by available modes gives the "composite time" for that link.

$$t_{ij} = \frac{-1}{\lambda_{ij}} \ln \sum_m \exp(-\lambda_{ij} t_{ijm}) \tag{3}$$

This composite time is used as the measure of deterrence fed into a formula similar to that of equation 1 to give an accessibility measure. The importance of destinations (W_j) is assessed on the basis of population, plus an index of business significance (based on international banks) and a further weight for national capitals. In addition a border effect variable (b_{ij}) was inserted which scales the deterrence effect if origin and destination are in different member states.

$$A_i = \sum_j b_{ij}. W_j. \exp(-\mu t_{ij}) \tag{4}$$

In this the deterrence measure, t_{ij}, is made sensitive to travel time differences through the parameter μ. The accessibility measure can then be multiplied by a measure of the origin's importance, E_i, reflecting employment in the relevant sectors to give a measure of total potential.

$$P_i = A_i E_i \tag{5}$$

This index essentially provides a second dimension to that of the standard Keeble analysis, especially for passenger transport. It does have certain problems, however. First, it has to be calibrated for each link since mode availability is not the same everywhere, and the range of destinations varies. Secondly, most modal choice models recognize characteristics other than speed as relevant choice variables. In an ideal situation such factors as comfort, price, etc. would be included since these may bear different relationships to speed in different situations. Third the choice of destinations is essentially arbitrary.

A Preferred Mode Index

The index developed by Lutter *et al.* (1992) uses a more subjective approach to define the best available mode for each link rather than estimating implicit link deterrence effects. This enables the construction of a more consistent index over the entire Community, although one which is based on a less complete analysis. In total 194 primary centres across Europe are used, but separate indices are calculated for access (termed the situation index) to this complete set, to the nearest three centres to any region (a measure of the wider regional situation), to the nearest of thirty-four major centres (a measure of proximity to major agglomerations) and also for accessibility to certain key sites such as nearest high-speed rail station or airport. These indices do not reflect differences in the importance of the various destinations, but accessibility to population is considered in a separate index which measures the population resident within certain time bands (3 hours being taken as the critical cut-off). Population is, as in the Aggregate Mode Specific index, based on the regional population which is then ascribed to zonal centroids (the main urban area) thus there are some problems with larger regions. This index also encompasses the importance of accessibility to, and accessibility along a network, but this time to defined destinations. Again accessibility is measured in terms of time, allowing for variations in quality along the network and including such elements as airport check-in and transfer times where appropriate. Variations in quality of service are allowed for between countries, e.g. car traffic speeds vary for motorways and some other roads.

An important innovation is the allowance for joint use of modes, instead of allocating all traffic to a main mode. Efficient transport from more peripheral regions often requires the use of more than one mode in combination. Developments using, for example classic and high-speed rail or high-speed rail and air are, as we have already seen, likely to play an increasingly important role. It is important that indicators reflect this. This is difficult to model, especially where it is intended to forecast changes in accessibility resulting from say new infrastructures, but without knowing how individuals will respond to such changes.

The ICON Index

The ICON index takes the connection time to each network in a NUTS Level III region and weights this by the relative importance of that network and a measure of the level of service. Ideally the weights should reflect the likely usage of each network by the activities of a region, e.g. for a region where the export of bulk raw materials is important, access to a port is more critical, for a region with a large financial services sector, access to airports and high-speed rail is more important.

The index used has the form:

$$\text{ICON}(I) = (1 + P_s)[T_m + T_u + (P_g \times T_g)]$$

where

T_m is the sum of times of connection to each network
T_u is a penalty for the absence of a particular network, in terms of extra time
T_g is a penalty for any discontinuities or gaps in the network
P_s and P_g are weights which reflect the importance of the mode and penalties for having to substitute an alternative.

Penalties are introduced for network discontinuities such as the need to use ferries (e.g. 5 h for UK; 10 h for Ireland) or because of rail track gauge differences (3 h for Portugal and Spain).

The index is used to define five levels of connectivity in terms of hours, viz: <0.5 h, 0.5–1.0 h, 1.0–1.5 h, 1.5–2.0 h, >2.0 h. Obviously these are somewhat arbitrary times, but it is interesting to note the relatively small number of regions which are more than 2 hours from a network.

Perhaps the major problem with ICON is its definition of accessibility independently of the transport needs of specific regions. Although modes are weighted, these weights are independent of a region's transport needs and reflect average usage of modes rather than potential usage. This is the opposite case to the Aggregate Mode Specific index which calibrates modal weights for each application. This causes problems for the ICON index where certain modes are not available in a region at all, access to a seaport may be irrelevant to the needs of a region, given its current production structure and trade flows.

REFERENCES

Aschauer, D.A. (1989) Is public expenditure productive? *Journal of Monetary Economics*, **23,** pp, 177-200.
Aschauer, D.A. (1990) Why is infrastructure important? in Munnell, A.H. (ed.) *Is there a Shortfall in Public Capital Investment?* Conference Series No 34. Boston: Federal Reserve Bank of Boston.
Biehl, D. (ed.) (1986) *The Contribution of Infrastructure to Regional Development.* Luxembourg:Office for Official Publications of the European Community.
Biehl, D. (1991) The role of infrastructure in regional development. in Vickerman, R.W. (ed.) *Infrastructure and Regional Development.* European Research in Regional Science 1. London: Pion.
CEDRE (1993) *Etude Prospective des Régions Atlantiques.* Report to European Commission. Strasbourg: Centre Européen du Développement Régional.
CERTE & TecnEcon (1994) *Future Evolution of the Transport Sector: Implications for Regional and Future Transport Planning.* Final Report to European Commission DG

XVI, Centre for European, Regional and Transport Economics, University of Kent/TecnEcon Ltd.

Clark, C., Wilson, F. and Bradley, J. (1969) Industrial location and economic potential in western Europe. *Regional Studies*, **3**, pp. 197–212.

European Commission (1993) *Growth, Competitiveness and Employment.* Luxembourg: Office for Official Publications of the EC.

Gramlich, E. (1994) Infrastructure investment: a review essay. *Journal of Economic Literature*, **32**, pp. 1176–1196.

Keeble, D., Owens, P.L. and Thompson, C. (1982) Regional accessibility and economic potential in the European Community. *Regional Studies*, **16**, pp. 419–432.

Keeble, D., Offord, J. and Walker, S. (1988) *Peripheral Regions in a Community of Twelve Member States.* Luxembourg: Office for Official Publications of the EC.

Lutter, H., Pütz, T., Spangenberg, M. (1992) *Accessibility and Peripherality of Community Regions: the Role of Road, Long-distance Railways and Airport Networks.* Report to DGXVI, Commission of the European Communities. Bonn: Bundesforschungsanstalt für Landeskunde und Raumordnung.

Munnell, A.H. (1990) How does public infrastructure affect regional economic performance? in Munnell, A.H. (ed.) *Is there a Shortfall in Public Capital Investment?* Conference Series No 34. Boston: Federal Reserve Bank of Boston.

Munnell, A.H. (1992) Infrastructure investment and economic growth. *Journal of Economic Perspectives,* **6**, pp. 189–198.

Newman, P. and Vickerman, R.W. (1993) Infrastructure Indicators and Regional Development: A Critique of Accessibility and Potential Measures. Paper to Regional Science Association, British & Irish Section, Annual Conference, Nottingham.

Newman, P. and Vickerman, R.W. (1994) Regional Impacts of Trans-European Networks, Transport Provision and Regional Development in Europe. Working Paper 1, CERTE. University of Kent, Canterbury.

Rietveld, P. (1989) Employment effects of changes in transportation infrastructure: methodological aspects of the gravity model. *Papers of Regional Science Association*, **66**, pp.19–30.

Simmonds, D.J. (1992) *Regional Impact of the Channel Tunnel and Associated Links.* Cambridge: David Simmonds Consultancy.

Spiekermann, K. and Wegener, M. (1994) The shrinking continent: new time-space maps of Europe. *Environment and Planning B: Planning and Design*, **21**, pp. 653–673.

Spiekermann, K. and Wegener, M. (1995) Microsimulation and GIS: prospects and first experience, in Klostermann, R.(ed.) *From Geographical Information Systems to Planning Support Systems.* Piscataway NJ: Centre for Urban Policy Research, Rutgers University.

Spiekermann, K and Wegener, M. (1996) Trans-European Networks and unequal accessibility in Europe. *EUREG. European Journal of Regional Development*, No. 4, pp. 35–42.

Vickerman, R.W. (1994*a*) Transport infrastructure and region building in the European Community. *Journal of Common Market Studies*, **32**, pp. 1–24.

Vickerman, R.W. (1994b) Regional science and new transport infrastructure, in Cuadrado Rouro, J., Nijkamp, P. and Salva, P. (eds.) *Moving Frontiers: Economic Restructuring, Regional Development and Emerging Networks.* Aldershot: Avebury.

Vickerman, R.W. (1995*a*) Regional impacts of trans-European networks. *Annals of Regional Science*, **29**, pp. 237–254.

Vickerman, R.W. (1995*b*) Location, accessibility and regional development: An appraisal of trans-European networks. *Transport Policy*, **2**, pp. 225–234.

Vickerman, R.W. (1996) Accessibility, peripherality and spatial development: the question of choice, in Reggiani, A. (ed.) *Accessibility, Trade and Location Behaviour.* Berlin: Springer.

Vickerman, R.W., Spiekermann, K. and Wegener, M. (1995) Accessibility and Economic Development in Europe. Paper presented to ESF European Research Conference on European Transport and Communications Networks, Espinho, Portugal.

Chapter 8

The Environment, Efficient Pricing and Investment in Transport: A Model and Some Results for the UK

John Peirson and Roger Vickerman

The environment has emerged, in the last decade, as a central issue in the UK transport policy debate (Royal Commission on Environmental Pollution, 1994; House of Commons Transport Committee, 1994). Important issues in this debate are the environmental impacts of transport, road building, road pricing, reducing demand for transport and the diversion of demand to more environmentally sensitive modes of transport. Deregulation and privatization of public transport have taken place at the same time as a greater public debate and concern over environment and transport. Even though the private sector will have a greater role in financing transport initiatives in the future, the public sector is likely to maintain an important role in funding public sector transport systems and investing in transport infrastructure in general. This chapter addresses these questions through the development of a model which estimates the full social cost of transport for each mode and uses the resulting efficient prices to predict shifts in demand in the short and long run. The full social costs are measured by estimating the marginal external costs of each transport mode and imposing these costs as taxes on the private costs of each mode. Where the demand for a mode increases, the model estimates the implied need for new investment in infrastructure. There are thus short-run and long-run solutions with associated tax revenues as well as implied investment needs and operational deficits.

The development of the model has revealed areas in which there are important deficiencies in information and theory. This chapter highlights these areas and makes recommendations. Informed policy debate would be improved by more research on: assessing and valuing the marginal external effects of transport, in particular on the effects of local and global air pollution, congestion and accidents; the degree of economies of scale in the provision of transport and, more generally, on the resource costs of all forms of transport; and the own and cross price effects on the demand for different transport modes.

The rest of the chapter is in four parts. First, an aggregate demand model is developed for application to the London and inter-urban passenger travel markets respectively. Secondly, empirical evidence on the external and internal resource costs of transport and demand elasticities are brought together for use in the demand models. Thirdly, the model is used to predict the consequences of efficient pricing on demand and investment needs in transport. The levels of demand, costs, revenues and implied investment in each mode are predicted. Finally, the key issues highlighted by the research are discussed and various recommendations and suggestions are made.

THE MODELS OF UK PASSENGER TRAVEL

The models developed in this study are only applied to the market for passenger travel in the UK. Two separate models are reported here for London and for inter-urban travel. The models consider the available modes and specify the effects of infrastructure, operating and external costs and demand elasticities. In particular, the consequences of applying efficient economic prices and investment are investigated.

The use of two independent passenger only models could be criticized. It is recognized that freight and passenger transport interact through their effects on congestion. We assume in effect that the volume of freight traffic is given independently of levels of passenger traffic and congestion. This is reasonable in the short-run since the volume of passenger vehicles is much greater than that of freight vehicles and freight traffic is less likely to be price sensitive. The interaction effects in the long-run are recognized to need further research. It is also recognized that many passenger journeys have both an urban and an inter-urban component. These two types of journeys were separated out to highlight the different issues in the two contexts. This does pose problems, but is essential to demonstrate the different capacity and externality effects in the two sets of markets. The link between the two is critical and clearly should be a topic for further research. These assumptions probably lead to an underestimation of external costs and the responses to the policies analysed.

The models specify the different modes available, but consider aggregate demand and supply. Network models that consider the flows and internal and external costs of different links could have been investigated. However, the available information on internal and external costs and demand is limited. Typically, this information is at best collected for specific representative parts of the transport network. The specification of internal and external costs and demand responses for each part of the network would represent a spurious disaggregation given the limited sources for these data. An important advantage of working at the aggregate level is it shows readily the consequences of pricing, management and investment and abstracts away from the problems of detailed management of networks. As more information becomes available, the use of network models will become more appropriate and informative. We assume that the London model can be treated as network neutral and are attempting to refine the inter-urban model to allow for variable congestion.

The model can be considered in three parts which are represented in figure 8.1. First, the available empirical evidence on the internal and external costs of each transport mode was assembled. These costs provided the basis for estimating efficient prices of transport. Secondly, simple demand models were calibrated using elasticities estimated in past studies. These were used with the efficient prices to estimate demand in the short and long run. The interaction of costs, investment and demand are allowed for in the model. Thirdly, for each mode, the implications of the prices and levels of demand were investigated for investment, taxes, costs and revenue.

Calibration was used rather than direct econometric estimation since this enabled an easy test of sensitivity to changing values. Since one of the

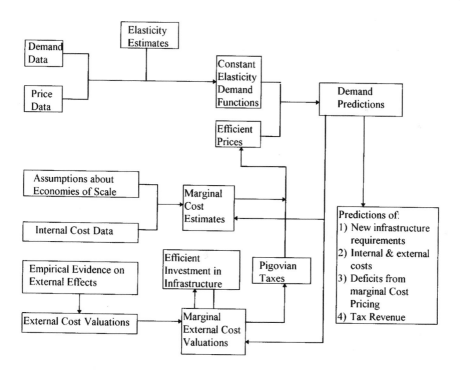

Figure 8.1. Structure of the model.

implications of changing the basis of pricing for the use of transport is to change behaviour, and hence elasticities, the use of directly estimated coefficients was not believed to be more appropriate in this case. Our primary interest is in the impact of changing prices rather than on the elasticities as such.

The efficient price of a transport mode is determined by adding the internal and external costs (with one important exception that will be explained). The appropriate measure of cost is the marginal cost for both internal and external effects. The degree of economies of scale is crucial to the results of the model for three reasons. First, marginal costs are estimated from average costs by making an assumption about the degree of scale economies. Secondly, where economies of scale exist, long run marginal cost pricing results in operating deficits. Thirdly, the theoretical literature on congestion shows that with constant costs and optimal investment, the inclusion of marginal congestion costs in prices produces revenues which cover the transport infrastructure costs. All three issues are investigated in the results section. As there is no consensus on the degree of economies of scale in transport, three different sets of assumptions about these economies were made and investigated.

An important objective of the study was to obtain accurate estimates of the external effects of transport. New estimates of the critical congestion and accident external effects were estimated (see Peirson, Skinner and Vickerman, 1994, 1996). Estimates for the external effects of local and global air pollution and noise were taken from the existing literature. Some new work was carried out on estimates of congestion and accident costs. The next section shows that there are areas of concern about the completeness and accuracy of the available estimates of external effects of transport.

The London passenger travel market includes car, bus, underground and rail. The model considers peak and off-peak demand separately. The inter-urban transport market was defined as travel in cars and coaches on motorways (the latter mainly operated by National Express) and travel on Intercity rail. Air travel was excluded as it only represents a small proportion of total inter-urban demand. The inter-urban model focuses on travel along the routes between the major conurbations in the UK rather than including all non-urban travel. Considering all non-urban passenger travel was not considered to be an appropriate level of aggregation.

The demand model uses passenger kilometres as the dependent variable and the constant elasticity demand takes the form

$$D_i = \alpha_i \prod_{j=1}^{n} [P_i] \beta_{ij} Y \gamma_i$$

where

D_i – demand for the ith transport mode in passenger kilometres
P_i – price of ith transport mode per passenger kilometre
Y – income

β_{ij} –price elasticity of ith demand with respect to jth price
γ_i –income elasticity of ith demand

(In the London model, the peak and off-peak own prices appear in each demand function.)

In the long run model, the income effects were estimated on the assumption that income growth was 2.5 per cent per annum for the next ten years. In the short run, income was assumed constant. The income and price elasticities were taken from a review of the literature. The equation was calibrated using information on present demands and prices – this allowed α_i to be calculated and then the parameters of the demand equation were fully specified.

The efficient price of each mode is given by adding the sum of the marginal external costs to the marginal internal costs. In the short run, the infrastructure is fixed (apart from one exception outlined below) and, thus, there are no associated marginal costs. The different marginal external costs are summed to give the Pigovian tax that should be imposed on transport users in order that they face the true marginal costs of use. The price of a transport mode calculated from the marginal internal and external costs at the present level of demand is not the efficient price. This price, and similar prices for other modes, will change the demand for all transport modes. These changes will in turn affect the marginal internal and external costs. The model solves for this problem with regard to congestion costs, both as an external cost and an internal cost in terms of the time taken to complete journeys. This an important factor for consistency, as shown by the feedback loops in figure 8.1, although in practice the adjustments for these effects were only of moderate importance. We consider that the variation in other external effects may be important. For example, as traffic volumes increase with fixed road capacity vehicle speeds fall and the accident rate per passenger kilometre decreases. The absolute number and severity of accidents may fall with lower traffic speeds (Peirson, Skinner and Vickerman, 1996). Another example is that air pollution emissions vary with the speed of traffic (Fergusson *et al.*, 1989).

Long run efficient pricing is complicated by the possibility of investment in new infrastructure and capacity. In the model, investment takes place to give an optimal balance between capacity and congestion for the road modes of transport. This balance is given when the marginal external costs of congestion are equal to the annualized cost of capacity. The model takes investment in roads as a sunk cost. If the cost of restoring roads to another use is less than the value of this other use, then road users should be faced with an efficient price that includes the maximum difference of the value of an alternative use and the restoration cost. It is assumed that this difference is never positive and the opportunity cost of land should not appear in the efficient price. (There is no major example of a modern road being explicitly returned to another use. However, there have been a number of cases of old railway lines being used for other purposes.)

The general issue of what is the efficient economic price of a transport mode has not always been clearly understood. For example, the Royal Commission on Environmental Pollution (1994) report suggests that congestion costs should not be considered as externalities. This appears to be based on an assumption that it is the environmental effects which are the current policy issue and that incorporating congestion effects simply swamps the estimates. The rather spurious argument is also raised that incorporating congestion effects overvalues new road construction. It would appear, however, that there is a need for a continuing debate on what constitute internal and external costs of transport.

There is also a continuing debate on the most appropriate way of evaluating environmental costs. We have followed the approach adopted by CSERGE (Maddison *et al.*, 1996) of estimating economic impacts discounted at an appropriate discount rate. Others have argued that this undervalues the environmental effects by undervaluing the future and not allowing sufficiently for future risk. Mauch and Rothengatter *et al.*(1995), for example, value a number of externalities in terms of the costs of reducing the environmental effects. This tends to produce higher estimates, but appears to involve an element of circular reasoning in which arbitrary emission level targets are set and then the environmental costs of the emissions valued in terms of the costs of reaching these targets. Since externally set targets are typically more stringent than those implied by any notion of optimal levels of environmental impacts, this tends to lead to an automatic increase in the estimated costs. There is a clear need for a continuation of this debate to which this model is a contribution (for further details of the model, see Peirson and Vickerman, 1996).

In the model, capacity adjusts to meet new demand in the long run. The consequent change in frequency of service for public transport, i.e. bus, coach, railway and underground, alters the demand for such modes. The model allows for this effect. There is an implicit assumption that the present relationship between supply and demand, i.e. occupancy rates, is optimal. The information does not exist to compute the optimal balance between supply and demand in a manner similar to that estimated for roads.

In the long run, as income increases, the valuation of external effects is likely to increase, the so-called Kuznets effect. For example, the value of time and accident injuries are likely to increase at approximately the same rate as income. This is allowed for in the model by including income elasticities for the value of external effects of transport.

The final output of the model is the public finance implications of policies of efficient pricing and investment. The new infrastructure capacity requirements of modes experiencing increases in demand are estimated. The magnitude of external and internal costs are estimated. The deficits resulting from economies of scale and marginal cost pricing are estimated. Finally, the tax revenues from efficient pricing are calculated. These predictions are important. A major objective of the study was to investigate whether the reallocation of demand from efficient pricing may be ineffective because of capacity constraints on those modes experiencing higher demands. For these restraints to be removed would potentially require large investments. The model provides estimates of these requirements and whether they could be funded from the tax revenues accruing from the entire transport system (see Peirson and Vickerman, 1993, for a fuller discussion of this point).

INFORMATION INPUTS TO THE MODEL

External and Internal Cost Estimates

The estimation of efficient prices has required a full investigation of the internal costs of the different modes and valuation of their external effects. Some of the external costs have been estimated for the United Kingdom in the past, e.g. Newbery (1987 and 1990), Pearce (1993) and Maddison *et al.* (1996). This study brought previous estimates together on a consistent and appropriate basis and constructed new estimates where necessary. For further details of the basis for all the cost estimations, see Peirson, Skinner and Vickerman (1994, 1995).

There are five externalities for which marginal external costs were estimated: local air pollution; global warming; noise pollution; congestion and accidents. The estimated values of the externalities are given in table 8.1. The figures suggest that, on average, current prices of inter-urban travel in the UK are reasonably close to the efficient prices. Cars have high external costs compared to those of rail. However, the high average internal costs of rail have to be compared with these external costs. The average congestion costs of cars include a wide range of different conditions, between the most heavily used motorways and those where use is much less. On the most crowded motorways, we estimated congestion costs for cars and coaches in the region of 2-3 and 0.5 pence per passenger km. In the case of London, congestion, local air pollution and accidents are the major external effects and these mostly affect road transport. Again the large average long run costs of rail and underground suggest that efficient pricing will only favour these modes if there are large economies of scale.

Table 8.1 presents the marginal external costs for each mode with the long run marginal costs, which are estimated for the two extreme assumptions of constant returns to scale and maximum economies of scale. The efficient prices that these costs imply are compared with the current prices.

The values of the externalities given in table 8.1 represent revised estimates from Peirson, Skinner and Vickerman (1995), following the work of Maddison *et al.* (1996). This has suggested that the health effects of local air pollution caused by emissions from road vehicles are much higher than previously estimated. The estimates for global warming are small relative to the other marginal external costs and appear to contradict the attention given to transport's effect on global warming, (e.g. in Royal Commission on Environmental Pollution, 1994).

Table 8.1. Marginal internal and external costs and prices of passenger transport (pence/passenger kilometre[1]).

Pence/ passenger kilometre	Global Wrm'g	Air Poll'n	Noise Poll'n	Congestion	Accdts	Total MEC	LRMC[2]	Eff't Price[2,3]	Eff't Price with EOS[3,4]	Current Price
Inter-urban										
Rail	0.01	0.12	0.02	0.04	0.03	0.22	9.67	9.89	5.05	7.11
Car	0.02	0.35	0.08	0.85	0.15	1.45	5.15	6.60	6.08	7.78
Coach	0.01	0.39	0.01	0.15	0.01	0.57	3.00	3.57	2.67	3.09
London										
Underg'd										
- Peak	0.01	0.13	0.09	0.72	0.03	0.98	45.18	46.16	10.02	10.12
- Off-Peak	0.01	0.13	0.09	0.00	0.03	0.26	15.80	16.06	8.16	8.94
Rail										
- Peak	0.01	0.13	0.09	0.80	0.03	1.06	20.11	21.17	11.12	6.88
- Off-Peak	0.01	0.13	0.09	0.07	0.03	0.32	12.55	12.87	6.59	6.88
Car										
- Peak	0.03	4.34	0.39	15.06	1.50	21.32	7.12	28.44	27.73	11.28
- Off-Peak	0.02	2.89	0.39	1.65	1.50	6.45	6.54	12.99	12.34	10.04
Bus										
- Peak	0.01	7.21	0.09	3.73	0.88	11.92	15.27	27.19	22.61	10.63
- Off-Peak	0.01	5.41	0.09	1.76	0.88	8.15	13.00	21.15	17.25	10.63

Notes
1. GB£0.01 = US$0.015 = ECU0.012
2. Assuming constant returns to scale
3. Efficient price is defined as LRMC + MEC
4. Assuming maximum returns to scale (see text for definition).

These costs are compatible with most estimates of the economic costs of global warming (e.g. Fankhauser, 1995). The estimates of the noise externalities of transport are similar to past estimates.

The largest external costs in table 8.1 are for congestion. London Transport 1993 data and regressions specifically for London were used to estimate congestion costs. These figures are close to those obtained by Newbery (1988 and 1990) using more aggregate data and regressions. Congestion costs were estimated from rail and underground data (see Peirson, Skinner and Vickerman, 1994, for full information on sources and methods).

The marginal external costs of road accidents were estimated in a model that considered the adjustment of drivers to more congested traffic conditions, see Peirson, Skinner and Vickerman (1996) for full detail. This procedure gave different estimates than the analyses of Newbery (1987, 1988), Jansson (1994), and Pearce (1993). Injuries and fatalities were valued using Department of Transport (1993) estimates.

Other external costs, such as the effects of transport on soil and water pollution, land and resource take and urban communities, are not readily quantifiable (see OECD, 1988; Commission of the European Communities, 1992; Whitelegg, 1993). Thus, the results of the studies have to be qualified by recognition of the omission of these presently unquantified external effects.

For the air pollution, global warming and noise external costs, it was assumed that marginal external costs were equal to average external costs. This is an important assumption, but the available information does not explicitly consider the variation in marginal external costs with the intensity of use of a mode. Additionally, it is assumed that no new technology is available that can reduce the marginal external costs.

The information for the estimation of capital and operating costs was obtained from a variety of published and unpublished sources (see Peirson, Skinner and Vickerman, 1995 for full information). Information on the degree of economies of scale was taken from surveying the limited information available for the British Isles. There is a debate on the extent of economies of scale in transport (see, for example, Button, 1993). This is reflected in the choice of three possible scenarios: one of constant costs and two of decreasing costs. These economies of scale are measured by comparing long run marginal costs with long run average costs. The maximum economies of scale that were assumed are: 0.5 for rail; 0.2 and 0.5 for capital and operating costs for Underground; 0.7 for buses and coaches; and 0.9 for cars. As far as possible, estimates of internal costs are based on incremental costs associated with greater use of that mode. Where possible such information underlies the assumptions about economies of scale considered above.

The elasticities used in the models were taken from a review of the literature. The sources most relied on were British Railways Board (1989), Fairhurst and Mack (1981), Fowkes (1992), Gilbert and Jalilian (1989), Glaister and Lewis

(1978), Goodwin (1992), Halcrow Fox and Associates (1993), Lewis (1977 and 1978), London Transport (1984, 1987 and 1993).

RESULTS

The study was used to consider many different assumptions. Tables 8.2 and 8.3 report the results for the case of large economies of scale. For the London model, there is shift in the short run to the more environmentally friendly modes

Table 8.2. Results for London passenger transport market using long run marginal cost pricing with large returns to scale.

(i) Demand changes (% changes from current demand)	Short Run Peak	Short Run Off-Peak	Long Run Peak	Long Run Off-Peak
Underground	6.0	10.9	17.5	24.8
Rail	-7.6	11.9	10.7	57.4
Car	-4.0	-4.6	19.7	31.1
Bus	-10.9	-14.9	-14.8	-15.3

(ii) Financial implications (£bn)

	New Infrastructure Capital Requirements (i)	Total Annual Price Revenue (excluding tax) (ii)	Annual Tax Revenue (iii)	Total Annual Internal Costs (iv)	Annual Surplus/ Deficit (ii)-(iv) (v)
Short Run Peak					
Underground	n.a	0.40	0.11	1.48	-1.08
Rail	n.a	0.51	0.23	1.02	-0.51
Car	n.a	1.30	3.80	3.17	-1.87
Bus	n.a	0.11	0.13	0.22	-0.10
Long Run Peak					
Underground	2.33	0.44	0.05	1.64	-1.20
Rail	1.07	0.61	0.08	1.23	-0.62
Car	4.58	1.62	4.56	3.97	-2.35
Bus	n.a	0.11	0.14	0.26	-0.15
Short Run Off-Peak					
Underground	n.a	0.25	0.01	0.92	-0.67
Rail	n.a	0.14	0.01	0.27	-0.14
Car	n.a	1.78	1.72	2.30	-0.51
Bus	n.a	0.24	0.20	0.36	-0.12
Long Run Off-Peak					
Underground	n.a	0.28	0.01	1.04	-0.76
Rail	n.a	0.19	0.01	0.38	-0.19
Car	n.a	2.45	2.80	3.31	-0.86
Bus	n.a	0.24	0.25	0.49	-0.25

of underground and rail. In the long run, the growth in demand for these modes is repeated, but the demand for car transport continues to grow. This pattern of growth is dominated by the high income elasticity of demand for urban car travel in both peak and off-peak periods. Large Pigovian taxes, particularly in peak periods, are not sufficient to force long run demand for car travel down.

In table 8.2, the column headed total price revenue refers to, for the case of road users, the purchase of private resources by road users, whilst internal costs includes these and the annualized cost of infrastructure. In the short run, rail and Underground make large losses in both the peak and off-peak periods. These losses can be funded by the tax revenues. This possibility is brought about by the large tax revenues accruing from road transport, which in turn are the result of the taxation of congestion, local air pollution and accident costs. In the optimal arrangement envisaged in this model, investment in capacity takes place up to the point at which marginal congestion cost equals the annualized long run marginal cost of capacity.

A similar picture emerges in the long run, with sizeable deficits which could be financed out of tax revenue. In the long run, there is a need for substantial

Table 8.3. Results for inter-urban passenger transport market using long run marginal cost pricing with large returns to scale.

(i) Demand changes (% changes from current demand)

	Short Run	Long Run
Rail	9.2	48.3
Car	2.9	42.4
Coach	-2.1	2.6

(ii) Financial implications (£bn)

	New Infrastructure Capital Requirements (i)	Annual Price Revenue (excluding tax) (ii)	Annual Tax Revenue (iii)	Total Annual Internal Costs (iv)	Annual Surplus/ Deficit (ii)-(iv) (v)
Short Run					
Rail	n.a	0.64	0.05	1.29	-0.65
Car	n.a	3.90	1.23	5.44	-1.54
Coach	n.a	0.57	0.15	0.87	-0.30
Long Run					
Rail	2.62	0.87	0.07	1.73	-0.86
Car	5.88	5.40	1.70	7.81	-2.41
Coach	0.01	0.60	0.16	0.90	-0.30

investment in transport infrastructure to meet increased demand for rail, Underground and car travel. The internal costs include the annualized cost of this new infrastructure. Thus, the tax revenues would more than cover the investment in new infrastructure. It should be noted that the value of external effects does not decline in the long run.

For the inter-urban model, in table 8.3, there are no substantial shifts in demand in the short run, in spite of the assumed large economies of scale in rail. In the long run, the elasticities of demand for rail and car travel result in large increases in demand. It is not possible to fund the deficits incurred in the efficient supply of transport. Even within the road sector taken by itself, this cannot be achieved.

CONCLUSION

This study set out to investigate the effects of efficient economic pricing of transport on inter-urban and London passenger travel. For the first time for the UK, marginal external and internal costs were estimated and put on a comparable basis. These figures were used to estimate efficient prices. These prices were used to predict the effects on demand, operators surpluses/deficits and tax revenues of efficient pricing and investment policies in the transport sector.

The major conclusion to be drawn from the study is that the external effects of transport may be important, especially for road transport in the urban sector, but efficient pricing does not result in substantial shifts away from the use of road transport. This result for cars is similar to that of De Borger *et al.* (1996) for a model of urban transport in Belgium that found a decrease in car demand in the region of 15 per cent, though bus/tram use increased by around 100 per cent. Their model only considered the short run and did not consider capacity constraints in the use of public transport, scale economies, costs of infrastructure provision, funding of transport, service elasticities and the availability of four modes of transport. In the long run, the results of the present models are mainly driven by income and demand for car travel continues to grow.

The London model shows that car and bus travel is currently substantially underpriced, particularly during peak periods. The under pricing of other modes depends on the views taken about the extent of economies of scale. Compared to full average costs, rail and Underground are underpriced. Moving to efficient prices, including long run marginal internal costs, would, in the presence of significant economies of scale, result in large deficits for the operators of rail, Underground and bus companies. However, the taxation of the large external effects of road transport would raise sufficient revenues to cover these deficits. This empirical result is over and above the standard transport economics result that an optimal congestion tax will exactly cover the costs of the optimal supply of road capacity, when constant returns to scale exist. The taxation of the external effects of road transport does not substantially reduce demand and in the long run the cost of these effects increases.

In the case of inter-urban travel, the external costs are not so important and there is at present an over supply of motorway capacity in aggregate. The revenue from taxing the external effects of road transport is not sufficient to cover the deficits of the coach and rail operators and the cost of investing in the road infrastructure.

The results concerning the small shift in demand away from road transport and the increasing level of road externalities are robust to varying assumptions. These results could be interpreted in four ways:

1. The costs of the external effects may have been under-estimated. It is notable that, in the last few years, the estimates of the external costs of road transport have risen sharply, e.g. see Mauch and Rothengatter (1995) and Maddison *et al.* (1996). We are concerned that the estimation of congestion costs is based on a weak theory and poor statistical estimation. This is especially true of inter-urban motorways where there are clearly growing localized problems of congestion within a network of more than adequate aggregate capacity. The estimates of local air pollution vary between 0.4 per cent and 3 per cent of GDP, see Pearce (1993) and Maddison *et al.* (1996). Estimates of the costs of global warming from transport appear to be very small. There are different methods for estimating the value of transport accident externalities.

2. The economies of scale for Underground, rail, bus and coach services may have been underestimated. The results given in this chapter show that they are robust to even assumptions of quite large economies. However, it is important to determine more accurately the extent of economies of scale in transport. There is a lack of research in this area.

3. The response of transport users and technology may be greater than assumed. It is clear that the evidence on cross price elasticities is poor and there is little evidence on price induced technological development. Anecdotal evidence from other countries suggests that it is possible to switch to a less road based transport system, but the costs of this switch and how it may be brought about are unclear.

4. The results could be interpreted as evidence of the ineffectiveness of price based polices in reducing the levels of the external effects of road transport. This is a controversial conclusion given the weight attached to such market mechanism based policies in, for example, Department of Transport (1993*b*), Royal Commission on the Environmental Pollution (1994), and Commission of the European Communities (1995).

In conclusion, this study suggests the need for information and agreement about various issues. The meaning of efficient pricing of transport modes still appears confused in certain policy suggestions and this technical economic debate should be resolved. Better information about the importance of all external effects of transport is required. In particular, more epidemiological and medical work on local air pollution and its relation to transport is required. A rigorous model of the external effects of congestion and accidents, and the relationship between them, is needed. With such a model, more dependable estimates of these two external effects could be obtained. The apparent lack of economic importance of global warming caused by transport requires further investigation. The response of consumers and technology to different transport prices should be examined more thoroughly than has been the case in the past, with particular attention being paid to cross-price effects.

REFERENCES

British Railways Board (1989) *Passenger Demand Forecasting Handbook.* London: British Railways Board.

Button, K.J., (1993) *Transport Economics.* Aldershot: Edward Elgar.

Commission of the European Communities (1992) *Green Paper on The Impact of Transport on the Environment – A Community Strategy for Sustainable Mobility,* COM(92) 46 final. Brussels: CEC.

Commission of the European Communities (1995) *Towards Fair and Efficient Pricing in Transport: Policy Options for Internalising the External Costs of Transport in the European Union.* Brussels:CEC.

De Borger, B., Mayeres, I., Proost, S. and Wouters, S. (1996) Optimal pricing of urban passenger transport: a simulation exercise for Belgium. *Journal of Transport Economics and Policy,* **30**, pp. 31–54.

Department of Transport (1993*a*) *Road Accidents in Great Britain 1992: The Casualty Report.* London: HMSO.

Department of Transport (1993*b*) *Paying for Better Motorways: Issues for Discussion.* London: HMSO.

Fairhurst, M. and Mack (1981) *Consequences and Causes of Changes in Road Traffic Level.* London Transport Economic Research Report R243. London: London Transport.

Fankhauser, S. (1995) *Valuing Climate Change: The Economics of the Greenhouse.* London: Earthscan.

Fergusson, M., Holman, C. and Barrett, M. (1989) *Atmospheric Emissions from the Use of Transport in the UK: The Estimation of Current and Future Emissions.* London: WWF and EER.

Fowkes, A. (1992) Segmentation of the Travel Market in London and Estimates of Elasticities and Values of Travel Time. ITS Working Paper 345. University of Leeds.

Gilbert, C.L. and Jalilian, H. (1989) The Demand for Travel and the Demand for Travel Cards on the London Regional Transport Network. University of Oxford Applied Economics Discussion Paper Series No.83.

Glaister, S. and Lewis, D. (1978) An integrated fares policy for transport in London. *Journal of Public Economics,* **9**, pp. 341–355.

Goodwin, P.B. (1992) A review of new demand elasticities with special reference to short and long run effects of price changes. *Journal of Transport Economics and Policy,* **26**, pp. 155–169.

Halcrow Fox and Associates (1993) *Road Pricing in London: Review and Specification of Model Elasticities,* prepared in association with ITS, University of Leeds and Accent Marketing and Research for the Department of Transport. London: DoT.

House of Commons Transport Committee (1994) *Charging for the Use of Motorways,* 5th Report. Session 1993/94, HC376. London: HMSO.

Jansson, J.O. (1994) Accident externality charges. *Journal of Transport Economics and Policy*, **28**, pp. 31–43.

Lewis, D. (1977) Estimating the influence of public policy on road traffic levels in Greater London. *Journal of Transport Economics and Policy*, **11**, pp.155–168.

Lewis, D. (1978) Estimating the influence of public policy on road traffic levels in Greater London: Rejoinder. *Journal of Transport Economics and Policy*, **12**, pp. 99–102.

London Transport (1984), *The London Transport Fares Experience*. Economic Research Report R259. London: London Transport.

London Transport (1987) *Traffic Trends Since 1970*. Economic Research Report R266. London: London Transport.

London Transport (1993) *Annual Report 1992/93*. London: London Transport.

Maddison, D., Johansson, O., Pearce, D., Calthrop, E., Litman, T. and Verhoef, E. (1996) *Blueprint 5: The True Cost of Road Transport*. London: Earthscan.

Mauch, S.P., Rothengatter, W. and others (1995) *External Effects of Transport*. Report by IWW, Karlsruhe and INFRAS, Zürich. Paris: International Union of Railways (UIC).

Newbery, D.M. (1987) Road User Charges in Britain. Centre for Economic Policy Research, Discussion Paper No.174.

Newbery, D.M. (1988) Road user charges in Britain. *Economic Journal,* **98** (Conference 1988), pp. 161–176.

Newbery, D.M. (1990) Pricing and congestion: economic principles relevant to road pricing. *Oxford Review of Economic Policy,* **6**, pp. 22–38.

OECD (1988) *Transport and the Environment*. Paris: OECD.

Pearce, D.W. (1993) *Blueprint 3: Measuring Sustainable Development*. London: Earthscan.

Peirson, J., and Vickerman, R. (1993) Environmental Taxes and Investment in Transport Infrastructure: The Case for Hypothecation. Paper presented to the Royal Economic Society Conference at York.

Peirson, J., and Vickerman, R. (1996) A Model of External Effects and the Efficient Supply of Transport. CERTE Discussion Paper 96/1. University of Kent at Canterbury.

Peirson J., Skinner, I. and Vickerman, R. (1994) Environmentally Efficient Transport Taxes and Investment. CERTE Discussion Paper 94/1. University of Kent at Canterbury.

Peirson, J., Skinner, I. and Vickerman, R. (1995) Estimating the external costs of UK passenger transport: the first step towards an efficient transport market. *Environment and Planning A*, **27**, pp. 1977–1993.

Peirson, J., Skinner, I. and Vickerman (1996) The Microeconomic Analysis of the External Costs of Road Accidents. *UKC Studies in Economics 96/6*. University of Kent, Canterbury.

Royal Commission on Environmental Pollution (1994) *Transport and the Environment, Eighteenth Report*. Cm 2674. London: HMSO.

Whitelegg, J. (1993) *Transport for a Sustainable Future: The Case for Europe*. London: Belhaven Press.

CHAPTER 9

CREATING THE SUSTAINABLE SUPPLY CHAIN: MODELLING THE KEY RELATIONSHIPS

James Cooper, Ian Black and Melvyn Peters

The concept of 'sustainability' emerged in the early 1980s. Since then the ideas of a sustainable society and sustainable development have played a key role in policy statements by national governments, the European Union, international conferences and the United Nations. Despite this widespread attention there is still no agreed definition of the concept, and perhaps more critically, little progress towards translating the idea of sustainability into clear policy targets. A widely quoted definition of a sustainable society is one 'that meets the needs of the present without compromising the ability of future generations to meet their own needs' (World Commission on Environment and Development, 1987). What this and other definitions have in common is a concern about the use of the world's renewable and non-renewable resources, and the effect of pollution emissions on the world's environment. Another strong theme in the discussion is the need to consider future generations – referred to as intergenerational equity.

A coherent strategy to respond to the aim of sustainable development clearly involves a consideration of all society's economic and social activities and their impact. A recent publication by the UK government (Department of the Environment, 1996) lists a set of indicators that might be used to assess 'whether our development is becoming more sustainable'. Within this set of over 100 indicators those of direct relevance to the supply chain are mostly related to transport and movement. The relevant indicators include *freight traffic, depletion of fossil fuels, road transport energy use, road building, emissions of greenhouse gases, road transport emissions of nitrogen oxides, carbon monoxide emissions, black smoke emissions, and materials recycling.* It is notable, as we shall see later, that noise pollution and road accidents are not referred to specifically in the document. Given the emphasis on transport found in this and other references to sustainability a clear policy stance on future transport consumption and its associated resource use and emissions is necessary.

The focus of this chapter is to examine the contribution of the supply chain to the demand for transport and to consider what policy responses might be desirable if the supply chain is to play its role in achieving a sustainable society, or sustainable development.

The first part of the chapter examines the interrelationship between all the components of the supply chain (sourcing, inventory and transport) and we consider the growing impact of logistics management – in which companies take an integrated approach to the supply chain and try to optimize the whole of it rather than each component part. Forces for change in supply chain design and operation are identified; the components are then examined to determine what contribution they make to increasing the length of haul for goods – a prime consideration in the generation of environmental impact.

We then turn to an examination of the relationships which connect economic activity, freight transport and the environment, with particular reference to published statistics.

The general increase in the use of heavy goods vehicles (HGVs) experienced in the last 40 years has been intimately connected with the growth in economic activity as measured by Gross Domestic Product (GDP). In the United Kingdom, for instance, GDP has grown at an average rate of 2.4 per cent per annum over the period 1952-95. If this increase had been simply an increase in production with the same mix of commodities and the same industrial structure then the growth in HGVs and new associated traffic should have followed a similar growth path. However, by its very nature, economic growth implies the adoption of new technology, the emergence of new products and the replacement of old industries. It can lead to a new structure of industrial production with greater levels of concentration of production, with more vertical integration in the production process and different patterns of interaction between the industry sectors. As economic growth proceeds, consumers' incomes increase and their pattern of consumption changes. The demand for movement of goods in an economy will be affected by all these factors. At the same time new technology in the form of improved vehicle design, material handling equipment and improved road performance (a combination of road design, vehicle design and the balance of supply and demand for road space) is affecting the supply side response of the freight industry.

Following these analytical sections the last section of the chapter examines what a strategic response, based on the concept of sustainability, to future growth in goods movement might involve.

SUPPLY CHAIN DYNAMICS

There is no reason to suppose that supply chain developments will be the same for all companies, irrespective of industry sector. For this reason, we sought to select companies for participation in the research programme with reference to the industry sector they represented.

We were guided in our choice of industry sectors by work undertaken by Cranfield in a major study for the US-based Council of Logistics Management (CLM)in 1992–33 (see CLM, 1993). That study covered developments in seven business sectors (retail, fast-moving consumer goods, consumer durables, business equipment, healthcare products, chemicals, and automotive).

We felt that it would be sensible to build on that early work by choosing several of the same industry sectors. But based on the CLM work, we chose to modify one of the sectors (e.g. channel management retailers rather than the broad spectrum of retailing). We also opted to include a sector previously not examined (food and agricultural products), which operates high capacity supply chains, to provide a new dimension for making comparisons between sectors. The final choice of six sectors studied as part of the research programme is therefore as follows:

1. Automotive
2. Business equipment
3. Fast-moving consumer goods
4. Chemicals
5. Food and agricultural products
6. Channel management retailers.

The choice of the manufacturing industry sectors was made to represent a variety of supply chain structures and operations. Automotive manufacturing represents a high volume and high value supply chain in terms of units of output at assembly plants. Moreover, it is a complex operation with around 3000 components being used in the manufacture of a single car, most of them being sourced from a variety of suppliers.

Business equipment companies (making computers, copiers etc) operate in a highly competitive market and many products have very short life-cycles of less than a year. In addition, production has, in recent years, been extremely footloose, with manufacturing of finished items being readily transferred from location to location.

Fast moving consumer goods (which includes a whole range of products from detergents to clothing) represent another high volume sector of the market but because the value-density of products is generally low, their supply chains often extend across relatively short distances.

Chemicals processing represents a growing sector, but one where the hazardous nature of many products places restrictions on how they can be moved and stored. Some chemicals, however, are highly specialized products which means that they are often moved over long distances from factories to customers.

Inclusion of the retail sector was warranted given the extensive control that many of the multiple chains now exercise over supply chain design and operation.

In interviews with managers representing companies in each of the studied sectors, we concentrated on two main areas of interest: the forces for change in supply chain structures (see Cooper *et al.*, 1995 for a full discussion of this topic) and what characterized the different logistics structures currently being used.

Figure 9.1 summarizes the components of logistics strategy in the different business sectors, as identified in the company interviews that formed a central part of the research programme. For the purpose of this chapter, the main interest in figure 9.1 is to relate transport needs to the different components of logistics strategy. In particular, are some components reliant on new ways of using

	AI	BEI	CMR	FMCG	FAP	CP
1. Improvements in customer service	↑	↑	↑	↑	↑	↑
2. Focused production	O	↑	-	↑	↑	↑
3. Modular products	↑	↑	-	↑	-	-
4. "Lean" supply chains	↑	↑	O	↑O	O-	O
5. Vertical integration (by ownership)	↓	↓	↓	O	O	O
6. Just-in-time systems	O	O	↑	↑	↑O	O
7. Postponement techniques	O	↑	-	↑O	↑	-
8. Extended organisations	↑	↑	↑	↑-	↑-	O
9. Reverse logistics	↑	↑	↑-	↑O	↑-	O
10. Pan-European sourcing	↑	O	↑	↑	↑	O

↑ increasing trend   ↓ decreasing trend   O not relevant   - no change

(A combination of the above symbols indicates that companies in the same business sector are developing in different ways).

AI   Automotive
BEI   Business Equipment
CMR   Channel Management Retailers
FMCG   Fast Moving Consumer Goods
FAP   Food and Agricultural Products
CP   Chemical Products

Figure 9.1. Components of logistics strategy.

transport and is it likely that greater environmental impact will be the expected consequence?

Using the framework of figure 9.1, we can begin to answer this key question by examining each component of logistics strategy in turn.

Customer Service

There are many dimensions to customer service, some of which have little bearing on the issue of transport demand. For example, better product availability is mainly an issue of inventory management; only when special delivery arrangements are made to complete orders will extra transport activity be created, but the scale of this is almost certain to be small, compared with mainstream delivery activities.

More frequent delivery (say, twice a week, rather than once a week) can, however, raise the transport requirement and lead to more environmental pollution. Two small vehicles, for example, may replace a single large one and their aggregate fuel consumption will exceed that of the larger vehicle. All other things being equal, this will mean more environmental pollution. Yet it is important to bear in mind the economic constraints to more frequent delivery; because it is often more expensive, customers do not always readily require it. This provides an important brake on increasing delivery frequency.

Hill (1994) lists the following as key components of customer service:

- Availability of stock
- Order cycle time
- Frequency of delivery
- On-schedule delivery
- Reliability of delivery

Order-cycle times, if shortened, will be related to frequency of delivery which has already been commented upon. Neither on-schedule delivery or reliability of delivery are likely to have a strong bearing on transport demand. It therefore follows that increases in levels of customer service will, in an overall sense, have but a modest impact on levels of transport demand, despite their occurrence in every business sector included in the study (see figure 9.1).

Focused Production

The move towards focused production has already occurred to a large extent in sectors such as automotive manufacture, which accounts for the 'no change' registered in figure 9.1. Individual automotive plants tend to specialize in perhaps one or two models, a pattern of production that has now been in place for some time.

However, in the other manufacturing sectors, focused production is on the increase (it does not, of course, apply to channel management retailers). A key consideration is that focused production, as practised by transnational companies does tend to distance production from many markets which may have once been served by a local production plant. So a growth in focused production across manufacturing does tend to suggest an accompanying growth in transport requirements and a resultant increase in environmental pollution, subject to critical assumptions on mode choice and similar issues.

The preceding qualification is an important one, because it is misleading to suggest that simple relationships link components of logistics strategy to transport requirements and, by extension, environmental pollution. For example, our research with one company revealed that they had changed the basis of shipping a particular product, when adopting the focused factory approach in Europe. Realizing that they were going to be paying much more for transporting the product (which was carried as a liquid), they arranged for it to be sent for local packing in a more concentrated form, and so halved the transport cost. As there was a reduced requirement for vehicles, the environmental impact was also less than it would otherwise have been.

In a similar vein, it is important to appreciate that there is not always a simple relationship between the increased distances over which companies move goods (following the adoption of focused production) and the price they have to pay for transport. This is because focused production will often lead to a heavier concentration of flows along certain routes, which gives the manufacturer considerable scope for negotiating price discounts with carriers. So focused factories may result in a level of environmental impact from transport which is disproportionate to the increase in transport price paid by the shipper.

Modular Products

A tendency towards modular products in several business sectors is the result of a number of supply chain and other considerations. In the first place, it can help to reduce inventory requirements when different countries have their own product specifications. Personal computers, for example, have different keyboard and electrical requirements, depending upon the destination country. By modularizing the PC into its constituent parts and 'picking-and-packing' at distribution centres, customer requirements can be satisfied without resorting to high inventory levels for finished PCs.

Secondly, in some businesses, especially those concerned with assembly, modularization comprises the supply of complete sub-assemblies from vendors. So instead of an automotive company receiving shock absorber components, springs etc from a variety of suppliers, a complete suspension unit may be sent from a first-tier supplier whose role it is to make the

constituent parts into a complete sub-assembly. In addition to inventory benefits there are also production advantages which result from this way of working. Thirdly, modularization is increasingly the result of environmental
legislation, particularly that which relates to recycling. Products need to be
'disassembled' quickly to make recycling operations economic, and modular-
ized construction helps in this respect.

Modular products are not, therefore, obviously associated with any increased
need for transport, compared with more traditional ways of making products
from components. As a developing component of logistics strategy, it seems
safe to say that modular products are 'transport neutral'.

'Lean' Supply Chains

A prime purpose of creating lean supply chains is to eliminate costly inventory
at every stage possible. The means for achieving this are various. Track-and-
trace information systems, for example, give a far clearer understanding of product movement along a supply chain and removes the need to keep inventory just
in case it is needed when deliveries fail to materialize. The integration of
management within organizations, perhaps through business process re-engi-
neering also makes it easier to eliminate wasteful or duplicated inventory in
supply chains.

Elimination of all kinds of duplication is at the heart of lean supply. While
inventory reduction is often the focus of lean supply, because of the many
opportunities for significant cost reduction, management initiatives may also
take the form of invoice elimination, or improved methods of expediting,
progress chasing and inspection.

To this extent, 'lean' supply chains are transport neutral. But other initiatives
may be less so. Take, for example, a common feature of lean supply chains,
which is to eliminate perhaps one or more echelon of warehousing from the
supply chain. The advantage of so-called warehouse 'centralization' is to reduce
inventory levels in safety stock by aggregating them (Maister, 1976; Sussams,
1986). But there is a well-known relationship linking warehousing and inventory
which suggests a rise in transport costs as warehouses are eliminated. The implication is that more transport demand is created by a move towards centralized
warehousing, since customers will be further away from points of supply and
'back-tracking' will occur to a greater degree in links between factory, warehouse and customer.

Another frequent feature of lean supply is just-in-time delivery. This is,
however, treated as a component of logistics strategy in its own right (see
below). So summarizing the contribution so far of lean-supply strategies to
higher levels transport demand, we can conclude that some aspects do appear to
have this effect to varying degrees of significance which are determined, for
example, by the degree of warehouse centralization that is chosen.

Vertical Integration

This particular component of logistics strategy is the only one listed that the research results show to be in decline, notably in the automotive, business equipment and channel retail sectors. The decline can be explained in a number of ways. Supporters of Williamson (1975) would point to transaction cost theory. Van der Ven *et al.* (1975) build upon inter-organization theory.

In essence, however, vertical integration has greater organizational importance than it appears to have for the transport demand. Whether a car seat, say, is assembled by the automotive company or its first-tier supplier of car seats has relatively little bearing on levels of transport demand within the overall supply chain. Vertical (dis)integration is, therefore, another component of logistics strategy which may be described as 'transport neutral'.

Just-in-Time (JIT) Systems

These are, of course, a facet of lean supply chains, which were discussed above. JIT can result, and often does, in more frequent deliveries of small consignments compared with re-supply practices based on traditional notions of economic order quantity.

It has been frequently pointed out that JIT can readily create more transport demand and so add to levels of environmental pollution (see, for example Allen, 1993). But it is also true that some adaptations of JIT, such as those used by several car manufacturers, do not necessarily result in increased transport demand with all its unwanted environmental impact. Companies like Ford, Rover and Nissan use a nominated carrier to collect consignments from suppliers in an operation which is designed around consolidated delivery. Not only can this be significantly less expensive than independent delivery by suppliers, but the transport operations can have many of the characteristics of bulk delivery (e.g. the use of large vehicles). Another initiative in JIT is that of co-location. Fiat and Nissan, for example, have encouraged certain suppliers to set up manufacturing locations close to their assembly plants (Hudson and Sadler 1992). Final delivery of components therefore has little in the way of transport requirement when suppliers are co-located. More important is the transport of inputs to component manufacture.

As a consequence it is difficult to generalize about the environmental impact of JIT. At best, it does not lead to high levels of transport activity and environmental pollution compared with traditional, bulk-consignment methods of re-supply. But, in its unmodified form, there can be no doubt that there is greater environmental impact from JIT-related practices, although not necessarily contributing to increased length of haul, which is an important concern of this chapter.

Postponement Techniques

Postponement techniques are principally rooted in inventory management and are closely related to modular production. In essence, postponement means leaving to the latest possible moment the decision on how to configure products for particular customers; it therefore works best when there is a modular construction of products in question. As a component of logistics strategy, postponement is similarly 'transport neutral'.

Extended Organizations

There are parallels between extended organizations and lean supply in that they both are based upon integration principles. Extended organizations have many facets and embrace various management ideas such as networking and 'co-makership'. Key considerations are to embrace change more quickly and to improve the dissemination of knowledge and understanding among network partners.

As far as supply chains are concerned, one of the more important ideas in extended organizations is that of 'integrated logistics asset management' in which buyers and suppliers jointly examine the possibilities for the deployment of assets to meet supply chain requirements. The reduction of empty running by backloading one another's vehicles is a possibility being explored by grocery retailers such as Sainsbury's in association with their suppliers.

This, then, is an example of where emergent supply chain strategies can result in a diminution of environmental pollution by driving down the demand for transport through an integrated approach to asset management.

'Reverse' Logistics

In focusing on the fate of unwanted packaging or life-expired products, there is always the danger that other environmental aspects of supply chain operation are overlooked. Transport is a case in point.

Regulations increasingly require companies to take responsibilities for their packaging and products and to arrange for their recycling or re-furbishment. This invariably implies, however, a new (and possibly more extensive) use of transport.

Much depends, of course, on the extent to which packaging and goods have to be moved as part of the recycling/refurbishment process. When it involves movement back to factories or to specialized disposal facilities the extra transport can be significant. This is (according to anecdotal reports) particularly so in Germany, where waste packaging that is in excess of the needs of recyclers is being exported to neighbouring countries, especially those to the east. By contrast, in France, the emphasis is often on local mass-burn units, which reduces the transport requirement, but can lead to understandable environmental anxiety over the unknown composition of emissions from the units.

So despite the best of intentions, there is little doubt that, overall, reverse logistics can add measurably to transport demand, particularly when the nature of materials for recycling does not lend itself to backloading. Much depends on the regulations locally which govern recycling and refurbishment schemes.

Pan-European Sourcing

An important consequence of increasing competition is the need to supply customers with higher quality products, in ever greater variety (Sargent and Creehan, 1993). For many industry sectors this has involved searching further afield to find suppliers who are able to help meet this need. The quality management programmes in automotive manufacturing, for example, have led many companies to source from those component suppliers which reliably make high quality parts; location is very much a secondary consideration when transport cost will often represent but a small element of the total supply cost.

In the automotive sector there is a steady trend away from local/national sourcing relationships, to ones which are constructed on a pan-European basis. This is particularly evident in Germany, when automotive companies have traditionally sourced mainly from Germany: now they are sourcing more from other countries as well. (Part of the reason for this is that German component manufacturers such as Bosch have established subsidiaries in neighbouring countries with a lower cost base.)

The picture is, however, a complex one, since sourcing needs are closely tied to manufacturing and supply chain management requirements. So some car assemblers such as Fiat and Nissan use co-located suppliers to expedite JIT delivery for certain components (see above). These are generally items which are high in variety and/or large in size, such as car seats (Cooper and Griffiths, 1994).

An increasingly trans-national approach to manufacturing is apparent in virtually all the case study companies along with an associated rise in pan-European sourcing for raw materials, component parts and sub-assemblies. This increase in pan-European sourcing (global for some companies) is closely associated with a new awareness of the strategic value of procurement in achieving competitive advantage. This advantage is provided by the supplier through cost reduction, service improvement (response) and technological innovation.

The move towards lean supply and lean production, most notably in the automotive and business equipment industries, has been accompanied by radical rationalization in the supplier base. Industrial customer/supplier relationships are being organized into tiered networks where any supplier below the first-tier operates as a sub-contractor to a first-tier supplier who is responsible for co-ordinating the flow of materials through the network and on to the end user. The vertical disintegration taking place in manufacturing places severe requirements on first-tier suppliers. Their increasing share in the value-added of the final product makes supplier selection of strategic importance and manufacturing companies are clearly willing to extend their search environment beyond national and local boundaries to secure capable suppliers.

In the one sector studied which is not part of manufacturing – channel management retailing – quality remains an important issue influencing supply, but variety is of almost equal importance in many product lines. Supermarket chains, for example, source fresh produce from around the world to offer more variety to ever more demanding customers. Beans from Kenya, strawberries from Spain and new potatoes from Egypt are far from uncommon sights on the shelves of most UK supermarkets. Clearly, the extra transport costs are more than balanced by the increased price shoppers are prepared to pay for out-of-season produce.

The quest for more quality and variety, and the forging of new relationships in procurement, has to be related to increased length of haul for goods. Local sourcing means relatively short lengths of haul. Now that commercial buyers are finding it necessary to source from across Europe (or sometimes even further afield) to achieve their aims, the implication is that length of haul is on the increase. When this translates, as it so often does, into longer trips by road, then greater environmental impact will be the inevitable result.

Environmental Implications of Logistics Strategy

The different components which go to make up logistics strategies in the six business sectors studied as part of the research programme are clearly not equally responsible for creating undesirable environmental impacts. The extent to which each contributes to increased transport demand and, by extension, more environmental pollution, can be summarized as follows:

Significantly promotes increased road transport demand/environmental pollution
  Focused production
  Pan-European sourcing

Marginally promotes increased transport demand/environmental pollution
  Customer Service
  Just-in-time
  Reverse logistics
  Lean supply chains

Components of logistics strategy which are 'transport neutral' and do not add to environmental pollution
  Modular products
  Vertical (dis)integration
  Postponement

Lastly, there is one component which contributes to reduced transport activity and environmental pollution
  Extended organizations (notably integrated logistics asset management)

It is, however, vital to appreciate that these overall conclusions do need to be qualified according to both industry sector and company; there is no single approach being taken to developing strategies in supply chain management and context is all-important. In particular, there needs to be careful consideration in any evaluation of how supply chain reconfiguration relates to environmental pollution from transport, and this theme is taken up in the next section of the chapter.

FROM ECONOMIC ACTIVITY TO THE ENVIRONMENTAL IMPACT OF FREIGHT

The previous section provided an analysis of the impact of changes in the supply chain on freight transport demand. This section examines the aggregate figures for freight movement in the UK economy as a whole in order to identify, and quantify, the contribution changes in the supply chain may have. Figure 9.2 provides an overview of the main factors that need to be considered in the relationship between the output of an economy (as measured by GDP) and the environmental impact generated by HGVs. Between GDP and Environmental Effects are four relationships that link these two variables. The first relationship refers to the change in tonnes of freight carried by HGVs in the economy (referred to as 'Tonnes Lifted'). Over the period 1952-94 in the UK economy goods movement using this definition has increased much more slowly than GDP.

Stability in the ratio of tonnes lifted to GDP up to 1962 was followed by a steady decline for almost twenty years with approximate stability since the early 1980s. Comparable figures for European countries also demonstrate a divergence between the two variables though not of the same pattern. The divergence must be explained by three broad reasons. Firstly the mix of commodities produced by the economy has changed over this period and given that there is a wide variation in the generation of goods movement (measured in tonnes lifted per unit of final output) then any change to this mix will affect the total tonnes lifted. This different propensity to generate goods movement applies not only to broad categories such as manufacturing and service industries but also within industry groups such as electrical and optical equipment. The second major factor affecting the relationship is any rearrangement of the structure of industry from raw materials through processing and distribution to final consumption – the supply chain. The processing of products and their assembly of products can take a number of stages. These stages may be separated by storage locations and the final distribution of the finished product may be direct to the customer or through intermediate stages of wholesale and retail locations. Changes in the design of the supply chain will have repercussions on the tonnes lifted in the economy.

Finally it should be recognized that goods movement is not only carried out by HGVs – Light Goods Vehicles, Rail, Pipelines and Shipping are also responsible

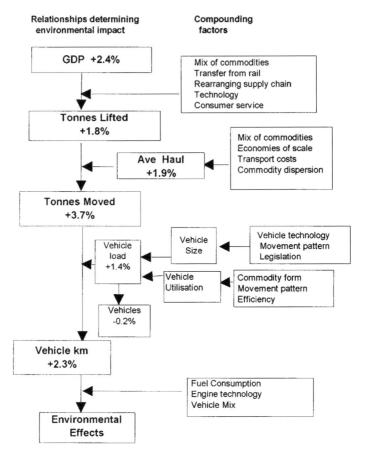

Figure 9.2.Heavy goods vehicle growth (figures show average annual percentage growth for the UK, 1952–94).

for goods movement. Changes in the relative attractiveness of these modes may lead to HGVs gaining a larger or smaller share of the total movement. In order to identify the relative contribution of these various factors annual growth in tonnes lifted can be broken down into three elements: that due to the growth in GDP (assumed in this context to be *pro rata*)

- that due the transfer from rail (based on the change in relative shares)
- that due to other factors (mix of commodities, change in industry structure).

Figure 9.3 shows this breakdown (together with the contribution from increasing average haul). The contribution of a declining rail share in tonnes lifted makes a modest contribution in the first decade up to the early 1960s. Most noticeably the contribution from 'structure' occurs in the 1970s. During

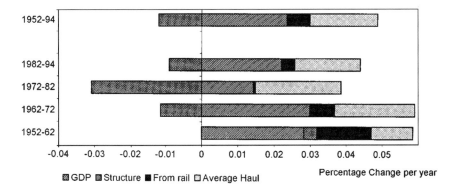

Figure 9.3. Contribution to growth of HGV tonne-km in UK.

the last 30 years the UK economy has experienced a decline in the proportion of GDP generated by the manufacturing sector. It could be argued that as this sector has a higher propensity to generate goods lifted per unit of output than the service sector (though not necessarily more than the other production sectors e.g. construction), then the relevant comparison should be between manufacturing output and tonnes lifted and not with GDP. Figure 9.4 plots the divergence between three possible output measures and tonnes lifted. If manufacturing industry output is used it appears that there is a divergence from about 1965 to 1976. However if the output from all production industries is used then the divergence is the same as for GDP – 20 years from 1965 to 1985. Ideally if it were possible to produce freight generation factors for each industry sector then the effect of the changing industrial mix could be accurately estimated and the contribution of 'other factors' determined.

A clear distinction is drawn in freight statistics between the amount of goods that are carried by goods vehicles (tonnes lifted) and the total movement of these goods taking into account distance moved (goods moved) which has units of tonne-km. The relationship between the two is an identity:

Goods Moved = Tonnes Lifted × Average Haul

Any explanation of the divergence in the growth of these two variables over time is therefore effectively an explanation of changes in average haul. In the UK over the four decades to 1994 the average length of haul has grown significantly at 1.9 per cent per annum, and therefore *Goods Moved* has grown faster than GDP, +3.7 per cent compared to +2.4 per cent per annum. This tendency is also found in other European countries over the last two decades. Figure 9.3 shows the annual contribution in average haul to tonne-km compared to the three factors referred to above. Figure 9.5 shows the steady upward trend from

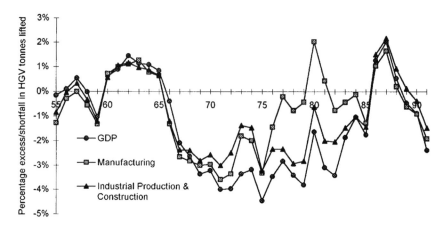

Figure 9.4. Tonnes lifted and three measures of output.

64 km in 1976 to 84 km in 1994. This graph also shows the length of haul by commodity and clearly shows how all commodity types have experienced significant increases.

The explanation behind the growth in average haul may be in a number of areas. As with Goods Lifted the change in the mix of commodities again may change the average length of move, if there is a variation between different commodities. Another reason suggested for the increase in average haul is the tendency for production to be concentrated in fewer sites. The explanation behind this is that the balance between the economies of large scale production and transport costs changes. Technological changes in production cost functions may favour large plants and reductions in transport costs mean that the cost of delivery to large market areas is not so onerous.

If Goods Moved (in units of tonne-km) represents the change in demand by the economy for movement by HGVs this may not be matched by the resources (material, human and environmental) consumed in their movement. Technological improvements in vehicle design, accompanied by improvements in road system performance, have led to larger vehicles, greater fuel efficiency and reduced environmental damage. Overall an average annual increase of 1.4 per cent in the load carried by an average vehicle over a 40-year period has meant that vehicle-km has grown by 2.3 per cent per year (vehicle-km = tonne-km/average load) – almost identical to the growth in GDP. The rapid increase in average annual activity of HGVs (in units km/year) has meant that the number of vehicles has actually declined in the period – an average of -0.2 per cent per year. Whilst the number has declined, the total carrying capacity in terms of tonnes (no. of vehicles × average Gross Vehicle Weight) has increased by 9 per cent – or 20 per cent if use is the weighting factor (vehicle-km × average Gross

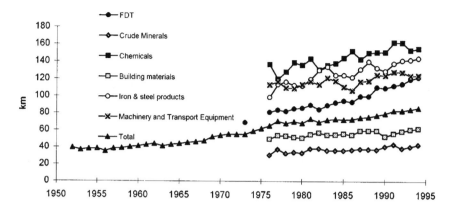

Figure 9.5. Average haul by main commodities, 1952–94.

Vehicle Weight). Although average load has increased over the period this has not kept pace with the increase in vehicle size and the average load *factor* (average load/average Gross Vehicle Weight by use) has actually fallen by 7 per cent. It should be noted that this analysis only considers weight as the critical factor. Volume is another attribute of vehicle loads and any change in the relationship between weight and volume (density – kg/m^3) over the period may have influenced the relative importance of weight and volume constraints on vehicle loading.

The three vital relationships are examined in much greater detail in Black *et al.* (1995). For the purposes of this chapter, the discussion is limited to the following: relocation of production; transport operating cost structures; average length of haul; vehicles and vehicle activity.

Relocation of Production

The subject of the location of facilities has a long history in economics and geography and a number of excellent surveys exist on the subject (e.g. Eiselt *et al.*, 1993 and Graitson, 1982). A major theme in this area is the relationship between economies of scale in production and the cost of transport. If, it is argued, there are significant economies of scale in the production process then plants will tend to be large. This implies that the journey from plant to final customers will also tend to be longer than if there are large numbers of plants scattered throughout a region. In examining the growth in average haul over the last four decades and prospects for the future a possible hypothesis is, therefore, that the trends were a result of changes in the production process that encouraged larger plants. We can firmly reject this hypothesis for manufacturing industry. The limited evidence for the last two decades on economies of scale shows no such tendency. And more importantly in the UK over the last 20 years the average size of plants in manufacturing industry has *de*creased. If economies of scale are not the explanation of the greater average haul then customers, or purchasers, throughout the supply chain must be obtaining goods and materials from more distant sources. The possible reasons for this are falling cost of movement (including transport, tariff and non-tariff barriers to trade in Europe) and the emergence of a wider range of products (which promotes the concept of the focused factory specializing in a selected part of the full product range), and greater consumer selectivity on the choice of product.

Transport Operating Cost Structures

Figure 9.6 provides a breakdown of changes in cost per tonne-km (constant prices) for 40 years divided (approximately) into 10-year periods. The average change per year is broken down as a function of changes in the four main determinants – standing cost, running cost, vehicle cost and vehicle-km per hour. Throughout the whole period the average annual change in unit cost was -1.37 per cent. The reduction in cost due to higher average speed and reduced running costs outweighed the increase in standing costs with the change in vehicle capital cost making a negligible contribution to the overall change. The increase due to standing costs is understandable given that increases in drivers' wages (which constitute the largest proportion) have consistently outstripped the increase in the price index. A reduction due to a fall in running cost, which includes maintenance and fuel, occurs during 3 of the 4 periods. The increase in average speed provides a consistent contribution to the reduction in costs over the period. The

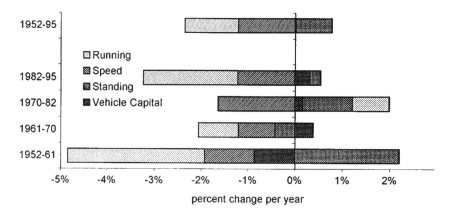

Figure 9.6. Contribution to cost change – 24 tonne rigid truck cost per tonne-km (constant prices).

speed increased from 10km/h in 1952 to 27 km/h in 1992. This increase derives from less idle time, reduced loading and unloading times as well as increased vehicle speed on the road.

Examination of other vehicle types which is only possible for shorter periods of time due to changes in definition, confirm the general picture of a decline in unit costs over the period (with a period of the 1970s being an exception).

Importantly, the figures above refer to the unit costs of a particular vehicle. If we take into account the change in the mix of vehicles, then the actual reduction in unit costs per tonne-km is much greater. During the period 1973 to 1993 (over which time consistent figures are available) for instance, the average size of vehicles has increased by 20 per cent due to the change in vehicle mix. Assuming the relative cost of vehicles remained the same over the period this change in vehicle mix would have led to a decrease in average operating cost per tonne-km of 13 per cent for the period. However this reduction poses a conceptual problem. It could be considered as a reduction of unit cost generated by the availability of larger vehicles due to technological developments combined with the relaxation of legal restrictions on size (weight and volume). Alternatively it could be considered in part at least *the effect* of other changes. The change in type of movement and the trend towards longer haul may have allowed the use of larger vehicles. It is clearly difficult to separate these two effects. For the entire period we have assumed that the effect of larger vehicles is to reduce the index of unit costs by 10 per cent.

Evidence on actual haulage rates is provided by a survey of FTA members. For the period 1985 to 1995 the index has grown on average at 4 per cent less per annum than the Retail Price Index. The nature of data collection may not pick up all the increases in rates but the source does seem to confirm the fall in transport unit costs, and a continuation of this trend into the mid 1990s.

Average Length of Haul

Estimates of average haul are derived from statistics collected on the Continuing Survey of Road Goods Transport and defined as tonnes moved (tonne-km) divided by tonnes lifted (tonne). (figure 9.5). Average haul for all commodities (total) has grown steadily since the mid 1950s. A detailed and consistent breakdown into commodities is available for the period 1973 to 1994. During this 20-year period all categories of products (except the small group *Other metal products)* have experienced a growth with most falling in the range 1 per cent to 2.2 per cent per annum (weighted average 1.6 per cent). There is a considerable difference in the distance by different commodities. *Chemicals* is over 150 km in the 1990s whereas two categories with a high weight to value ratio (*Crude Minerals* and *Building Materials*) are less than 60 km. Both the last two categories have experienced growth in the average haul over the last twenty years.

Quantifying the reasons behind the continuing growth of average haul is fraught with difficulties of interpretation. As noted above the simple explanation of larger and fewer production units could, under the most generous interpretation of the impact of focused factories and larger distribution centres, explain only a small part of the increase. A potentially important influence is undoubtedly the fall in transport unit costs outlined above. Simple time series analysis (not surprisingly given the long response times) offers no clear evidence of the impact of unit cost changes. The alternative method of using cross section analysis at a point in time to analyse the deterrence of distance can be used, but needs to be used with extreme caution and qualification. Using this approach our research and modelling exercise suggests an elasticity of average haul with respect to unit costs of -0.7. Even if we accept the elasticity, it still fails to explain all the change observed. Additional effects, or even substitutes to the cost argument, are concerned with the proliferation of products and the general reduction in barriers to trade (particularly relevant in the case of international trade). It is worth noting that the official journal of the EC (1989) stated that 'Completion of the internal market is inconceivable without . . . an increase in demand, in volume and in qualitative terms for all types of transport'. Both these may have contributed to the phenomenon but at the moment there is no strong evidence to suggest that they are the major factors behind the growth in average haul within Great Britain. The importance of unit transport costs therefore remains by default if not by the evidence adduced by our cross section model. This last model illustrates the importance of transport costs in the cross section context with its implication that if distance was not a deterrent then the random distribution of products would imply an average haul of 240 km.

Vehicles and Vehicle Activity

The increase in average GVW over the last two decades should imply that fewer vehicle kilometres are required to carry a given level of goods moved (tonne-km). This conclusion is dependent on any changes in the load factor (defined as the average load carried (in tonnes) divided by the carrying capacity in tonnes). For convenience it is assumed that the average carrying capacity is two-thirds of the GVW. This is approximately true for all HGVs and there has been no change in this general rule over the last 15–20 years. Inspection of the load factor clearly demonstrates a decline during the 1980s and 1990s. To some extent, therefore, this decline counteracts the impact of higher GVW. The reasons behind this fall are not easy to identify. The percentage of empty running has actually declined over this period and this therefore implies the average load factor on loaded journeys has also declined. This overall fall may be due to a changing pattern of demand with a greater emphasis on volume limiting the load carried rather than tonnes, or it may reflect poorer utilization of the vehicles. In total the trend is equivalent to a decline of 7 per cent over the period compared to an increase in GVW (in use) of 20 per cent. The implication of the combination of these two figures is that a 38 per cent increase in tonne-km was achieved with an increase of 24 per cent in vehicle-km.

Vehicle Activity determines the number of vehicles required. The growth in annual kilometres per vehicle has been continuous over the period from 18,400 km in 1952 to over 50,000 km in 1994. This represents a growth of 2.4 per cent per annum. In the later years the increase has been even faster, 3 per cent per annum in the 1976 to 1994 period. This greater intensity of use of all types of vehicle is partly due to longer hours of operation, less time loading and unloading and faster speeds on the road. A comparison with an earlier study (Tweddle and Cooper, 1985) concerned with truck operation in the night hours 2000 h to 0600 h shows that activity during these hours has increased modestly between 1973 and 1992. Based on the Department of Transport's census of vehicles at 200 points located throughout the UK, the comparison shows that in 1973 8.4 per cent of lorry movements occurred between these hours. In 1992 this figure had increased to 9.2 per cent. Estimates of average traffic speeds are scarce and often based on limited and biased samples. Some studies (see for instance CEBR, 1994) suggest a small decline in average road speeds from the early 1980s to the early 1990s whereas others (DoT, 1994) suggest a continued increase. Whilst increased road speeds may have contributed to the increase in earlier years, the greater utilization over the last 10 to 15 years must have been mainly generated by more hours of operation. The translation from vehicle-kilometres per year to number of vehicles required depends solely on the vehicle activity per year. The implication of the change in distance covered by an average HGV (in conjunction with vehicle-km required) is that the number of vehicles registered decreased from a peak of 605,000 in 1967 to 416,000 in 1994. This figure is below the estimated number of registered HGVs in 1952 of 457,000.

FORECASTS

Components

A forecast for freight movement and environmental impact for the UK based on our analysis is presented below together with a comparison with two other forecasts. The first was made by the UK government (Department of Transport, 1989) to assist in road transport infrastructure investment, and the second by a Dutch consultant (NEA, 1994) for the International Road Transport Union (IRU).

The starting point of these forecasts is GDP. The assumption for the NEA study that covered Western Europe assumed an average growth rate of 3.1 per cent compared to a mean 2.5 per cent in the official UK study. In this study the prediction of tonnes lifted used the mean rate for the UK of 2.5 per cent combined with an adjustment to cater for the mix of output moving away from the production industries towards the service sector. This leads to a somewhat slower growth in tonnes lifted. It also assumes that the modal split between road and rail will remain the same as today.

On the question of changes in the average haul, the reduction in operating costs per tonne-km in the past and the opening up of markets in Europe can be expected to continue this trend. However there seems a likelihood that road speeds may fail to increase in the future and may actually fall (CEBR, 1994); it also seems unlikely that technological improvements can provide significant improvements in vehicle capital and maintenance costs. The study forecasts, therefore, assume a reduction in the rate of growth of average haul but, recognizing the long term nature of the response in this area, that it will not be a significant factor before the end of the century. Using the elasticity estimates identified in the study, a forecast is also provided making the assumption that the price of fuel is doubled by taxation.

The increase in average haul provides an opportunity for hauliers to use larger vehicles and therefore the growth in vehicle-km is rather lower than tonne-km. The growth in tonne-km is partially counterbalanced by the increase in average load leading to a slower growth in vehicle-km.

The end result of these assumptions can be seen in figure 9.7. The current study's forecast falls approximately midway between the Department of Transport's *High* and *Low* forecast. It is considerably less than the forecast for Europe as a whole; the main difference seems to be due to the difference in GDP assumption, a significant movement away from other modes of transport and a more modest increase in vehicle size in Europe. The impact of tax that doubles the price of fuel can be seen to reduce the growth in vehicle-km to the *Low* forecast of the Department of Transport.

Environmental Impact

The key to forecasts of pollutant emissions is the growth in fuel consumption and legislation defining limits on individual vehicle emissions. Fuel consumption per tonne-km can be expected to decline for three reasons: greater fuel efficiency per vehicle, the movement to larger vehicles (with their greater efficiency per tonne-km), and the increase in average haul (operating at more efficient speeds and on less congested roads). In combination they should yield a reduction in fuel consumption per vehicle-km of approximately 0.5 per cent per year compared to vehicle-km (see figure 9.8). Carbon dioxide (CO_2) emissions from HGVs are of particular relevance for global warming. They are intimately related to fuel consumption and should therefore grow in line with this forecast.

The pollutant emissions of major concern are nitrogen oxide (NO_x), hydrocarbons (HC), carbon monoxide (CO) and particulates (Eggleston, 1992). Maximum individual vehicle emissions for diesel engines in commercial vehicles

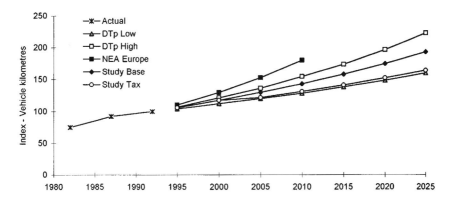

Figure 9.7. UK HGV forecasts.

have been defined for the European Union Directive 91/542/EEC. The standards for new vehicles started on the 1st October 1995 – the Euro 2 standard. If these standards (defined in terms of g/kWh) are met by all new vehicles then, given the average life of commercial vehicles, within 10 years over 90 per cent of vehicles will meet these standards and some will perform better. There is also the prospect that further legislation will bring in more stringent requirements. The forecast shown in figure 9.8 assumes that the figure achieved in 2005 is the standard as defined in the 1991 Directive without further legislation. The index is based on the weight of all the four pollutant emissions (not including CO_2) described above.

POLICY RESPONSE

Past Trends and Future Prospects

The relationships which connect economic activities to the environmental impact for freight transport are complex. In this chapter we have focused on how heavy goods vehicles contribute both to supply chain operations and environmental impact, using past and current data alongside an overview of developments in logistics strategy. We can conclude that changes in supply chain design and operation have had important consequences for transport, most notably through increasing the average length of haul for goods.

However, it becomes much more difficult to establish how new requirements for goods movement translate into vehicle movements, which are the basis for causing environmental pollution. Projections of vehicle-km, for example, have to be based to a large extent on simple extrapolation of trends. Yet there is nothing in the available data which suggests there will be a halt in the increase of vehicle-km.

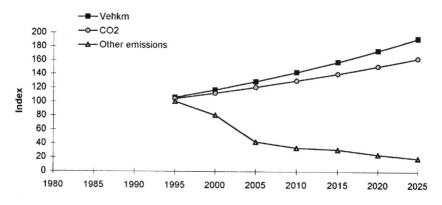

Figure 9.8. Emissions – UK HGV forecasts.

The consequence will be a corresponding rise in carbon dioxide emissions, which are closely related to vehicle-km. More encouragingly, but solely thanks to legislation, the emission of four other major pollutants (NO_x, HC, CO and particulates) looks set to fall.

But air pollution from the engine exhausts from lorries represents but one aspect of environmental impact. For example, at the indirect level, an increase in vehicle-km contributes to the rising demand for roadspace and the construction of new infrastructure. This, too, must be taken into account when the full environmental impact of supply chain changes is assessed.

Sustainability

How do these forecasts square with the achievement of sustainability? Given the elusiveness of a precise definition of the term there is clearly room for disagreement. The dramatically reduced rates of pollution emissions can be seen as a clear positive move towards sustainability. The continuing increase in fuel consumption and carbon dioxide production must be seen as a further consumption of non-renewable resources combined with an increasing risk of environmental degradation associated with global warming.

A recent report from the EU (1996) certainly expresses no doubts about such projections. Referring to transport as a whole in the EU it considers that ' . . . on current policies alone, transport trends are unsustainable'. No definition of sustainable is provided. Indeed the document clearly diverts the argument away from problems of definition and targets. Instead it follows the economists' line of argument concerned with externalities and pricing. Transport movements are seen as imposing costs (their list includes congestion, noise pollution, air pollution, and accidents). If consumers are aware of these costs when making decisions about transport then, it is argued, these individual consumers' actions will guide the use of resources devoted to transport in an optimal way. Whilst this approach certainly forces recognition of the immediate consequences of the demand for transport, it may not (depending on what method is used) respond clearly to long-run concerns about non-renewable resources and long run dangers such as global warming.

The Cost of Externalities

The Green Paper estimates the level of current costs associated with the externalities of accidents, noise, air pollution, and climate change due to road freight vehicles at between 32 and 56 billion ECU for EU-15. In the latter figure noise contributes 12BECU, accidents 21BECU and the remainder 23BECU is attributed to air pollution and climate change. It should be emphasized that these figures have a wide margin of uncertainty. The methods that are used to derive them do not have universal support. In addition they may change in the future; in particular the costs attributed to air pollution should fall dramatically as the impact of stricter emission controls emerges.

If users of the road transport network are to be made aware of these external costs the Commission prefers the emphasis to be placed on pricing rather than regulatory measures, though it does concede that a mixture may be the optimal response. Such pricing, or charging, measures could be based on vehicle ownership, vehicle use, fuel consumption or even, as they suggest, a vehicle's propensity to produce emissions.

No detailed breakdown of the figures is given but it is possible to estimate the external costs in the UK at up to 7BECU which is about twice the revenue generated by current vehicle taxation. Note that this estimate of externalities does not include congestion costs, which, for transport as a whole, is estimated to be equal to the sum of accident, noise and air pollution external costs.

If a 'fair and efficient' pricing policy based on these, or similar figures, were to be introduced into Europe this would clearly mean a significant increase in freight transport charges with consequent implications for the structure of supply chains. A complete forecast of future trends in transport costs must also take into account developments in technology, the impact of further deregulation in Europe (including cabotage) and trends in road speeds. Overall it appears likely that the imposition of charges based on external costs (albeit gradually) could see a period of rising transport costs and charges.

It appears therefore that transport costs could rise by 20–25 per cent as a result of EU policy. Based on the price elasticity estimates referred to above this might reduce growth in tonne-km in the longer term by somewhat under 20 per cent, with the main effect falling on a reduction in average haul. One other important effect would include a transfer to other modes. How any increase in charges might impact on the actual rate of growth in tonne-km (or vehicle-km) depends on the phasing of its introduction. With a gradual introduction it might lead to a standstill in the rate of growth for say 5–6 years rather than an average growth of 3–4 per cent as seen in Europe and the UK over the last two decades.

Using the analysis from the second section of this chapter it is possible to speculate that the impact of such an increase in transport cost on the supply chain structure would be the following:

Slowing down or reversal of trends towards
   Focused production
   Pan-European sourcing

Small impact on
   Customer Service
   Just-in-time
   Reverse logistics
   Lean supply chains

No impact on
   Modular products
   Vertical (dis)integration
   Postponement
   Extended organizations

Responsibility

The development of a coherent and systematic strategy towards a sustainable supply chain, and in particular transport along its links, must consider not only the objectives to be pursued and an evaluation of possible policy initiatives, but also the appropriate response and role of different institutions. The scope of institutions in the context of sustainability range from supra-national bodies through the EU, national governments, local governments, private companies down to individuals. As far as the growth in heavy goods vehicles and their emissions is concerned a prime responsibility is taken by the EU. This stems from the Treaty of Rome's requirement for a common transport policy and environmental responsibilities derived from the Single European Act of 1987 and the Maastricht Treaty of 1992. The UK government's approach to transport policy is, therefore, to some extent constrained as a member of the EU, but at the same time it can influence a wide range of measures such as the level of roadbuilding, taxation and legislation concerned with such issues as road charging. Local authorities also have responsibility for land use policy which can influence the location of activities and the consequent demand for transport. Local initiatives can also take place in areas of lorry bans or restrictions on access.

At the corporate level companies are committed to the idea of environmental audits and a related environmental management system. Transport demand does figure in these audits with emphasis on factors such as environmentally friendly vehicles, fuel saving and to a limited extent local sourcing. How far this process can go in limiting the growth in vehicle-kilometres (both car and goods vehicles) is constrained by the need to compete effectively in the market place. Local rather than European wide sourcing, or supply chains with the lowest demand for transport may not be in the long term interests of the company.

Individual responsibility (and its associated cost) is accepted for some environmental issues such as recycling). If we accept that the idea of a sustainable supply chain must address a major source of goods vehicle growth – the increasing average haul – then individuals could contribute by increasing the proportion of locally sourced goods. A major problem is the lack of information provided and the complexity of information that would be needed.

Transport Strategy

In discussing a strategy for the supply chain that responds to the search for sustainable development, the nature and extent of the framework adopted for analysis is critical. One complication is that transport policy must consider the intimate links between passenger and freight transport. Investment decisions for roads must consider the demands of both people and goods. Taxation policies on fuel may not be able to distinguish between different vehicle types, and must therefore impact both passenger and freight movement. Transport policy also encompasses a wide range of possible issues and instruments. These should be co-ordinated and used in a balanced policy response. In its report *Moving Forward: A Business Strategy for Transport*, the CBI (1995) considers there are three essential elements of a coherent strategy for transport. These are a clear investment strategy ('Develops strategic transport links to key domestic and international markets . . . increased public . . . and private sector investment.'), pricing policy('. . . signals to users about the costs of their actions . . .'), and better management of transport ('. . . reducing the transport intensity of economic growth.(and) the environmental impact of transport for any given level of intensity, . . . promoting . . . business best practice'). All of these components can contribute to a balanced and co-ordinated policy. All impinge to some extent on the design and operation of supply chains via the implications of policy for the cost and performance of freight transport.

Even within the framework outlined by the CBI there is still considerable scope or uncertainty about the precise levels of investment desirable, the precise level of 'fair and efficient' prices, and the opportunities offered by technology and better business practice for more efficient use of resources in transport. On balance, it appears, that the cost of freight transport through a combination of road congestion and taxation policies (responding to environmental pressures and arguments about sustainability) may increase in the future relative to other costs in the economies of Western Europe. This would reverse the trend of the last four decades. Just as the decline in cost has affected the design of the supply chain, a reversal would also, in the long run, lead to adjustments in the structure of networks and sourcing.

REFERENCES

Allen, J. (1993) Just-in-Time Transportation and the Environment. Internal Paper, University of Westminster, London.

Black, I. Richards, R., Clark, J. and Peters, M. (1995) Modelling the Links between Economic Activity and Vehicle Kilometres. CCLT Research Report No.1.

CBI, (1995) *Moving Forward: A Business Strategy for Transport.* London: CBI.

Centre for Economics and Business Research, (1994) *Roads and Jobs,* London: CEBR.

Chisholm, M and O'Sullivan, P. (1973) *Freight Flows and Spatial Aspects of the British Economy.*Cambridge: Cambridge University Press.

Cooper, J. Peters, M. and Bence, V. (1995). Supply Chain Dynamics and the Environment – A Study of Six Industry Sectors. CCLT Research Report No. 1. Cranfield University.

Cooper, J. and Griffiths, J. (1994) Managing variety in automotive logistics with the rule of three. *International Journal of Logistics Management,* **5**(2).

Council of Logistics Management (1993) *Reconfiguring European Logistics Systems.* (Prepared by Andersen Consulting and Cranfield School of Management). Oak Brook: CLM.

Department of the Environment (1996) *Indicators of Sustainable Development for the United Kingdom.* London: HMSO.

Department of Transport (1989) *National Road traffic Forecasts.* London: HMSO.

Department of Transport (1994) *National Travel Survey,* 1994. London: HMSO.

EC (1989) *Official Journal of the Economic Community.* C318, Dec 1989, Brussels.

European Union (1966) *Towards Fair and Efficient Pricing in Transport.* Brussels: EU.

Eiselt, H *et al.* (1993) Competitive location models: A framework and bibliography. *Transportation Science,* **27**(1).

Graitson, D. (1982) Spatial competition à la Hotelling: A selective survey. *Journal of Industrial Economics,* **31**, pp. 13–25.

Hill, G. (1994) Assessing the cost of customer service, in Cooper, J (ed.) in *Logistics and Distribution Planning.* London: Kogan Page, chapter 2.

Hudson, R. and Sadler, D. (1992). 'Just-in-Time' production and the European automotive components industry. *International Journal of Physical Distribution and Logistics Management,* **22**(2).

Maister, D.H. (1976) Centralisation of inventories and the square root law. *International Journal of Physical Distribution,* **6** (3).

NEA and Cranfield University (1994) Future Logistics Structures: The Development of Integrated Supply Chain Management across Six Industry Sectors. Centre for Logistics and Transport, Cranfield University.

Sargent, M.H., and Creehan, K.P. (1993) Managing the complexities of product proliferation. *Mercer Management Journal ,* No 1.

Sussams, J. E. (1986) Buffer stocks and the square root law. *Focus on Physical Distribution and Logistics Management,* **5**(5).

Tweddle and Cooper, J.C. (1985) Recent trends in lorry traffic by night. *Traffic Engineering and Control,* January.

Van der Ven, A. H., Emmit, D. C. and Koenig, R. (1975) Frameworks for interorganisa-
tional analysis, in Negandhi, A.R. (ed.) *Interorganizational Theory.* Kent, OH: Kent
State University Press.
Williamson, O.E. (1975) *Markets and Hierarchies.* New York: The Free Press.
World Commission on Environment and Development (1987) Our Common Future (The
Brüntland Report). Oxford: Oxford University Press.

CHAPTER 10

IMPROVING AIR QUALITY: LESSONS FROM CALIFORNIA

Wyn Grant

Urban areas of California, in particular the Los Angeles metropolitan area, have the worst air quality in the United States. From 1992 to 1994 the Southland experienced an average of 103 days a year above the federal standard for ozone, compared with thirteen days in the next most polluted city (Houston) and four in New York. The sunshine which makes California such an attractive place to live also contributes to its high pollution levels. These chronic air pollution levels have led to a series of innovative policies in California designed to improve air quality which have attracted worldwide attention. However, as this chapter shows, these policies have encountered a number of difficulties and have so far made a relatively small contribution to the improvement of air quality.

Air quality has improved substantially in Los Angeles over the last quarter of a century because of vehicle emission controls which have been required on new vehicles in California since 1966 and the closure of many factories that were stationary sources of air pollution. The number of days above the federal health standard for ozone decreased from 208 in 1987 to 98 in 1995. These gains have been achieved despite a substantial increase in population in smog prone areas such as Los Angeles and Sacramento, with vehicle-miles travelled increasing twice as fast as population. In 1995 there were only thirteen ozone episodes in the South Coast Air Quality Management District (SCAQMD, covering metropolitan Los Angeles) compared to twenty-three in 1994, and fifty-nine ozone advisories (lower grade alerts) compared with ninety-six in 1994. The year's highest ozone reading, 0.26 parts per million, was also the lowest recorded in twenty years. If air pollution had remained at 1980 levels, the summer weather in 1995 would have resulted in eighty ozone episodes rather than thirteen. However, largely because of climatic factors, there were fifteen health advisories and two Stage 1 episodes in the first five months of 1996.

Despite some progress, much remains to be done before pollution standards are attained, the deadline having been extended to 2010 for the South Coast in the State Implementation Plan approved by the US Environmental Protection Agency in September 1996. Los Angeles remains the smoggiest region of the nation where ozone health standards are violated on approaching one day in three. On the worst days, ozone levels are two-and-a-half times the federal standard. Recent health studies have suggested that residents suffer adverse health effects when exposed for several hours at levels below the current federal health standard of 0.12 ppm. The US Environmental Protection Agency is expected to propose a new ozone standard at 0.07 to 0.09 ppm averaged over eight hours. Such a standard would have the effect of increasing the number of days the South Coast exceeds the federal ozone standard from about 100 to 120 days a year. Summing up the progress achieved, the Chief Executive Officer of the SCAQMD, James Lents, has commented, 'Our greatest success to date has been wiping out days with very high levels of ozone. We must continue to reduce the high number of days that residents are exposed to unhealthful levels of ozone above the federal standard' (Press statement, 20 October 1995).

There is increasing evidence from a long term study of 3,600 schoolchildren across the state that children who live in smoggy areas are moving into adulthood with an already impaired lung function. Such findings are consistent with an earlier study which examined homicide and accident victims among young adults in Los Angeles. Nearly all the lungs examined had some form of chronic bronchitis and 76 per cent showed some degree of inflammation. 'In addition, about one-third of subjects had some degree of chronic interstitial pneumonia, a form of the disease found deep within lung tissue' (California Air Resources Board, 1991, p.4).

It should be stressed that the air pollution problem is very much seen as a local one with adverse health effects, and with impaired landscape visibility a secondary concern. Typical SCAQMD press releases feature joggers or mountain bikers whose activities are threatened by smoggy conditions. The air pollution debate in California pays little attention to global warming. 'The idea that addressing concerns about global warming might be one of the main objectives of air pollution policy was responded to in [research] interviews with reactions that varied from bafflement to an acknowledgment that the balance of policy concerns might be different in Europe from the United States' (Grant, 1995, p.21). A California Air Resources Board official responded, 'there is not a whole lot that is based on the global climate issue'. An air quality management official in San Francisco commented, 'We all realize that global warming is linked to transportation, but from a formal agency point of view, and in terms of the California Clean Air Act, global warming is not something we work on or deal with'. An environmental lobbyist commented, 'Europe generally has been more aggressive on global warming . . . we have for political reasons and economic reasons simply not been able to really revive the global warming issue in a meaningful fashion.'

Policy measures are therefore addressed primarily to reducing ozone formation and other forms of local air pollution. The central part of this chapter reviews four of the policy measures used in California: encouraging the production and use of electric vehicles; attempts to foster higher levels of occupancy per vehicle; efforts to secure the repair of highly polluting vehicles; and the use of reformulated gasoline. This does not exhaust the range of policy measures used, but it includes those seen as experimental and innovative or those thought likely to have a significant impact on pollution levels.

BATTERIES NOT INCLUDED: THE ELECTRIC VEHICLES PROGRAMME

We would love to sell electric vehicles the same way they sell electric toys –'batteries not included'. (Bob Lutz, President of Chrysler, Sacremento Bee, 7 April 1995)

California has received flattering world wide media coverage for its pioneering zero emission (i.e. electric) vehicle programme. From the 1998 model year, 2 per cent of the vehicles sold in the state by the seven leading manufacturers (the 'Big Three' plus the four main Japanese companies) were supposed to be zero emission vehicles. This would mean an initial level of 20,000 vehicles a year. The zero emission vehicle level would increase to 5 per cent from the 2000 model year, so that by 2010 there would be a fleet of 1.1 million electric vehicles in California. Any manufacturer that failed to meet its target would be subject to a fine of $5,000 a vehicle. An impressive and stringent programme indeed, and one that was bound to be challenged by big oil companies and by Detroit as the crunch time approached.

Thus, at its December 1995 meeting the California Air Resources Board had on its agenda an item to 'modify the zero-emission vehicle program in a market oriented manner consistent with clean air goals'. Translated out of bureaucratic prose, this meant finding a fudge that would satisfy the auto manufacturers while still claiming to be pursuing the original programme goals. The outcome 'is a clear victory for the world's seven biggest motor groups, and California's big oil companies'(*Financial Times*, 20 November 1995). A number of elements contributed to this climbdown, but they may be summarized as a change in the atmosphere of state politics in a less environmentally friendly direction.

In the late 1980s, the political atmosphere in California, particularly in the Democratic controlled legislature, was a favourable one for new environmental initiatives. The landmark California Clean Air Act was passed in 1988 and in 1990 voters passed two measures providing substantial additional funding for rail transport. As California moved into recession, however, a recession deepened by the major downturn in the defence industry after the end of the cold war, voters became less enthusiastic about environmental measures. Evidence of the changing climate of public opinion is provided by the fact that the 1992 rail bond suffered a 2 per cent defeat, and the 1994 rail bond lost by a two to one margin.

In 1994 Kathleen Brown attempted to become the third member of her family to be governor of California. Her disorganized campaign was routed by Governor Pete Wilson who was encouraged to run for President. His campaign eventually ended in failure, but while he was running, he felt obliged to shift his position on electric cars which up until then had been broadly supportive. In April, four Midwestern governors, three of whom had March 1996 primaries, wrote to Wilson telling him that California's commitment to electric vehicles would cost jobs in their state. In an not untypical piece of doublespeak, Wilson said that he remained committed to California's clean air goals, but had become very concerned about the electric vehicles mandate. Wilson, who is an astute politician, then made a clever move. Knowing that the battery technology is the Achilles heel of the electric car, he requested the state Air Resources Board to conduct an audit of the progress made in electric vehicle battery technology. If the audit, as expected, revealed unsolved problems, sound arguments would be available for suspending the programme.

Political support for the programme from a significant source was also weakened. Sensing a significant new market, the electricity utilities had been key industrial supporters of the electric vehicles programme. The four leading utilities sought to raise electric and gas rates (initially by $632 million) to promote the introduction of natural gas and electric cars. Given that electricity rates in California were already 50 per cent above national average, opposition emerged from consumers. Toward Utility Rate Normalization (TURN) organized alongside such diverse organizations as the Congress of California Seniors, the National Manufacturers' Association, and the Congress of Racial Equality in Californians Against Utility Company Abuse. Perhaps the most significant member of this coalition was the powerful Western States Petroleum Association: it was the public relations firm representing the oil companies which initially organized the coalition. All this effort paid off. In a judgment by the state Public Utilities Commission, Judge Steven Weissman struck down proposals for the utilities to pay for the special wiring needed in residences to recharge cars, and reduced the amount the utilities were allowed to spend on their vehicle programmes to $166.6 million.

With the utilities to some extent neutralized, the auto manufacturers started to marshall their forces. When research interviews were being carried out in 1993, the auto companies only occasionally turned up in Sacramento for special hearings on electric vehicles. The running on the issue was left to the oil companies, long term economic and political players in California and, unlike the auto companies, major contributors to state election campaigns. While the oil companies engaged in 'Astroturf' lobbying (creating artificial grass roots organizations), the car companies exerted influence behind the scenes, making some use of dealer networks when they wanted to mobilize in legislators' districts.

By the autumn of 1995, the auto manufacturers were approaching a crucial few months. They would have to start installing production capacity if they were to meet a 2 per cent target in 1998. An official at the American Automobile Manufacturers' Association commented, 'We are getting towards crunch time' (*Financial Times*, October 1995). The automobile manufacturers started a radio advertising campaign to state their case and made sure they were effectively represented at any CARB hearings. The panel convened by the ARB to conduct the review of battery technology, which had been set up in August with four individuals with a research science background as members, was seen as pivotal.

The reason why it was pivotal needs careful examination for both political and substantive reasons. There are four main arguments that have been advanced against the electric car programme: the emission gains are less impressive when one takes account of the effects of electricity generation; manufacturers do not want to make them; consumers do not want to buy them; and the technology is not ready. The first argument does not really hold up, unless one makes the unrealistic assumption that electricity is generated by coal fired stations. Even critics of electric cars state 'When total emissions from EVs (power generation included) are compared to total emissions from gasoline-powered cars, EVs look good. On a per-vehicle basis the reductions in individual pollutants are substantial, ranging from 75 per cent to 99 per cent depending on the scenario and assumptions' (Gordon and Richardson, 1995, p.15).

The argument that manufacturers do not want to make them is significant only in the political sense that the auto companies are a powerful lobby: it is not a policy argument against electric cars. The arguments about consumer reaction are of greater concern from a policy perspective and cannot be fully rehearsed here (see Grant 1995 for an extended discussion). The main limitations of an electric vehicle from a consumer perspective are that they have a limited range; they are dependent on a charging infrastructure which does not yet exist; and, although much improved, they have some inferior performance characteristics. The range issue is a significant one, because in practice many journeys, even many commuting trips, are relatively short, 'Drivers place great value on being able to accommodate their expected *maximum* use rather than a high probability of meeting their *average* use' (Gordon and Richardson, 1995, p.9).

Consumers would be faced with paying more for a vehicle that offers less. For example, Ford plans to sell an electricity powered Ranger pick-up truck with a range of 58 miles for urban driving, which will cost $30,000 compared with the normal price of around $10,000. General Motors is launching its EV1 in 1996 at a cost of around $35,000. The range is 70 to 90 miles before recharging for three hours. Forty per cent of the weight in the two seater vehicle is accounted for by the lead acid batteries. Another drawback is that the lead acid battery has an average life cycle of 15,000 to 20,000 miles and would need replacing every two years at an approximate cost of $1,500. In order to encourage purchases, the

SCAQMD decided to offer $5,000 discounts to the first 1,200 purchasers of electric vehicles in the Los Angeles basin.

Electric car advocates accept that in practice many initial sales would be fleet sales, for example to state and local government and utility companies. It is envisaged that sales to private individuals would principally be as a second (or, in California, third or fourth) vehicle that would be used mainly for local shopping and recreational trips. There are enough ecologically minded wealthy Californians around to buy such vehicles as a novelty item. The problem is that if concern about vehicle range limited their use, their contribution to emission reductions would be correspondingly less.

Against this background, it is not surprising that the California Air Resources Board (CARB) hearings in 1995 produced estimates of sales in 1998 that varied from 3,500 to 98,000 vehicles. Toyota estimated sales at 5,800 and General Motors forecast 3,500, increasing to 10,000 with additional incentives and infrastructure, i.e. 10,000 below the state target. A research group at the University of California, Davis, has produced more optimistic estimates based on a survey of California households which suggests that there is a viable near-time market for electric cars. They told the CARB hearings that consumer demand for electric vehicles was at least 7 per cent of the annual market and would increase to 15 per cent if mid-size models with longer range were available (*Sacramento Bee*, 29 June 1995). The difficulty with survey evidence is that it is based on stated intentions which may not accurately predict purchase decisions. Studies of buyers' actual behaviour suggests a preference for high performance vehicles (Gordon and Richardson, 1995, p.6).

The really crucial problem is, however, whether sufficient advances have been made in battery technology to produce commercially viable electric cars in significant numbers. This is a complex technical issue which will have to be treated here in a summary fashion. One point that has to be emphasized is that there is a big difference between developing a new battery technology in laboratory conditions or placing it in a prototype vehicle, and actually putting it into commercial production. A significant and time consuming intermediate stage is constructing the plant to construct a few hundred batteries which can then be used in a pilot vehicle programme on the road. It is important in particular to satisfy safety requirements and it is noticeable that as the electric vehicle deadline in California has approached, chiefs of fire departments have expressed their concern that what would happen to electric vehicles involved in road traffic accidents should be fully considered in their appraisal.

Lead acid batteries are the principal available option for volume production of electric vehicles in 1998. Lead acid batteries are heavy and bulky and in a two seater vehicle offer a range at best of 100 miles which would be significantly reduced in unfavourable weather conditions. A lead acid battery model is thus unlikely to meet what is regarded as the minimum acceptable standard of a 100 mile range in an urban/suburban duties cycle. The other immediately available option is a nickel cadmium battery which offers a longer range and faster recharging than lead acid. However, they are more expensive to produce than lead acid. Thus, both the batteries currently available have serious performance limitations.

More advanced batteries are likely to be available in the medium to long term, although it is unlikely that even in ten years time there will be a system available which will meet the United States Advanced Battery Consortium goal of giving a car a range of 200 to 250 miles between recharging. These advanced batteries would be more expensive than a lead acid battery system, but this additional cost would be offset by a longer life cycle.

The established battery makers have focused on lithium-ion and nickel metal hydride batteries because they are in principle similar to existing systems. However, each of these systems requires progress in the area of finding substitutes for costly materials which are essential to their successful performance, e.g. cobalt oxide in the case of lithium-ion. Less conventional high temperature systems, zebra (sodium nickel chloride) and sodium sulphur have attracted developers from outside the battery industry, but these systems are probably five years away from being available commercially. If left standing for a month these high temperature batteries would freeze up and the materials would have to be renewed. They also raise safety issues.

The evidence collected by the independent expert panel suggested that serviceable, high performance batteries would not be available until 2001 at the earliest. These findings were welcomed by the auto companies, Frank Schewibold of General Motors commenting that the panel 'have done us all a favour' (*Financial Times*, 13 October 1995). However, one should not imagine that all that was involved was the dispassionate assessment of the relevant scientific evidence. There was also a major political battle involved. Dan Walters, one of the state's most experienced political commentators, noted, 'The stakes – socially, environmentally, politically and financially – are almost incalculably huge, and the political/public relations war is growing more intense by the minute'(*Sacremento Bee*, 19 October 1995).

Within CARB, staff members were concerned that starting the programme with a technology similar to that of ordinary car batteries might damage the longer term acceptability of electric vehicles:

> I think the staff came away from this discussion concerned that it's important that the first vehicles that are put out by the big manufacturers are good ones. In other words, you don't want to have a situation where you introduce vehicles into the market which don't do what they're purported to do and, therefore, turn off the consumer market. (Transcript of CARB hearing, Sacramento, 26 October 1995)

The chairman of CARB commented, 'A vehicle without a buyer does nothing to meet air-quality goals' (*Sacramento Bee*, 22 December 1995). It was therefore no surprise when California suspended its programme in December 1995, also affecting the adoption of similar regulations in other states. It was agreed that the mandate would be suspended until 2003 while manufacturers built a small demonstration fleet of 3,750 vehicles to test the technology and consumer reactions to it. These cars would be demonstration vehicles sold to utilities as part of a pilot programme to test the technology.

Observers of the California political scene would not find it surprising that the auto manufacturers and oil industry largely succeeded in their objectives, particularly against the background of a voting public which was giving less priority to environmental issues. The electric vehicles programme was an innovative one, but it ran ahead of the development of the technology and consumer demand. Even when better technology is available, subsidies will probably be necessary to persuade consumers to buy the vehicles. The electric vehicle programme therefore had to abandon its stated objectives. However, it did act as a catalyst for the development of battery and electric vehicle technology. As one expert commented, 'I've been in batteries for a long time and I've never seen the rate of progress before that I've seen in the last five years' (Transcript of CARB hearings, Sacramento, 26 October 1995).

FROM REGULATION XV TO RULE 2202

Seagriff notes how, against the background of the recession which enhanced business concern about the cost of complying with air quality rules, SCAQMD's approach altered considerably in the 1990s. 'The 1991 Plan was very much one of 'command and control' the 1994 Plan is much more considerate to local economic needs.' (Seagriff, 1995, p.160).

This trend is exemplified by the fate of Regulation XV. This regulation was an attempt to increase average vehicle ridership in Los Angeles. The measure was a process rather than performance based measure. Employers with more than 100 employees at any place of work were required to submit plans for reducing vehicle emissions through trip reduction programmes every two years, with information on progress being submitted in the intervening year.

One of the drawbacks of this approach was that it was administratively costly with over forty staff at the SCAQMD being employed on work relating to the regulation:

> What we found we need[ed] was a lot of data collection capability to cover 5,500 work sites in the air basin, at one time it was 6,200 before the economy had a recession. That's an awful lot of file space, an awful lot of people opening envelopes and trying to track dates, and they have to be reviewed each year. (Interview, SCAQMD, 1 April 1993)

As one might expect with such a regulation, there have also been problems with the definition of key terms such as work site and employee. A work site is defined as a site that is under the control of an employer that is not separated by more than one public thoroughfare. There have been problems with construction sites and whether they are under the control of the contractor or the various subcontractors. Temporary employees have also caused problems:

> Employers say, wait a minute, if they work for a temporary service company, we have no control or responsibility, and the temporary agency people say we've got three people at this place, and two over here, and another half a dozen out there, I can't get them together in a ride sharing program. (Interview, SCAMD, 1 April 1993).

In a context where federal tax law encourages employers to provide free parking, it is not surprising that this rather bureaucratic regulation had little impact on ride sharing levels. The goal was to achieve 1.5 persons per vehicle at designated work sites, but between 1987 and 1995, the actual increase was from 1.13 to 1.28, representing less than half the stated goal. Moreover, the programme focused on the commuting trip, but the long-term trend is for work trips to decline as a proportion of all trips. The freeways in Los Angeles are congested throughout the day and 'non-work trips are the most rapidly increasing component of peak hour traffic'. (Guiliano and Wachs, 1992, p.13).

In 1995 state legislation was passed (SB 437, Lewis) which released employers from the requirement to submit ridesharing plans. Lewis is a conservative Republican from Orange County and his measure was sponsored by a coalition of large retail stores who had found the ride sharing regulation particularly onerous. Following this change in state law, Regulation XV was replaced in December 1995 (by a nine to three vote on the SCAQMD board) by a more flexible and less costly alternative, Rule 2202, On-road Motor Vehicle Mitigation Options. Businesses will still be required to meet annual emissions targets based on their number of employees in order to avoid sanctions under the federal Clean Air Act. However, instead of submitting a lengthy ridesharing plan every two years, companies will be able to send in a one-page registration form outlining their chosen vehicle emission reduction option. They could, for example, scrap pre-1981 vehicles; use remote sensing devices to identify and repair highly polluting vehicles; or convert on or off road vehicles to alternative fuels. Alternatively, emission reduction credits earned when, for example, a plant is shut down could also be used to meet the employer requirement.

As Marvin Braude, an SCAQMD board member admitted, their approach to the problem had failed:

> We tried to push the state of the art with this strategy and we failed. Now we need a new approach. What government was really doing was asking industry to impose changes on people's lifestyle and behavior. That was something that government itself was unwilling to do. (Sacremento Bee, 20 November 1994)

THE GROSS EMITTER PROBLEM

It has been estimated that some 50 per cent of vehicle emissions in California come from around 10 per cent of the total vehicle fleet. These are either very old vehicles or newer vehicles that have developed faults or been tampered with by their owners in an effort to improve performance. The implication of this finding is that by targeting a minority of vehicles through enforced repairs or voluntary scrapping programmes it would be possible to make a significant impact on air pollution levels.

Motorists in California have been required to take their cars once every two years for a 'smog check' carried out by facilities trading under names such as the 'Smog Wizard'. It has been suggested that some of these facilities do not have enough trained staff, and that the equipment does not permit sufficiently stringent tests. There have also been allegations of fraud. The federal Environmental Protection Agency sought to impose on California a new system whereby motorists would have to take their cars to centralized state run testing stations. This led to an intense political battle which is fully described in Grant (1995). Eventually, the White House became involved as it is always sensitive to any issue which might offend California's crucial voters. A compromise was arrived at which does, however, open up new possibilities in the area of coping with the gross emitter problem.

Progress has also been made possible by new remote sensing technology which was developed in the late 1980s. Remote sensing is a technique for instantaneously measuring emissions from vehicles' tailpipes as vehicles drive by. Each machine used for this purpose costs around $150,000. A 6 inch diameter infrared beam is projected horizontally across a single lane of traffic – a popular location for doing this is at a single lane freeway ramp, or on a surface road where traffic can be narrowed to a single lane. As vehicles drive by, the beam passes through the tailpipe exhaust, which absorbs some of the infrared light. A sensor and computer translate this into an emissions level. The pollutants measured are carbon monoxide, carbon dioxide and hydrocarbons; some units also measure nitrogen oxide emissions. At the same time, an electronic licence plate reader uses a video camera and computer automatically to record the vehicle licence plate. The equipment offers an accuracy of plus or minus 5 per cent for carbon monoxide and plus or minus 15 per cent for hydrocarbons. However, if a vehicle's engine is cold or if the vehicle is accelerating, emissions may be considerably higher than if the vehicle is cruising at a steady speed. There is also some evidence that the equipment may not work well under wet conditions when there is splashback from the road surface.

Remote sensing is seen to be particularly important as a potential contributor to reducing vehicle emissions in Sacramento which is afflicted by smog but has little scope for reductions in air pollution from stationary sources. In the summer of 1995 remote sensing devices were placed on freeway ramps and streets to check passing cars. It is estimated that almost all of the 800,000 vehicles registered in Sacramento County were checked in this way. To double check the information obtained, 6,000 names were extracted from Department of Motor Vehicles records and the owners had to take their vehicles to a test station under threat of a $250 penalty. The results from both sets of tests will be used to profile the make, model and year of the 15 per cent of cars that emit the greatest levels of pollution. Owners of vehicles that match the profile will have to go to a state certified test only station to obtain a smog certificate. Owners whose vehicles fail the test must have repairs done elsewhere and then return to the state certified stations for a further test before the Department of Motor Vehicles will renew their registration. After its initial application in Sacramento in 1995, the programme was extended in 1996 to the Los Angeles basin, along with other areas that violate federal air quality standards such as Fresno, San Diego and Ventura county.

On the south coast a pilot study was carried out at two sites in Orange County in May 1995 with 39,000 vehicles checked. Up to 8 per cent of vehicles measured were found to be high polluters with tailpipe emissions far exceeding state air quality standards. Checks revealed that up to 28 per cent of vehicles had been tampered with, resulting in high emissions. A quarter of the 600 motorists stopped agreed to turn over their vehicles on the spot for repair and emissions testing (they were provided with rental cars while their vehicles were being fixed). The cost of repairs ranged from $42 for a simple inspection to $2,800 to replace an entire engine, with an average cost of $630. Motorists who were pulled over but chose not to leave their vehicles for repair had much higher tamper rates. Highlighting one of the problems facing the air pollution programme, SCAQMD chief executive James Lents commented, 'Unfortunately, some people still believe the myth that cars will run better if emissions controls are disconnected' (SCAQMD press release, 20 December 1995).

With new technology and new enforcement mechanisms, tackling the gross emitter problem is one way of seeking to reduce emissions of smog precursors. However, such an approach is not without its limitations. Indeed, in some ways its principal limitation is that it is the kind of 'quick fix' or 'silver bullet' which is attractive to decision makers seeking speedy and relatively costless solutions to intractable problems. If air pollution is caused to a significant extent by gross emitters, it ceases to be everyone's problem and becomes the other guy's problem – the one driving that old clunker or the high performance vehicle with out of state plates that has had its emission system tampered with. No painful choices about lifestyle are therefore necessary.

The implementation of measures to tackle the gross emitter problem also poses difficulties. Calling in those cars that are thought most likely to be gross emitters makes sense until one recalls that many cars are unregistered (as many as 20 per cent, according to one interview respondent) and those that are not registered may be among those which are the most polluting because they have not been properly maintained. Scrapping programmes which pay bounties for old vehicles is another policy option which is increasingly used. However, they face the 'additionality' problem familiar to public policy makers in a number of contexts: one may be paying people to do what they would have done anyway.

The bounties paid are insufficient to pay for a replacement vehicle: $600 is a typical figure. Drivers of old cars tend to be the poorest sections of population who may have difficulty getting to work without their own vehicle.

It is worth noting that the nearly 100-page booklet issued to drivers in California makes hardly any mention of driving practices or maintenance failures which might contribute to higher levels of air pollution. Indeed, the opening message from the governor emphasizes the importance of mobility to the California lifestyle. Chronic traffic congestion is identified as 'the California commuter's biggest headache' (Department of Motor Vehicles, 1995, p.61). Commuters are urged not to eat, groom in the rearview mirror or read newspapers while driving as such behaviour can contribute to congestion. There is just a very brief mention of engine tune up as a practice that can help to reduce emissions that pollute the air. This omission is not accidental: it reflects the centrality of the car in American culture and its link with notions of freedom (note the importance of the 'road movie' in American cinema). Americans do want cleaner air, but land use patterns and deeply ingrained cultural preferences make it difficult to achieve.

REFORMULATED GASOLINE

Since June 1996 all gasoline sold in California has had to meet CARB's cleaner burning requirements. It is estimated that cleaner-burning gasoline, known officially as California Reformulated Gasoline, will reduce smog-forming emissions from motor vehicles by around 15 per cent. This is the equivalent of taking 3.5 million vehicles off the roads or drivers leaving their car at home for one day a week. 'A major strength of reformulated gasoline as a means to alleviating mobile source emissions is that it can be produced, distributed and marketed in a cost-effective manner. Because it can be used in currently available vehicles and distributed through the existing gasoline distribution system, the effects of its use will be immediate' (Gordon and Richardson, 1995, p.17). It should be noted, however, that the impact will be on evaporative and exhaust emissions of volatile organic compounds, nitrogen oxides, carbon monoxide and sulphur dioxide. 'Since any form of gasoline contains about the same amount of carbon as any other, changing the formula of gasoline would not lessen the greenhouse effect in any way' (Nadis and MacKenzie, 1993, p.63). Its effect on smog forming emissions may be reduced by the increase in the speed limit from 55 to 65 miles per hour.

Prior to the introduction of reformulated gasoline, oxygenated gasoline was already widely used in the state. 'The extra dose of oxygen makes combustion more complete, thus reducing emissions of carbon monoxide and unburned hydrocarbons' (Nadis and MacKenzie, 1993, p.62). Reformulated gasoline does offer 1 per cent less average gas-mileage than oxygenated gasoline and 3 per cent less than non-oxygenated gasoline. Production costs are between 5 and 15 cents more a gallon compared to conventional gasoline, so motorists can expect to pay an extra dime a gallon. Nevertheless, reformulated gasoline provides one of the least costly remaining ways of achieving substantial emission reductions. Road tests show that it presents few performance problems, except perhaps for the fuel systems of some older, high mileage vehicles. Motorists thus go on driving the same vehicles which they fuel at the same locations and which offer them similar performance characteristics. There are thus none of the problems that would arise with electric vehicles. Nevertheless, there was clearly some concern about consumer resistance. When reformulated gasoline was first introduced at six gas stations in Sacramento, their location was kept secret to avoid 'drivers looking for problems'(*Sacramento Bee*, 12 March 1995).

Tackling the gross emitter problem and introducing reformulated gasoline should bring about further reductions in air pollution, but these measures by themselves are unlikely to enable federal or state air quality standards to be met. Even these gains are threatened by a continuing increase in state population which is matched by a larger increase in registered vehicles and an even greater increase in vehicle-miles travelled. Sprawling land use patterns, the location and design of shopping and recreational facilities, and prevalent values all encourage a high level of dependence on cars. Considerable funding has been put into light rail and subway systems, but negative attitudes towards public transport remain, while the relative unimportance of journeys into a central business district limits the impact of investment in new rail systems. Ninety-five per cent of all trips are still by car and investments in public transport have not been very cost effective, particularly as many light rail users have transferred from bus services (for a fuller discussion, see Grant 1995; Seagriff, 1995).

CONCLUSION: A WARNING

California's high profile zero emission vehicles programme has had to be curtailed in the face of political opposition from the oil and auto industries; a weakening of political support at the state level; and problems with technological feasibility and consumer resistance. The ride sharing programme was characterized by a rather inflexible command and control approach and new state legislation has forced the programme to be abandoned in its original form. These policy failures have led to a new emphasis on what can be achieved by gross emitter programmes and the introduction of reformulated gasoline.

Comparative public policy research usually reveals that policy advances which have been trumpeted in the media are less effective than is claimed. The real problems arise not when a policy is devised and formulated, when political resistance may be weak because its operational effects are some years away, but when the time for implementation arises. This certainly applies to the zero emission vehicles programme in California. That does not mean, however, that there is no value in examining the Californian experience. There is a good scientific understanding of the causes and mechanisms of air pollution, and increasing knowledge about its effects on health as well as the processes of global warming. 'Scientific understanding is weakest regarding effective strategies to improve air quality' (Kirlin, 1990, p.163). It is in this area that social science research has a contribution to make.

Practical lessons to be drawn from Californian experience are that effective electric vehicles at a competitive price are some way off. Obligatory ride sharing programmes are difficult to enforce. The gross emitter problem is also found in Britain, and this is one possible area of action for the new Air Quality Management Areas (Department of the Environment, 1995, pp. 18-19). Given that these Air Quality Management Areas may be formed by groups of authorities, there is a direct institutional analogy with the Californian model. They could benefit from Californian experience with remote sensing techniques, even though the climatic conditions in which they are applied are rather different. The potential of reformulated gasoline should also be seriously considered.

However, it has to be recognized that many of these measures are palliatives rather than solutions. Some of the most draconian restrictions on car use have been imposed in Singapore which has a relatively authoritarian governing regime. In circumstances where the car plays a central part in the working and recreational lives of the majority of the population, it is difficult to introduce effective curbs on its use in a democracy. Even on the Isles of Scilly off the south-west coast of Cornwall, where there are only 9 miles of public road on the main island, parking, traffic management and speeding is becoming a problem which has provoked much public debate but little in the way of effective solutions (*The Scillonian*, various issues).

Use of the price mechanism in terms of both petrol prices and road charges is one area where the debate is at a more advanced stage in Britain than in California where gas prices are low and congestion charging schemes are very controversial. The fundamental problem remains one of attitudes and behaviour: our own attitudes and behaviour from which the writer is not exempt (who when driving in central London recently in congested conditions noted a sign stating that he was in an air quality monitoring zone). In making a choice between transport modes, one faces a collective action problem in which the conditions of use are relatively fixed and one's own decision not to drive may lead to considerable personal inconvenience without having any perceptible effect on levels of air pollution. 'Economic instruments . . . will influence those attitudes. However, there needs to be a more deep-rooted cultural change in the way people view car speed and performance' (Royal Commission on Environmental Pollution, 1994, p.144). Public policy measures can help to structure the context within which individual economic actors make their decision about using different transport modes, but governments cannot – and should not– shape lifestyles.

REFERENCES

California Air Resources Board (1991) *Facts about Air Pollution and Health.* Sacramento: Air Resources Board Public Information Office.

Department of the Environment (1995) *Air Quality: Meeting the Challenge.* London: Department of the Environment.

Department of Motor Vehicles (1995) *1995 California Driver Handbook.* Sacramento: State of California.

Gordon, P, and Richardson, H.W. (1995) *The Case Against Electric Vehicle Mandates in California.* Los Angeles: Reason Foundation.

Grant, W. (1995) *Autos, Smog and Pollution Control: The Politics of Air Quality Management in California.* Aldershot: Edward Elgar.

Guiliano, G. and Wachs, M. (1992) A Comparative Analysis of Regulatory and Market-based Transportation Demand Strategies. School of Urban and Regional Planning, University of Southern California.

Kirlin, J.J. (1990) Command or incentives to improve air quality, in Kirlin, J.J. and Winkler, D.R. (eds.) *California Policy Choices*, Vol 6. Los Angeles: University of Southern California.

Nadis and Mackenzie (1993) *Car Trouble.* Boston: Beacon Press.

Royal Commission on Environmental Pollution (1994) *Transport and the Environment.* London: HMSO.

Seagriff, E. (1995) Southern Californian air quality plants in the 1990s and the effects on transport policy. *Transport Reviews*, **15**(2), pp. 141–165.

PART 3: *Local Aspects*

The final part of the book examines more particular issues and methods at the local scale and reports on innovative data capture methods and some disturbing empirical findings. Peter Headicar and Carey Curtis have carried out a detailed survey on new patterns of travel resulting from new housing development. In their study of five contrasting locations in Oxfordshire, they conclude that local planning authorities can exert a major influence on the amount of car based travel. The average figure of 27 miles travelled per adult each weekday varies by location (± 15 to 20 per cent). This variation is not affected by accessibility or by socioeconomic attributes. They conclude the income differences between the new housing locations are not the primary source of the variations in work related car travel between the five locations. These results are disturbing as the amount of car based travel has not been seen as a factor in decisions on housing location. Variation in travel has traditionally been based on the variation in household characteristics, principally income. With the current debate over where 4.4 million new homes should be located in England (to 2016), the importance on travel patterns must be raised if sustainable mobility objectives are to be strengthened.

It is not just in the Shire counties that these questions are being raised. Andy Gillespie and his colleagues have strongly criticized standard predictive modelling philosophy, saying that it is inappropriate for an understanding of contemporary change in cities. They develop a more qualitative understanding through interviews with the relevant actors – the 'supply' institutions, the developers and managers of the city, and people. The researchers have explored the fragmentation of the city (Newcastle) and the conurbation (Tyneside) through the ending of the integrated planning and transport supply regime; they have examined the spatial restructuring of the conurbation; and they have investigated the polarization and segmentation of society through their patterns of movement and mobility. Even though travel is becoming more dispersed and trip lengths are increasing, Tyneside has been able to live with and accommodate the car. The conurbation has not been turned inside out or forced towards car dependence. Brownfield sites within the city have been redeveloped as part of the inner city regeneration and the density and scale of metropolitan Tyneside conforms to the sustainable city ideal. The question here is whether these findings are unique or can be replicated in other cities.

One key determinant to change at all levels is the link between attitudes and behaviour. Margaret Anderson and her team have developed an innovative survey instrument, the Green Journey Guide. Respondents in Ashford (Kent) have been confronted, challenged and convinced (?) about the importance of limiting car use. The experimental methodology which mixes quantitative and qualitative responses in a participation exercise has been contrasted with more traditional questionnaire surveys. Response rates and understanding seem to have been enhanced through the two way communication and interaction. Behaviour does change over time, and it is influenced by external sources of information, by greater understanding and by positive and negative inducements (local encouragement and national discouragement). However, the dependence on the car is very strong, and together with its symbolism, it makes real change in behaviour problematical. Nevertheless, by highlighting the costs of using the cars and the benefits provided by the car, together with the alternative choices that could be made, some progress on the breaking down of barriers has been made.

Questions are also raised about the economic basis of consumer preferences. Robert Sugden uses a range of contingent valuation methods to express preferences about particular choices. Survey bias can be controlled, but there is increasing evidence that some of the underlying economic theories are limited. Through a series of carefully controlled experiments, it is demonstrated that willingness to pay and willingness to accept are not symmetrical, that there are part-whole inconsistencies and that reported valuations are very sensitive to the elicitation method used. So even if we have good survey methods and we ask the right questions, there are limitations to the analysis methods used. It is suggested that reference dependent preferences should be used and that there is an emerging convergence between methods based in economics and those based in psychology.

This questioning of standard transport analysis methodology and the acceptance of the limitations of economic analysis is refreshing. The final chapter from John Henneberry and his colleagues argues for closer links between transport planning and local land use planning. The Sheffield 'Supertram' has been justified on the basis of the substantial non-user benefits that arise from a major transport investment. These benefits include accessibility benefits to road users, economic benefits through regeneration, greater flexibility in local labour market conditions, changes in land and property prices, and positive benefits from the enhanced image of the city. These non-user benefits are very difficult to measure and quantify, as new time based methodologies are required. Their scale is often small with complexity in the range of actions, and there are also questions over whether the benefits are really generated or merely redistributed. These benefits are becoming an increasingly important component of evaluation as the conventional time savings used in transport analysis are limited in congested urban networks.

Throughout this book established methods and conventional wisdom have been questioned. This is refreshing and reflects the new seriousness with which the environmental debate in transport is now being addressed. It is no longer acceptable to say that we will stick with traditional methods. Nor is it acceptable to say that it is too difficult to include environmental factors in transport analysis. This book has demonstrated new ways of thinking and it has made steps (even strides) forward in developing and testing appropriate methods. In these ways the research reported here has made a substantial contribution to both asking the difficult questions on transport and the environment, and in giving answers to those questions.

CHAPTER 11

THE LOCATION OF NEW RESIDENTIAL DEVELOPMENT: ITS INFLUENCE ON CAR-BASED TRAVEL

Peter Headicar and Carey Curtis

The Environment White Paper of 1990 signalled renewed interest by the government in the relationship between land use and transport planning (Department of the Environment, 1990). With increasing public concern at the environmental implications of long-term traffic growth the government was looking to land use planning as one of the means by which the projected growth might be contained. Research was commissioned to review available evidence in this field (Departments of the Environment and Transport, 1993). On the basis of this revised planning policy guidance concerning transport (PPG 13) was published in 1994, followed by a 'Guide to Better Practice' a year later (Departments of the Environment and Transport, 1994 and 1995).

We begin by reviewing briefly the research context for this policy initiative. We then report on our research which was carried out in 1993–94. This focuses solely on new residential development and utilizes the results of specially designed surveys to identify the significance for car-based travel of the location of major new housing areas. We explain the objectives and methods of the research, present its findings and consider possible explanations for the variations in travel behaviour identified by location. Finally we report our conclusions and comment on their implications for planning policy.

BACKGROUND: RESEARCH EVIDENCE AND GOVERNMENT POLICY

The government's desire to reduce the need to travel and to issue guidance to planning authorities on how this may be achieved has to contend with the lack of clear evidence as to the efficiency of different urban forms and settlement patterns. Available evidence has been reviewed, notably by ECOTEC

(Departments of the Environment and Transport, 1993), Banister (1995) and Breheny (1995) and each of these authors has added their own original work and offered overall conclusions. The subject is complex in itself and is further complicated by the fact that ultimately transport is only one of several factors contributing to the sustainability or otherwise of different urban forms (Owens, 1991).

Taking the full range of possibilities concerning the size and density of individual settlements there is clear evidence from National Travel Survey data in Great Britain that the volume of travel and the proportion by car decreases with population density, although the absolute number of trips is remarkably constant. The proportion of trips by car also decreases with settlement size, but the beneficial effects of this are offset by the greater trip lengths associated with the largest cities. This seems to be the main reason why the shift in population out of the main urbanized areas which has characterized the last three decades of itself has contributed surprisingly little additional car travel (Breheny, 1995).

The practical value of these conclusions is however offset by two factors:

1. The extremes of settlement size and density which are present in the existing settlement pattern are not serious policy options for future planning – nobody is suggesting recreating anything like the existing conurbations on the one hand or the myriad of dispersed rural settlements on the other.

2. Within the range that *is* practicable there is very much less variation. For example urban areas within a range from less than 25,000 to over 100,000 only vary by about 10 per cent from the all area average of 100 miles per person per week and the proportion by car only the odd percentage point from the all area average of 71 per cent (ECOTEC, based on 1986 NTS data). Similar observations apply to density.

For practical planning purposes it is *increments* to the existing settlement pattern which is the salient issue. ECOTEC carried out a number of simulations of alternative development patterns. They concluded that:

> concentrated, relatively centralized development options are likely to be more efficient from an emissions perspective than lower density, decentralized more peripheral patterns of development. However there is a clear indication, taking the simulations as a group, that the potential benefits are dampened and could in practice be outweighed by the rerouting and reduced vehicle operating efficiencies resulting from the increased congestion associated with the former types of option.

The proviso is very important given the increasing pervasiveness of congestion which may be expected in future years. It also highlights a more general observation (noted in the work of Banister et al 1994) that relationships which may be observed between urban characteristics and travel at the aggregate level do not necessarily apply in the case of individual towns. Not only will the physical configuration of particular towns be significant (e.g. the relationship between land uses and between built development, transport routes and internal open space) but also the capacity of the inherited road system and – increasingly important – the policies adopted by local authorities to the management of the available road and parking space.

Whilst broad principles governing the planning of development can therefore be deduced, there remains considerable uncertainty (or interpreted another way, policy discretion) as to the application of these principles in particular urbanized regions. The guidance issued by the Government – although important in signalling a change of principle – is only able to indicate a number of broad tenets. These include channelling the majority of new development to or within larger urban areas, to locating major generators of travel demand in existing centres, and in siting development where it is accessible by means other than the private car. The latter is consistent with the Government's overall objective of providing travel *choice* and in reducing the *need* to travel (by car) – not necessarily synonymous with reducing travel itself. The importance of this distinction is returned to at the end of this chapter.

PROJECT OBJECTIVES AND RESEARCH DESIGN

The source of our project was the perceived mismatch between most research (which has studied urban form or settlement patterns as a whole) and the areas of influence available to local planning authorities (which centre on the increments of development or redevelopment likely to occur over a 15 year time horizon). At a strategic level the 'choice' which these authorities have is in the spatial distribution of these increments – their number, size and relationship to existing areas of development and transport routes.

Notwithstanding the research and guidance which has been published to date there remains a dearth of evidence for generating options and making choices about these increments. Does it make a difference where new development is located, in terms of the amount of car-based travel likely to result, and if so, by how much? Planning authorities are weighing up options in relation to a wide variety of objectives, as well as accommodating local political pressures. However strong their support in principle for lessening car-based travel, unless clear evidence is available as to why one particular spatial pattern should be preferred to another it is unlikely that the issue will sway the choices made.

In focusing our project on new development we also concentrated on one of the major land uses, viz housing. The identification of land for housing development is arguably the most important single element in the preparation of development plans, not simply because of the amount of land needed but because the requirement for housing is the only one which is specified by Central Government in its Regional Planning Guidance and which authorities are obliged to try and meet.

The allocation of land for new housing is especially important in South-East

England where the scale of the requirement is greatest and where existing development is already most extensive. Current projections anticipate an increase of over 1.4 million households in London and the South-East over the period form 1991 to 2011. The recent upward revision of these projections has however increased the significance of land for new housing as a national issue (Department of the Environment, 1995; Hall and Breheny, 1996).

New housing areas are not only very specific in their location, they also tend to attract particular sections of the population and thus have distinctive travel-generating characteristics. In order to accommodate both issues it was considered essential to undertake primary research in a sample of such areas. We drew our sample from the area around Oxford – Oxford being a freestanding city of about 110,000 population and a sub-regional centre in the fast-growing outer part of South-East England, some 60 miles west of London.

We selected five major housing estates which had recently been developed and which provided examples of the sorts of locational options typically available to planning authorities. They differ in their relationship to the core city (Oxford) and to major transport routes serving the area and linking it with the regional and national centre (London). The five locations (shown in figure 11.1) are:

1. Periphery of built-up area of city (Botley);
2. Dormitory settlement close to city (Kidlington);
3–5. Freestanding towns approximately 10–15 miles from the city served by:
    national motorway (Bicester)
    InterCity rail service(Didcot)
    neither of these (Witney)

Except for Botley (which is in effect a suburban neighbourhood of Oxford with a population of 4,100) all the other estates lie within settlements of between 14,000 and 20,000. Bicester, Didcot and Witney are three of four so-called 'country towns' designated by Oxfordshire County Council as places where the bulk of new housing is being concentrated. By contrast most open land within a ring approximately five miles around Oxford has been designated as Green Belt where there is a strong presumption against new development. Although the estates at Botley and Kidlington have been completed in recent years they therefore represent locational types which are unlikely to be replicated within the existing County Council strategy (Oxfordshire County Council, 1996).

The basic principle governing the research design was to select estates and households which differed in their locational attributes but which, as far as practicable, were similar in all other respects likely to affect the propensity to travel (Curtis and Headicar, 1994). The initial part of the survey, based on a random sample of about 400 addresses on each estate, enabled residents' characteristics as a whole to be determined and provided the information from which certain categories of household could be selected for detailed interview.

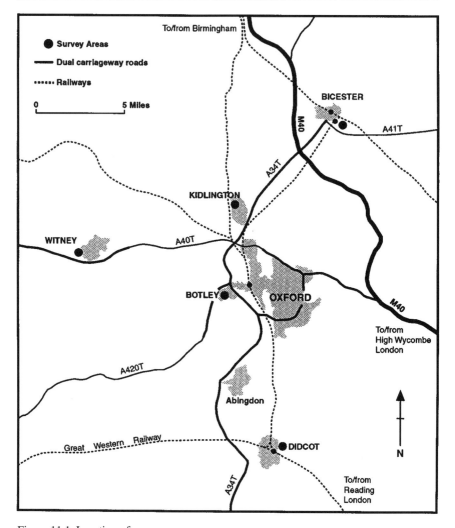

Figure 11.1. Location of survey areas.

The bulk of the survey was conducted with these 'selected households' (about 110 on each estate) drawn from four of the most common categories defined in terms of:

- number of adults;

- the employment status of each adult (full-time, part-time or not employed);

- the presence of children and whether the youngest child was aged under 10 (a threshold age linked to the ability to travel independently).

The four selected categories all contained two adults, at least one of whom was in full-time employment, and together comprised 61 per cent of all households present on the surveyed estates.

This process of selection enabled the surveyed households on the five estates to be standardized as far as a number of composition variables likely to influence travel behaviour was concerned. In addition the survey results reported here are weighted so that the mix between the selected categories is the same on each estate (equivalent to the average distribution found on all five). Only adult travel behaviour is quoted, although it should be noted that only 1 in 8 of all households contained a child aged 10 or more who might be likely to undertake independent journeys. (The car-based elements of their travel would generally be picked up by information from their parents acting as 'chauffeurs' anyway).

SURVEY RESULTS: VARIATIONS IN TRAVEL BEHAVIOUR BY LOCATION

The surveys obtained information on individual's travel behaviour in two forms:

1. (By direct interview) all regular journeys, defined as those made to the same destination for the same purpose at least once a week.

2. (By self-completion) all trips made on a single day (a Thursday during school term).

All modes and travel purposes were included except business trips which did not start or finish at home.

The two sources have different virtues. The record of regular journeys enables the basic patterns of activity and travel within a household to be studied, including links between household members, whilst removing the vagaries of day to day variation. The travel diary on the other hand provides a snapshot of all trips actually made on a single day. The most important weekday journeys - to work and to school – figure in both sources and since the findings on regular journeys have been reported elsewhere (Headicar and Curtis, 1994) they will only be reviewed briefly here.

1. Regular Journeys

In all the adults in our survey make an average of 7.5 return journeys a week travelling 142 miles (see table 11.1). The number of journeys is similar at all five locations but the distance travelled varies widely. The average for residents of the Bicester estate (182 miles) is almost double that of Kidlington (94 miles).

In terms of travel mode the car is used for 81 per cent of all regular journeys (71 per cent as car driver) and walking and cycling 14 per cent. Public transport caters for only 5 per cent. However walking and cycling journeys are typically much shorter so that the proportions of travel *distance* by car and

Table 11.1:   Regular journeys – distance travelled by location (miles per adult per week, selected household categories, all modes).

Survey area	All	Botley	Kidlington	Bicester	Didcot	Witney
Total Distance *	142	123	94	182	145	162
Return journeys*	7.5	7.6	7.8	7.2	7.4	7.3
% car journeys+	81	78	67	96	82	85
Car distance+	108	97	65	172	102	152

Notes
* All regular journeys - including mixed mode and multi-purpose journeys.
+ Does not include mixed mode or multi-purpose journeys.

public transport are therefore greater – 85 per cent and 13 per cent respectively. There are major differences in the use of travel modes at the five locations. At one extreme (Bicester) the car is used for 96 per cent of regular journeys; at the other (Kidlington) it is used for only 67 per cent.

The combined effect of differences in journey distance and the use of transport modes produces even more striking contrasts in the overall amount of car-based travel at the different locations. Kidlington residents generate only 38 per cent of their Bicester counterparts – 65 miles a week compared with 172. The other locations show a range of results between these two extremes.

Table 11.2 shows the breakdown by journey purpose distinguishing between work and home-based business journeys and the remainder. Overall, work purposes contribute rather more than a half of all regular journeys but four-fifths of the distance travelled. It is the variation in work journey distances which is the pre-eminent source of the differences in overall distance travelled between the five locations. Between Kidlington and Bicester the difference for work-related purposes is 80 miles a week (76 per cent of the all-area average) compared with only 6.5 miles (26 per cent) for all other purposes.

Table 11.2:   Regular journeys – distance travelled by location and purpose (miles per adult per week, selected household categories, all modes).

	All areas	Botley	Kidlington	Bicester	Didcot	Witney
WORK AND HOME-BASED BUSINESS JOURNEYS:						
Total distance (miles)	105.6	88.1	64.5	114.6	108.6	121.9
No. of return journeys	3.9	3.9	3.9	3.8	3.9	3.7
OTHER HOME-BASED JOURNEYS						
Total distance (miles)	24.7	26.1	20.6	26.0	23.4	27.1
No. of return journeys	3.0	3.0	3.2	2.9	3.0	3.1

Note: Return journeys which involve a mix of modes and/or purposes are not included: the sum of the purpose totals does not therefore equal the overall totals in table 11.1.

2. One Day Trips

The survey of all trips on one weekday revealed a very similar pattern (see table 11.3). Variations in total distance travelled, in the percentage of trips by car (as driver or passenger) and in the distance by car showed the same ordering of the five locations. The range of difference was however somewhat less marked. Thus the average daily distance travelled by car by people in Bicester is reduced to 1.94 times the distance of people in Kidlington (compared with 2.64 in respect of regular trips). The car-based share is reduced from 96 per cent to 91 per cent in Bicester whereas in Kidlington it increases slightly from 67 per cent to 68 per cent.

This mitigation of the extreme differences is because there is much greater similarity between the five locations in non-work/business travel which forms a larger proportion of all trips on a weekday than it does of regular journeys during a week. Work and home-based business purposes account for 57 per cent of journeys and 81 per cent of the distance travelled on a regular basis. They only account for 46 per cent of trips and 74 per cent of the distance travelled on a single weekday.

Table 11.3:   One-day travel by location (weekday per adult, selected household categories, all modes).

	All	*Botley*	*Kidlington*	*Bicester*	*Didcot*	*Witney*
Total distance (miles)	**31.5**	28.7	22.3	36.7	34.3	35.4
Number of trips	**3.55**	3.76	3.53	3.12	3.51	3.83
Per cent of trips by car	**78**	72	68	91	79	84
Car distance (miles)	**27.2**	24.9	17.9	34.9	25.8	33.1

Table 11.4:   One-day car travel by purpose (weekday per adult, selected household categories).

	All Areas	*Botley*	*Kidlington*	*Bicester*	*Didcot*	*Witney*
WORK AND HOME-BASED BUSINESS JOURNEYS:						
Number of car trips	**1.29**	1.24	1.01	1.53	1.25	1.45
Total distance (miles)	**15.1**	14.2	9.9	18.0	14.9	16.5
No. of return journeys	**19.5**	17.6	10.0	27.5	18.6	23.7
Ratio of all areas mean		*0.91*	*0.51*	*1.41*	*0.96*	*1.23*
OTHER HOME-BASED JOURNEYS						
Number of car trips	**1.49**	1.44	1.41	1.32	1.54	1.76
Total distance (miles)	**5.2**	5.1	5.3	5.7	4.7	5.3
No. of return journeys	**7.7**	7.3	7.4	7.5	7.2	9.4

Note that the weighted data incorporates approximately 9 per cent of adults on all estates who are non-workers; the trips and distances *per worker* are correspondingly higher (see tables 11.8–11.10).

Table 11.4 confirms that the variation in work-related travel between the five locations (equivalent to 17.5 miles per adult per day in the extreme) is attributable to a combination of differences in the number of car trips and their average length. By comparison the patterns of car travel for the other purposes are remarkably similar. Analysis reported elsewhere (Headicar, 1996) has shown that this overall similarity arises from a mix of shorter journeys for 'home-town' destinations and longer journeys for external ones in the case of the freestanding towns counter-balanced by the opposite in the city-periphery locations. (Such equalization would not of course be likely if an area's settlement geography differed markedly from that of Central Oxfordshire's). Nevertheless if the object of concern is the volume of car-based travel it is clearly in terms of *work-related purposes* that explanations must be sought.

POSSIBLE EXPLANATIONS FOR TRAVEL VARIATION BY LOCATION

Two main reasons can be offered for the variations in work-related travel reported above:

1. Differences in the accessibility characteristics of the five locations.

2. Differences in the basic socio-economic attributes of the populations at the five locations (ie. in variables other than those which were controlled for in the sampling and weighting procedures);

1. Differences in Accessibility

The survey locations vary in four main respects as far as accessibility is concerned, each of which exerts an influence on travel behaviour:

- availability of local employment
- proximity of other major sources of employment
- proximity to Oxford City as an employment location
- proximity to strategic transport routes.

The limited influence of *local employment* can be seen in the proportion of residents who have their workplace within their 'home town' – i.e. the settlement in which their housing estate is situated (table 11.5). The low figure at Botley is not surprising given its small size and suburban character. What is more remarkable is that in the other locations – especially the freestanding 'country towns' – only about 1 in 5 adults work in their home town. This is in spite of the fact that the towns are of a substantial size and have been deliberately planned as 'balanced communities' (i.e. with a mix of housing, jobs and other facilities). Furthermore, being new estates their residents have made a deliberate choice to move to them.

Table 11.5: Present workplace location by survey area (percentage of regular work trips).

Workplace:	Botley	Kidlington	Bicester	Didcot	Witney
'Home town'	10	22	18	16	21
Oxford City	53	48	22	15	26
Rest of Oxfordshire	21	22	23	34	33
External Metropolitan*	10	5	24	27	10
External Other*	6	4	13	8	10

Note

*External = outside Oxfordshire; 'metropolitan' is Greater London plus the sector of SE England (mainly Outer Metropolitan Area) between it and Oxfordshire.

Given the low utilization of local jobs amongst all the surveyed estates, the *proximity of other major sources of employment* is clearly likely to have an influence on the distances travelled by the majority of working adults.

Botley and Kidlington have a clear advantage in this respect because of their location just outside Oxford City which represents by far the largest concentration of employment in the area. About half their residents have workplaces within the City and this is the principal reason for them having a much higher proportion of shorter distance work trips than the country towns (table 11.6).

Amongst the other towns Oxford City figures as a workplace to a relatively small extent, given these towns' long-standing links with the city and the lack of major alternatives. Of the three Didcot has a higher proportion of work trips under 10 miles due the greater number of intervening opportunities within this distance, notably the town of Abingdon and other employment concentrations to the south of it within the A34 corridor.

The proximity of other major sources of employment is also reflected very clearly in the median work trip distance from each of the estates. The median distances of Bicester and Witney residents are three times those of Botley. (Other factors influence the upper half of the journey length distribution and hence alter the pattern of overall *average* distances from the estate. These are discussed below.)

Table 11.6: Trip length distribution by home location (work and home-based business trips, all modes).

	Botley	Kidlington	Bicester	Didcot	Witney
Proportion of work trip ends within 5 miles	50%	40%	31%	29%	26%
Proportion of work trip ends within 10 miles	80%	79%	36%	47%	38%
Median distance of trips (miles)	4.8	7.2	14.8	11.0	14.7
Mean distance of trips (miles)	10.4	7.8	18.3	15.5	15.9

Proximity to Oxford City as an employment source influences not only trip length but also trip mode. The combination of relatively short distance, slow peak-period speeds for private cars, a deliberate policy of restraint on commuter parking in and around the city centre and of priority for buses and cycling, creates a situation in which the use of these non-car modes becomes significant in Botley and Kidlington. They account for 24 per cent and 23 per cent of work and home-based business trips respectively from those estates compared with less than 4 per cent in the three estates of the country towns. This therefore compounds the effect of shorter average trip length in contributing to their lower volume of car-based travel overall.

The effect of *strategic transport routes* can be seen in comparing travel behaviour from the three country towns. An analysis of workplace opportunities in terms of travel *time* by car showed that Bicester is 17 per cent better than Didcot and 61 per cent better than Witney. Although not particularly well placed geographically with respect to employment the Bicester estate's easy access to both the M40 and A34 facilitates car commuting over longer *distances*. Witney by contrast has no equivalent links and suffers from serious peak-period congestion along the single carriageway A40 link to Oxford, the A34 and M40.

Analysis of commuting trips shows that 23 per cent from Bicester are greater than 25 miles compared with only 14 per cent from Witney. It is this difference in the upper half of the journey length distribution (given that the median distances from the two estates are virtually identical) which explains why Bicester has the longer *mean* distance for commuting trips shown in table 11.6 and, in turn, the greater total work-related travel by car (table 11.4).

The figures for Didcot also illustrate the influence of a strategic transport route although in this case it is the high-speed rail service to Reading and London Paddington. There are similarities in the role performed by this service in the travel patterns of the Didcot residents as with the M40 in the case of Bicester. A third of the long-distance commuting trips (which at Bicester are made almost exclusively by car) are at Didcot made by train. This is the main reason why although Didcot residents travel almost as much in total as their Bicester and Witney counterparts (table 11.3) their distance by car is substantially less. Nine per cent of work and home-based business trips from Didcot are made by rail, with an average distance in excess of 30 miles.

2. Differences in Socio-Economic Characteristics

Several of the socio-economic variables likely to influence travel behaviour were explicitly controlled for in the research design, viz number and gender of adults, their employment status, and the presence of children over or under aged 10. Further analysis of the surveyed population showed very close similarities between the five locations in average ages of both adults and children and in number of children.

Table 11.7:   Average house price, household incomes and household vehicles.

	All	*Botley*	*Kidlington*	*Bicester*	*Didcot*	*Witney*
Average house price (£000)	**78.4**	95.6	60.5	85.7	72.0	78.4
Ratio to all areas mean		*1.22*	*0.77*	*1.09*	*0.92*	*1.00*
Av. gross h'hold income (£000)	**27.7**	29.8	23.5	31.2	24.9	29.1
Ratio to all areas mean		*1.08*	*0.85*	*1.13*	*0.90*	*1.05*
Av. vehicles per household	**1.68**	1.61	1.42	1.92	1.68	1.84

The possible influence of three further variables, not explicitly controlled for, will be explored here:

- household income
- household car availability
- personal use of an employer's car.

When the five estates were first selected for surveying their variation in average house price (imputed from Council Tax banding) suggested that there would be a similar variation in household income. This is confirmed by the information obtained from the selected households although the extent of variation in income (as a percentage of the mean) is less than house price (table 11.7). In addition Bicester swaps places with Botley at the top of the rank order.

To test the effect of variation in income the bands used in interviewing were grouped to form approximate quartiles amongst respondents. As would be expected successively higher income groups exhibit greater travel propensity (table 11.8). But within each group there is a wide variation between the five locations.

The scale and pattern of this variation is not entirely consistent (the degree of disaggregation inevitably introduces some vagaries). Overall however this form of analysis (which standardizes the number of respondents in each income group on each estate) produces much the same relationship between the five estates as the non-standardized results quoted earlier (table 11.4). In other words income differences are *not* the primary source of the differences in work-related car travel between the five locations.

The *number of cars* available for use by members of a household is generally a further important factor influencing the propensity to travel by car. However in seeking to explain variations in travel behaviour by location it is important to note the link between location itself and car ownership and hence, indirectly, with car travel.

Comparison of the estates close to Oxford with those in the country towns shows this locational effect. The average car availability at Kidlington (1.42 per two-adult household) is 15 per cent less than at Didcot (table 11.7 earlier) even though the profile of the two sets of households in terms of income and

Table 11.8. Work-related car travel by income group.

	All*	Botley	Kidlington	Bicester	Didcot	Witney
GROUP 1 (<£23,000 pa gross)						
Percent of households	**29**	16	49	22	34	22
Distance per worker**	**15.02**	5.96	9.00	17.31	18.22	27.91
Ratio to average of areas		*0.40*	*0.60*	*1.15*	*1.21*	*1.86*
GROUP 2 (£23,000-£28,999)						
Percent of households	**27**	30	25	26	35	21
Distance per worker**	**18.76**	23.18	9.72	40.45	13.19	17.71
Ratio to average of areas		*1.24*	*0.52*	*2.16*	*0.70*	*0.94*
GROUP 3 (£29,000-£37,999)						
Percent of households	**22**	31	17	24	14	27
Distance per worker**	**21.47**	11.44	18.82	28.23	25.70	26.67
Ratio to average of areas		*0.53*	*0.88*	*1.31*	*1.20*	*1.24*
GROUP 4 (£38,000+ pa gross)						
Percent of households	**22**	23	9	30	18	29
Distance per worker**	**30.32**	30.32	9.68	37.85	31.73	30.00
Ratio to average of areas		*1.00*	*0.32*	*1.25*	*1.05*	*0.99*
Average of four group ratios		*0.79*	*0.58*	*1.47*	*1.04*	*1.26*
Unstandardized ratio from						
table 11.4		*0.91*	*0.51*	*1.41*	*0.96*	*1.23*

Notes
* Average of the five locations, ie equalizing the actual distribution of incomes
** Miles per weekday

employers' cars – and in this analysis, composition by definition – is virtually identical. Likewise car availability at Botley is lower than at Bicester and Witney by a similar margin.

The significance of these differences in household car availability lies in their link with the amount of work-related car travel. On average, amongst otherwise similar two-adult households, workers in those with 2+ cars generate 41 per cent more work-related car trips and 51 per cent longer ones, resulting in 113 per cent greater car distance overall (table 11.9). The proportion of such households varies between the estates but differences in car distance per worker are evident amongst *both* 0 and 1 and 2+ car households.

The pattern of variation is broadly as noted before but there are some distinctive features. Amongst 0 and 1 car households work-related car travel is *lower* in Botley than in Kidlington, as one might expect given the greater proximity of Botley to central Oxford. However, amongst 2+ car households travel from Botley is disproportionately high (relative to 0 and 1 car households) whilst at Didcot it is disproportionately low. In the case of Botley this is attributable to the effects of company car motoring (discussed below) whilst at Didcot the

Table 11.9:   Work-related car travel by household car availability.

	All	*Botley*	*Kidlington*	*Bicester*	*Didcot*	*Witney*
0 and 1 Car Households*						
Percent of Households	**37**	41	56	17	42	25
Car Trips per Driver	**1.11**	0.88	0.97	1.61	1.15	1.28
Distance per Trip (miles)	**11.02**	5.79	8.76	12.88	14.95	12.96
Car Distance per Worker	**12.28**	5.04	8.49	20.77	17.45	16.67
2+ Car Households						
Percent of Households	**63**	59	44	83	59	75
Car Trips per Driver	**1.57**	1.59	1.32	1.67	1.50	1.65
Distance per Trip (miles)	**16.65**	17.38	10.98	18.97	14.92	17.37
Car Distance per Worker	**26.10**	27.54	14.59	31.80	22.32	28.61

Note
* The proportion of 0 car households is 1.3 per cent overall and between 0 and 3 per cent on the individual estates.

explanation lies in the 'substitution' by rail of a proportion of longer distance journeys noted previously.

Personal use of an employer's car is a factor which might be expected to be associated with higher volumes of car travel, and variation in this form of car availability between the five locations therefore needs to be explored.

Overall nearly 9 out of 10 workers have personal use of a car and of these a quarter use one which is owned by their employer. However, workers living in 2+ car households are four times more likely to have access to an employer's car (52 per cent as against 13 per cent).

On average those with use of an employer's car make 2.2 times the car travel for work-related purposes as those with personal use of a private car. Almost all the difference is attributable to greater trip length rather than to a greater number of car trips (table 11.10). Thus in the comparison of 2+ with 0 and 1 car households above the element of greater work-related travel derived from *longer* (as opposed to fewer) car trips is attributable to this association with employer's cars rather than to multiple vehicle ownership as such.

At Kidlington and Didcot (the estates with lower average incomes) those with use of an employer's car make more travel than their private car-using peers compared with the same groups at Bicester and Witney. Witney is remarkable in that although it has the highest proportion of workers with an employer's car amongst the five estates their travel is little more (only 17 per cent) than those using private cars. At the other extreme people with an employer's car at Botley travel 4.4 times more! This difference represents the combined effect of two distinct factors – the relatively large amount of work-related car travel by those with private cars at Witney and the low additional amount by those with employer's cars coupled with exactly the opposite situation at Botley.

Further examination shows that the behaviour of people with employer's cars

Table 11.10. Work-related car travel by use of private and employer's car.

	All	*Botley*	*Kidlington*	*Bicester*	*Didcot*	*Witney*
Use of Private Car						
Percent of Workers*	**64**	64	66	64	70	56
Car Trips per Worker	**1.52**	1.35	1.31	1.82	1.48	1.62
Distance per Trip (miles)	**11.67**	7.84	7.57	14.17	11.71	15.61
Car Distance per Worker	**17.70**	10.63	9.95	25.81	17.30	25.16
Use of Employer's Car						
Percent of Workers*	**24**	26	16	29	16	34
Car Trips per Worker	**1.62**	1.66	1.30	1.57	1.61	1.79
Distance per Trip (miles)	**24.12**	28.29	19.82	29.01	26.36	18.22
Car Distance per Worker	**39.00**	47.00	25.33	45.25	41.93	32.70
Trips less than 10 miles		48%	58%	23%	40%	39%
Trips more than 25 miles		50%	33%	45%	39%	19%

Note
* A further 12 per cent of workers live in non-car households or have shared or non-priority use of a single household car

at Botley is in fact similar to their peers at Bicester with at or near a half of all work-related trips being 25 miles or longer. (Both estates have almost direct access to uncongested dual-carriageway routes). By contrast at Witney – only 10 miles further west than Botley – the proportion is under a fifth. It is difficult to believe that such differences are not linked with Witney's relatively poor highway accessibility. However whether this exerts an influence by constraining Witney's residents once they have moved or alternatively on the people who choose to move there (discouraging those anticipating high work-related mileage) is something we have yet to determine.

Whatever the reason it is certainly true that these differences in trip length distribution amongst the minority of people who have an employer's car 'distort' the basic features of work-related travel amongst residents generally at the five locations. Together with the differences in the proportion of such people on each estate they are the principal reason for the irregular overall relationship of average to median distances noted previously in table 11.6.

CONCLUSIONS

A number of conclusions may be drawn from the research and these are listed below. The particular figures quoted necessarily reflect the circumstances of the case study area. It should be also be emphasized that the conclusions derive only from fieldwork conducted on households of a certain composition, although there is no reason to suppose they do not broadly characterize all households containing one or more employed adult. However they will not apply to the minority of households (around 10 per cent of the total) who have no employed member.

1. Amongst comparable groups of households living on recently developed housing estates within the same sub-region the amount of car-based travel varies very considerably by location. On a single weekday the average amount of car travel per adult ranges between 18 and 35 miles. The lower level is attributable to a combination of lower overall distance travelled (22 miles against 37) and a greater proportion by non-car modes (32 per cent as compared with 9 per cent).

2. On a single weekday just under a half of all trips and three-quarters of the distance travelled is associated with work and home-based business purposes. However it is these purposes which account for almost all the difference in car travel between the surveyed locations.

3. Only a fifth of workers who have moved to a new estate have their workplace within the same settlement (given settlement sizes in the survey area of 14,000–20,000 population). The geographical relationship of a settlement to other principal employment opportunities influences both prospective distance and modal choice and is therefore of great importance as a factor in overall commuting behaviour.

4 Compared with the alternative of freestanding towns within the same sub-region residential locations at or near the periphery of the core city contribute to the lessening of work-related car travel for three reasons:

(*a*) A large proportion of residents' workplaces are located within the city, reducing the number of medium and long distance commuting journeys. (Within the survey area city periphery locations had 80 per cent of such journeys less than 10 miles – double the proportion of the freestanding towns.)

(*b*) Amongst comparable (two adult) households at these locations car ownership is some 15 per cent lower. Non car ownership is virtually absent at all locations but the significance of one car households is that they generate only half the work-related car travel of their 2+ car owning peers.

(*c*) City periphery locations create the opportunity (given appropriate local transport policies) for a substantial element of commuting by non car modes even from high income households. One of the surveyed locations (Botley) provided evidence of more than a quarter of work-related trips by walk or cycle from an estate where almost 60 per cent of households had 2 or more cars.

5. As a general rule public transport has little or no significance for residents of new estates regardless of the transport opportunities available. Within the survey area public transport use on any scale was confined to very particular situations, viz bus travel to the core city from a well-served estate some 6–7 miles distant and long distance travel to London by high speed train from an estate within

walking distance of a principal station. In both cases however the modal share was less than 10 per cent and applied only to work-related journeys.

6. Apart from effects attributable to location in terms of the position of an estate within the settlement pattern of a sub-region, location with respect to strategic transport routes has an additional influence. Developments at locations with easy access to motorways or dual carriageway trunk roads have a higher proportion of longer distance journeys, resulting in higher car mileage overall. The converse applies to poorly served locations.

7. The significance of location relative to strategic highways appears to be accentuated by the travel behaviour and home location choices of the minority of workers who have use of a company car. Overall these people generate more than twice the amount of car travel as those with personal use of a private car.

POLICY IMPLICATIONS

Caution must obviously be applied in attempting to generalize from a relatively small scale research exercise conducted within a single case study area. Oxford itself is renowned for a car restraint policy which is 'severe' by contemporary standards amongst English cities of its type although it represents a direction in which many others are now moving. However, the significance of this policy should not be exaggerated as far as the research results are concerned. The importance of location in relation to the city lies more in the likelihood of shorter-distance journeys (and hence non-car modes also) rather than through the effects of car restraint, which are largely confined to the city centre.

The 'country towns' in any case have relatively little connection with Oxford City and certainly with the city centre (except for specialized activities). Their characteristics are arguably no different from the large number of similar expanding towns in the outer South-East and adjacent shire counties. The distinctive travel behaviour of residents living on their new estates reported here is also likely to be replicated in the expanding shire towns within commuting range of the country's other main conurbations although probably operating over somewhat shorter distances on average.

In such contexts the case study evidence taken at its face value implies that local planning authorities *can* exert a substantial influence on the amount of car-based travel through the strategic location of new housing. Overall locational differences would appear to account for plus or minus 15 to 20 per cent around the study area average of 27 miles per adult per weekday, i.e. a difference of the order of 10 miles.

This estimate is conservative in that it derives from a sample of locations which is narrower than the full range available to a shire county. Development locations *within* the built-up area of larger towns on the one hand and in rural areas but outside the expanded country towns on the other could be expected to show greater differences. In particular, differences would start to emerge in non-work as well as work-related travel. Differences in car-based travel for non-work purposes could also apply to locational types which *were* included in the present study if they were situated within a sub-regional settlement pattern markedly different from that of the Oxfordshire case study area.

In the context of the case study area and the types of locations surveyed the evidence suggests that for a new estate of, say, 500 dwellings locational differences could represent something like 1.5 million vehicle miles per year.[1] If this were true it would clearly be a major consideration for planning authorities to set alongside other factors pertinent to strategic housing decisions in areas such as Oxfordshire. However, for planning authorities to be able to exploit such differences (i.e. locating housing only or predominantly in places which minimized the likely amount of car travel) it would be necessary to assume that potential occupants were indifferent to location within a sub-region. In other words there would have to be nothing inherently different about the *types of people* choosing one housing estate rather than another and that they or their peers would be equally prepared to occupy a new house somewhere else.

Such indifference is implausible on three counts:

1. Within any sub-region a proportion of households will only consider moving to, within or near a particular town (eg because of their own background, the location of relatives, children's schools, workplaces etc).

2. Amongst those households who *are* prepared to consider more than one town there are likely to be preferences (eg concerning social or environmental attributes) which in aggregate are not neutral. These preferences will be reflected in the prices of equivalent properties and this in turn becomes a source of discrimination between potential residents.

3. No sub-region – at least within the central urbanized core of England – functions as a self-contained housing and employment market. Each potential housing location varies in its attractiveness with respect to other, overlapping markets – in Oxfordshire's case those of Greater London and centres in the Outer Metropolitan Area in particular.

Insofar as some locations are more attractive than others to people drawn from these different groups the question arises as to whether there are systematic differences in car-travel propensity between them. If so, then the travel behaviour which is observable at particular locations is in part at least attributable to the *people who have chosen to occupy them* rather than to the accessibility characteristics of the places themselves. In our case study examples might be the London rail commuters at Didcot, the long-distance motorway commuters at Bicester and the 'low-mileage' company car users at Witney.

If this 'circularity' argument has any substance (and we are pursuing the issue in further research) then simply altering the location of developments will not necessarily bring about a change in behaviour amongst people who will be 'forced' to occupy them. (Locating new estates at Oxfordshire's country towns for example does not currently transform their occupants into leading the locally orientated, 'self-contained' lives traditionally associated with such places.) Upon such questions hung the practical value of the previous Conservative government's policy of locating development where it offers 'transport choice', but where in reality people pre-disposed to using cars extensively will continue to do so.

Whatever the truth of these arguments the scope for planning authorities to influence the location of development is in practice conditioned by local patterns of housing demand – whether these derive from people's attachment to a particular town, from relative preferences between different towns in an area, or from the pressures exerted on it by the 'overspill' of demand from adjoining, more urbanized areas. Together these create an inertia which for both political and economic reasons authorities have to be responsive to. At a broader spatial scale the same principle of responsiveness to projected demands operates in setting the county-wide housing figures contained in Regional Planning Guidance (Curtis, 1996). The result is that planning authorities tend to adopt spatial allocation policies which follow the inherited distribution of population, reinforcing the existing settlement hierarchy (Oxford Brookes and W. S. Atkins, 1996).

For authorities to move away from past trends and to attempt to locate housing where it will contribute to less car travel (in line with PPG13) the research undertaken in Oxfordshire has two very clear, but problematic pointers :

1. It is highly desirable that development other than that which is practicable within existing built-up areas should be located at or close to the periphery of a main urban area (as opposed to smaller freestanding towns). However this flies in the face of Green Belt and similar policies of 'urban containment' which have been applied to many cities such as Oxford over several decades. The political attachment, local and national, to these policies is such that even public *discussion* of their applicability into the twenty-first century is barely possible. In these circumstances authorities are forced very much into second best options – for example to country towns such as Oxfordshire's or (rather wishfully as far as actual travel behaviour is concerned) to settlements in rail served corridors.

2. It is important to locate development not so much where it offers the choice of public transport but where it is likely to *discourage* extensive *car* use. To achieve this implies locations remote from motorway interchanges and similar access points on to other dual-carriageway routes. Such a policy may seem rather perverse in that it denies occupants of new development the opportunity to capitalize on the accessibility offered by the primary route network. An alternative view would be to see this policy as a necessary surrogate in the absence of effective direct pricing of the highways themselves.

The evidence from the case study (where all the estates surveyed would satisfy PPG13 criteria) indicates that unless these principles are adhered to housing location strategies will seriously under-achieve in their their potential to contribute to less car-based travel.

NOTE

1. Assuming 65 per cent of households contained 2 or more adults with an average of 2 workers of the kind surveyed in this research (which covered 61 per cent of households) this would present 650 workers x 10 miles a day (90 per cent as car driver) x , say, 220 working days a year = 1.287 million vehicle miles. To this would need to be added the travel generation of a further 25 per cent or so of households which contained a single working adult (i.e. 125 persons). On a pro rata basis (not confirmed in this research) this would amount to 1.535 million vehicle miles in all.

REFERENCES

Banister, D., Watson, S. and Wood, C. (1994) The Relationship Between Energy Use in Transport and Urban Form. Working Paper 12, Planning and Development Research Centre, Bartlett School of Planning, University College, London.

Banister, D. (1995) The research evidence, in Godfrey, K. (ed.) *Reducing the Need to Travel* Oxford Planning Monographs Vol. 1, no. 2. Oxford: School of Planning, Oxford Brookes University.

Breheny, M. (1995) Counter-urbanization and sustainable urban forms, in Brotchie, J. *et al* (eds.) *Cities in Competition.* Melbourne: Longman Australia.

Curtis, C. and Headicar, P. (1994) The Location of New Residential Development: Its Influence on Car-based Travel: Research Design and Methodology. Working Paper 154. School of Planning, Oxford Brookes University.

Curtis, C. (1996) Can strategic planning contribute to a reduction in car-based travel? *Transport Policy*, **3**(1/2).

Department of the Environment (1990) *This Common Inheritance,* Cmnd 1200. London: HMSO.

Department of the Environment (1995) *Projections of Households in England to 2016.*London: HMSO.

Departments of the Environment and Transport (1993) *Reducing Transport Emissions Through Planning* (Report by ECOTEC Research & Consulting Ltd). London: HMSO.

Departments of the Environment and Transport (1994) *Planning Policy Guidance Note 13: Transport.* London: HMSO.

Departments of the Environment and Transport (1995a) *PPG13: A Guide to Better Practice.* London: HMSO.

Hall, P. and Breheny, M. (eds.) (1996) *The People: Where Will They Go?* London: Town and Country Planning Association.

Headicar, P. (1996) Settlement size: It's not size but location that matters, in *Proceedings of 8th Annual TRICS Conferenc.* London: JMP Consultants Ltd.

Headicar, P. and Curtis, C. (1994) Residential development and car-based travel: Does location make a difference? in *Proceedings of Seminar C (Environmental Issues)* 22nd European Transport Forum. London: PTRC.

Owens, S. (1991) *Energy Conscious Planning.* London: Council for the Protection of Rural England.

Oxford Brookes University and W. S. Atkins Planning Consultants (1996) Land Use Effects of Planning Policy Guidance and Increasing Congestion (Report to the Department of Transport).
Oxfordshire County Council (1996) *Deposit Structure Plan to 2011*. Oxford: Oxford City Council.

CHAPTER 12

MOVEMENT AND MOBILITY
IN THE POST-FORDIST CITY

Andrew Gillespie, Patsy Healey and Kevin Robins

Profound changes are occurring in the economic, social, cultural and spatial organization of the contemporary city. This chapter attempts to explore the implications of these changes for patterns of movement and mobility, and also considers the ways in which changing travel patterns and behaviours are themselves integral to the broader transformations taking place in ways of urban living and working. Having developed a set of propositions concerning these themes, the chapter draws on a study of a particular city, Tyneside, in the north-east of England, to examine their validity.

The study is intentionally exploratory, both in terms of the conceptual framework which it embodies and in terms of the approach to explanation it adopts, and was borne out of a sense of dissatisfaction with what we contend is the excessively narrow conceptual and methodological paradigm which dominates urban transport studies. At the root of the problem appears to be an approach to social scientific enquiry that, faced with the enormous complexity of travel behaviour, and within the context of very close professional links between research and practise, has tended to eschew *understanding* in favour of *prediction*. There are a number of inter-related features of transport research, which seem to stem from this predictive or forecasting objective, which we contend are undermining its intellectual credibility and hampering its ability to cope with the challenges it is facing, which primarily concern developing a better understanding of travel behaviour in a period of rapid change.

Firstly, the over-riding aim of predicting travel behaviour *outcomes* has resulted in a modelling approach which tries to hold as many other 'variables' as possible constant. In the idealized, normative decision-making context in which transport research has evolved, 'models are estimated to replicate a transport system provided most external conditions remain more or less stable' (Ortúzar and Willumsen, 1991). The purpose of transport modelling is thus to:

> identify a 'most likely future' under the assumption that current conditions, attitudes and mechanisms would continue to evolve as they have in the past or in line with known trends. Sensitivity testing is intended to explore the effect of changing these assumptions, so that some of the underlying trends which control the model behaviour may be taken to be quite different from those observed in the past. (Webster, Bly and Paulley, 1988, p.27)

Although sensitivity testing may be an effective means of examining the robustness of a travel demand model's assumptions, it does not help us to understand the nature of change in travel behaviour. The assumption of holding 'external conditions' stable (they are external only in the sense of a very narrow conception of the system being studied) is particularly problematic at a time when the city is undergoing such rapid spatial, social, economic, political and cultural change.

A second problem with the conventional approach (which Wachs, 1996, has gone as far as describing as obsolete), is its narrow focus on the individual trip as the unit of analysis and prediction. The classic four-stage transport model (of trip generation, trip distribution, modal split and route assignment) masks the underlying causal patterns which could 'make sense' of travel behaviour: 'information about the dynamics of behaviour, interrelationships within the household and among different trip makers, and relationships to other quality of life aspects are all absent from the models' (Stopher *et al.*, 1996, p.296). Increasing calls have been made by transport researchers, dissatisfied with the conventional trip-based approach, for the development of activity-based frameworks for understanding travel behaviour (e.g. Jones *et al.*, 1991; Spear, 1996; Kitamura *et al.*, 1996). Stopher *et al.* (1996) suggest that 'a paradigm shift is called for, focusing not on travel but on the behaviours, needs and roles that generate it', and they conclude that 'progress in transportation will not come if the discipline continues along the present path of pursuit' (p.310).

A third and related problem concerns the modelling approach itself, and the highly restricted theoretical base which underlies transport models. Aggregate level models rely on gravity or entropy maximizing approaches to predicting trips, while at the individual level micro-economic or random utility theory approaches to predicting behaviour are the norm (Webster *et al.*, 1988). Despite the critique, from the 1970s onwards, of the legitimacy of quantitative modelling of human behaviour, which has caused a major re-think of methodology within the social sciences (Sayer, 1984), transport research remains largely locked-in to a quantitative modelling paradigm (Banister *et al.*, 1990). This paradigm seems in the transport field to derive either from the systems analysis approach of engineering or from neo-classical micro-economics, with its highly questionable assumptions concerning utility-maximizing behaviour and economic rationality. Although such approaches enable quantitative predictions of travel behaviour to be made, they contribute little to understanding the complexity of travel behaviour. As Handy (1996, p.164) argues, 'the low level of explanation . . . of the disaggregated models that have been generated so far suggests that there is still a great deal left to understand about travel behaviour'. She advocates bringing new methodologies to bear (in the sense of new to transport research), such as attitudinal surveys, stated preference surveys and focus group discussions, in the hope that these 'may allow for the behavioural analysis which has been lacking' (Handy, 1996, p. 163-164).

The pursuit of an almost mechanistic approach to travel prediction, at the expense of understanding or explanation, is reflected then in the conceptual frameworks and the methodologies which constitute the dominant paradigm. Ironically perhaps, the close links between transport research and transport planning practise, which appear to be responsible for the former's prediction imperative, now pose a threat, due to the latter's crisis of legitimacy. The 'predict and provide' philosophy which has dominated transport policy, in which demands are projected, equated with need and met by infrastructure provision, has become untenable (Owens, 1995; Banister and Button, 1992). The current attempts to re-think transport policy and to embrace what Goodwin *et al.* (1991) have termed a 'new realism', which would break the cycle of road building in response to forecasts of car travel growth, require, in our view, new ways of conceptualizing and of studying travel behaviour, for the conventional paradigm of transport research is singularly ill-suited to the task in hand, being itself part of the problem.

The study reported here was devised with the aim of contributing, in an exploratory way, to the espousal of new conceptual frameworks and new approaches to analysis in the transport field. We begin firstly with a consideration of the hypothesized transition from a so-called Fordist city to a post-Fordist city, and in so doing raise a number of questions concerning the changing influences upon travel behaviour.

TOWARDS THE POST-FORDIST CITY?

'Fordism' is a term used to describe a particular conjuncture of economic, social and institutional characteristics which together made up a stable 'model of development' during the 1950s, 1960s and early 1970s (Lipietz, 1987). The economic basis of this model was mass production and mass consumption,[1] regulated and sustained through a combination of collective wage bargaining, the dominance of large corporations, Keynesian demand management and the welfare state. It has been argued that this particular model of development suffered a series of set-backs in the 1970s which undermined its continued viability, leading to a so-called 'crisis of Fordism'. For many commentators, the 1980s and 1990s have signified a break with the Fordist model, and have been characterized by various attempts to construct a new model of economically and socially sustainable growth.

Although there is as yet no clear consensus as to whether such a 'post-Fordist' growth model has been achieved (see Amin, 1994, for a review), commentators can at least agree on some reasonably clear features of the transition which are pointing towards it. These features include a strong emphasis on product innovation and on achieving flexibility in production; a growth in outsourcing; individualized wage determination and flexible labour markets; more differentiated consumption patterns, and much greater reliance on market forms of regulation.

While the transition from Fordism to post-Fordism is usually seen as occurring at the macro-level of national and international economic and regulatory systems, it is also postulated to have expression at the level of the city, affecting not only the economic base of the city but also the reality of daily living and working and even urban culture and aesthetics. Elements of the hypothesized transition from Fordist to post-Fordist city (and, in the cultural sphere, from modern to post-modern) include:

• the shift in the economic base of the city away from production towards what Castells (1989) has termed the 'informational mode of development' and hence the 'informational city';

• the shift from manufacturing to service employment and from stable forms of employment to more precarious forms, with an attendant growth in part-time working, contract, temporary or casual labour, and self-employment;

• an accentuation of the city's role as a centre of consumption, spectacle and cultural activities (Featherstone, 1991), and the associated emergence of new spaces of consumption and leisure, and, through, gentrification, new residential spaces as well (Zukin, 1988);

• a greater degree of social polarization, due to changes in labour markets and in welfare provision, leading to the emergence of 'dual cities' (Mollenkopf and Castells, 1991);

• a demographic shift away from stable nuclear families towards more single parent and single person families, leading towards what Mingione (1991) has termed the 'fragmented society';

• cultural transformations associated with what Baudrillard (1983) has described as 'hyperreality', a world of simulated experiences represented in and by TV soaps, video games and shopping malls;

• political transformations, associated with the politics of differentiation and the rise of new social movements, and the shift 'from managerialism to entrepreneurialism' in urban governance (Harvey, 1989a);

• the increasingly privatized, rather than collectivized, provision of urban services;

• the increasing hegemony of market forms of regulation, rather than management by the (national or local) state.

Clearly there are too many and too complex changes above to be ascribable to a single cause, or to be meaningfully captured by the Fordist/post-Fordist label; nevertheless, there is a degree of consistency running through many of the changes, which are reflective of patterns of living and working which are becoming more highly differentiated. Cooke (1990, p.341) has summarized these inter-related changes as 'a growing pluralization of culture, economic activities, consumption practises and processes of control'.

The Spatial Organization of the Post-Fordist City

How is this growing pluralization reflected in the spatial organization of the post-Fordist city? Although there is no simple or single spatial outcome, unsurprisingly given the range and complexity of the changes alluded to under the post-Fordist banner, one aspect of the post-Fordist city upon which there is a degree of consensus is that of the 'disorganization' of its spatial structure. Gibelli (1988), for example, contrasts the fluidity and ambiguity of what she terms the 'post-modern metropolis' with the clearly structured and organized 'Fordist metropolis', which was

> characterized by the strict relationship between form and function, by specialized zones of industry, administration and residential quarters, with a cultural-symbolic centre, and with a regular pulse, beating like a heart, everyday sending flows of commuters from the outskirts into the centre and back again. (Gibelli, 1988, quoted in Qvortrup, 1992, p.102)

She argues that the post-modern metropolis, heavily reliant on 'network co-operation' within flexible information-based activities, will lose the association between particular buildings and locations and particular functions, and instead will be characterized by an architectural and spatial structure displaying flexibility and multi-purpose adaptability. Continuing this theme, Qvortrup (1992, pp. 102) sees the post-Fordist/post-modern city as mixing up office work quarters, shopping centres and leisure quarters, 'with the 'intelligent home' as the symbolic node of home-working, home-shopping, home-banking, and home-based leisure'.

Just as the spatial regularity of the Fordist city is giving way to a more fragmented and complex spatiality, so it is the case with temporal regularities. The rhythm of the conventional working day is giving way under a variety of flexible working practises, leisure and consumption activities are no longer allocated their set times but rather are extending temporally into the '24 hour city' (Lovatt *et al.*, 1994), while in the realm of goods production and distribution, 'just-in-time' principles have become firmly established. The post-Fordist city thus displays more complex activity patterns, both spatially and temporally.

The theme of fragmentation of an earlier, clearly-defined spatial structure has been identified by many commentators on post-Fordist urbanization. Harvey (1989*b*), for example, comments on the retreat from master-planning and its replacement by the 'design of fragments', in which the city is akin to a collage. Dear (1991) comments upon the 'amazingly variegated microgeography' of Los Angeles, the paradigm case for the post-Fordist metropolis, a feature of that city which Soja (1989) has also remarked upon. He draws attention to the Los Angeles Transportation Department's 'city identification programme', in which '433 signs [have been erected] which bestow identity within the hyperspace of the City of Los Angeles' (Soja, 1989, p.245). Soja argues that 'never before has the spatiality of the industrial city become so kaleidoscopic, so loosened from its nineteenth century moorings, so filled with unsettling contrariety' (Soja, 1989, p.187).

In addition to the argued fragmentation of the previously ordered and spatially structured Fordist city, another aspect of the transition towards the post-Fordist city which has been remarked upon, in the North American context at least, is that of a simultaneous 'decentering and recentering of urban nodalities' (Soja, 1989, p.188). On the one hand, the central city has been rejuvenated as a site for spectacle, consumption and, through the process of gentrification, middle class housing, while on the other the city turns itself inside out through the development of 'amorphous agglomerations that defy conventional definition of urban-suburban-exurban' (Soja, 1989, p.188). Garreau (1991) has coined the term 'edge cities' to describe this form of urbanization. He argues that:

> today, we have moved our means of creating wealth, the essence of urbanism – our jobs – out to where most of us have lived and shopped for two generations. This has led to the rise of the 'Edge City'. (Garreau, 1991, p.4)

Clearly the trends leading towards a spatially fragmented and de-centred metropolitan structure are identified most clearly with North America, particularly with those cities which are creations of the twentieth century and which have, like Los Angeles, organized themselves around the private automobile as a 'complete way of life' (Dear, 1991, p.38). Nevertheless, even in Europe many of the same *trends* in urban spatial re-organization can be discerned, particularly in countries such as the UK in which previously restrictive planning regulations have been relaxed, allowing market forces to play a much more prominent role in shaping the process and pattern of urban development.

Changes in Movement, Mobility and Travel Patterns

The study was concerned with exploring the intersection of the above postulated features of the transition towards post-Fordist cities with issues concerning movement, mobility and urban travel. The interest lay both in the *implications* of the above changes in urban ways of living and working and in spatial organization for travel patterns and characteristics, but also in the way in which changes in movement and mobility are themselves *constitutive* of these new ways of living and working and of new spatial structures.

The types of question we were interested in addressing thus included:

• How are any shifts in the sectoral composition and contractual status of employment reflected in the spatial pattern or temporal incidence of travel to work?

• What impact is the development of 'new spaces of consumption' having upon urban travel, and upon the access to these facilities by different groups within the urban population?

• How are any increases in social polarization finding expression in differentiated levels of movement and mobility?

• What are the implications of changing demographic and family structures for urban movement and mobility?

• Is there any evidence that the rise of an electronically-mediated 'hyperreality' is impacting upon movement and mobility, for example by suppressing travel from the home for leisure purposes?

• What are the movement and mobility implications of the privatization and deregulation of public transport services?

• What are the implications of less (local or national) state planning and the increasing reliance on market forms of regulation in the urban development arena for the location of work, retailing and leisure activities, and for the journey patterns associated with these activities?

• Is there any evidence for the hypothesized 'fragmentation' of the urban structure, and for the demise of the relatively ordered patterns of movement which previous structures engendered?

• To what extent do movement and mobility patterns reveal evidence for the 'de-centering' of urban spatial structures?

• To what extent is rising car ownership, usage and dependency integrally implicated in new ways of urban living and working?

Figure 12.1 attempts to represent schematically the nature of the hypothesized transition from Fordist to post-Fordist city, focusing on the locational and transport-related themes. On what might be described as the land use and transport planning 'supply side', the transition would be marked by a shift away from planning, integration and regulation towards a more deregulated, market-driven and, perhaps, fragmented supply environment.

	'FORDIST' CITY	'POST-FORDIST' CITY
Planning framework	Ordered, planned	De-regulated, market-driven
Public transport provision	Integrated, regulated	Dis-integrated, fragmented
Work location	Large workplaces, concentrated spatially	Smaller workplaces, dispersed spatially
Shopping location	Local and town centres	Edge of town
Leisure location	Local and town centre	Edge of town/dispersed?
Movement patterns	Ordered, centred	Dis-ordered, de-centred
Mode of travel	Public transport and walk	Car

Figure 12.1. Planning, location and travel in the Fordist and Post-Fordist cities.

Concerning the location of work, retailing and leisure activities, trends would be likely to be discernible towards more spatially dispersed and edge of town locations, with a commensurate weakening of the dominance of city centre locations for these activities. In movement and travel terms, these trends would be likely to find expression in more disordered and de-centred travel patterns, with the city centre becoming just one node among many. Under such circumstances, a marked modal shift away from public transport towards car travel would be likely to emerge.

CHANGING MOVEMENT AND MOBILITY: A TYNESIDE CASE STUDY

On the face of it, Tyneside would not constitute an obvious choice of a city with which to examine evidence for post-Fordist tendencies, given that Los Angeles has been advanced as the paradigm example of the new model. However, there are a number of reasons why Tyneside provides an appropriate and interesting choice for investigating the transitional features in urban change, within the clearly very different context of the UK.

Firstly, Tyneside, and in particular the city of Newcastle, came to exemplify in the post-war period many of the classic characteristics of the *Fordist* city; planned, regulated and embodying an overtly modernist vision of urban development. This vision reached its apotheosis in the 1960s and 1970s, under the political leadership of the leader of the Council, T. Dan Smith, and his Chief Planner, Wilfred Burns, and was captured in Smith's only partly rhetorical desire to re-create Newcastle as the 'Brasilia of the North'. The modernization ethos which underlay the comprehensive plans for Newcastle's redevelopment is conveyed by Burns (1967, p.2): 'the [regional] capital city must be at the head of renewal, and in the forefront in providing what modern man expects in a modern environment'. The rational planning features of 'Fordist' Tyneside included:

• an employment structure dominated by large workplaces in state-owned industries (shipbuilding) and state administration (the then Department of Health and Social Security office complex at Longbenton in Newcastle, the 'nerve centre' of the county's social security system, was described one time as the 'largest administrative complex in the world after the Pentagon'!) (Robinson, 1988);

• the comprehensive re-development of the central area of Newcastle, including the development of the Eldon Square Shopping Centre, one of the largest shopping centres in the country and an early example of public-private partnership;

• major programmes of slum housing clearance in the areas adjoining the riverside industrial areas and their replacement by large-scale council housing schemes, including the 'Byker Wall' re-development;

• the planned provision of new housing and industrial development areas, including the development of Killingworth New Town on the northern fringe of the conurbation, and, south of the Tyne, the development of Washington New Town between Gateshead and Sunderland;

• a massive planned programme of new road building, including urban motorways and rigid vehicular/pedestrian separation (see figure 12.2, reproduced from Burns, 1967), not of all which came to fruition (thereby saving some of Newcastle's original city centre);

• the planning of a fully integrated public transport system, involving the construction of a light railway system (the Metro) and the re-organization of the bus network to become feeders for the Metro. The system was planned in the 1970s and fully implemented by the early 1980s.

The second main justification for choosing Tyneside for the empirical investigation is that in the 1980s, this embodiment of the state-planned, regulated Fordist city began to display features indicative of the 'post-Fordist transition', partly at least as a consequence of increasingly urgent attempts to develop a new economic base for the conurbation in the aftermath of the rapid decline in the late 1970s and early 1980s of its heavy engineering industries (Robinson, 1988). These features included:

• the attraction of new economic activities displaying 'post-Fordist' characteristics, including Japanese production activities in the broader region and financial services 'back offices' and call centres in the conurbation itself;

• the development of new centres of consumption and leisure, exemplified by John Hall's MetroCentre in Gateshead, the largest shopping centre development

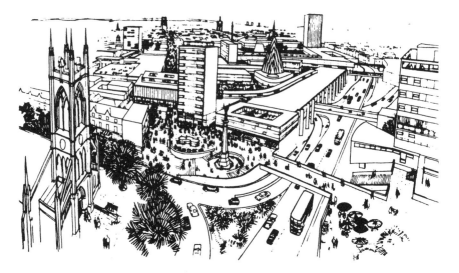

Figure 12.2. Planned vehicle/pedestrian segregation, and urban motorways, Newcastle upon Tyne (Source: Burns, 1967)

in Europe, accompanied by the consolidation of Newcastle's role as a service centre and consumption node rather than a production base;

• 'waterfront' regeneration projects, such as the Newcastle Quayside, the St Peters Basin marina and housing development, and the re-development of North Shields Fish Quay, serving to bring middle class housing back into the riverside areas;

• heightened social deprivation, after more than a decade of Thatcherism, one tangible expression of which were the riots on the Meadowell Estate and in Benwell;

• new institutional frameworks, involving the down-grading of the role of the local state (expenditure capping on the districts and the abolition of the strategic planning authority, Tyne and Wear County Council), and their displacement by quangos (notably the Tyne and Wear Development Corporation (TWDC) and Tyneside Training and Enterprise Council) and private-public partnerships such as The Newcastle Initiative;

• the relaxation and streamlining of planning controls on development through the creation of Enterprise Zones and the TWDC;

• the de-integration, with the abolition of the County Council in 1986, of the integrated public transport system, and the deregulation of bus services.

Although a number of changes have thus occurred on Tyneside which could be argued to represent features of an 'ideal type' Fordist to post-Fordist city transition, there are a number of particularities of Tyneside which will limit the extent to which this transition model can be expected to apply, especially with respect to changing spatial organization and travel patterns. Tyneside has a very distinctive spatial structure (figure 12.3), with important implications for the nature of its travel patterns. The conurbation is effectively a coalescence of previously separate riverside communities (Newcastle, Wallsend and North Shields on the north bank of the Tyne, Gateshead, Hebburn, Jarrow and South Shields on the south bank). The conurbation is thus characterized by a 'double-linear' rather than concentric form, and is multi-nodal. Further, the nature of the area's economic development resulted in the riverside communities being relatively self-contained, with, traditionally, very short journeys to work. The demise of shipbuilding and marine engineering since the 1960s has led to a forced restructuring of this spatial organization and of the travel patterns associated with it. The Metro system has had the effect of greatly facilitating this restructuring, connecting the riverside communities with each other and with the conurbation's increasingly dominant centre, Newcastle (University of Newcastle upon Tyne, 1990).

A second distinctive feature of Tyneside which is relevant to the investigation is that car ownership levels, while rising in line with national trends, remain remarkably low (51.8 per cent of Tyneside households did not have a car in 1991, compared with only 33.4 per cent of GB households), whilst the quality of

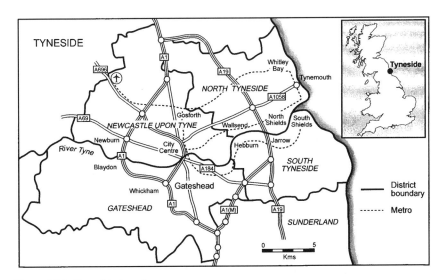

Figure 12.3. Tyneside location map.

public transport provision (bus as well as Metro) is relatively high, a legacy of the previous era of high investment and the strategic planning of transport provision.

Methodology for the Study

The overall objective of undertaking a study of Tyneside was to develop a better understanding of how changes in transport provision, in the location of activities and in economic and social processes are being reflected in changes in travel behaviour. Our interest was not in *measuring* these changes, nor in building econometric *models* of their inter-relationships, but rather in developing a *qualitative understanding* of them, through the perceptions of the relevant actors.

More specifically, we wished to explore, through a series of semi-structured interviews with different types of actors, how, firstly, the fragmentation of Tyneside's previously integrated and planned transport supply regime; secondly, the spatial re-restructuring of the conurbation, with respect to work, consumption and leisure activities; and, thirdly, the increasing differentiation, polarization and segmentation of ways of life, all come together in changing patterns of movement and mobility. The interviews were held with three main groups of actors:

1. The Transport 'Supply-Side' Institutions

Interviews were held with representatives of all of the main institutional actors with interests in the supply, regulation or control of transport, public and private, on Tyneside. These included the local authorities (highway engineers, land use planners and the Passenger Transport Authority); the Passenger Transport Executive, responsible for running the Metro system; the bus companies; the Department of Transport; and transport engineering consultancies active in the area.

These interviews were designed to elicit information on the ways these transport supply-side actors perceived that movement and mobility on Tyneside have been affected by the institutional fragmentation of the transport sector and the effective demise of strategic transportation planning, and the manner of their responses to these changes. Further, we were also interested in exploring the extent to which the types of changes in living and working which were labelled above as 'post-Fordist' were recognized and integrated (or not, as the case may be) into their 'mental models' of the conurbation, or at least those aspects of such models which impinged upon their professional domains.

2. Developers and Managers of New Nodes of Employment, Retail and Leisure Activities

Information on the spatial restructuring of the conurbation, from the perspective of those responsible for this restructuring, was obtained from interviews with

Tyne and Wear Development Corporation and with the developers and managers of new workplace locations (such as the Newcastle Business Park and companies located on the Park, such as IBM); new sites of consumption (such as the operators of the MetroCentre, companies located there such as Marks and Spencer, and superstore operators); and new sites of leisure activity (such as up-market health clubs, multiplex cinemas and new leisure experiences such as the Wet and Wild water park in North Shields).

In these interviews, we sought to examine how assumptions about travel behaviour – particularly in relation to private car and public transport usage – were built into the design and implementation of the various nodes, and the extent to which these assumptions have been borne out by subsequent experience of actual travel behaviour.

3. Households

Interviews were held with members of a number of households, supplemented by travel diary information, in order to explore perceptions concerning ease of movement, accessibility to various facilities (work, school, shops and leisure facilities), the role of travel in different lifestyles, the extent of car dependency, perceived generational differences in travel behaviour, etc. The interviews took place with households located in different parts of the conurbation, in order to encompass a range of socio-economic and locational contexts. In order to impose a degree of commonality between the limited number of households interviewed, the selection was restricted to families with one or more teenage children.

The interviews were achieved through contacts with four secondary schools in Newcastle and North Tyneside (the schools being located in Kenton, Gosforth, Heaton and Wallsend). Daily travel diaries, covering weekdays and weekends, were first obtained from the children of selected classes (through the good offices of teachers of Geography!), and, wherever possible, similar diaries for parents and other household members were sought, using the children to administer the diaries to their other household members. In total, some 1470 separate journeys were covered by the dairies, covering basic information such as journey purpose, time of journey, mode of travel, etc. The diary exercise was followed up by home-based interviews with a small number of families, on a voluntary basis. The interviews, twenty-five in number, were not in any sense 'representative' of an assumed broader population, though we did attempt to ensure, through the selection of schools, that a reasonable range of household types would be represented.

In retrospect, this part of the methodology proved least successful, with a considerable amount of effort required to achieve a small number of household interviews, which varied much in quality (depending largely on the inter-personal dynamics within each household!). Focus group discussions with groups of varying age, gender and socio-economic status would probably have proved a more cost-effective means of obtaining the type of material we were looking for.

In the sections which follow, the main findings to emerge from the empirical work are summarized.

FRAGMENTATION OF PUBLIC TRANSPORT SUPPLY?

The thesis being explored here is that the shift from an integrated, planned approach to transport provision, to a less-planned, more market-driven approach, signified by the abolition of the County Council and by bus de-regulation in the mid-1980s, will have fragmented the supply of public transport services, fuelling a modal shift towards car travel for those with choice and resulting in deteriorating mobility levels for those without.

The evidence from the supply side institutional actor interviews certainly confirms the contention that a major fragmentation has taken place in the system of transport planning and regulation, well understood by the actors concerned to be part of a broader shift towards a neo-liberal governance agenda in Britain which has taken place since the end of the 1970s. This fragmentation has taken a number of forms, including the loss of forced bus-Metro integration; the loss of through ticketing between buses and Metro; the rationalization and subsequently privatization of the bus operators; the falling into a state of 'disrepair' of the Tyne and Wear multi-modal model (a classic symbol of the 'golden age' of rationalist, centralized, 'Fordist' transport planning); the loss of a strategic planning level resulting in more inter-district conflicts; and more conflicts between local authority highways engineers and the bus operators, notably over the restraint on bus operation in the centre of Newcastle.

The question remains, however, of to what extent the undoubted fragmentation in the top-down strategic *planning* of transport has detrimentally affected the level and quality of actual transport *provision*. The loss of integration between Metro and bus with bus deregulation, coupled with fares increases in 1986 following the abolition of Tyne and Wear Council, did certainly lead to a marked fall in Metro patronage (and, indeed, overall public transport patronage) (University of Newcastle upon Tyne, 1990). However, patronage levels soon stabilized, albeit at a lower level. Further, a number of other observations suggest that the assertion that a generalized fragmentation in service provision has taken place is difficult to sustain. These include:

• The integration between bus and Metro at major interchanges (such as Regent Centre and Four Lane Ends) has slowly re-appeared, due to travel demand to which the bus operators have responded on the basis of commercial logic.

• Very few services have been lost through deregulation, with the continuation of supported services by the PTA enabling socially desirable services to be maintained. Moreover, cost rationalization by the bus operators has meant that many fewer services now require support than in the previous regime.

• Innovation has occurred in public transport provision, notably through the use of mini-buses and more rapid responses to demand changes.

• Little 'cut-throat' competition, which could have brought about fragmentation, has in practise emerged, due at least in part to the 'municipal corporatism' of the dominant bus companies, which has prevented new entrants from becoming established.

• Some attempts have been made to re-introduce co-ordination, albeit with lower level objectives, through the central government promoted 'Package Approach' of integrating policies for roads and for public transport, and through joint working arrangements.

Despite, therefore, the pressures for fragmentation, the quality of public transport provision on Tyneside has not been as severely affected as might have been predicted; indeed, in certain respects at least, the supply of service has been improved in a more market-responsive environment (as one respondent put it, the trouble with the old approach, embodied in the PTE, was its Stalinism!).

CHANGES IN THE LOCATION OF WORK, RETAILING AND LEISURE ACTIVITIES

The thesis under investigation here was that the 'post-Fordist' transition of the Tyneside economy, with a shift towards smaller workplaces, in offices and services rather than production activities, coupled with commensurate shifts in the location of retailing and leisure activities, would be leading towards much more decentralized and dispersed travel patterns and towards greater car dependency.

The Location of Workplaces

The specificities of Tyneside, with employment historically concentrated along both banks of the Tyne, and with a tradition of localized journeys to work, has indeed resulted in marked changes in work locations and in travel patterns associated with economic restructuring. A number of facets of change can be identified:

• The virtual demise of shipbuilding and marine engineering has brought to an end the localized patterns of work travel which characterized the riverside communities. The Metro system, which runs along both sides of the river, is widely recognized to have played an important role in 'helping people get used to commuting'. The decline of riverside employment strengthened the *relative* importance of Newcastle city centre as an employment location, though actual growth in full-time employment in the 1980s favoured non-central locations such as Washington New Town, north west Newcastle, around the airport, and the northern suburbs of North Tyneside (Newcastle upon Tyne, 1990).

• In the 1990s, the non-central location of workplaces has become more marked. Changes in working practises and in office space requirements are fuelling a widespread growth in office development outside of the city centre in high specification office parks, such as Newcastle Business Park and the Fifth Avenue Business Park on the Team Valley. Work-related travel requirements are an integral element of this locational shift. As one influential institutional actor put it: 'Cities have to flex, and this hasn't been encouraged in Newcastle city centre. Office accommodation which has no car parking is simply not meeting needs. Office uses are changing, particularly in professional companies – you go to your client or your client comes to you'. Although in non-central locations, many of these new office developments are nevertheless within the existing built-up area, due to the lure of urban regeneration subsidies in Enterprise Zones and the Development Corporation area.

• The modal shift to the car reflected in this statement is being accentuated by the development of 12 or 24 hour working in a number of major new office employers, notably telephone call centres, which are also concentrated in business park locations (Richardson and Marshall, 1996). Nevertheless, public transport services are being provided to the new business parks, with the developers being keen to improve access by bus in order to maximize labour availability, and with the bus companies recognizing the need to 'capture' ridership even if services have to be provided, for a period at least, ahead of commercial viability. Although in non-city centre locations, the business parks do not represent the type of spatially diffused workplaces which would be very difficult to serve by public transport; the Newcastle Business Park, for example, is a concentration of 4000 jobs, while the Fifth Avenue Business Park is located within a major concentration of nearly 20,000 jobs on the Team Valley.

In summary then, changes in workplace location associated with economic restructuring and the decline of the riverside concentrations of employment have resulted both in a stronger orientation towards Newcastle city centre, and, more recently, to a growth of new non city centre workplace locations. Significantly, however, these new locations are primarily in Enterprise Zones and in the areas of the Tyne and Wear Development Corporation; these are nearly all brownfield sites, usually at the heart of the conurbation, rather than greenfield sites on its periphery, and have been subsidy-driven (Healey, 1994).

The Location of Retailing

Retailing too has become much less localized, with the sharp decline of neighbourhood shopping centres and the traditional 'high streets' in the riverside towns. Retail provision has become much more spatially concentrated, in two main phases. Firstly, the construction of the Eldon Centre shopping centre in Newcastle in the 1970s and the opening of the Metro system in the early 1980s (which could be argued to be a device for facilitating travel from all parts of the conurbation to the centre of Newcastle) led to a considerable concentration of new retail investment in Newcastle's town centre. The second phase, which is still continuing, was marked by the opening of the MetroCentre in Gateshead in the mid-1980s and by a proliferation of new superstore building, with companies such as Safeways, Tescos and Asda predominating. The second of these phases focused on non-town centre/high street locations, and had the car user very much in mind.

Nevertheless, a combination of factors has meant that the conurbation has not been 'turned inside out' by these latter developments, and has managed to accommodate the interests of non car-owners to a perhaps surprising degree:

• There has been no generalized decline of retailing in Newcastle city centre attendant upon the opening of the Gateshead MetroCentre, despite the impressive scale of the latter. Indeed, new rounds of retail investment are currently taking place in the centre of Newcastle, such as the doubling in size of the Marks and Spencer store, already the second largest in the country after Oxford Street. Whereas other major new 'out of town' shopping developments close to existing centres, such Meadowhall/Sheffield, Lakeside/Romford and Merryhill/Dudley, have had demonstrably negative impacts upon the level and quality of town centre retailing, this has not occurred in Newcastle both because the city centre was considerably more robust to begin with and because the MetroCentre has attracted new shoppers which have not simply been diverted from the centre of Newcastle, reflecting the particular geography of the region and location of the MetroCentre with respect to major roads. Nevertheless, there is growing evidence of weakness in the non-prime city centre locations, and a number of secondary retail centres in the conurbation have undoubtedly been detrimentally affected by the MetroCentre.

• The locations in which the new retail capacity has been built have tended not to be on the edge of the conurbation, due in part to Green Belt restrictions and the tightly bounded nature of the conurbation in local government terms, with the adjacent Northumberland County Council wishing to restrict the sprawl of the built-up area any further north. As with new office developments, however, the main factor explaining the location of new retail investment is the existence of government subsidy on brownfield sites; in a weak property market, commercial property development has followed the subsidy (Healey, 1994). The main

developments have thus taken place in Enterprise Zones, explaining the locations of the MetroCentre and Team Valley's Retail World, and, for superstore
locations, a number of sites at the interstices between the separate towns which
make up the conurbation. These major new retail developments have thus been
accommodated largely *within* the existing fabric of the conurbation, rather than
at or beyond its edges.

• Partly because of these locational characteristics, the new retail facilities are
not completely car-based, although car usage clearly predominates. In the case
of the MetroCentre, for example, the developers intended to make no provision
at all for public transport, though a re-think was forced by Marks and Spencer,
whose decision to construct their first out-of-town centre store was crucial to the
overall venture. More than 20 per cent of MetroCentre users currently arrive by
public transport, primarily bus (despite the name, the MetroCentre is not on the
Metro!). The scale of the MetroCentre means that it has become a major node in
the Tyneside bus network, largely due to the commercial decision-making of the
bus companies. Broadly similar modal splits are evident for the superstores; the
Tesco at Kingston Park, for example, located within a primarily ABC1 catchment area, has a significant number of public transport users, in this case primarily arriving by Metro.

The Location of New Leisure Activities

Even more clearly than for the trends in workplace and retail location, recent
years have seen a decline in localized facility provision and a growth of larger
scale, concentrated facilities, dependent upon conurbation-wide catchment areas.
Examples include the demise of the high street cinema and the growth of large
multiplex cinemas (the MetroCentre UAI apparently has the world record for
ticket sales in one day!); the contraction of municipal local swimming baths and
the concentration into a fewer number of much larger 'leisure pools', and the
emergence of private-sector 'water theme parks', notably 'Wet and Wild' on the
Royal Quays site in North Shields, with its 300 car parking spaces and 350,000
visitors per year; or the advent of new leisure facilities, such as the Kingston
Springs health club at Kingston Park in Newcastle, which requires a catchment
area of 300,000 people in order to attract its target membership of 3000.

Journeys to such facilities are, of course, very much longer on average than
the types of localized journeys which they have functionally replaced, and are
much more likely to be made by car. Trends in leisure journeys on Tyneside
seem to exemplify well the main problem with respect to travel behaviour and
the environment; it is not that more journeys are being made, rather that they are
longer, and are more likely to be made by car (Jones, 1993). Most of the
members of Kingston Springs, to take a decidedly non-representative example,
are members of two-car households and, as the manager put it, 'those who have

difficulty getting here couldn't afford to be members anyway'. Seventy-four per cent of visitors to the Wet and Wild water theme park arrive by car, and many of the remainder arrive in organized parties by coach and mini-bus. Nevertheless, although the facility has been described as 'being in the middle of nowhere', it is in fact close to the riverside and can be reached by both bus and Metro, as well as attracting a number of local residents from the neighbouring, socially deprived, communities, who are offered heavily discounted admission prices. Its location is explained by being part of the Tyne and Wear Development Commission's Royal Quays flagship regeneration project, which enables it to benefit from TWDC grants.

In conclusion, the major use of brownfield sites for new office, retail and leisure facilities, largely as a result of the availability of EZ and TWDC subsidies, has meant that the conurbation has not been 'turned inside out' by the new developments. Developments which would normally be associated with out-of-town or 'edge city' locations have been accommodated within the fabric of the metropolitan area, often indeed at the very heart of the conurbation. This has enabled public transport to remain a viable option for reaching the new workplaces, retail centres and leisure facilities, an option which the bus companies appear to have responded vigorously towards maintaining.

In terms of the post-Fordist de-centering and spatial dispersal thesis, it must be concluded that the specificities of Tyneside's spatial structure have resulted in restructuring taking a rather different form. Indeed, it could be argued that, in terms of its travel patterns at least, Tyneside has moved from a 'pre-Fordist' to a Fordist phase, with much less local travel centred on relatively discrete riverside communities, and much more evidence of conurbation-wide travel. Evidence does though suggest that more decentralized, dispersed travel patterns are beginning to become established, though their impact is very much lessened by the locational peculiarities of the predominately brownfield forms of development discussed above.

CAR DEPENDENCY OR CAR INCORPORATION?

One of the main themes explored in the household interviews concerned the extent to which car owning households perceived that their lifestyles were car dependent, indeed that these lifestyles might even be built around the car, and the extent to which non-car owners (or those individuals with restricted car access) perceived that their access to different types of facility was impaired.

For the non-car owning families, it would be difficult to sustain the thesis of impaired mobility or limited accessibility, at least in the family's own perceptions. Activity patterns did tend to be much more localized than for car owning families, with more use of local shops and primarily local family and social relationships. Nevertheless, public transport was seen to be perfectly adequate for meeting their travel needs, and, indeed, the level of service was perceived as having improved since deregulation. Changes in the pattern of retail provision (or indeed in health care provision, which we also examined) which were leading towards more centralized facilities, perhaps in less accessible locations, were accommodated by means of a range of relatively simple coping strategies, such as undertaking a monthly shop at a superstore by taxi. Significantly, there was little evidence from the interviews that non-car owning households aspired to car ownership.

For car owning households, 'mixed modal' patterns pre-dominated, rather than complete car dependency. Different journey purposes were associated with different modes, but relatively few journeys were completely dependent upon car usage; the main exception to this was work-based travel, in which car-usage has clearly become integral to a wide range of occupations. For home-based travel, the car has become incorporated into people's lifestyles, but these lifestyles appear not to have been built around car dependency.

Interestingly, there was no evidence from the interviews of children's 'daily activity spaces' having become truncated due to fears over the safety of travel (though this observation is based only on families with teenage children). Indeed, parents perceive that their children travel far more widely than they used to do at equivalent ages, reflecting both the greater opportunities for travel, and the greater distances to desired leisure facilities such as cinemas, sports facilities and swimming baths. The travel diaries reveal that children in car owning households benefit considerably from car usage; in total, of the journeys undertaken by 10-14 year olds, 37 per cent are by car, while 30 per cent of journeys by 15-19 year olds are by car (table 12.1). However, earlier statements concerning less localized travel patterns need to be tempered by the recognition that walking remains by far the dominant mode of travel for young people, accounting for 46 per cent of journeys in the 10–14 age group, and for 44 per cent of

Table 12.1:   Modal split between car and foot, for different age groups (percentages of total travel for each age group).

Age	Car %	Foot %
10–14	37.1	46.2
15–19	29.6	43.7
20–24	51.1	17.8
(30–34)	(84.6)	(7.7)
35–39	54.8	30.8
40–44	68.4	26.3
45–49	66.3	16.7
50–54	69.6	25.5

Source: Travel diaries (NB. 30-34 age group has low numbers in this band).

journeys in the 15–19 age group. Even for adults, with their much greater levels of car usage, walking constitutes a significant mode of travel, accounting for 31 per cent of journeys in the 35–39 age band, and for 26 per cent of journeys for those aged 40–44.

The continued importance of walk journeys on Tyneside, embedded within people's daily activity patterns, reflects of course a form of urban spatial organization which has not yet become designed around the assumption of universal car access. This is perhaps unsurprising, given that it is only in the 1990s that car ownership has reached a majority of Tyneside's households.

CONCLUSIONS

In terms of the post-Fordist transition thesis, there is certainly evidence to suggest that significant changes are occurring in the nature of employment and of daily life on Tyneside which are associated with new forms of spatial organization and new patterns of movement and mobility. From the evidence obtained from interviews with key actors and from Tyneside families, activity locations appear to be becoming increasingly dispersed and journeys increasingly long. There is clearly a need to complement the exploratory qualitative interview research reported here with more 'conventional' quantitative research. This complimentary research needs itself, however, to be exploratory, in the sense of not embodying assumptions about the nature of, or motivation for, travel behaviour. Changes in urban spatial and societal organization appear to be occurring on a sufficient scale to suggest that models which attempt to predict future outcomes from past regularities are likely to have little predictive utility.

In terms of the policy implications of the research reported here, care obviously needs to be taken in attempting to draw broader policy lessons from the case of a single city. There are, nevertheless, a number of interesting features pertaining to the Tyneside example which warrant further consideration, particularly within the context of the shift which is occurring in transport and planning policy towards sustainability (Owens, 1995).

The first, and most obvious lesson, concerns the way in which Tyneside has learnt to live with and accommodate the car, and the role of urban policy land use planning, broadly conceived, in facilitating this accommodation without either turning the conurbation inside out or forcing car dependency. As a result of Enterprise Zones and the Development Corporation, coupled with planning restrictions which have limited development on the periphery of the conurbation, the major new developments – offices, retailing and leisure – have occurred primarily on sites. As a result, the heart of the conurbation is in the process of being successfully re-generated (at least in land re-use terms), and accessibility for the non-car owning minority (only just a minority remember) has been maintained. The conurbation appears to have managed, to date at least, to achieve its 'need to flex', by accommodating new types of primarily car-based office, leisure and retail facilities, within the confines of the built-up area. Ironically then, the 'planning free zones' of the EZs and UDC area appear to have achieved highly desirable (planned?) outcomes. In a property market such as Tyneside at least, the availability of public subsidies in particular brownfield locations appears to be able to exert sufficient leverage on private development to achieve locational outcomes desired by the planning system. Within the context of new planning guidelines, such as PPG13, there is perhaps much to be learnt from the Tyneside experience. An issue for the future is whether planning tools alone, without development subsidies, could achieve these desired outcomes.

If sustainable transport and planning policies *are* to be devised, it seems clear to us that there will need to be a deep-seated political and cultural shift towards the promotion and facilitation of urban, particularly metropolitan, living. Only in cities, with their density, scale and public transport provision can the car be accommodated and absorbed into ways of living and working, without the generation of excessive amounts of car-based travel.

NOTE

1. There is a direct link between transport and the term 'Fordism', which is a reference to the model of mass production and mass consumption which is said to have originated with Henry Ford. Not only did his River Rouge car plant in Detroit revolutionize production with its assembly line principles, but by paying his workers high wages ('$5 a day') in return for their high productivity he also recognized the need to establish the basis by which mass *consumption* could develop (Meegan, 1988).

REFERENCES

Amin, A. (1994) Post-Fordism: models, fantasies and phantoms of transition, in Amin, A.(ed.) *Post-Fordism: A Reader.* Oxford: Blackwell.

Banister, D. and Button, K.(1992) *Transport, the Environment and Sustainable Development.* London: E & F Spon.

Banister, D., Gillespie, A., Hay, A., Jones, P. and Williams, H.C.W.L.(1990) United Kingdom, in Nijkamp, P., Reichman, S. and Wegener, M.(eds.) *Euromobile: Transport, Communications and Mobility in Europe.* Aldershot: European Science Foundation and Avebury.

Baudrillard, J. (1983) *Simulations.* New York: Semiotext(e).

Burns, W. (1967) *Newcastle: A Study in Re-planning at Newcastle upon Tyne.* London: Leonard Hill.

Castells, M. (1989) *The Informational City.* Oxford: Blackwell.

Cooke, P.(1990) Modern urban theory in question. *Transactions of the Institute of British Geographers* NS, **15**, pp. 331–343.

Dear, M. (1991) Taking Los Angeles seriously: time and space in the postmodern city. *Architecture California*, **13**(2), pp. 36–42.

Featherstone, M. (1991) *Consumer Culture and Postmodernism.* London: Sage.

Garreau, J. (1991) *Edge City: Life on the New Frontier.* New York: Doubleday.

Gibelli M.C. (1988) Urban planning strategies and tools to cope with technological and socio-economic change in metropolitan areas, in *Urban Development and Impacts of Technological, Economic and Socio-Demographic Changes.* Paris: OECD, pp. 88–104.

Goodwin, P., Hallett, S., Kenny, F. and Stokes, G. (1991) *Transport: The New Realism.* Report to the Rees Jeffreys Road Fund. Oxford: University of Oxford Transport Studies Unit.

Handy, S. (1996) Methodologies for exploring the link between urban form and travel behaviour. *Transportation Research* D, **1**(2), pp. 151–165.

Harvey, D. (1989*a*) From managerialism to entrepreneurialism: the transformation of urban governance in late capitalism. *Geografiska Annaler*, **71**, pp. 3–17.

Harvey, D. (1989*b*) *The Condition of Postmodernity.* Oxford: Blackwell.

Healey, P. (1994) Urban policy and property development: the institutional relations of real-estate development in an old industrial region. *Environment & Planning* A, **26**, pp. 177–198.

Jones, G. (1993) Planning and the reduction of transport emissions. *The Planner*, **10**(26), pp. 8–20.

Jones, P.M., Dix, M.C., Clark, M.I. and Heggie, I.G. (1991) *Understanding Travel Behaviour.* Aldershot: Gower.

Kitamura, R., Pas, E.I., Lula, C.V., Lawton, T.K. and Benson, P.E. (1996) The sequenced activity mobility simulator (SAMS): an integrated approach to modelling transportation, land use and air quality. *Transportation*, **23**, pp. 267–291.

Lipietz, A. (1987) *Mirages and Miracles: the Crises of Global Fordism.* London: Verso.

Lovatt, A. with O'Connor, J., Montgomery, J. and Owens, P. (1994) *The 24 Hour City, Selected Papers from the First National Conference on the Night-Time Economy.* Manchester: Manchester Institute for Popular Culture.

Meegan, R. (1988) A crisis of mass production? in Allen, J. and Massey, D. (eds.) *The Economy in Question.* London: Sage.

Mingione, E. (1991) *Fragmented Societies: A Sociology of Economic Life Beyond the Market Paradigm.* Oxford: Blackwell.

Mollenkopf, J. and Castells, M. (1991) *Dual City.* New York: Russell Sage.

Owens, S. (1995) From 'predict and provide' to 'predict and prevent'? Pricing and planning in transport policy. *Transport Policy*, **2**(1), pp. 43–49.

Ortúzar, J. de Dios, and Willumsen, L.G. (1991) Flexible long range planning using low cost information. *Transportation*, **18**, pp. 151–173.

Qvortrup, L. (1992) Telework: visions, definitions, realities, barriers, in *Cities and New Technologies.* Paris: OECD, pp.77–108.

Richardson,R, and Marshall, J.N. (1996) The growth of telephone call centres in peripheral areas of Britain: evidence from Tyne and Wear. *Area*, **28**(3), pp. 308–317.

Robinson, F. (1988) Industrial structure, in Robinson, F. (ed.) *Post-industrial Tyneside: An Economic and Social Survey of Tyneside in the 1980s.* Newcastle upon Tyne: Newcastle upon Tyne City Libraries and Arts.

Sayer, A. (1984) *Method in Social Science: A Realist Approach.* London: Hutchinson.

Soja, E.W. (1989) *Postmodern Geographies: the Reassertion of Space in Critical Social Theory.* New York: Verso.

Spear, B. (1996) New approaches to transportation forecasting models: a synthesis of four research proposals. *Transportation*, **23**(3), pp. 215–240.

Stopher, P.R., Hartgen, D.T. and Li, Y. (1996) SMART: Simulation models for activities, resources and travel. *Transportation*, **23**(3), pp. 293–312.

University of Newcastle upon Tyne (1990) The Longer Term Effects of the Tyne and Wear Metro. Report to the Transport and Road Research Laboratory, Department of Transport. University of Newcastle upon Tyne.

Wachs, M. (1996) A new generation of travel demand models, Guest Editorial. *Transportation*, **23**, pp.213–214.

Webster, F.V., Bly, P.H. and Paulley, N.J. (eds.) (1988) *Urban Land Use and Transport Interaction: Policies and Models.* Farnborough: Avebury.

Zukin, S. (1988) The postmodern debate over urban form. *Theory, Culture and Society*, **5**(2–3).

CHAPTER 13

GREENER TRANSPORT TOWNS: PUBLICLY ACCEPTABLE, PRIVATELY RESISTED?

Margaret Anderson, Julia Meaton, Clive Potter and Alan Rogers

The premise behind the work outlined in this chapter is that if the implementation of greener transport measures is to be successful it needs the acceptance and co-operation of the public. There is little doubt that in recent years public attitudes towards the apparently inexorable rise in road traffic have begun to change. Surveys (for example, Lex Service plc, 1995) indicate that people are increasingly recognising the adverse effects of pollution, congestion and road building and thinking that alternatives to personal car-borne mobility are a good idea. The realization that the unfettered use of the private car can no longer be taken as a given in transport policy is gaining ground.

There is an assumption, however, that changing attitudes will be translated into changing behaviour; that those who agree with cycle lanes and better bus services will use them when they are provided. This research was designed to look critically at this assumption: to find out if there is any real link between *attitude* and *behavioural change*; whether knowledge and understanding of the problems will influence people's personal travel decisions; and which measures seem to be not only the most acceptable but the most effective for bringing about change.

The researchers based their work on a number of assumptions: firstly that while many people may have general knowledge of the negative impacts of car use, most are unlikely to have specific information, either on how they are personally affected or on how their individual travel decisions increase or decrease the impacts; and secondly, that if they have such information it will have some effect on their travel decisions, but that a major change in behaviour will only be likely to occur if the circumstances relate directly to the people concerned.

There is now increasing recognition that while environmental problems may be generated nationally, or even internationally, many of the solutions must be implemented locally. This is in line with the philosophy of Agenda 21 (Chapter 28) and is particularly important in relation to transport, given the relevant responsibilities of local authorities. The vital role of local government in 'educating, mobilising and responding to the public' is likely to be a determining factor in achieving the Agenda's goals (Earth Summit, 1992). In practical terms, however, officers need to find time and cost efficient ways to initiate debate and build public support, especially with personal mobility where private decisions on travel behaviour are being made locally every day, but many of the decisions on how and where transport means and modes will be provided, are being made in a national context.

Putting all this together, the research team proposed a project based on the idea of developing an innovative survey methodology that would bring together information, problems and solutions in a local context and which would involve participants in seeing situations in relation to their own decisions and subsequent outcomes. In this way it was hoped to overcome the hypothetical nature of some stated preference surveys and draw the public into the transport and environment debate. The experimental survey document that was developed is called *The Green Journey Guide* (figure 13.1). Being a survey relevant to local people it was based in a particular location, however, it was anticipated that once tested and refined the methodology could be adapted for use anywhere.

The case study town chosen was Ashford in Kent. The research team brought to bear on the discussions its previous experience in developing and carrying out research in Ashford that had encouraged local people to understand the problems and constraints involved in planning for major urban expansion (Anderson, Meaton and Potter, 1994). The lessons from that project were the inherent reasonableness of people once they were cognizant of the wider situation, and their willingness to participate and express ideas in an informal situation.

The philosophy behind *The Green Journey Guide* was three-fold. Firstly to confront people with both the impact of their own current travel decisions and the cumulative effects of all the myriads of similar decisions made by others. Secondly to challenge them to consider their attitude towards the introduction of greener transport measures and whether their introduction locally would have any effect at all on the travel decisions they made. Finally to find ways to engage the interest of participants and to convey the seriousness of the issues, without antagonising them with abstract threats of doom and gloom. The *Guide* therefore attempted to make connections: between respondents' own travel behaviour and that of other members of their families; and between the benefits they derive from using the car and the costs imposed on others (and ultimately themselves). In other words, it aimed to encourage people to acknowledge that

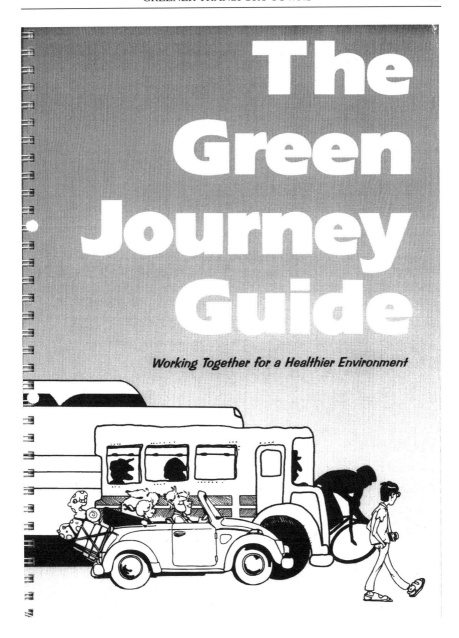

Figure 13.1. The cover of *The Green Journey Guide*.

they are not only part of the problem, by giving them information, but that they can also be part of the solution, by suggesting ways in which they could, through their own actions, contribute to a cleaner, safer environment. It was believed that from the research a group of respondents would be revealed whose greener attitudes and behaviour could be harnessed to lead change to more environmentally friendly transport modes.

To the extent that the methodology, in its experimental form, has outputs that can be measured, the research team have concluded that the project was successful in revealing local, and reinforcing national, trends in the use of cars and the likelihood of the public accepting, and changing to, greener forms of transport. Perhaps more importantly it has highlighted the importance of relating work in the field of transport behaviour to that of behavioural studies in other areas of research.

DEVELOPMENT OF THE METHODOLOGY

Rationale

The stated aim of the research was to develop an innovative methodology designed to explore the reactions of the public to a range of policies or measures intended to reduce both the use of cars and their environmental impacts. There were a number of reasons for deciding that a new methodology was required. The main one was that it was believed that there was no existing survey format that could satisfactorily combine the breadth and type of information the researchers wanted both to impart and to receive with an interactive presentation, drawing participants into the transport/environment debate as it specifically affects them.

Additionally, Local Agenda 21 is encouraging the search for new methodologies which will 'educate and entertain' and be sufficiently 'lightly engineered' to have wide appeal. Previous research by the authors (Anderson *et al.*, 1994) has suggested that the vehicle through which the information is delivered to the public can be influential in gaining public understanding and support.

The team therefore set itself three main objectives related to what information *The Green Journey Guide* would give and receive and how it would be designed.

1. *Obtaining information from respondents*:
(*a*) their existing patterns of travel and private car use;
(*b*) their *attitudes* to a variety of measures for encouraging greener travel behaviour and their *willingness to change their behaviour* if the measures were implemented;
(*c*) their existing knowledge and understanding of the environmental impacts of travel, particularly car use;

(d) their socio-economic and other characteristics (in order to identify the types of people most in favour of and most antagonistic to greener transport solutions, with the ultimate aim of targeting policy persuasion).

2. *Supplying information to respondents*:
(a) confronting respondents with an estimate of the environmental costs of their personal journeys;
(b) providing information on the reasons for the need to reduce car use;
(c) providing information on greener travel measures and how they would provide environmental and personal benefits.

3. *Basing the survey on a number of premises*:
(a) that the more people understand about a situation the more likely they are to work with solutions than against them;
(b) that people take more interest when they can see the relevance of the costs and the benefits in their own lives;
(c) that people learn by doing things as well as by reading and hearing; participative learning is therefore more effective than passive;
(d) that people will learn more, work harder and concentrate longer if they are enjoying themselves.

In following these objectives the team's discussions on the content and format of *The Green Journey Guide* drew on the findings of research by social psychologists. In particular the design of the *Guide* considered the importance of persuasive communication and the presence of inducements in the establishment of links between attitude and behavioural change. Consideration of these points and the relationship of these research findings to the *Guide* are discussed in more detail in the final section at the end of this chapter.

The Travel Pack

Before decisions could be made on the content of *The Green Journey Guide* it was considered necessary to conduct a local travel survey. The survey was designed to collect new data on how people were travelling around Ashford and how they were using the current transport systems. Its purpose was two-fold: to provide detailed 'baseline' information on travel activity; and to provide information for use in *The Green Journey Guide* in order to relate the *Guide* as closely as possible to the respondents' circumstances in Ashford. For example, instead of basing calculations of resource use or pollution levels on national data they would be based on more local information.

There are a variety of ways of collecting personal travel information. One of the more popular methods has been the travel diary but since the 1980s transport researchers began exploring the possibilities of activity diaries (Stopher, 1992; Kitamura, 1988). These are similar to travel diaries but, instead of just asking for information on travel, they aim to elicit information on a much wider spectrum of the respondents' behaviour and so reduce the difficulties respondents frequently encounter in remembering all their trips. As the forgotten trips are often those of short duration and/or are on foot their omission makes it very difficult for researchers to understand the complete travel behaviour of respondents. Activity diaries are designed so that this under-reporting can be minimized by requesting respondents to keep a record of *all* their activities throughout the day. This not only means that shorter, non-motorized trips are likely to be remembered, but it also allows the full pattern of travel activity to be revealed and consequently studied (Bonnel, 1995; Jones, Dix, Clarke and Heggie, 1991; Van der Hoorn, 1979). Barnard (1986) and Clarke, Dix and Jones (1981) have compared travel and activity diaries revealing advantages and disadvantages for both. Probably the most important drawback of activity diaries is that they can be time consuming, so busy households may not be willing to respond. However, for this research it was important that as little information as possible was omitted, so activity diaries were favoured over travel diaries. It was also believed that as respondents were to be self selecting to a certain extent, and therefore forewarned, they would be more likely to complete the diaries than might be the case with large random samples. As well as respondents' travel behaviour the research project also needed to collect information on perceptions of environmental and financial costs and awareness of accident risks.

A 'Travel Survey Pack' was therefore developed for the research which incorporated three elements: an activity monitor (or diary), a journey recorder and a questionnaire. The Activity Monitor was designed to collect general information on the half-hourly activities of each respondent. They ticked whether they were at home or away, and if they were away, where they were and what they were doing. Every time they marked 'away' they were instructed to fill in the Journey Recorder, which collected detailed information on each trip, no matter how short. The Activity Monitor therefore served as a memory jogger. The Questionnaire collected a variety of ancillary information on car ownership, annual mileages, attitudes towards cars, changes in travel behaviour, use of alternative modes and socio-economic characteristics.

The travel survey ran over two days, a Friday and a Saturday. This maximized the possibility of gaining complete, unfalsified accounts, uncorrupted by respondent fatigue and diminished motivation (Golob and Meurs, 1986). The sample frame was targeted at employees of firms and organizations in Ashford broadly representative of the employment structure of the town and reflecting variations in type, location and size. The participating firms publicized the project to their employees who volunteered to participate. An attempt was made to distribute the diaries throughout all 'levels' of organization, ranging for example from part-time cleaners to top management. Two hundred and eleven employees agreed to participate and they were asked to encourage all members of their households also to complete a diary. It was hoped that, as a result, the survey would be completed by a reasonably representative sample of people working in and around Ashford.

The 211 households received 847 Travel Packs of which 398 (47 per cent) were returned, recording detailed information on a total of 3,552 journeys over the two study days. Respondents made an average of five journeys each on Friday, and four on Saturday. Of these journeys 73 per cent were made by car, 21 per cent by foot and fewer than 3 per cent by public transport; 53 per cent of the journeys were less than 2 miles and 70 per cent were under 4 miles. The three main journey purposes were work, shopping and leisure, which together accounted for 90 per cent of all trips recorded. Only 10 per cent of households had no car, with 33 per cent having two cars or more, while 93 per cent of individual respondents would not consider living without a car.

Following the results of the Travel Survey it was decided that *The Green Journey Guide* should focus on the three main journey purposes of work, shopping and leisure. These became the basis upon which baseline positions could be set at the start of the *Guide* and also the foci of the method for recording stated behavioural change as respondents progressed through the *Guide*. The means by which respondents were able to calculate a personal travel 'score' was also influenced by the diary findings. Towards the end of the *Guide* information from the activity diaries was used to help respondents appreciate the financial and environmental savings they could make.

In addition to the travel survey information, the Ashford Local Plan, the Transport Plan for Kent, and the draft Ashford Transport Strategy were studied (Ashford Borough Council, 1990; Kent County Council, 1993; Ashford Borough Council and Kent County Council, 1993); public transport providers were consulted and many facts and figures on the impacts of car traffic were collected. All these eventually helped the research team to make decisions on the content of *The Green Journey Guide*.

The Green Journey Guide – Design

At the outset the research team had plenty of ideas but no fixed conception of the form which *The Green Journey Guide* would take. In fact there was some discussion about whether it would be preferable to design a 'road show', or a 'planning-for-real-type' pack with face-to-face interaction, or perhaps to undertake illustrated structured interviews, rather than attempt to diversify and amplify a questionnaire-type format. However, these kinds of activities have already proved their value and an important part of the research was to explore a different approach.

They also tend to work best in fairly small areas such as neighbourhoods. Reactions to transport policies for the wider area of a town or region need to come from larger numbers of respondents representing the variety of locations, users and journeys. The research team therefore decided to develop *The Green Journey Guide* as a postal survey document. The problem was how still to retain for respondents the interactive, probing and enjoyable nature of face-to-face activity through the more impersonal medium of a questionnaire.

Basic decisions were also needed on such matters as which of the many facets of the transport debate to include; how to present them in a way which would involve participants in thinking about, rather than just reacting to, proposed changes in transport provision; how to keep up the interest; and how to make the outcomes easily analysable. Long and sometimes circular discussions ensued.

The wide variety of possible car-reducing measures suggested in the literature, and in some cases already implemented, needed to be whittled down to a manageable and relevant number. Choices had to be made even within a main policy, for example amongst different means to encourage cycling or increase the availability of public transport. Recognition had to be given to practical factors of implementation, such as relative cost (from cheaper to very expensive), the timescale (from immediate to long term) and organization (from simple to very complicated). Overall, measures had to be applicable to Ashford where a major new local transport development (such as a metro link) would not be viable but greater use of the existing rail network might be. In this regard too it was necessary to consider the dual role of public and private transport providers and their possible contributions to changing travel behaviour.

Eventually the choice of measures was decided by their relevance to the participants' local transport patterns and were based on three main sources: information from the Travel Survey on current travel behaviour; the Transport Plan for Ashford; and possible national policies such as road pricing. The options presented to participants were therefore realistic and confronted them with choices they could envisage and understand. They came under the main headings of: cycling; buses and trains; car pooling, parking and park and ride; petrol pricing; and road tolls.

The second major set of decisions the team needed to take related to the information to be supplied to respondents in order to provide a context for the introduction of, and necessity for, greener transport measures. These decisions were based on the overall message the team wanted to convey and on the information needed to explain the various measures proposed. The first hurdle the team had to overcome was the one of academic neutrality. *The Green Journey Guide* was not, by its very nature, intended to be a balanced treatise on the pros, cons and uncertainties of the debate surrounding the contribution of cars to global climate change or the social and economic impacts of congestion. It was designed on the premise that car use needs at least to be controlled, and preferably reduced, and ways and means need to be found to achieve that. The information to be given, therefore, needed to answer the question why? And to answer it in as broad and comprehensible a way as possible.

Pollution was covered in some detail, along with the counter arguments such as the introduction of cleaner cars and fuels. Car accidents and speed controls; health and safety related to the greener solutions of cycling and walking; the monetary costs of congestion; and the land use impacts of new roads were all considered to be necessary to include. The amount of material, and the way it was presented, were important considerations; too many facts would over-load and bore the participants; too relentless and gloomy a review could be counter-productive. As far as possible therefore information was referred to in local situations, relevant and amusing ways were found to visualize statistics, such as two tonnes of carbon dioxide (figure 13.2*a*), and the material was put across using quizzes, games and 'conversations'.

The third determining factor in the design of the *Guide* was how to make the links between (*i*) the participants' current travel behaviour, (*ii*) their responses to the proposals for greener travel and (*iii*) the effects of any decisions they made to change behaviour. It was felt to be essential that on completing the *Guide*, respondents should have some simple way to sum up, for themselves, the level of their commitment to greener transport measures. In this way they could conclude the *Guide* by relating back to their current behaviour.

The solution to this problem was achieved when a decision was made on how to record respondents' replies to the questions on the proposed new measures. They were asked first for their *attitude* to a policy, giving an answer disagree, don't know, or agree, and giving reasons. Secondly they were asked whether implementation of the measure would result in any *change in travel behaviour* for their working, shopping or leisure journeys and if so, how. In order to carry the traffic theme through the *Guide* these questions were accompanied, not by a series of boxes to tick or cross, but by a composite 'traffic light', 'signpost' and 'road symbol' (figure 13.2*b*). The attitude questions were answered on the traffic light using coloured dot stickers (red for disagree, amber don't know and green agree). Behavioural changes for different journey types were answered on the appropriate signpost(s) by adding a 'mode sticker' (for example a bicycle – figure 13.2*c*). The 'road' was a space in which to write any explanations. Instructions for the traffic light were given on a pull-out card. When they had completed the *Guide* respondents were asked to count up the number of their remaining red and green dots to give an indication of their overall *attitude*, and also to check back and count mode stickers to see how often they expected to *change their behaviour* in response to new policies. The use of coloured stickers had three purposes: they were considered more fun than ticking boxes; they also required more deliberate choice than might occur when respondents, pen in hand, can just tick or cross their way down the page; and they provided an easy way for respondents to check their answers at the end.

While the information content and measurement system were being worked out there was also an on-going discussion about how to make *The Green Journey Guide* a coherent and enjoyable experience. It was anticipated that participants might have to commit at least an hour, and, as there was no inherent incentive for them to keep going, the maintenance of interest was a high priority. A host of more or less feasible ideas were put forward, from virtual reality,

(a) livening up the statistics

Carbon dioxide is one of the worst gases contributing to climate change - how much carbon dioxide do you think a typical car in Ashford produces each year?

Circle which one you think-
a) 10kg   b) 200kg   c) 2 tonnes   d) 4 tonnes

The answer is   **Peel Off**
                     to Reveal Answer   a hippo   Were you right?

(b) recording answers on a 'traffic light'

Trains

Trains are also a good alternative to using a car, especially for longer journeys. Ashford is lucky to have five railway lines converging at its centre.

The map below shows these lines. Imagine that there is a regular half-hourly train service from all stations within 20 miles of Ashford, running from 7.00am to 11.00pm. What do you think of this idea? Show us on the traffic light -

Would you change any part of your TRAVELMAP? If so, REMEMBER to use the sign post and write underneath -

Work
Shopping
Leisure

(c) mode stickers

Car   Bus   Train   Motorbike   Bicycle   Foot   Taxi

(d) Smogbuster and Manic Motorist exchange views

Enforcing speed limits not only helps to save lives, it also helps the environment.

If the 70 mph speed limit were STRICTLY enforced, substantial amounts of fuel could be saved and less pollutants would be pumped into the air!

I DON'T CARE

J LIKE DRIVING FAST!

Figure 13.2. Illustrations from *The Green Journey Guide*

video games and isometric maps to overlays, scratch and sniff and show cards. The final choices were inevitably influenced by the constraints of money, time, skill and practicality.

The eventual design of *The Green Journey Guide* was given interest and coherence mainly by the interaction of two cartoon characters, Smogbuster and Manic Motorist (figure 13.2*d*), who led participants through the *Guide*, presented information, discussed the issues raised, answered questions that might well occur to participants and commented on the summary of points at the end.

The Green Journey Guide in its final form, is an A4 spiral bound booklet with a cover in shaded green (figure 13.1). On its 41 pages are information, questions, quizzes and challenges. Its design, content and presentation are intended to elicit thoughtful responses from the participants and convey a serious message in a relatively light-hearted way. As Newby has said (1996) 'We need to accept that end-of-the world depression mongering is not enough to persuade most people to act. There are serious messages to convey, but adding a little fun, sparkle and humour (does) not go amiss'.

The Green Journey Guide – Content

The Green Journey Guide falls roughly into four parts relating to respondents' current travel for work, leisure, and shopping; their response to measures for greener travel; a review of their responses; and a questionnaire.

Respondents started by recording their current travel behaviour on a map of Ashford. They located their home, work-place, usual shop and favourite leisure place and used coloured pens and mode stickers to record the regular route, the mode used and the mileage of each journey. Respondents then moved on to three related 'games' which were designed to give some measure of the impact of each journey. Figure 13.3*a* shows how the scores for the games were calculated. These scores were added together using the Trafficator, or ready reckoner (figure 13.3*b*). The traffic light pointer changed colour from green, through amber to red as scores mounted up. This section ended with comments on the implications of the scores and the suggestion that *The Green Journey Guide* might help to bring scores down in future.

The main section of *The Green Journey Guide* contained the proposals for greener transport measures. There were 39 in all of which 25 were 'carrots' and 14 were 'sticks'. A full list of the measures is given in table 13.1. They started with relatively simple local measures for improving facilities for cyclists, and moved through public transport (buses and trains), car pooling, parking (cost and space), park and ride and on to national policies for increased petrol taxes and road pricing (as they might apply in Ashford). Each measure was explained, with maps if appropriate, and reasons given for its implementation. Each proposal required a composite answer from respondents recorded on the 'traffic light' as described above.

(a)   The Work Journey "Game": the method used to achieve an "impact score" for each type of journey.

Game 1 : Work Journey

Think about the typical journey to work you've drawn on your TRAVELMAP. Look at the game board on the facing page. Starting at your house, choose the route that most closely resembles the way you travel to work. Mark your route with a RED cross.

You'll notice there are several hazard warning lights along each road - these lights indicate the level of pollution and pedestrian accidents caused by the different ways of travelling - How many have you passed on your route? Write the answer in the empty box.

Now MULTIPLY this number by the number of miles you travel between your home and your workplace, and write the answer in the empty box -

DOUBLE IT - to include the return journey, and write the figure in the box -

Finally, MULTIPLY this by the number of times a week you make the journey to work

Your answer is your WORKSCORE

Example: -

Mrs Motor drives all the way to work and so passes 20 hazard warning lights on her route.

20

She lives 5 miles from work so 5 x 20 = 100.

100

Multiply 100 x 2 (to include return trips) = 200.

200

Mrs Motor goes to work 5 days a week - so, 5 x 200 = 1000

1000

So, her WORK SCORE is 1000.

When you have calculated your Work Score, write it on the score panel of your workplace on the picture. Take your TRAFFICATOR and move the pointer to record your score.

Work Journey

(b)   The Trafficator: a ready reckoner for calculating total "impact scores".

Figure 13.3. Illustrations from *The Green Journey Guide*

Table 13.1:   List of policy options in The Green Guide and parallel questionnaire

**CYCLEPATHS	–	provision
**CYCLEPATHS	–	and showers/lockers at work
**CYCLEPATHS	–	and more secure bike parks
**CYCLEPATHS	–	and help to purchase bikes
**BUSES	–	local $\frac{1}{2}$ hour servlce 7am–11pm
**BUS SERVICES	–	and more routes
**BUS SERVICES	–	and later/earlier times
**BUS SERVICES	–	and priority lanes
**BUS SERVICES	–	and subsidy (av. £1 return – 10 mile radius)
**BUS SERVICES	–	and subsidy (av. 50p return – 10 mile radius)
**BUS SERVICES	–	and more frequent times
**BUS SERVICES	–	and more comfort
**BUS SERVICES	–	and advance knowledge at bus stops
**TRAINS	–	$\frac{1}{2}$ hour service within 20 miles, 7am–11pm
**TRAIN SERVICE	–	and subsidy (£2 day return)
**TRAIN SERVICE	–	and subsidy (£1 day return)
**TRAIN SERVICE	–	more frequent
**TRAIN SERVICE	–	and more comfort
**TRAIN SERVICE	–	and more stations
**BUS/TRAIN	–	integrated times
**BUS/TRAIN	–	integrated fares
**CAR POOLS	–	with parking subsidy (50%)
**CAR POOLS	–	with petrol subsidy (5%)
**PARK AND RIDE	–	with 10 minute buses £1/day
**PARK AND RIDE	–	service and priority bus lanes
PARKING	–	@ 25p/hour after 3 hours at ALL car parks
PARKING	–	@ 50p/hour after 3 hours at ALL car parks
PARKING	–	@ £1/hour after 3 hours at ALL car parks
QUEUE	–	to park average 10 minutes
QUEUE	–	to park average 20 minutes
QUEUE	–	to park average 30 minutes
PETROL	–	price rise of 8p/litre
PETROL	–	price rise of 15p/litre
PETROL	–	price rise of 50p/litre
PETROL	–	price rise of £1/litre
INNER RING ROAD	–	daily charge 20p
INNER RING ROAD	–	daily charge 50p
INNER RING ROAD	–	daily charge £1.00
INNER RING ROAD	–	daily charge £2.00 ** indicates 'carrot' policy

The third section of the *Guide* asked participants to look back at their responses and assess their overall acceptance of the greener measures. In particular the *Guide* attempted to demonstrate how a change to greener travel for only one journey a week, if implemented by the whole population of Ashford, could amount to considerable reductions in pollution and savings of money.

Throughout *The Green Journey Guide* the individual measures were each introduced to respondents separately. In reality, of course, an integrated policy combining a number of measures would be needed. In recognition of this, the last task respondents were given was to select from the list of measures an acceptable mix which, if introduced in Ashford, would enable people to leave their cars at home, sometimes at least.

Finally, *The Green Journey Guide* ended with a brief socio-economic questionnaire.

CONDUCT OF THE SURVEY

The Green Journey Guide formed the core of the research. The survey was therefore designed primarily to gauge reactions to this experimental methodology, although it was also expected that the information obtained would provide some useful indicators of public reactions to greener transport measures. Following a pilot study *The Green Journey Guide* was sent to 222 people in the Ashford area. They had all been respondents for the Travel Survey and had indicated their willingness to give further help with the project. One hundred and seven *Guides* were completed, a return rate of 48 per cent. At the same time, the research team produced a parallel questionnaire consisting of all the questions in *The Green Journey Guide* relating to the 39 proposed transport measures, and the socio-economic questions. The Parallel Questionnaire followed a standard format, with boxes to tick, and with no additions in the way of explanations, maps or illustrations. The sample which received this questionnaire was drawn from people who had completed the team's earlier participative exercise in Ashford in 1991 (Anderson *et al.*, 1994). Two hundred and one questionnaires were despatched to this group and 112 were returned, a response rate of 56 per cent. The purpose of the questionnaire was to provide a response contrast to the innovative format of *The Green Journey Guide*.

Subsequent analysis of the two samples, based on the main socio-economic indicators of sex, age, employment status and income, revealed some significant differences between them. *The Green Journey Guide* group was more likely to contain young people, those in full-time work and people with incomes of £20,000 or more. The Questionnaire group, on the other hand, was more likely to contain retired people, part-time workers and those with lower incomes (less than £15,000). There was no significant differences between them for the other variables within these indicators or for gender.

RESULTS

The research team recognized that there were inherent difficulties arising from the use of two different samples for *The Green Journey Guide* and the Parallel Questionnaire. However, in considering the aims of the research, firstly to test the methodology and only secondly to gain some information on attitudes and behaviour, the socio-economic differences between the samples were seen to have some positive advantages. In testing the methodology the data from the *Guide* were looked at separately and then compared with those from the Questionnaire. For the analysis of the data on the acceptability of individual policies, however, the two sets were taken together.

The outline of results and their discussion which follows looks first at the joint analysis of responses to the 39 proposed measures, as they provide the background for the subsequent discussion and assessment of *The Green Journey Guide*.

The Public Acceptability of Greener Transport Measures

The overall conclusion to be drawn from the analysis of the responses from both *The Green Journey Guide* and the Parallel Questionnaire is that the most accept-able way to reduce car use in Ashford would be to combine *local* encourage-ment with *national* discouragement. This would mean at the minimum providing a network of cycle paths in and around the town to make cycling easier and faster; ensuring that bus services were more convenient and cheaper to use; and that trains were more convenient. Local measures to make driving more expen-sive, through road tolls and higher parking charges, could however be counter-productive by encouraging people just to drive elsewhere to avoid the increased costs. Large nationally imposed increases in the price of petrol (50p or more per litre) are likely to be more effective in reducing car use (Anderson and Meaton, 1995). These conclusions are based on the combination of the *attitude* responses, which demonstrated support for local infrastructure improvements, and the *willingness to change* responses which showed that even willing people will need to be pushed into actually using the facilities provided.

The data have been summarized in figures 13.4 and 13.5 which show very clearly that there is a distinction between *attitude* and *behaviour*, in other words between *acceptance* and *effectiveness*.

The 'carrot' policies attained a high level of acceptance, 18 out of the 25 were agreed with by 50 per cent or more of the respondents up to a maximum of 82 per cent for cycle paths with secure bike parking. All of the other 'carrot' policies achieved a score of 20 per cent or higher. 'Sticks' on the other hand fared badly. The highest level of agreement was 28 per cent for the introduction of charges for *all* car parks (including employers') at 25p per hour after three hours. No other 'stick' achieved agreement higher than 17 per cent. The six policies at the bottom

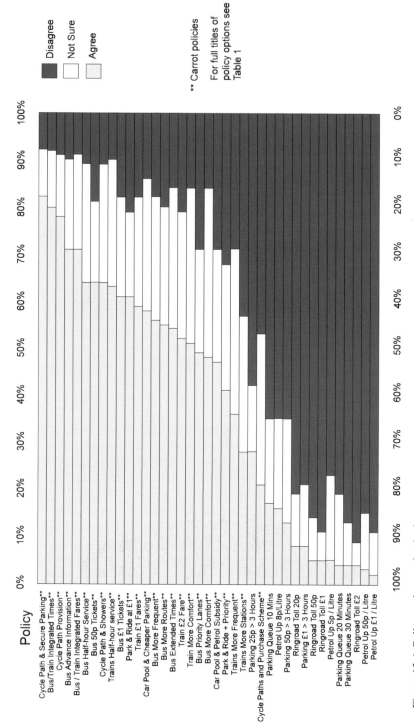

Figure 13.4. Policy options and attitudes.

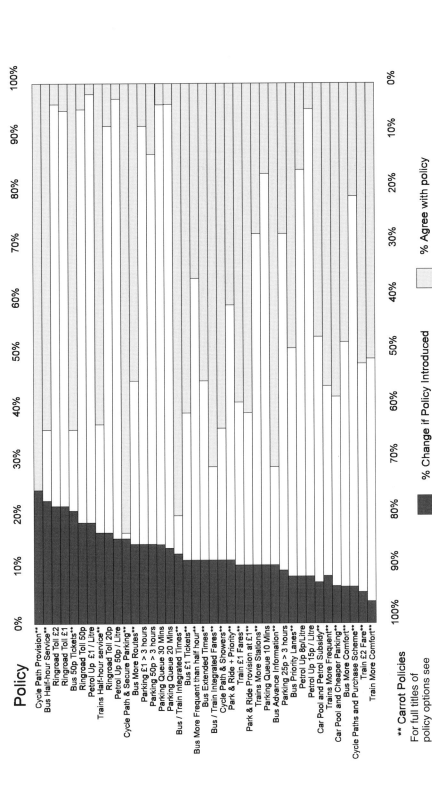

Figure 13.5. Percentage changing behaviour if policy implemented compared to percentage agreement with policy.

of the poll, with less than 5 per cent agreement each, were high petrol price increases, long queues for car parks and the highest charge to use the ring road. There were no policies with which nobody agreed.

Conversely there were no measures that would have no effect on behaviour. However, whereas 'carrots' scored highly for acceptability, 'sticks' were more likely to be effective in changing behaviour. Ten of the 16 policies most likely to cause change, with scores between 14 and 25 per cent, are 'sticks' but they are also the most draconian and disliked: all four of the proposed daily ring road charges (£2, £1, 50p and 20p); the highest petrol price increases (£1 and 50p more per litre); the highest parking charges after 3 hours (£1 and 50p); and the longest likely queuing times (30 and 20 minutes).

However, apparently more effective than any of these 'sticks' are two of the 'carrots'. Cycle path provision could be expected to encourage 25 per cent of respondents to change behaviour and a regular half-hourly bus service on specified routes between 7am and 11pm, 23 per cent. Other bus-related policies in the top 16 were subsidized 50p fares (21 per cent) and more bus routes (15 per cent). Regular half-hourly train services polled 17 per cent and cycle path provision with secure parking (the most popular policy on the attitude scale) polled 16 per cent.

With a few exceptions, therefore, it seems as though tough 'sticks' are likely to be more effective at changing behaviour than most 'carrots', even if they are less popular. However, this statement requires some qualification. Looking at *how* behaviour would change shows that for all 'carrot' policies people would expect to change from cars to greener modes of transport. For all *local* 'stick' policies, on the other hand, some people at least expected to use a different route around Ashford altogether, thereby possibly using the car more not less. For a *nationally imposed* and largely unavoidable 'stick', such as higher petrol prices, this sort of reaction almost disappears. There is an indication, however, that expensive petrol might encourage respondents to think more carefully about the way they drive and the fuel efficiency of their cars.

Having outlined the level of effectiveness of policies and the likely resulting changes in behaviour, the fact remains that even in the best case, cycle path provision, 75 per cent of respondents still did not expect to alter their travel behaviour and in the worst cases it was more than 95 per cent. This does not mean that if the measures were introduced people would not change, they might find themselves forced to or, more happily, they might be encouraged by the improved conditions provided by a less car-clogged town. What it does mean is that simply providing alternatives to the car, or restricting its use, will probably do little to alter the fundamental reasons why most people use cars for most journeys and do not want to change.

Answers to questions in the *Guide* and Questionnaire show that for 82 per cent of the respondents the car was their preferred mode of transport, the most commonly given reasons being convenience (46 per cent), speed and independence

(10 and 9 per cent), and comfort and cost (7 per cent each). As a result 65 per cent used the car to go to work, 78 per cent to go shopping and 76 per cent for leisure journeys. The next most popular mode was walking, with cycling, public transport and other modes coming a poor third. Yet, in common with similar surveys elsewhere this one revealed that most journeys made are quite short, averaging 12 per cent under one mile and 66 per cent under 5 miles.

Respondents whose preferred mode of transport was *not* the car tended also to stress convenience, 'no parking problems', and the positive aspects such as 'I enjoy walking', 'biking is non-polluting and relatively faster than walking', 'I can relax on a train journey, and walk around'.

Asked why they would not change behaviour in response to the introduction of new or improved alternatives, the car users gave answers ranging from the expected one of 'convenience' to 'laziness' or 'I can't be bothered'. More specifically, for not walking or cycling respondents mainly referred to distance, carrying, health and safety, making comments such as:

'it's too far to walk when I'm on my feet all day'
'I can't carry a month's shopping on my bike or my head!'
'walking is unpleasant with all the pollution'
'there is no safe or easy route'

'Convenience' and 'inaccessibility' generally sum up the reasons why respondents would not change to better public transport. 'Inflexible' and 'restricted to a timetable' were frequent comments. Again there was the problem of carrying children and shopping. The point was also made that 'other forms of transport are usually necessary to complete the journey, e.g. walk or taxi'.

The responses to the 'stick' policies mirrored the reasons for using the car in the first place, but quite a number of additional comments were made which generally followed three themes: the effect on the town's economy; the effect on other people; and the action other people might be expected and take. Some typical comments were:

'a good way to kill the town' (parking fees)
'people would not bother to go to shop' (queues)
'would kill businesses inside the ring road' (tolls)
'the idea is good but there are still people who need to use cars, pregnant women, disabled people' (parking fees)
'will make living in rural areas more expensive and diminish the viability of rural communities' (petrol prices)
'will create stressed and irritable customers for shop assistants' (queues)
'they don't queue, they abandon and in places they shouldn't' (queues)
'people would absorb the price' (petrol prices)
'people would increase journey miles and time to avoid the ring road' (tolls)

Concern for the environmentally negative effects of some of the policies was

also evident. Several respondents, for example, questioned the increased pollution: from long car park queues and from more frequent buses waiting in the
town centre and 'belching out fumes' from often poorly maintained engines;
some were worried about security at Park and Ride sites; and others were not
convinced that higher petrol prices were the right way either to curb car use or
raise revenue.

Overall, it is clear that even where attitudes are favourable, it will take more
than the introduction of greener policies to bring about a big change in current
travel behaviour decisions. Whether a methodology like *The Green Journey
Guide* can have a positive influence on these decisions will now be considered.

Comparison of Responses from the *Guide* and Questionnaire

Significance testing of the data from the two groups demonstrated some important differences in their responses. In terms of *attitude, The Green Journey
Guide* respondents (GJGs) were more likely to agree than the Parallel
Questionnaire respondents (PQs) with 11 of the measures. Five of these were
'carrots', all of which related to public transport provision except one,
cyclepaths with assisted purchase schemes (table 13.2*a*). The six 'sticks' related
to parking fees, the lowest petrol increase and the two shorter queuing times.
The PQs on the other hand, were more likely to agree with four measures, all of
which were 'carrots': integrated bus and train times; cyclepath provision; half-
hourly bus services; and more stations. For the other 25 policies there were no
significant differences in response.

Overall, therefore, it seems that GJGs are more likely to have a positive *attitude* to policies than PQs, but the pattern of agreements differed. GJGs tended to
represent the extremes, the participants registering either a few positive attitudes
(6-15 out of the 39 policies) or many (more than 31). This could be attributed to
people's reactions to the *Guide* itself which might either have reinforced negative attitudes (like 'Manic Motorists' the advantages and pleasures of driving
outweighing any described disadvantages) or encouraged respondents to see for
themselves the positive reasons for the introduction of the measures. PQs on the
other hand were more consistent, most of them agreeing with 15–25 of the policies. This more middle-of-the-road response could also have resulted from the
type of questionnaire which provided no information likely to influence the
response in any way.

Testing of the data on likely *behavioural change* again revealed significant
differences in response. As table 13.2*b* shows, PQs were more likely to change
their behaviour than the GJGs for 12 of the 'stick' policies: all the ring road and
parking charges; all the petrol price increases except the lowest (8p); and all the
car park queuing times except one (20 minutes). For 'carrots' the differences are
more evenly divided, the PQs being more likely to change behaviour for four of
them (both park and ride schemes and both integrated bus and train schemes)

Table 13.2. Significant differences in responses to the 39 proposed greener traffic measures (1) between respondents completing the *Green Journey Guide* and the Parallel Questionnaire.

(a) ATTITUDES: respondents more likely to agree

Rank (2)	*% (3)*		
2	80	**	Integrated bus and train times
3	78	**	Cyclepath provision
6	68	**	Bus half-hour services
9	68	**	*Train half hour services*
12	58	**	*Train £1 fare*
17	52	**	Train £2 fare
22	42	**	*Park and ride with priority*
24	28	**	Train, more stations
25	28		*Parking queue 10 minutes*
26	20	**	*Cyclepaths and purchase schemes*
27	17		*Parking queue 10 minutes*
28	16		Petrol up 8p/litre
29	14		*Parking fee 50p > 3 hours*
31	8		*Parking fee £1 > 3 hours*
37	4		*Parking queue 20 minutes*

No significant differences between the two groups for 24 policies

(b) BEHAVIOUR: respondents more likely to change

Rank (4)	*% (5)*		
3	22		Ring road toll £1
5	22		Ring road toll £2
6	19		Ring road toll 50p
7	19		Petrol up £1/litre
9	17		Ring road toll 20p
10	16		Petrol up 50p/litre
13	15		Parking fee 50p > 3 hours
14	15		Parking fee £ > 3 hours
15	15		Parking queue 30 minutes
17	13	**	Integrated bus and train times
19	12	**	*Buses, more frequent services*
22	12	**	Integrated bus and train fares
24	11	**	Park and Ride
26	11	**	Park and Ride with priority
28	11	**	Parking queue 10 minutes
29	10		Parking fee 25p > 3 hours
30	9	**	*Bus priority lanes*
32	9		Petrol up 15p/litre
37	7	**	*Cyclepaths and Purchase Schemes*

No significant differences between the two groups for 20 policies

Notes
** denotes carrot policies
italics Green Journey Guide respondents
(1) See Table 13.1 for the full list of measures
(2) Rank order of agreement (all respondents, Figure 13.4)
(3) Percentage agreeing (all respondents, Figure 13.4)
(4) Rank order of behaviour change (all respondents, Figure 13.5)
(5) Percentage changing behaviour (all respondents, Figure 13.5)

whereas the three most likely to influence GJGs were two bus policies (more frequent services and dedicated bus lanes) and the provision of cyclepaths with associated bike purchase schemes. There was no significant differences between the groups' responses for the other 20 policies (18 'carrots' and 2 'sticks').

Comparison of tables 13.2a and 13.2b seems to indicate that while the policies GJGs are more likely to agree to than PQs include quite a number of 'sticks' the pattern is reversed where changing behaviour is concerned. In this regard, PQs seem to be more widely influenced than GJGs. To explore these differences further, and to test for any relationship between greater likelihood to agree and greater likelihood to change behaviour, cluster analyses were carried out on the data. The research team was particularly interested to see whether a recognizable 'green' group would be revealed that might be targeted to help encourage greater use of non-car modes of transport.

When the data on *attitudes* were subjected to cluster analysis three distinct groupings emerged. The 'greenest' group, that is those who were the most inclined to agree with all the policies except the most draconian (for example an extra £1/litre on petrol or a £2 daily charge to use the ring road), was more likely to be full-time workers. The second group contained people with mixed reactions to both 'carrots' and 'sticks' and they were more likely to be students or part-timers. The third group, the people inclined to disagree with most policies, were more likely to be housewives/husbands or retired. Further analysis of these three clusters revealed that both the 'green' group and the middle group were more likely to be the GJGs, whereas the cluster most likely to disagree was more likely to include PQs.

These findings on *attitude* would seem to confirm the influence of the differences between the characteristics of the two samples rather than the differences between the type of questionnaire. However, the distinction is not as clear cut when consideration is given to the data on *behavioural change*. Although three clear clusters again emerged, the behaviour clusters were not the same as those for attitude. The behaviour clusters were divided between those agreeing with policies and willing to change, those very unwilling to change and an inbetween group. The only significant socio-economic difference between the three groups related to age. The youngest and oldest respondents seemed unwilling to change and were less likely to have agreed with policies. The 26–45 year olds, on the other hand, were most willing to change and agreed with more policies. Otherwise, whereas for *attitudes* the cluster most likely to agree with policies was also more likely to contain GJGs, for *behaviour change* the 'very unwilling' cluster was the one most likely to contain GJGs.

The statistical evidence differentiating response for the GJGs and PQs is therefore mixed and sometimes contradictory and it is difficult to see the clear pattern that the researchers hypothesized would emerge. It is possible to argue that the experience of working through the GJG made its respondents more thoughtful in their replies. They seem to be more definite (positively or negatively) in their attitudes and more willing to accept 'sticks' such as tougher parking restrictions and higher petrol prices. They are, however, more ambivalent towards the challenge of changing their behaviour which may reflect a more realistic response than the arguably more 'tick happy' PQs.

Conclusions from the Comparisons of Results

The results from *The Green Journey Guide* and the Parallel Questionnaire, both severally and together, were not quite what the research team had expected. In the first place it had been hypothesized that GJGs with all the information and explanations, would come out 'greener' than the PQs. Generally speaking this proved to be true for attitudes, but it was the PQs who displayed more of a tendency to change behaviour. It was also anticipated that it would be possible to isolate clusters of people whose characteristics would enable them to be identified as having different sets of attitudes or different levels of willingness to change their travel patterns. Unfortunately although a relatively 'green' group did emerge from the combined samples, it was small in size and only weakly differentiated from the other respondents. Even in the cases where a clear cluster was identified with respect to attitude it did not carry through in respect of the related behaviour changes.

It seems therefore that it is not possible to make clear distinctions between the responses from *The Green Journey Guide* and the Parallel Questionnaire, nor can their responses be attributed, either separately or together, specifically to their socio-economic characteristics. Throughout the testing of the data, both for significance and for clusters, the results gave mixed messages. It would appear from this that travel behaviour is dictated by the perceived advantages of the car which, in the end, cut across not only personal characteristics but also attitudes to alternative modes of travel. Possible explanations for these contradictions between attitude and behaviour will be discussed in the next section.

DISCUSSION AND CONCLUSIONS

The Green Journey Guide Methodology

The Green Journey Guide (GJG) was developed as an innovative methodology for this project and the survey was essentially a pilot stage which yielded useful information on aspects for future improvement. For example more room needs to be made for feedback from respondents on the use they make of the information provided and to test whether focusing directly on such aspects as personal safety or child health would be likely to have more influence on travel decisions than, say, details of pollution or of rising monetary costs. Equally, it would have been helpful to have elicited more specific information from participants on the 'whys' and 'hows' of their responses to the proposed measures than was actually achieved, and on their overall reaction to greener transport as a way for the future. An attempt was made in the *Guide* to tackle the problems of the interdependence of transport decisions by proposing single policies in the main text and then asking respondents to make a choice of interconnected policies at the end. More thought needs to be given to this aspect as it seems likely that the choices made were more related to respondents' previously stated attitudes than to any vision of the transport system as an integrated whole.

The pilot project, however, demonstrated success for the GJG in its aim of testing the public acceptability of measures to reduce car use. The responses show that the provision of many of the alternative and greener modes of travel would be generally acceptable but that this positive attitude is not a clear indicator of an equal level of behavioural change. The reasons why this is the case are partly explained by the direct barriers (convenience, distance etc.) that respondents said stood between their positive attitudes and their *ability* to change behaviour. The possible influence of less tangible barriers, that were not acknowledged by respondents, will be considered in the final section of this chapter.

Despite the difficulties respondents indicated a willingness to make *some* changes to travel patterns if the situation with respect to alternatives were improved. The most positive response of all was to the provision of a network of cyclepaths, preferably accompanied by securer arrangements for parking and the provision of showering and changing facilities at destinations. Similarly, improved public transport, especially a good network of cheaper and more frequent buses, seems likely to encourage a change in favour of its use, particularly for work and school journeys. The implementation of these measures could therefore be expected to effect some voluntary changes in travelling behaviour. On the other hand the measures designed to coerce the public into changing their behaviour by hitting directly at their personal expenditure of money (ring road, parking and petrol charges) or time (long queues at car parks) are not, except at a minimal level, generally acceptable to the public, even though they are likely to be more immediately effective in inducing changes in behaviour. Unfortunately, past experience has shown that car drivers are remarkably resistant to increases in costs so that the effects could well only be short-lived as drivers adjust to new prices. Whether, if this short-term reaction coincided with the introduction of cyclepaths and better public transport, the public would turn more permanently to greener modes, is not clear.

The aim of the GJG was not only to provide information on public responses to greener transport modes but also, and more importantly, to open up for respondents the debate on the need for car reduction policies. In this respect the research team believe the experiment had considerable value. The GJG proved to be a channel for two-way communication. It was rooted in the local situation, it raised counter-arguments such as technological fixes and it demonstrated that even small changes in behaviour can accumulate to larger benefits. Respondents therefore would have had difficulty in replying to the questions without also having some personal responses to the information provided. Forty eight per cent of those receiving the GJG took the time and trouble to complete it and, as the results show, they were by no means people already convinced of the need to accept changes in their travel behaviour.

The Links between Attitude and Behaviour

The more intangible barriers that stand between attitudes and intended or actual behavioural change have long been the study of social psychologists. Their research has shown that ultimately reluctance or enthusiasm for voluntary change are often more related to innate feelings than to the immediate reasons people give for continuing with their existing behaviour, even when their attitudes to the behaviour may be changing. What causes people to change behaviour and maintain the change has therefore been the subject of many studies (for example Rajecki, 1939 and 1990; De Young, 1993). The GJG was proposed and designed on the premise that behaviours do change over time and that these changes can be influenced by external sources such as information, understanding and inducements (both positive and negative).

The conflict that the survey results showed between a 'yes' attitude to the provision of greener transport modes and 'no' to behavioural change is typical of the social problems characterized by the puzzle of 'the prisoners' dilemma' or, in an environmental context, Hardin's 'tragedy of the commons' (1968). If respondents really believe that car use has undesirable impacts, then they should reduce them by driving less and using alternative modes more. The problem for any *individual* is that the positive outcomes of this change could be long term and hard to see, whereas the impact on her or his way of life might be expected to be immediate and negative. Only if *everybody* changes to alternative modes will the effects become obvious sooner, not only environmentally but also in general improvements to the alternatives. The dilemma therefore lies in the fact that individuals are personally better off by not co-operating but, in the end, all individuals will be better off if they act together for the common good (Dawes, 1980).

The dilemma is very clear in relation to car use. The question is, is it possible to persuade people to co-operate to reduce car use and, if so, how? One way of approaching this has been through 'persuasive communication' (Cook and Berrenberg, 1981) of which the GJG would be a good example. The information included in the GJG, coupled with the attempt to relate the *Guide* to respondents' own lives throughout, assumed that the more people understand about a problem the more likely they are to accept the need for change. The work by Petty and Cacioppo (1986) seems to support this view. They believe that changes are more enduring if they result from advocacy, 'as a result of a person's careful and thoughtful consideration of the true merits of the information' (p.3). They term this the 'central route' for persuasion, as opposed to the 'peripheral route' where change occurs as the result of a single cue, such as the endorsement of the attitude by a famous person. Research in this field also indicates that even though the relationship between attitude and behaviour may not be direct there is evidence that greater knowledge may influence overall attitudes and behaviour in related areas of activity (Cook and Berrenberg, 1981). The research team believes that the GJG experience would, at the very least, have left residual knowledge with the respondents which could not have been acquired by participants given the Parallel Questionnaire. The influence and endurance of this residual knowledge requires further testing.

Other common methods of inducing behaviour change are the presentation of incentives or disincentives, either material or social (Cook and Berrenberg, 1981). In the GJG these are exemplified by the division between 'carrot' and 'stick' policies. Most of these were material incentives which took the form of actions to make non-car alternatives more attractive while at the same time attempting to reduce the attractiveness of car use. Financial inducements were also aimed at reversing the perception of car use as being low cost and public transport as high cost (Cook and Berrenberg, 1981).

Social inducements are divided by Cook and Berrenberg (1981) into three types: social recognition and approval for actions and achievements; commitment by individuals to engage in action; and the involvement of individuals in group decisions to act. It was difficult in the GJG to put much emphasis on social inducements because it was not an activity being undertaken publicly or in groups. The GJG attempted, however, to relate each respondent's own travel behaviour to wider car related problems through the initial 'Trafficator' measures of the impacts of their accumulated journeys and, at the end, their totting up of responses throughout the *Guide*. Social inducements, particularly the making of commitments by individuals or groups, coupled with persuasive communication, are increasingly being recognized as means of encouraging co-operation for behavioural change (for example, Tertoolen, 1994). Dawes (1980) describes experiments where the standard two-person prisoners' dilemma games were extended to three or more people and 'the salutary effects of communication are ubiquitous' (p.185). Levels of co-operation of over 90 per cent were achieved in games where participants were allowed to communicate with each other, but were as low as 30 per cent in non-communication groups. Dawes recognizes three facts of face-to-face discussion that facilitate co-operation: humanization (the participants get to know each other); discussion (of the dilemma); and commitment (from self and others), all of which interact. Such direct interaction is not possible with a postal survey like the GJG and during the design stage the research team surmised that one role of the GJG in the future could be to open up the debate across a wide spectrum of a local population, ahead of more focused group meetings that might follow.

Even when the circumstances permit, and attitudes and willingness to change behaviour seem to coincide, intentions (like New Year resolutions) still do not always result in the desired action. In fact intentions to use cars less, like intentions to eat less, smoke less or achieve many other seemingly desirable behaviours, may actually result in an increase in the previous behaviour (Tertoolen, 1994). This outcome is the result of internal conflict or 'cognitive dissonance', i.e. a situation where a person's attitude and behaviour are not consistent (Festinger, 1959). Festinger based his theory of cognitive dissonance on the observation that people generally wish to be consistent within themselves, which is manifested by consistency (or consonance) between what people know or believe and what they do. Where there is inconsistency (or dissonance) between belief and behaviour, people feel uncomfortable and try to re-establish consonance, while at the same time avoiding situations and information that might increase the dissonance. To achieve this satisfactory state people make trade-offs between attitude and behaviour. Depending on the strength of their attitude, or the attractiveness of the changed behaviour, the individual will move the balance to make one or the other dominant. For example, people whose knowledge tells them that increasing car use has widespread disbenefits for themselves and others, and that changing behaviour towards the use of greener travel modes would be beneficial, yet who still continue to use their car as much as before, can only resolve the dissonance by making one of two choices. They can *either* line up their behaviour with their beliefs, which would mean leaving the car at home more often (or even removing dissonance altogether by not having a car), *or* they can manipulate their knowledge in order to rationalize their behaviour by emphasising, for example, the necessity of using the car, the lack of alternatives and the marginal impact that their changes would have on either the local or the global problem. In either case, they have manoeuvred their understanding of the situation, their 'cognition', out of a position of dissonance into one of consonance. In so doing they will either have strengthened their behavioural change or, as is more frequently the case where car travel is concerned, they will have adjusted their attitude and probably increased their car use in the process. The fact that in the GJG the most popular 'carrot' policies (cyclepaths and better bus services) also featured amongst those most likely to change behaviour may hold out some hope that if these facilities were provided the dissonance might be resolved in their favour, for some journeys at least.

Cognitive dissonance theory has another ally in the theory of psychological reactance (Brehm, 1966). Psychological reactance is aroused when what is seen as a traditional freedom is threatened or eliminated. The magnitude of the reactance will depend on a number of factors, particularly the importance of the freedom to an individual both by itself and compared to other freedoms, and the pressure to comply. It is clear that this theory is very relevant to any policies that suggest curtailing the 'freedom' of the road and the car. The reactance manifests itself in an increasing desire for the freedom, an inclination to encourage others to enjoy the freedom also, and a tendency to become threatening. The latter point is exemplified by the fact that the people who completed *The Green Journey Guide* were generally quite calm in their responses to questions about 'carrots' but when asked about 'sticks' some of them clearly became more agitated, using words such as 'rubbish', and 'disaster' and stating that 'people should be allowed to drive where they please', that price increases would be 'unacceptable' and 'I'm getting fed up with people trying to stop me using my car!'.

For a behaviour as deeply ingrained as car use is, and as reinforced by external circumstances (for example the location and road accessibility of most desired destinations and the social prestige of one's 'wheels'), the combination of cognitive dissonance and social reactance makes attempts to engender major changes to car use an uphill task. The GJG attempted to test which of persuasion or coercion is the more likely to overcome these psychological resistances. Results from the combined answers of GJGs and PQs indicate the coercive 'stick' measures may be more immediately effective, even if unpopular, than 'carrots'. Coercion, however, does little to overcome personal resistance, and may indeed increase it, witness those who would continue to use their cars even in the face of strong deterrents.

Recent research in the Netherlands, a country well known for its priority provisions for cyclists and its good public transport (Potter and Smith, 1995), has demonstrated that questions of dissonance and reactance need to be addressed more fully. Vertoolen's work (1994, p.20) has shown that even when researchers employed the most powerful instruments available in psychology (giving individually directed feedback; self-registration [of intention to use car less]; and commitment [to use car less])' there was no change in behaviour.

What is it about car use that seems to be even more resistant to change than other behaviours considered to be undesirable, such as smoking? Car use not only has positive internal reinforcement for individuals (personal mobility, prestige, comfort, convenience, cost etc.), and a negative perception of the alternatives, but it is also strongly and increasingly reinforced by the external forces of society which have placed car-borne accessibility at the centre of land use planning for 50 years and provided it free at the point of use for all consumers. Inevitably therefore for those who have them, cars have become the 'best' and 'only' way to travel for the majority of their journeys and, although the environment is seen as important, it seems unlikely to replace the central role of the car, at least in the near future.

A major problem is the gross under-estimation by car owners of the private costs of driving a car and, even more so, the widespread ignorance of the external or environmental costs. The costs of making a journey by car are therefore seen as marginal to both possessing the car and paying for the journey. The rationale for using the car can be summed up as 'have car, will travel'.

Ultimately, perhaps, the only way to break the habit is to remove the car altogether. Clearly this solution is not immediately practicable so the alternative may be to change the balance of the payoffs. If, for example, car use is made more expensive, less convenient and slower while the alternatives become cheaper, faster and more convenient, then it might be expected that 'greener' travelling habits would be engendered and that these could then be reinforced by changes in the priorities of land use planning. Vertoolen and his colleagues, however, question the extent to which this happens. It is possible that psychological reactance to the loss of 'freedom' may result in people travelling more, i.e. switching to alternatives for some journeys but retaining their 'have car, will travel' urge and making up for the loss of car use for one type of journey with additional or longer journeys of other types. Vertoolen (1994) has therefore concluded that it is 'the image of the car as a symbol of independence and individual freedom (that) needs to be changed' and that 'the illusion that car driving offers 'unlimited freedom' needs to be questioned more in publicity campaigns' (p. 19).

The authors of *The Green Journey Guide* addressed the question of freedom only obliquely (through discussion of accidents and congestion) having felt that the argument was too complicated to fit within the format chosen. However, they made the basis of the *Guide* as personal and local as possible with the intention of encouraging respondents to identify with the problems and the solutions. The Dutch research indicates however that identification and commitment are still not enough. Possibly they will only be effective if people's positive attitudes can actually be used in the design and implementation of local solutions. This is the thrust of Local Agenda 21. De Young, in his review of conservation behaviour (1993, p. 493) concludes that when people are allowed 'to conduct their own explorations, rather than being in the midst of someone else's large experiment (they) perceive a role for themselves (and) have a sense that their contribution is not optional but a necessity'. As a result, not only is a powerful behaviour change force made available but it is also argued that 'when people are expected to play a role in change, they may feel an obligation or responsibility to help the change succeed' (Folz, 1991).

The Green Journey Guide in its format and content addressed many of the issues raised in this discussion. The researchers believe it was successful in helping people to make connections between their use of cars and the wider costs that cars impose, and in taking the issues and solutions into participants' own lives. However, the results have also illuminated the gap that exists between positive attitudes and the likelihood of correspondingly positive changes of behaviour. The researchers do not believe that the *Guide* could be used as a tool for behavioural change, *per se*. They do think that it could be refined as a technique for opening up new debates with the public on the future pattern of transport provision. Local Agenda 21 provides an opportunity for such inclusion of local people in widespread and comprehensive discussions on the development and promotion of greener travelling behaviour. De Young (1993) has concluded that such involvement can be accompanied 'by a sense of challenge and excitement on the part of the public' and looks forward to 'a future where individuals are satisfied, and even enjoy, the process of forging a conserving society' (p. 501).

REFERENCES

Anderson, M. Meaton, J. and Potter, C. (1994) Public participation: an approach using aerial photographs at Ashford, Kent. *Town Planning Review*, **65**(1), pp. 41–58.

Anderson, M. and Meaton, J. (1995) Green transport in carrot and stick mix. *Planning*, No.1103, pp. 8–9.

Ashford Borough Council (1990) *Ashford Local Plan, First Review*. Ashford: The Council.

Ashford Borough Council and Kent County Council (1993) *The Ashford Transport Strategy: Consultative Draft*. Ashford: The Councils.

Barnard, P.O. (1986) Use of an Activity Diary Survey to examine travel and activity reporting in a home interview survey. *Australian Road Research Board*, **13**(4), pp. 329–358.

Bonnel, P. (1995) An application of activity-based travel analysis to simulation of change in behaviour. *Transportation*, **22**, pp. 73–93.

Brehm, J. (1966) *A Theory of Psychological Reactance*. New York: Academic Press.

Clarke, M., Dix M, and Jones, P. (1981) Error and uncertainty in travel surveys. *Transportation*, **10**, pp. 105–126.

Cook, S. and Berrenberg, J. (1981) Approaches to encouraging conservation behaviour: a review and conceptual framework. *Journal of Social Issues*, **37**(2), pp. 73–107.

Dawes, R. (1980) Social dilemmas. *Annual Review of Psychology*, **31**, pp.169–193.

De Young, R. (1993) Changing behaviour and making it stick. *Environment and Behaviour*, **25**(4), pp. 485–505.

Earth Summit (1992) The UN Conference on Environment and Development: Chapter 28: *Local Authorities' initiatives in support of Agenda 21* (page 200). London: Regency Press.

Festinger, L. (1959) *A Theory of Cognitive Dissonance*. London: Tavistock Publications.

Folz, D. (1991) Recycling program design, management, and participation: a national survey of municipal experience. *Public Administration Review*, **51**(3), pp. 222–231.

Golob, T.F. and Meurs, H.J. (1986) Biases in response over time in a seven day travel diary. *Transportation*, **13**, pp. 163–181.

Hardin, G. (1968) The tragedy of the commons. *Science*, **162**, pp. 1243–1248.

Jones, P., Dix, M.C., Clarke, M.I. and Heggie, I.G. (1991) *Understanding Travel Behaviour*. Aldershot: Gower.

Kent County Council (1993) *Transport Plan for Kent*. Maidstone: The Council.

Kitamura, R. (1988) An evaluation of activity-base travel analysis. *Transportation*, **15**, pp. 9–34.

Lex Service plc (1995) *Lex Report on Motoring: What drives the Motorist?* London: MORI.

Newby, L. (1996) Limiting factors to environmental action. *Environmental Guidelines*, **2** (1), pp. 2–4.

Petty, R. and Cacioppo, J. (1986) *Communication and Persuasion: Central and Peripheral Routes to Attitude Change*. New York: Springer Verlag.

Rajecki, D. (1939 and 1990) *Attitudes* (1st and 2nd eds.). Sunderland, Mass: Sinauer Associates.

Stopher, P.R. (1992) Use of an activity-based diary to collect household travel data. *Transportation*, **19**, pp. 159–175.

Tertoolen, G. (1994) Free to move. . .?! A Field Experiment on Attempts to influence Private Car Use and the Psychological Resistance it evokes. A Policy Orientated Report. Utrecht University, Section of Social and Organisational Psychology (typescript).

Van der Hoorn, T. (1979) Travel behaviour and the total activity pattern. *Transportation*, **8**, pp. 309–328.

CHAPTER 14

ANOMALIES AND BIASES IN THE CONTINGENT VALUATION METHOD

Robert Sugden

Public debate about transport projects often focuses on their environmental impacts. In Britain, however, such effects are not included in the formal economic evaluation of transport projects by the Department of Transport. The Department of Transport's procedure for evaluating road projects takes account of construction costs, changes in travel costs and changes in accident risks, while the assessment of environmental effects is handled through the quite separate procedure of Environmental Impact Assessments.

There is now a large body of research which elicits individuals' valuations of environmental benefits and disbenefits using the contingent valuation (CV) method, in which individuals express their preferences by answering questions about hypothetical choices. The CV method offers an apparently promising method of integrating environmental evaluation into conventional cost-benefit analysis. However, the CV method has been subject to serious criticism, particularly as a result of theoretical and experimental research by psychologists and economists into the problems of eliciting preferences. This work has revealed that individuals' responses to CV questions are in certain predictable respects inconsistent with the received theory of preferences. In this chapter, I review the evidence of such anomalies in CV surveys, and compare two alternative approaches to the problem of explaining this evidence. One approach interprets anomalies as the result of survey biases that are in principle correctable; the other interprets them as evidence of failures of the received theory. I then briefly describe a series of experiments, which were designed to discriminate between these two kinds of explanation.

ANOMALIES AND BIASES

One of the most fundamental assumptions of economics is that individuals have preferences over alternative bundles of consumption goods. In addition, these preferences are usually assumed to have certain properties of internal consistency or well-behavedness: they are assumed to be complete, transitive, continuous and convex. Thus, in the familiar two-good case of economic textbooks, preferences can be represented by a map of downward-sloping indifference curves, convex to the origin. I shall call such preferences *Hicksian* in recognition of Hicks's (1943, 1956) work in formulating the modern theory of consumer behaviour.

These assumptions are so basic to economics that they often are not even stated. When economists try to find ways of giving advice to policy-makers, they typically presuppose that individuals have Hicksian preferences. There are, it is thought, two main problems to be overcome in policy evaluation. The first is to find a theoretically valid method for drawing conclusions about social welfare from information about preferences. This problem is the subject matter of welfare economics. The second problem is to find a practical method for *eliciting* preferences – for discovering sufficient information about preferences to allow conclusions about social welfare to be drawn. The CV method is seen as one way of eliciting information about preferences for environmental benefits and disbenefits.

However, the data generated by CV surveys often turns out to be inconsistent with the Hicksian assumptions about preferences. In this chapter, I focus on three such *anomalies*. I shall describe these in more detail later, but briefly, they are: divergences between willingness-to-pay (WTP) and willingness-to-accept (WTA) valuations; part-whole similarities; and the sensitivity of reported valuations to the elicitation method used. I use the word 'anomaly' to convey the idea that these properties of responses are contrary to received theory; at this stage, I do not want to presuppose any particular explanation for them.

As a way of approaching the idea of bias, consider an analogy. Suppose we use survey research methods to try to measure the consumption of cigarettes among the members of some social group. Our survey has two questions: respondents are asked to report how many cigarettes they smoked in the previous day, and how many they smoked in the previous week. The survey is randomized so that one-seventh of respondents are interviewed on each day of a given week. Averaging over all respondents, we should expect that, apart from normal sampling variation, consumption over a week is seven times greater than consumption over a day. But suppose we find that reported weekly consumption is significantly less than seven times reported daily consumption. Then, relative to our prior conceptual scheme and prior background assumptions (for example, that total weekly cigarette consumption is approximately constant over time), the information we have elicited is internally inconsistent.

In principle, it is possible that our background assumptions are at fault. For example, if the survey had been carried out in the week after Christmas, the results might be telling us that cigarette consumption is lower at Christmas than at other times. But unless there is some obvious peculiarity about the timing of the survey, it is much more plausible to infer that for at least one of the questions, responses are subject to *bias*: they are systematically different from the truth. One possibility is that respondents' memories of the previous day are more reliable than their memories of the previous week, and that people consciously or unconsciously fill in gaps in their memories in the way that they wish were true (or in the way that they think their interviewer would most like to be true). On this hypothesis, responses to 'previous week' questions are systematically biased downwards; if this bias is significant, surveys which use 'previous week' questions are unreliable.

Now compare an anomaly found in CV surveys – the tendency for WTA valuations to be much greater than WTP valuations. As in the cigarettes case, the data generated by surveys are internally inconsistent, *given a particular set of background assumptions*. According to the received theory of preferences, the maximum amount of money that a person is willing to pay for a given increment of a good should be approximately equal to the minimum amount he would accept as compensation for forgoing that increment (see the next section). Thus the WTP data seem to be telling us that people have relatively weak preferences for the good *vis à vis* money, while the WTA data are telling us that the *same* preferences are relatively strong – an inconsistency.

One possible interpretation is that the survey instrument is biased. For example, it might be that, for some reason, respondents to WTA questions tend to overstate the minimum amount of compensation that they *really* would be willing to settle for. If this is so, then anyone who wants to use CV to elicit preferences needs to understand the nature of the bias and then to refine CV survey methods so as to eliminate that bias. (For example: if it was found that the WTA-WTP disparity was entirely due to the overstatement of WTA, then we could elicit preferences using only WTP questions.)

However, the fact that WTA-WTP disparities are inconsistent with the received theory of preferences does not imply that *necessarily* there is a bias in our survey methods. It is possible that it is the theory, and not the survey methods, that is at fault. A typical respondent is telling us that the maximum amount he would be willing to spend to buy some good, if he did not already possess it, is much less than the minimum amount of money for which he would sell it, if he *did* already possess it. In itself, this is not internally inconsistent: a person could behave in this way. The inconsistency arises only when we try to map what the respondent is telling us on to the Hicksian theory of preferences. Thus it is at least possible that we are not dealing with survey bias at all: we may be finding evidence that the Hicksian theory is an inadequate model of people's actual decisions. If this is the case, then the WTA-WTP disparity should not be thought of as a problem in the CV method; rather, it is a much more general problem for consumer theory and for welfare economics, which CV research has merely uncovered.

The work reported in this chapter was carried out in a project entitled

'Identifying and correcting for biases in the contingent valuation method'. As this title suggests, the project team began with some expectation that the anomalies found in CV studies were biases, and with the belief that the problems caused by those biases could be overcome by improvements to CV design. However, as we reviewed the existing literature, and as our research progressed, we became increasingly aware of the possibility that anomalies might reflect failures of Hicksian theory. Thus, the focus of our research shifted towards testing whether the anomalies found in CV studies were biases or not.

DISPARITIES BETWEEN WILLINGNESS TO PAY AND WILLINGNESS TO ACCEPT

Apparent disparities between WTP and WTA valuations are a well-known problem for the CV method. When CV surveys elicit both WTP and WTA valuations of the same good, the mean and median values of WTA are often found to be several times higher than the corresponding WTP values. A typical example is Rowe, d'Arge and Brookshire's (1980) study of the value of visibility to the residents of an area in New Mexico. Respondents were asked to compare visibilities of 75 miles (the existing state of affairs) and 50 miles (the potential impact of a coal-fired power station). When they were asked to state their WTP to retain high visibility, the mean response was $4.75 per week; when they were asked to state their WTA for accepting low visibility, the mean response was $24.47 per week.

Whether such differences between WTP and WTA are consistent with Hicksian theory has been a matter of controversy. Some environmental economists have argued that, when respondents are valuing public goods which have few substitutes, large differences between WTA and WTP are compatible with the theory. The best-known exponent of this view is Hanemann (1991), whose analysis is based on the work of Randall and Stoll (1980). Along with many other commentators, I find Hanemann's argument unconvincing, for reasons which I set out in Sugden (1997b). Here, I shall give only a very informal account of the controversy.

In most CV surveys, respondents are asked to imagine that they retain their current money income. For example, in the case of the New Mexico study, a WTP respondent was effectively asked to envisage a *status quo* in which she had her existing money income but, unless something was done, visibility would be only 50 miles (that is, the power station would be built). She was asked to state the maximum amount of money she would be willing to pay out of her weekly income in order to secure 75 miles visibility. A WTA respondent was asked to envisage a *status quo* in which she had her existing money income and 75 miles visibility; she then had to state the minimum amount of money she would accept as a supplement to her weekly income as compensation for a reduction in visibility to 50 miles. Consider a respondent whose weekly disposable income is $400, and who gives the mean responses: her WTP valuation is

$4.75 and her WTA valuation is $24.47. If these responses are treated at face value and mapped on to a Hicksian theory of preferences, we have elicited two pieces of information about the respondent's preferences. Let (x, y) stand for the 'bundle' of x visibility and y per week expenditure on private consumption goods. From the respondent's WTP response, we can infer that (50 miles, $400) is indifferent to (75 miles, $395.25). From her WTA response, we can infer that (50 miles, $424.47) is indifferent to (75 miles, $400). Given a strict interpretation of the Hicksian assumptions, these two preferences are not inconsistent with one another: we can draw an indifference curve diagram with two convex indifference curves, one passing through the first two points and one passing through the second.

However, a Hicksian explanation of such a WTA-WTP disparity has some further implications which seem highly implausible. To say that (50 miles, $424.47) is indifferent to (75 miles, $400) is to say that, had the respondent's income been $424.47 per week and had the *status quo* visibility been 50 miles, her WTP for an increase in visibility to 75 miles would have been $24.47 per week. But we know that her WTP for exactly this increase in visibility, given her actual income of $400 per week, is $4.75. So if we are to maintain the Hicksian explanation, we have to suppose that a 6.1 per cent increase in income would lead to a 315 per cent increase in WTP!

The elasticity of WTP with respect to income (approximately +52 in this example) is sometimes called the *price flexibility of income*. Randall and Stoll (1980) show, as a theorem within Hicksian consumer theory, that if the price flexibility of income is not too far from zero (say, in the range from –2 to +2), and if WTP is small relative to income, then the difference between WTA and WTP will be small. By *a priori* argument, Hanemann (1991) tries to persuade us that very high values of price flexibility of income are plausible for some public goods. But in fact, CV studies often estimate the relationship between WTP and income. I know of no case in which the elasticity of WTP with respect to income has been found to be anywhere near the magnitude that would be consistent with a Hicksian explanation of WTA-WTP disparities.

The following conclusion is, I suggest, warranted: if WTP is only a small fraction of income (as it is in most CV studies), then for a Hicksian consumer, the divergence between WTA and WTP can be expected to be very small – at most, a few per cent. The divergences described at the beginning of this section are *not* consistent with Hicksian theory. Whether they should be interpreted as the result of biases in CV methods or as failures of Hicksian theory remains to be resolved.

PART AND WHOLE

Another well-known problem for CV is an apparent tendency for individuals' valuations of public goods to be unresponsive to the quantity of the good that is (hypothetically) on offer. A telephone survey reported by Kahneman and Knetsch (1992) provides an illustration. In this survey, respondents were asked to think about the environmental services provided by federal and provincial governments in Canada. Then they were asked questions such as the following: 'If you could be sure that extra money collected would lead to significant improvements, what is the most you would be willing to pay each year through higher taxes, prices, or user fees, to go into a special fund to improve environmental services?' Different respondents were asked about different classes of environmental services, some classes being subsets of others. For example, some respondents faced the question presented in the previous section, involving a special fund 'to improve environmental services'; they were told that environmental services' included 'preserving wilderness areas, protecting wildlife, providing parks, preparing for disasters, controlling air pollution, insuring water quality, and routine treatment and disposal of industrial wastes'. Other respondents were asked a similar question, but in relation to 'a special fund to improve preparedness for disasters'. In both cases, the median WTP was $50. Kahneman and Knetsch interpret this and other similar results as evidence of an *embedding effect*: reported WTP for a whole (environmental services) is no greater than reported WTP for a small part of that whole (preparing for disasters). More evidence of such effects in CV studies is provided by Boyle *et al.* (1994).

Are such observations consistent with Hicksian theory? As in the previous section, consider an individual who has preferences over bundles (x, y), where x (a vector) denotes public goods and y denotes private consumption. Let x_0 be the initial provision of public goods; let $x_2 - x_0$ be the 'whole' and let $x_1 - x_0$ be the 'part'. Thus, for example, x_0 might be the status quo level of water quality in two lakes A and B, x_2 an improved level of water quality at both lakes, and x_1 the improved level at A but the *status quo* level at B. Let $WTP_{01}(y)$ denote the individual's willingness to pay for a move from x_0 to x_1, given an endowment of y of private consumption; $WTP_{02}(y)$ and $WTP_{12}(y)$ are defined in a similar way.

Hicksian theory implies the following relationship between these valuations, for any value of y:

$$WTP_{01}(y) + WTP_{12}[y - WTP_{01}(y)] = WTP_{02}(y). \tag{1}$$

The right-hand side of this equation measures WTP to move from x_0 to x_2 (i.e. WTP for the whole). The left-hand side measures the sum of (*a*) WTP to move from x_0 to x_1 (i.e. WTP for the part) and (*b*) WTP to move from x_1 to x_2, given that the individual has already paid an amount equal to her WTP for the move from x_0 to x_1 (i.e. WTP for the complement of the part, given that the part has already been bought).

Notice that this equation does not rule out the possibility that $WTP_{02}(y)$ is only slightly larger than $WTP_{01}(y)$ – that is, that the valuation of the whole is only slightly larger than that of the part, as in many reported instances of embedding effects. For example, the component parts of the whole might be close substitutes for one another, so that the individual has a strong preference to consume one part but, given that she is consuming one part, has little desire to consume its complement in addition. Strictly speaking, then, similarities between part and whole valuations are not incompatible with Hicksian theory. But a Hicksian explanation of the part-whole similarities found in CV surveys does not seem very plausible. For example, it is difficult to see why 'preparedness for disasters' should be an almost perfect substitute for all the other environmental services on Kahneman and Knetsch's list.

RESPONSE MODES

CV studies have used a wide range of elicitation methods. Among the ways in which elicitation methods differ is in terms of their *response modes* – that is, in terms of the kind of response that is required from the individual whose preferences are being elicited. There is a large amount of evidence that reported valuations are systematically affected by the response mode.

The most direct elicitation method is the *open-ended* question. Here, for example, if the object is to elicit WTP for some good, each respondent might be asked 'What is the largest amount of money that you would be willing to pay for . . . ?' Another method is to present each respondent with a single *binary choice* problem such as: 'Would you be willing to pay £20 for . . .?' By posing different binary choices to different respondents, it is possible to infer the distribution of WTP valuations in the sample as a whole. A third method is *iterated bidding*. Here, a respondent is first asked, say: 'Would you be willing to pay £20 for . . . ?' If the answer is 'Yes', the question is repeated, but with a higher price, say £40; if the answer is 'No', it is repeated with a lower price, say £10. This process continues until the respondent's WTP has been bracketed in a sufficiently narrow band (for example: he is willing to pay £35, but not £40).

The available evidence suggests that binary-choice questions tend to elicit higher WTP valuations than do open-ended ones. For example, reporting work linked to our project, Bateman *et al.* (1995) analyse responses from a very large CV survey, designed to elicit valuations of the prevention of salt-water flooding of the Norfolk Broads. Open-ended and binary-choice WTP questions had been given to independent samples of respondents. Each format can be used to construct a WTP *survival function* (that is, a function which for each positive amount of money, v, tells us the proportion of the sample for whom WTP is greater than or equal to v). At all values of v, the binary-choice survival function lies above the open-ended one. Similar discrepancies are reported by Sellar *et al.* (1985) and by Kristöm (1993).

The starting-point effect is another well-attested property of CV surveys. This effect has most often been reported in the context of iterated bidding: respondents' final valuations are found to be positively correlated with the first amount of money they are asked to consider (e.g. Boyle, Bishop and Welsh, 1985;

Roberts, Thompson and Pawlyk, 1985). A striking example is reported by Loomes (1994). Piloting a CV questionnaire to elicit valuations of vehicle safety features, Loomes used a visual aid which consisted of a plain card with a window cut out to reveal a single sum of money. This sum could be changed by rotating a disc. The interviewer rotated the disc until the respondent was just willing to pay the amount shown in the window. For half the respondents, the first amount displayed in the window was £25; for the other half, it was £75. Depending on the risk-reduction scenario being valued, the mean WTP elicited with the £75 starting point was between 1.9 and 2.9 times greater than that elicited with the £25 starting point.

Clearly, such response mode effects are inconsistent with Hicksian theory. If different survey methods generate different measures of what, in the Hicksian theory, is a single magnitude, then either the theory is an inadequate representation of reality or at least one of the survey methods must be biased.

SURVEY BIASES

Why might CV surveys be biased? Many applications of the CV method elicit preferences for *public* goods, and critics have pointed to the special difficulties involved in eliciting individuals' preferences for such goods. In the present context, the distinguishing feature of a public good is that if it is supplied to any individual, it is supplied to everyone. Thus it is difficult to construct a credible scenario in which people make hypothetical decisions as individuals about whether or not to pay for a public good.

Some commentators have suggested that CV respondents believe that the responses they make *as individuals* may determine the tax payments they make *as individuals* (or, in the case of WTA questions, their responses may determine the compensation they receive). Of course, this belief is false: it must be false if, as CV respondents are always assured, their responses will be treated anonymously. Even so, the belief may be held. If it is, it is likely to impart a bias towards the understating of WTP and the overstatement of WTA (Hoehn and Randall, 1987; Mitchell and Carson, 1989, pp. 153–170), and this bias might contribute to observed divergences between WTP and WTA.

A further problem in eliciting preferences for public goods is that CV questions may invoke the kind of reasoning that individuals use to make decisions about voluntary contributions to charities. As a result, respondents may fail to report their preferences for the relevant public goods themselves, but instead use their answers as a way of expressing their commitment to particular ethical values. Very high WTA valuations may be used as a way of registering a protest against the idea of selling a public good (see, for example, Mitchell and Carson, p. 34). As Kahneman and Knetsch (1992) argue, expressive responses may also generate embedding effects, since the expressive value of a contribution to an inclusive cause, and the expressive value of a contribution to a representative subset of that cause, are likely to be similar to one another. The wording of Kahneman and Knetsch's telephone survey, inviting respondents to express willingness to contribute to general-purpose 'funds' but without specifying what services would be provided in return (see p. 303), may have made the analogy with charity particularly salient. But, given the inevitable artificiality of questions about willingness to pay for public goods, it is difficult to ensure that respondents report their preferences rather than expressing their moral values.

Other sources of potential bias are independent of whether the good for which preferences are being elicited is public. One such source of bias is the use of misplaced strategic heuristics – *strategic bias* for short. Consider the position of a respondent who is asked to state the largest amount of money he is willing to pay for some good. Whatever the reality of the survey situation, such a question may induce him to think about other contexts in which he might be called on to say how much he is willing to pay for something. One of the most obvious such contexts is bargaining – for example, buying a second-hand car. In situations of bargaining, it is often a good tactical move to try to appear less willing to trade than you really are; one such move is to claim that you are willing to pay no more than some amount of money which is less than the maximum you really are willing to pay. Conversely, if you are a seller, you might claim that you will accept no less than some amount of money which is greater than the minimum you really are willing to accept. Even if your bargaining opponent insists that his stated position is final, and that he will make no more concessions, you should not necessarily believe him.

In bargaining, then, people are likely to use heuristics (that is, mental routines or rules of thumb) which lead them to understate WTP, to overstate WTA, and to discount information which purports to tell them that they are facing take-it-or-leave-it offers. Such heuristics may then be imported into situations which resemble bargaining, even if in those situations, the heuristic is misplaced (see, for example, Knez, Smith and Williams, 1985). This seems particularly likely to happen when the bargaining-like problems the individual faces are unfamiliar, since the less familiar the type of problem, the less likely it is that the individual will have learned heuristics which are well-adapted to tackling it. For most respondents, of course, taking part in a CV survey is a very unusual experience. We might expect strategic bias to be particularly significant in the case of open-ended questions, since the idea of stating the least favourable terms on which one is willing to trade is similar to that of deciding on a strategy for bargaining. Binary-choice questions seem more likely to invoke the heuristics that people use when trading at fixed prices – for example, in supermarkets. However, since most people in developed economies have much more experience of buying at fixed prices than of selling at fixed prices, we might also expect strategic heuristics to have a greater impact on WTA than on WTP. Thus, the hypothesis that CV respondents use misplaced strategic heuristics offers a potential explanation of WTA-WTP disparities, and of the tendency for reported WTP valuations to be greater when elicited through binary choices that when elicited by open-ended questions. In addition, we might expect binary-choice WTA valuations to be *less* than open-ended ones, but I know of no evidence on this issue (other than the results of our own experiments, to be described later).

ALTERNATIVES TO HICKSIAN THEORY: REFERENCE DEPENDENCE

In this section and the next, I shall consider whether anomalies in CV responses might reflect limitations of Hicksian theory. I shall begin by looking at an alternative model of preferences – the theory of *reference-dependent preferences*, proposed by Tversky and Kahneman (1991). This is an extension of the same authors' earlier theory of choice under risk: *prospect theory* (Kahneman and Tversky, 1979), and incorporates hypotheses first proposed by Thaler (1980).

A fundamental idea in these theories is that individuals understand the options in decision problems as *gains or losses relative to a reference point*. The reference point is to be understood as the current asset position of the individual. Each individual is assumed to have a preference ordering over consumption bundles, conditional on the reference point; if the reference point changes, preferences over given bundles may change. In Hicksian theory, in contrast, options are interpreted as absolute levels of consumption, and the concept of a reference point is not recognized.

Tversky and Kahneman impose two conditions on the way in which preferences can change as the reference point changes. One of these conditions is *diminishing sensitivity*. The idea behind this condition is that 'marginal value decreases with the distance from the reference point' (Tversky and Kahneman, 1991, p. 1048). If we are working in the domain of gains (i.e. if we are evaluating bundles which dominate the reference point), diminishing sensitivity is analogous with the familiar assumption of diminishing marginal utility in conventional consumer theory. In contrast, in the domain of losses (i.e. if we are evaluating bundles which are dominated by the reference point), diminishing sensitivity is analogous with *increasing* marginal utility.

Tversky and Kahneman's second condition is *loss aversion*. This represents the psychological intuition that 'losses . . . loom larger than corresponding gains' (Tversky and Kahneman, 1991, p. 1047). The main implications of this condition are illustrated in figure 14.1. Here A, B, C and D are four bundles made up of different quantities of two goods, X and Y; think of X as being some specific good for which we might want to elicit valuations, and think of Y as standing for 'money' or 'consumption of all other goods'. Consider the preference ranking of A and D, as viewed from each of the possible reference points A, B, C and D. As the reference point moves from A to B, any change in the preference ranking of A and D is in favour of D. The idea here is that D is better than A on the X-dimension; this difference will have greater psychological impact when it is interpreted as a potential loss (i.e. when the reference point is

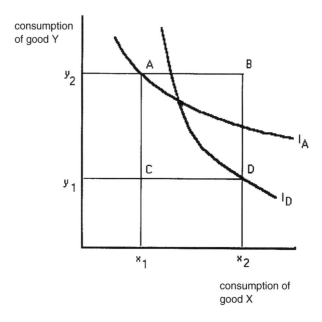

Figure 14.1. Divergencies between WTP and WTA.

B) than when it is interpreted as a potential gain (i.e. when the reference point is A). Similarly, changes in the reference point from B to D, from A to C, and from C to D, all tend to shift the preference ranking of A and D in favour of D.

Figure 14.1 illustrates how loss aversion can lead to divergences between WTP and WTA of a kind that are incompatible with Hicksian theory. Consider the indifference curves I_A and I_D: I_A is defined relative to the reference point A, while I_D is defined relative to the reference point D. That these two curves cross as they do is consistent with loss aversion: A is preferred to D when the reference point is A, but D is preferred to A when the reference point is D. Notice that if the individual is endowed with A, his WTP for an increase in consumption of good X from x_1 to x_2 is less than $y_2 - y_1$. In contrast, if he is endowed with D, his WTA for a decrease in consumption of good X from x_2 to x_1 is greater than $y_2 - y_1$.

Reference-dependent theory may also have implications for the relative valuation of parts and wholes. Consider the case, discussed on pp. 302–304, in which the 'whole' is made up of two 'parts'. In order to establish the existence of a part-whole effect in WTP which contravenes Hicksian theory, we have to compare three measures $WTP_{01}(y)$, $WTP_{12}[y - WTP_{01}(y)]$, and $WTP_{02}(y)$. Here, $WTP_{01}(y)$ is the individual's WTP for the 'first part', as viewed from a *status quo* in which he is endowed with neither part. $WTP_{02}(y)$ is his WTP for the 'whole', as viewed from the same *status quo*. $WTP_{12}[y - WTP_{01}(y)]$ is his

WTP for the 'second part', as viewed from a reference point at which he is endowed with the first part, but with correspondingly less of the composite commodity. Because the first two of these measures are made from one reference point, while the third is made from another, reference-dependent theory does not imply that $WTP_{01}(y) + WTP_{12}[y - WTP_{01}(y)] = WTP_{02}(y)$. In other words, part-whole effects are consistent with the theory. Unfortunately, reference-dependent theory does not generate firm predictions about the direction of part-whole effects. Essentially, this is because diminishing sensitivity applies both to the specific good (or goods) being valued and to the composite commodity.

Reference-dependent theory is still at an early stage of development, but it seems to offer a way of integrating some important psychological insights into a relatively simple and tractable model. Ultimately, it may be able to provide a unified explanation of divergences between WTA and WTP and of part-whole effects.

ALTERNATIVES TO HICKSIAN THEORY: THE CONSTRUCTION OF PREFERENCES

In the Hicksian model (and, indeed, in Tversky and Kahneman's model of reference-dependent preferences) an individual comes to a decision problem equipped with a complete preference map, from which decisions can be 'read off'. But do *real* individuals have such preferences? An alternative approach, favoured by some psychologists, is to think of the individual as *constructing* her preferences in response to specific decision problems. Different ways of presenting what, in a Hicksian perspective, is the same decision problem may evoke different strategies for constructing preferences. As a result, the preference that is constructed may differ according to the way the problem has been presented (Payne, Bettman and Johnson, 1992). It is important to notice that, from this *constructive processing* viewpoint, such differences are *not* the result of biases. To think in terms of bias is to presuppose that there are 'true' preferences which an ideal, unbiased elicitation mechanism would discover. But the constructive processing approach rejects this presupposition.

In the context of CV, two dimensions of problem presentation are particularly significant. One is the distinction between *choice* tasks and *valuation* tasks. In a choice task, a respondent is offered a number of options and asked to choose one of them. In a valuation task, she is shown one option and is asked to value it on some scale. In CV surveys, open-ended WTP or WTA questions are valuation tasks, while binary-choice questions are choice tasks (iterated bidding might be thought of as a hybrid of choice and valuation). Focusing on valuation tasks, the second dimension is the scale on which valuations are expressed. In CV surveys, valuations are almost invariably expressed in terms of money; but in principle, it would be possible to use other scales – for example, respondents might be asked to say how much travelling time they would be willing to incur to reach a national park.

Several psychological theories about the effects of problem presentation use the general idea of *response compatibility* (Slovic and Lichtenstein, 1983; Tversky, Sattath and Slovic, 1988; Tversky, Slovic and Kahneman, 1990). Different strategies for constructing preferences, and different pieces of information which might be used in the construction process, vary in the extent to which they are compatible with the kind of response that is required. Here, 'compatibility' is understood in terms of ease of mental processing; it is hypothesized that individuals tend to use decision-making strategies which economize on mental processing.

One difference between choice problems and valuation problems is that there are various simple heuristics which apply to the former but not to the latter. In particular, when facing a binary choice between two options which differ on two attributes, a decision maker may focus on the attribute which she sees as the more important, and choose the option which is better in terms of this attribute. This heuristic avoids the need to make quantitative trade-offs between one dimension and another, thus economizing on mental effort. However, it is not applicable to valuation problems, in which trade-offs have to be made.

In a typical CV survey, the options can be thought of as having two main attributes: monetary cost and non-monetary benefit. Discussing choice tasks involving public programmes to improve road safety and to clean up beaches, Tversky, Sattath and Slovic (1988, pp. 373–374) hypothesize that non-monetary benefit (safety or health) is viewed as a more important attribute than monetary cost. If this is generally true, then the theory of response compatibility implies that binary-choice WTP questions ('Would you be willing to pay £y for . . . ?') will tend to evoke affirmative answers. Thus, the binary-choice response mode might be expected to elicit responses which imply relatively high money valuations of non-monetary benefits. Since open-ended questions invoke heuristics for making trade-offs between dimensions, these will tend to elicit lower money valuations for the same non-monetary benefits.

In relation to valuation questions, Tversky, Sattath and Slovic (1988) hypothesize that any given attribute is given more weight in determining a response if the required response is on the same scale as the attribute than if the scales are different (*scale compatibility*). Thus, asking respondents to value non-monetary benefits in money units will tend to elicit relatively high money valuations. Take the case of road safety. Here what is required is a trade-off between safety and money. According to the scale-compatibility hypothesis, asking for a response in money units will induce respondents to give greater weight to the money dimension, and hence to express relatively low money valuations of safety. This effect tends to reduce valuations that are elicited by open-ended methods, thus compounding the effect described in the previous paragraph. Notice that, unlike the misplaced strategic bias described in the section on Survey Biases, these effects tend to reduce open-ended WTA valuations as well as open-ended WTP ones.

A related, but slightly different, hypothesis about the effects of problem presentation is that of *anchoring and adjustment* (Tversky and Kahneman, 1974). Here, the idea is that if an individual faces a task which requires him to respond on some given scale, he will begin by looking for some point on that scale that can serve as an 'anchor', and then arrive at a response by 'adjusting' from that point. Adjustment does not completely eliminate the influence of the original anchor: the higher the anchor point, the higher the response. As with the hypotheses about response compatibility, the underlying idea is that decision makers use heuristics which economize on mental effort. If the anchoring-and-adjustment hypothesis is correct, responses to open-ended CV questions will be particularly vulnerable to what Mitchell and Carson (1989, pp. 240–246) call *implied value cues*. The common feature of implied value cues is that respondents make inappropriate use of information that happens to be salient for them at the time. For example, an iterated bidding procedure might start by asking a respondent whether she would be willing to pay £20 for some permit. The respondent might then think of £20 as a potential answer, and ask herself how much more or less than £20 she is willing to pay. If respondents use this kind of anchoring-and-adjustment process, WTP and WTA valuations elicited by iterated bidding may be positively related to the amount of money referred to in the opening question – the phenomenon described in the section on Response Modes as the 'starting point effect'.

Binary-choice questions may be subject to a related effect. By stating a particular price for a good and then asking a respondent whether she is willing to pay this, we may be inducing her to think of that price as in some way reasonable. On this hypothesis, the price which is built into a binary-choice question is acting as a kind of 'anchor' for the respondent's reasoning, even though the response is not arrived at by a process of 'adjustment'. To the extent that this effect exists, there will be some tendency for binary-choice questions to elicit the answer 'Yes' (i.e. I am willing to trade on the terms offered) when responses to open-ended questions would lead us to expect the opposite answer. Thus WTP valuations elicited by binary-choice questions will tend to be higher than those elicited by open-ended ones, while the opposite will be the case for WTA valuations. This effect is sometimes called *yea-saying* (e.g. Mitchell and Carson, 1989, pp. 240–241).

EXPERIMENTS

The experiments carried out by the project team were designed to try to discriminate between the two types of explanation of CV anomalies – that is, between the hypothesis that anomalies result from failures of survey instruments, and the hypothesis that they result from failures of the standard theory of preferences.

Our broad strategy was to elicit the preferences of experimental subjects by asking the same kinds of questions as in CV surveys, but with two main differences. First, we elicited preferences for well-defined private consumption goods, rather than for public goods. Second, our subjects made real decisions, not hypothetical ones: thus, for example, if a subject stated his WTP for a good, he was making a potentially binding commitment to buy at any price up to that amount. Our aim was to eliminate as far as possible the potential sources of bias described on pages 298–301. By using private goods and by using an appropriate elicitation method (see later), we removed the incentives for preference misrepresentation that are inevitable in CV studies of public goods. By using straightforward consumption goods (such as cans of Cola, or Belgian chocolates) with no obvious moral content, we hoped to eliminate any tendency for respondents to think in terms of charitable donations, or to use their answers as a way of expressing moral commitments.

Although we cannot be sure that we eliminated biases due to misunderstanding, we were able to give our subjects detailed instructions and plenty of practice. Since the subjects were making real decisions which determined the amount of money and/or goods they left the experiment with, they had a clear incentive to understand the procedures. If anomalies persist in these circumstances, this would tend to suggest that those anomalies are not due to biases in CV methods, but instead reflect the limitations of the received theory of preferences. We investigated the four main issues discussed below.

Divergences between WTA and WTP, and Reference Point Effects

We elicited subjects' valuations for two private consumption goods (Belgian chocolates and Cola). To ensure that our subjects had no incentive to misrepresent their preferences, we used an elicitation mechanism first proposed by Becker, De Groot and Marschak (1964), and now widely used in experimental economics. Take the case of a WTP question. The respondent tackles this as an open-ended question, and states the maximum amount of money he is willing to pay for the relevant good. After he has responded, a price is generated at random from some given probability distribution of prices. If the randomly-generated price is less than or equal to the person's stated maximum, he is required to pay that price, and receives the good in exchange. If the price is greater than the respondent's stated maximum, no trade takes place. The mechanism for eliciting WTA valuations is a mirror-image of the WTP mechanism.

Four different measures of valuation were elicited: WTP, WTA, *equivalent gain* (EG) and *equivalent loss* (EL). The equivalent gain for an increase in consumption of a good is the extra money that would be just as desirable as the extra consumption; the equivalent loss for a decrease in consumption is the loss of money that would be just as undesirable as the decrease in consumption. Our experiment differed from most other investigations of divergences between WTA and WTP in two respects: first, because it included EG and EL as well as

WTP and WTA; and second, because it controlled for the income and substitution effects which Hanemann (1991) invokes to explain WTA-WTP divergences in CV studies (see pages 301–302).

The principles of our experimental design can be described in terms of figure 14.1. Think of good X as a consumption good (say, cans of Cola) and of good Y as money. In our experiment, a subject was endowed with one of the combinations A, B, C or D. If she was endowed with A, she was asked to state her WTP for $x_2 - x_1$ extra cans of Cola. From her answer to this question, we can impute her preference between A and D. (That is, if her WTP is greater than or equal to $y_2 - y_1$, she prefers D to A; if it less than $y_2 - y_1$, she prefers A to D.) If the subject was endowed with D, she was asked to state her WTA for giving up $x_2 - x_1$ cans of Cola. If she was endowed with C, she stated her EG for an $x_2 - x_1$ increase in Cola. If she was endowed with B, she stated her EL for an $x_2 - x_1$ decrease in Cola. From each of these valuations, we can impute the subject's preference between A and D.

If Hicksian theory is correct, each subject has a fixed preference between A and D, which can be elicited by any of the four methods. In contrast, reference-dependent theory implies that preferences between A and D may differ according to whether the subject is endowed with A, B, C or D. Any given subject is most likely to prefer A to D if her initial endowment is A, and least likely to have this preference if her endowment is D. To put this another way, WTP will generate the lowest valuations of the change in consumption of Cola; WTA will generate the highest valuations; EG and EL will generate intermediate valuations.

The results confirmed the predictions of reference-dependent theory. For example, with A = (two cans of Cola, £3.00) and D = (six cans of Cola, £1.50), and with groups of 76–80 subjects answering each valuation question, the proportion of subjects reporting a preference for A over D was 60.0 per cent when the endowment point was A, 50.0 per cent when it was B, 26.3 per cent when it was C, and 15.8 per cent when it was D. We found a very similar pattern for a different specification of A, B, C and D, in which subjects reported their valuations of Belgian chocolates.

Recall that WTA-WTP disparities can arise from the use of misplaced strategic heuristics. Could this bias, rather than reference-dependent preferences, explain our results? Although our subjects were making decisions for real, and thus had an incentive to understand our procedures, those procedures were obviously unfamiliar to them (apart from the practice subjects were given as part of the experiment itself). Thus, we cannot reject *a priori* the possibility that significant numbers of them thought about the tasks they were given as though these were bargaining problems.

One benefit of eliciting EG and EL as well as WTP and WTA is that by doing so, we can control for strategic biases. Compare EL and WTP for Cola. In the WTP case, the subject is endowed with A = (two cans of Cola, £3.00) and is asked to state the maximum amount of money she would be willing to give up in return for four extra cans of Cola. In the EL case, she is endowed with B = (six cans of Cola, £3.00) and is asked to state the maximum amount of money she would give up in return for keeping the six cans of Cola, rather than losing two of them. Notice that these two choice problems are *exactly* the same, apart from the way they are framed in terms of gains and losses. In each case, the subject will finish up *either* with two cans of Cola and £3.00, *or* with four cans of Cola and £3.00, less an amount of money she has paid to the experimenters. In each case, she has to state the largest payment such that she still prefers the second outcome to the first. From a 'strategic' point of view, both framings seem to have the same power to suggest (wrongly) that it might be in the subject's interest to understate the amount of money she is willing to give up. Thus, I suggest, differences between WTP and EL cannot plausibly be explained in terms of misplaced strategic heuristics. The same goes for differences between WTA and EG. The fact that we found such differences, and that these differences were in the direction predicted by reference-dependent theory, suggests that some kind of reference-point effect was at work, independently of any strategic bias.

Scale Compatibility and Strategic Bias

The experiment described above had another novel feature. As well as asking subjects to value increments of consumption of a good in terms of money, we also asked them to value increments of money in terms of the good. For example, take the case in which A, B, C and D are combinations of money and Cola, with A = (two cans of Cola, £3.00) and D = (six cans of Cola, £1.50). Suppose we wish to impute a subject's preference between A and D from the reference point A. One way to do this is to give her A as an endowment, and ask her to state the maximum amount of money she is willing to pay for four extra cans of Cola: this is the WTP measure discussed in on pp. 312–314. From this valuation, we can infer whether she prefers A to D or vice versa. Alternatively, we could give the subject the endowment A, but then ask her to state the minimum amount of Cola she would be willing to accept as compensation for giving up £1.50. This is a WTA valuation of money in terms of Cola. From this measure, too, we can infer the subject's preference between A and D.

Recall that the hypothesis of scale compatibility implies that if options are described in terms of two attributes, and if a task requires responses on the same scale as one of those attributes, respondents will tend to give greater weight to that attribute. In our experiment, 'giving greater weight to money' implies a greater tendency to prefer A to D, while 'giving greater weight to Cola' implies a greater tendency to prefer D to A. Thus, we can test the scale compatibility hypothesis by investigating whether implicit preferences between A and D vary systematically with the response scale.

In the experiment, we elicited preferences between A and D using each of the four reference points (that is, eliciting each of WTP, WTA, EG and EL), for each of the two response modes. As far as reference-point effects are concerned, the broad pattern of results is the same for both response scales: the proportion of subjects reporting a preference for A over D is greatest when the reference point is A, and least when it is D, with intermediate proportions when the reference point is B or C. But we found no systematic scale-compatibility effects.

The hypothesis of strategic bias gives us a reason to expect a different pattern of reported preferences across response scales. In relation to strategic bias, the crucial distinction is between questions in which the subject reports a maximum willingness to pay on some response scale (i.e. WTP and EL questions) and those in which she reports a minimum willingness to accept on some response scale (i.e. WTA and EG). If there is strategic bias, this will impart a downward bias to WTP and EL responses, and an upward bias to WTA and EG responses. When the response scale is money, a downward bias in responses implies a bias towards reporting a preference for A relative to D. (Remember that switching from A to D involves giving up money in return for the specific good – say, Cola.) But when the response scale is Cola, a downward bias in responses implies a bias towards the *opposite* preference – for D relative to A. Whatever the response scale, these biases will tend to favour a preference for A when the reference point is A, and a preference for D when the reference point is D. As noted above, our experiment cannot distinguish between these biases and refer-ence-point effects.

However, the other two reference points are more interesting. Suppose the reference point is B. Then the valuation measure that is elicited is EL. This is true, whether the response scale is money (in which case the subject reports her willingness to accept a loss of money as an alternative to a fixed loss of Cola) or Cola (in which case she reports her willingness to accept a loss of Cola as an alternative to a fixed loss of money). Thus if the response scale is money, strategic bias will favour a preference for A relative to D, while if the response scale is Cola, the same bias will tend to favour a preference for D relative to A. In fact, we find exactly this pattern, although its quantitative impact is not particularly great. When the reference point is B, the proportion of subjects reporting a preference for A over D is 50.0 per cent when the response scale is money and 43.7 per cent when it is Cola. When the refer-ence point is C, the figures are 26.3 per cent and 35.5 per cent. The same pattern is found for chocolate: when the reference point is B, the proportion of subjects preferring A to D is 92.1 per cent when the response scale is money and 75.0 per cent when it is chocolate; when the reference point is C, the figures are 70.0 per cent and 81.6 per cent. The implication seems to be that responses are influenced both by reference-point effects and by strategic bias.

Part-Whole Effects

We investigated part-whole effects by eliciting subjects' WTP and WTA for two kinds of voucher. The elicitation methods were similar to those of the experiment described on pages 312 and 314. One 'red' voucher gave an entitlement to a main course at a pizza restaurant; the other 'blue' voucher gave an entitlement to a dessert course at the same restaurant. Each of these vouchers may be interpreted as a 'part'; the combination of the two is the 'whole'. In the case of WTP, we elicited (*a*) WTP for a red voucher by subjects endowed with no vouchers, (*b*) WTP for a red voucher by subjects endowed with a blue voucher, (*c*) WTP for a blue voucher by subjects endowed with no vouchers, (*d*) WTP for a blue voucher by subjects endowed with a red voucher, and (*e*) WTP for both vouchers by subjects endowed with none. If income effects are negligible, the sum of (*a*) and (*d*) should equal the sum of (*b*) and (*c*), and both sums should equal (*v*). By varying endowments of money between subjects, we were able to estimate the magnitude of any income effects, and thus control for them. WTA measures for parts and whole were elicited in a similar way.

The main finding was that the sum of WTP for the two parts, whether using (*a*) and (*d*) or (*b*) and (*c*), was significantly greater than WTP for the whole. For example, we elicited (*a*) and (*e*) from one group of 37 subjects; the mean WTP for the red voucher was £2.18 and for both vouchers was £3.00. If preferences are reference-independent, the implication is that for this group of subjects, the mean WTP for a blue voucher, given a red one (i.e. the mean value of (*d*)) is £0.82. Another group of 36 subjects stated (*d*) directly; the mean value was £1.32. We found similar results for WTA: the sum of WTA for the two parts was significantly greater than WTA for the whole. These differences could not be explained by income effects.

As far as we know, ours is the first study to investigate part-whole effects for private consumption goods. These findings are significant, because they suggest that the part-whole effects found in CV studies are not wholly the result of the public characteristics of the goods for which preferences are being elicited. Our results raise the possibility that part-whole effects may be related to reference-point effects (see pp. 312-314).

Open-Ended versus Binary-Choice Questions

We ran an experiment which elicited WTP and WTA valuations for private consumption goods (bottles of sparkling wine, and packets of tea bags), using open-ended questions for one group of subjects and binary choice questions for another group. As in the other experiments, an incentive-compatible design was used. The main results were that WTP valuations were higher for binary-choice questions than for open-ended ones, but WTA valuations were *lower*. For example, in an open-ended question, one group of subjects were asked to state their

WTP for a bottle of wine. Of these subjects, 62.0 per cent stated amounts of £1.50 or more, while 17.2 per cent stated amounts of £3.00 or more. Another group was asked a binary-choice question, effectively asking: 'Are you willing to buy the wine at a price of £1.50?'; 85.5 per cent said they were. Members of a third group were asked if they were willing to buy the wine at a price of £3.00; 39.7 per cent said they were. In the case of WTA, 85.5 per cent of open-ended respondents stated WTA valuations of £5.50 or less, and 47.8 per cent stated valuations of £3.00 or less. However, 96.6 per cent of binary-choice respondents chose to sell at a price of £5.50, and 60.3 per cent chose to sell at a price of £3.00.

These results are interesting, particularly since, as far as we know, comparisons between open-ended and binary-choice response modes have not previously been made for WTA valuations. Taken together, these results are consistent with the anchoring (or yea-saying) hypothesis. That hypothesis implies a tendency to accept whatever terms of trade are offered in binary-choice questions: thus binary-choice respondents appear to be willing to pay relatively large amounts and to accept relatively small ones. They are also consistent with the hypothesis that there is strategic bias, and that this bias has more impact on open-ended responses than on binary-choice ones (see pp. 304–305). The results are *not* consistent with the response compatibility hypothesis, which implies that binary-choice questions will generate higher valuations than open-ended ones, irrespective of whether WTP or WTA is being elicited.

CONCLUSIONS

There can be little doubt that the responses elicited by CV surveys show systematic patterns that are not compatible with the standard economic theory of preferences. In particular: willingness-to-accept valuations are greater than willingness-to-pay valuations to a degree that cannot be explained by income and substitution effects; responses can be strongly influenced by what (from the perspective of a theory of rational choice) is irrelevant information, such as the starting point for iterated bidding; binary-choice questions tend to elicit higher willingness-to-pay valuations (but possibly lower willingness-to-accept valuations) than do open-ended questions; and when a good can be broken down into parts, the sum of the valuations of the separate parts tends to be greater than the valuation of the whole.

Experimental research (of which our experiments are just a small part) seems to be showing that these anomalies are not specific to CV surveys. The same effects can be generated in controlled experimental settings in which individuals make decisions involving real trades in private consumption goods. Thus these anomalies cannot be attributed solely to the hypothetical nature of the questions in CV surveys, or to the difficulties in eliciting preferences for public goods. To some degree, the experimental evidence supports the hypothesis of 'misplaced strategic bias': respondents seem to be using rules of thumb which lead them to conceal the full extent of their willingness to trade; these rules of thumb are appropriate in real-life bargaining situations, even though they are misplaced both in the context of CV and in the experimental setting. To the extent that CV responses are subject to such bias, there is scope to refine CV methods.

Even after allowing for strategic bias, however, significant anomalies remain. The best available explanations for these anomalies, I suggest, are provided by psychologically-based theories of decision-making, such as the theories of reference-dependent preferences and of anchoring. The challenge for economics is to develop new models of individual choice which take account of the insights generated by psychological research and which are consistent with the available evidence.

REFERENCES

Bateman, Ian J., Langford, Ian H., Turner, R. Kerry, Willis, Ken G. and Harrod, Guy D. (1995) Elicitation and truncation effects in contingent valuation studies. *Ecological Economics*, **12**, pp. 161–179.

Bateman, Ian J., Munro, Alistair, Rhodes, Bruce, Starmer, Chris and Sugden, Robert (1997*a*) A test of the theory of reference-dependent preferences. *Quarterly Journal of Economics,* forthcoming.

Bateman, Ian J., Munro, Alistair, Rhodes, Bruce, Starmer, Chris and Sugden, Robert (1997*b*) Does part-whole bias exist? An experimental investigation. *Economic Journal*, forthcoming.

Becker, Gordon M., DeGroot, Morris H. and Marschak, Jacob (1964) Measuring utility by a single-response sequential method. *Behavioral Science*, **9**, pp. 226–232.

Boyle, Kevin J., Bishop, Richard C. and Welsh, Michael P. (1985) Starting point bias in contingent valuation surveys. *Land Economics*, **61**, pp. 188–194.

Boyle, Kevin J., Desvourges, W.H., Johnson, F.R., Dunford, R.W. and Hudson, S.P. (1994) An investigation of part-whole biases in contingent valuation studies. *Journal of Environmental Economics and Management*, **27**, pp. 38–64.

Hanemann, W. Michael (1991) Willingness to pay and willingness to accept: how much can they differ? *American Economic Review*, **81**, pp. 635–647.

Hoehn, John P. and Randall, Alan (1987) A satisfactory benefit cost indicator from contingent valuation. *Journal of Environmental Economics and Management*, **14**, pp. 226–247.

Hicks, John R. (1943) The four consumer surpluses. *Review of Economic Studies*, **8**, pp. 108–116.

Hicks, John R (1956) *A Revision of Demand Theory*. Oxford: Clarendon Press.

Kahneman, Daniel and Tversky, Amos (1979). Prospect theory: an analysis of decision under risk. *Econometrica*, **47**, pp. 263–291.

Kahneman, Daniel and Knetsch, Jack (1992) Valuing public goods: the purchase of moral satisfaction. *Journal of Environmental Economics and Management*, **22**, pp. 57–70.

Knez, Marc, Smith, Vernon L. and Williams, Arlington W. (1985) Individual rationality, market rationality, and value estimation. *American Economic Review*, Papers and Proceedings, **75**, pp. 397–402.

Kriström, B. (1993) Comparing continuous and discrete valuation questions. *Environmental and Resource Economics*, **3**, pp. 63–71.

Loomes, Graham (1994) Valuing Health and Safety: Some Economic and Psychological

Issues. Paper presented at Seventh International Conference on the Foundations of Utility, Risk and Decision Theory, Oslo.

Mitchell, Robert Cameron and Carson, Richard T. (1989) *Using Surveys to Value Public Goods: The Contingent Valuation Method.* Washington, D.C.: Resources for the Future.

Payne, John W., Bettman, James R. and Johnson, Eric J. (1992) Behavioral decision research: a constructive processing perspective. *Annual Review of Psychology,* **42**, pp. 87–131.

Randall, Alan and Stoll, John R. (1980) Consumer's surplus in commodity space. *American Economic Review,* **70**, pp. 449–455.

Roberts, Kenneth J., Thompson, Mark E. and Pawlyk, Perry W. (1985) Contingent valuation of recreational diving at petroleum rigs, Gulf of Mexico. *Transactions of the American Fisheries Society,* **114**, pp. 214–219.

Rowe, Robert D., d'Arge, Ralph C. and Brookshire, David S. (1980) An experiment on the economic value of visibility. *Journal of Environmental Economics and Management,* **7**, pp. 1–19.

Sellar, Christine, Stoll, John R. and Chavas, Jean-Paul (1985) Validation of empirical measures of welfare change: a comparison of nonmarket techniques. *Land Economics,* **61**, pp. 156–175.

Slovic, Paul and Lichtenstein, Sarah (1983) Preference reversals: a broader perspective. *American Economic Review,* **73**, pp. 596–605.

Sugden, Robert (1997*a*) Public goods and contingent valuation, in Bateman, Ian and Willis, Ken (eds.) *Valuing Environmental Preferences.* Oxford: Oxford University Press.

Sugden, Robert (1997*b*) Alternatives to the neoclassical theory of choice, in Bateman, Ian and Willis, Ken (eds.) *Valuing Environmental Preferences.* Oxford: Oxford University Press.

Thaler, Richard (1980) Toward a positive theory of consumer choice. *Journal of Economic Behavior and Organization,* **1**, pp. 39–60.

Tversky, Amos and Kahneman, Daniel (1974) Judgment under uncertainty: heuristics and biases. *Science,* **185**, pp. 1124–1131.

Tversky, Amos and Kahneman, Daniel (1991) Loss aversion in riskless choice: a reference-dependent model. *Quarterly Journal of Economics,* **106**, pp. 1039–1061.

Tversky, Amos, Sattath, Shmuel and Slovic, Paul (1988) Contingent weighting in judgment and choice. *Psychological Review,* **95**, pp. 371–384.

Tversky, Amos, Slovic, Paul and Kahneman, Daniel (1990) The causes of preference reversal. *American Economic Review,* **80**, pp. 204–217.

CHAPTER 15

NON-USER BENEFITS FROM INVESTMENTS IN URBAN LIGHT RAIL: EVIDENCE FROM SHEFFIELD

John Henneberry, Paul Lawless and Peter Townroe

Over recent years the cost benefit appraisal technique used by the Department of Transport in the United Kingdom to evaluate prospective investments in inter-urban trunk road schemes, the COBA technique, has been criticized on a number of counts. The core of the COBA approach lies in attaching a money cost to a time saved value for users of a new road, with the number of users rising over time on the basis of national forecasts of road traffic volumes. The fixed matrix basis of the forecasts provides for changes of route but not of the relative significance of origins and destinations. This has given rise to much discussion on the significance of, and benefits to, induced traffic growth on a new link and the use of a variable matrix basis for the forecasts (e.g. SACTRA, 1994). At the same time the COBA approach has received criticism for not encompassing the environmental impacts of road schemes. Detailed suggestions have been put forward as to how to incorporate systematically environmental factors into the overall investment evaluation (SACTRA, 1992; Bateman *et al.*, 1993).

Even a variable trip matrix basis for traffic forecasts will not encompass all possible generated traffic, induced by the construction of a new road. For over time land uses change, particularly those in proximity to and with good access to the road. These prospective changes introduce uncertainty into the anticipated trip demand patterns: they are difficult to model, having a close interdependence with the evolution of policy decisions by the local governments responsible for land use development control. But such changes should not be ignored. That was the basis of the minority letter and commentary to the 1994 SACTRA report on induced traffic generation by one member of the Committee, Ms Audrey Lees (SACTRA, 1994, pp. 235–242).

Ms Lees pointed out that the Committee had received submissions from a number of important bodies drawing attention to the need to move closely related transport planning to local land use planning. These bodies wanted to broaden trunk road planning in particular to encompass an assessment of the interaction of transport and land use. Submissions arguing for this came from the Royal Institution of Chartered Surveyors, for example, from the Town and Country Planning Association, from the Countryside Commission, from the Council for the Protection of Rural England, and from the Royal Town Planning Institute. Ms Lees also quotes from the Joint Memorandum from the Departments of Environment and Transport to the Royal Commission on Environmental Pollution in 1992; and points to Planning Policy Guidance Note 13; issued by both Departments. PPG13 refers to the need to coordinate transport planning with land use planning at the regional guidance, structure plan and local plan levels.

The interrelationship between transport investments and land use developments is perhaps most marked in peri-urban locations. Patterns of employment and of residence will be pulled about by the new contours of accessibility, if land use changes are allowed to take place. The SACTRA (1994, p. 157) report quotes the Halcrow Fox modelling study of the Norwich Northern Distributor route as an example of this. 'Filling-in-out-to-the-bypass' has been the experience of new building on the edges of many communities. And there will be lifestyle gains and losses from such new roads to local residents: from the loss of through traffic, less pollution, higher property values etc, as well as from improved accessibility, to set against the loss of open countryside, unwanted new development etc. Changes such as these non-user costs and benefits from a trunk road investment, can be paralleled by similar changes from a major public transport investment within an urban area. The recently completed initial investment in the Sheffield urban light rail system, the Sheffield 'Supertram', and in related major urban road schemes, provides an excellent case study for the examination of these non-user benefits.

THE SHEFFIELD INVESTMENTS

The mid-1990s has seen the completion of five major transport investments within the city boundaries of Sheffield; with one further delayed project, the STOL airport, now looking to be operational by early 1998.

Four of the schemes involve new and improved roads. The Mosborough Link Road, a £27 million scheme, was completed in 1994, providing a new access to developing industrial and residential suburbs to the south east of the city and enhancing access to the M1 motorway via the Sheffield Parkway (a major dual highway completed in 1968). The road was built in three stages, over six years, with 50 per cent funding from the European Regional Development Fund. The £16 million upgrade to a section of the Outer Ring Road provides for improved access to the airport and to several industrial areas. The £18.5 million Penistone

Road upgrade improves the major arterial route, the A61, to the north west of the city centre. This road leads out past the Sheffield Wednesday football ground at Hillsborough to the important link over the Pennines to Manchester, the Woodhead Pass. It runs along the floor of the Upper Don Valley, a key industrial area, and serves large residential suburbs to the north of the city.

The £33 million Don Valley Link Road is rather different. Completed in 1996, this 4.4 km improvement provides a key dimension to the strategy of the Sheffield Development Corporation for the industrial regeneration of the Lower Don Valley. This area remains the steel making heart of Sheffield, but now with dramatically fewer people employed in both steel and the related engineering and metals industries. A major restructuring of the employment base has been required, with major physical redevelopment. The enhanced Link Road runs from the city centre to the M1 junction close to the Meadowhall Shopping Centre. It passes the stadium and the arena both constructed for the 1991 World Student Games and a further shopping area; but more importantly it runs beside a series of industrial sites, cleared, de-contaminated and prepared by the Development Corporation. The cost of the road included extensive land organization for the road itself. The Corporation invested a similar additional total in the principal sites. Construction of new factories, a hotel, and several office developments has now occurred on a number of these sites, bringing new industrial and commercial life to the Valley.

The STOL airport has been delayed. The 50 ha site is a former steelworks. The basic development cost has been met by the opencast mining of some 1.5 million tonnes of coal. The original developers went into receivership at the end of 1992 but the site for the runway has been prepared. Finance for the associated business park is now being assembled, and this will bring the package together to provide airport business and short-haul flights off a 1200 m runway and to stimulate related business activity on 800,000 sq ft of industrial and commercial space. The estimated cost of the airport development is £13 million.

The £240 million Supertram investment parallels the road schemes. The 29 km route has three arms. The longest of these runs out to the south east of the city centre, leading eventually to the Mosborough suburbs. The other two arms lead along the Upper and the Lower Don Valleys. The background to the investment is set out and discussed in some detail in Townroe (1995) and in Lawless and Dabinett (1995). The system started to carry passengers in March 1994 on the first section to be opened, running down from the city centre to the Meadowhall Shopping Centre. All sections were open by the end of 1995. The build up of patronage has been slower than anticipated; and the disruption caused by the construction of the half of the route that is on-street led to much local complaint and controversy (Hay and Haywood, 1994). However, the system is path-breaking in terms of the British experience. It is of a different character to its two principal comparators: the Tyne-Wear Metro and the Manchester Metrolink. This is partly because of the topography of Sheffield, partly because of the on-street running, but especially because of the role the investment is intended to have in the social and economic regeneration of Sheffield.

The financial appraisal and the technical evaluation of the proposed investment in the Sheffield light rail system in 1985 was complemented by a wider cost-benefit analysis. This analysis provided grounds for a capital grant from central government under Section 56 of the 1968 Transport Act. Approval for this grant finally came in December 1990, following the necessary legislation passing through Parliament in 1988. The cost-benefit analysis also provided information to support the contribution of £13 million towards the cost of the line in the Lower Don Valley from the IDOPs Programme of the European Community. In addition, the Sheffield Development Corporation contributed to this part of the investment, following an evaluation which suggested that up to 2000 additional jobs would be created along a 400 metre corridor of the track on land owned by the Corporation.

From its initial conception, the Sheffield Supertram investment was viewed as having the potential to offer significant non-user benefits. In large part, these benefits would fall to urban road users in the city, to the extent that passengers on the tram would otherwise have travelled by car or by bus. In that sense, the tram enhances the accessibility capacity of the city. But the Supertram was also envisaged as providing other indirect benefits to the Sheffield economy, in offering a stimulus to economic regeneration. This stimulus was seen as going beyond the contribution of local expenditures from the construction activity. The Supertram, it was thought, would offer a new flexibility in the local labour market; it would enhance land and property values; and it would add an important dimension to those factors which might attract additional industrial and commercial investment to the city. If these non-transport benefits prove to be significant, then the case made by other cities for light rail investments of various kinds could be strengthened. As construction started, it was seen therefore as clearly desirable that an evaluation should be undertaken of the non-user impacts of the Supertram investment, taking account of the related road improvements. The research described below came from this understanding.

THE RESEARCH APPROACH

The Sheffield Supertram has been the subject of extensive research. In 1992 consultants Atkins Wootton Jeffreys together with the Transport Studies Unit of the University of Oxford assessed the transport impacts of the Supertram investment, on the use of the road system in Sheffield, and on the numbers of passengers on bus routes in competition with the tram or affected by the tram lines.

This research reported in this chapter investigates the non-transport impacts of Supertram investment and takes account of the recent major road investments in Sheffield.

The approach taken for this non-user evaluation of the Sheffield transport investments has been presented in some detail in Dabinett and Lawless (1994), Lawless and Dabinett (1995), and in Townroe (1995). In summary, the research approach has seen four groups of actors as potentially being influenced by the light rail investment and the parallel road schemes: *households and individuals*, particularly in the context of their shopping habits and their participation in the local labour market; *companies*, also in the labour market but in addition using the road system to bring in supplies, to offer access to customers, and to transport out manufactured goods; *investors*, particularly non-local property companies and their agents; and *enablers and regulators*, with particular attention to agencies promoting new investment and to the operation of the local land use planning system. These actors interact through three market places: that for land and property, that for labour, and that for the local market for goods and services. The key outputs to be observed from these interactions are in physical development, in changing property prices, in new, additional or retained jobs, and changes in the levels of business operations. In each of these areas the research team has turned to both available sources of secondary data and to information collected from a number of separate before-and-after survey exercises.

Evidence from other transport investment studies (e.g. Huddleston and Pangotra, 1990; or the work on the impact of the Tyne Metro, CURDS *et al.*, 1990; and of the Manchester Metrolink, Forrest *et al.*, 1995) suggests that the secondary non-user benefits are small relative to the values gained by users. It is therefore tempting to leave any assessment or forecasting of such benefits out of the reckoning in the appraisal of a proposed investment. However, the evidence from other studies does attribute significance to these non-user benefits, especially when considered from the perspective of the local urban community involved. This is particularly so when the investments are seen as important components of an overall urban economic and social regeneration strategy; but many of the benefits will be generated in even the most prosperous urban areas (where of course the user benefits are also likely to be relatively high). There are however the particular research problems which will occur in any evaluation of these non-user benefits.

The first of these is the issue of *timescale*. Benefits from the workings of the labour market and especially the property market take time to work through. There is therefore not only the issue of waiting once the new investment is operational for inputs to emerge, but also the issue of assembling comparable data across two or more fairly widely spread points in time. Arguably, the Sheffield research could revisit key data sources with benefit five and ten years hence. A second issue is timing the data collection to allow a *before-and-after comparison*. In this the Sheffield work has been successful, both in the collection of primary and of secondary data. But there is an issue here in establishing an appropriate base-line. It should also be stressed that the study is not a 'one-off' evaluation. A third issue relates to *identification and limitation*. There are many indirect effects where the benefits are not only long term, but essentially fall to individuals, businesses and households located outside the city involved; and where it is difficult to identify all impacted-upon parties within the city boundaries. The Sheffield study is confident that it has encompassed the major secondary effects. The fourth research issue here is the standard problem in any investment impact study or export policy evaluation: the problem of *attribution*. Over the period of construction of a large transport project and over the period in which local market forces are absorbing its impact, the rest of the world is not standing still. Other social and economic pressures are present and are changing over time. The interpretation of the Sheffield data has tried to maintain an awareness of the significance of these parallel changes to the local economy and to local society.

DATA COLLECTION

The process of data collection in this research exercise falls into five parts under the headings of the five themes in the original research design:

1. Image

Major new urban transport investments provide an opportunity for a city to reinforce its strategy in selling itself as a location for business investment, both to local investors and to potential external investors. But how significant is the impact of this particular dimension of city marketing? The Sheffield case has been investigated with two before-and-after surveys. Ten Sheffield based developers, agents and recent inward investors were interviewed in 1993 and early in 1994, together with ten key national relocation advisers in major property companies. This survey activity was repeated early in 1996.

Indirect evidence has also come from a fairly large survey (linking in with another study) of day-trip and overnight visitors to Sheffield in 1996. The survey work was complemented by an analysis of the marketing activity of the two principal development agencies in the city: the Sheffield Development Corporation and the Department of Employment and Economic Development of Sheffield City Council.

2. Land and Property Values

If new transport infrastructures and the associated services result in an enhancement of land values and a rising demand for property, reflected in both the capital and the rental values of property, then not only is there a local welfare gain to the local land and property owners but there is a market signal of attraction to investors, local and non-local. This impact has generated some controversy in the literature, for the impact on some properties close to a new facility might be negative (e.g. the house under the flight path, the cottage beside the bypass). And it is important to distinguish impacts upon residential properties from impacts upon commercial and industrial property. The present study does this. There are three elements here.

The first has used a monthly data series on asking prices for houses in Sheffield, offered for sale by local estate agents. The data set includes information on the physical characteristics of each house (number of beds, type, key features). The distance to the Supertram line and the nearest stop was calculated for houses within a 1 km corridor each side of the line. Each property was also assigned a neighbourhood variable, drawing upon the local housing market areas across the city which local estate agents use in their selling details. This overall data set for 1988, 1993 and 1996 covers 4,800 cases: about 1,600 for each date. It was subject to hedonic regression analysis.

Similar information for the same years was collected for non-residential property within the same corridors. Rateable values of shops, offices and industrial buildings were used as the price variable. Some 165 observations have been generated here.

The detailed statistical analysis of price information was complemented in this part of the study by nine detailed property development case studies in the Lower Don Valley, the Upper Don Valley, the city centre and Mosborough undertaken in 1995 and early in 1996. An additional overview was obtained via the establishment of a Delphi Panel of thirty-two local property agents. Participants were surveyed in 1994 and 1995.

3. Land Use and Development

Two types of data have been used in this part of the study. The intention was to look for implied causal links between the transport investment and land use changes, by looking in particular at spatial patterns of new developments and at the influence of local land use policies under the statutory planning system.

Land use surveys were undertaken along the tram and road corridors in the Upper and Lower Don Valleys, and also in the City Centre, on a before-and-after basis. In the Upper Don Valley information was collected in 1993 and 1995, in the Lower Don Valley in 1992 and 1995, and in the city centre in 1994 and 1996. The data was collected 'on the ground' by students walking the streets and in the case of the city centre put onto a GIS database.

At the same time (and with considerable difficulty) information on planning applications in the transport corridors has been down-loaded from the Sheffield City Council PLANAPPS system, for 1992 and 1993.

4. Business Operations and Location

The focus in this part of the study has been on the influence of the transport investments on the operations of existing businesses. Improvements in transport may have an influence on local relocation; or, in a more limited way, in profitability from lower costs of production. This may come from less congestion, from a more direct routing, from improved access to suppliers and access to customers. Conversely, the same improvements provide easier access from competitors. Specific data on these changes are very difficult to collect. The Sheffield study has had to rely therefore on two survey exercises obtaining more impressionistic findings; and on the values that may be obtained from GOAD Plus.

The principal survey activity here has been two telephone-contact surveys of businesses in three areas: the Upper Don Valley and the Lower Don Valley, and in Mosborough, the rapidly growing suburb to the south east of the city, at the end of the tram line and of one of the major road schemes. A before survey gained a response from 234 establishments in October 1993. An after survey gained a response from 331 establishments in the same areas in July 1995.

This survey has been complemented by information from a city centre panel of retail establishments, before and after; and from case studies of six relocations. The GOAD Plan analysis has been undertaken as follows, in the four principal shopping centres:

City Centre	1990	1994	1995	1996
Hillsborough	1991	1993		
Crystal Peaks	1990	1994		1996
Meadowhall	1991	1994	1995	1996

5. The Labour Market

Any transport improvement will influence patterns of individual mobility. In the Sheffield case it was expected that this would be the case for both the tram and the road investments. In linking these investments to urban regeneration, it is potential geographical mobility in the labour market that is important. The Sheffield study considered this area of impact using three sources of data.

The first source was a before and after data collection exercise on the residential post codes of ten major organizations located in Sheffield city centre. These organizations employed 13,000 people between them (they included Sheffield Hallam University and parts of the City Council). Broken down by sex and broad occupational category, a before and after comparison, of 1994 compared to 1996 is possible, using GIS techniques.

This major (and innovative) data analysis exercise is completed by two surveys. One is of locational choice of job and home and of journey-to-work mode of new recruits to these organizations. The second is a survey of 250 job seekers. A before survey was undertaken in 1994, in Job Centres, Careers Centres and local community centres. This survey was repeated in 1996. Again GIS techniques are being used to help in the analysis of patterns of job search.

RESEARCH FINDINGS

A summary of the research findings so far may be presented under the same five headings:

1. Image

The two surveys of property agents and consultants, locally in Sheffield and national, demonstrated:

• An increased volume of activity and interest in Sheffield as an investment location in 1995 compared with 1993.

• The image of the city in a general sense is an important factor in investment decisions, set alongside the specific requirements of sites, accessibility, labour supply etc.

• The image of Sheffield as an investment location had improved over the two years, because of the success of Meadowhall, publicity given to sporting events and the environmental improvements in the Lower Don Valley.

• The Supertram contributed to this image, as a modern, clean, new facility; but in making investment choices, the improved road accessibility from the four major road schemes was more important.

• The *relative* standing of Sheffield as an investment location amongst its peers of comparable cities did not improve between 1993 and 1995.

• The proposed airport was not thought to be important for an improved image of Sheffield.

Among the comments received from interviewees was the reflection that the tram is more significant for *office* investments, the roads for *manufacturing* investments; that it did provide a very modern image; that it demonstrated that local transport problems were being addressed; but transport infrastructure and services stood alongside many other attributes of the image of a city to a potential investor, and alongside many other basic locational requirements. The tram in particular was just a one positive addition to other positive changes occurring in the city.

2. Land and Property Values

The hedonic regression analyses of the price and building characteristics of residential and non-residential property along the route corridors, using 1988, 1993 and 1996 data, showed a significant impact of the transport investment on residential property values, but failed to show a significant impact on non-residential property values.

In 1988 the distance of a house being offered for sale from the future route of the Supertram and the asking price for that house had a modest inverse relationship i.e. the nearer the route, other things being equal, the higher (slightly) the price. In 1993 the opposite was the case. Houses away from the route, towards the edges of the delineated corridors, showed a tendency to be higher priced, ceteris paribus. In 1996 the location of a house in relation to the Supertram route had no statistically significant influence on its price.

It seems that anticipation of Supertram in 1993 reduced house prices, perhaps because of a fear of poorer road access, or because of a fear of the local disruption in the building of the system. This latter factor was given much local publicity at the time. Upon completion of the South Yorkshire Supertram system part of this price reduction was removed. It may be that, over the longer term, Supertram will have a positive impact on house prices but more research would be necessary to establish this effect.

A further unpicking of the data may demonstrate a difference in the Supertram corridor effect for cheaper houses than for more expensive larger properties, given different patronage rates for the use of public transport. There may be a related student effect, in a city where over 10 per cent of the resident population are students in either higher or further education.

The inconclusive results for the non-residential property may just reflect very weak market conditions during the study period. The Delphi Panel of 32 property intermediaries argued for a strong positive effect, but it is difficult to assess how far these opinions were based on hard results rather than on hopes and expectations. Perhaps the important finding here is that opinion was positive rather than negative, particularly given the negative press locally for both the tram and road improvements during construction for retailing and for commercial enterprises in particular.

3. Land Use and Development

Counter to expectations, the work on land use changes and related land use policies found a lack of response in advance of construction of the roads and of the tramway, both in the pattern of planning applications and in the formulation of local land use plans. The latter improved in the early 1990s with the work of the Sheffield Development Corporation as development control agency in the Lower Don Valley. The impact of the Lower Don Valley Link Road on the take up of prepared sites by both property developers and companies building for themselves is now clear. But even there, the impact has only emerged as the road investment nears completion. Very little impact could be detected in advance of construction, even when the plans and the funding were agreed (and when land values were lower). Land use planning policies, arguably, would have benefited from an earlier introduction of the 'Package Bid' approach to the funding decisions on transport improvements.

The land use policies outside the Lower Don Valley have now (post 1992) started to respond more strongly both to the road and to the tram investments. The successful Single Regeneration Budget bid of 1995, for example, played to the strengths and the potential impact of both road and tram investments, following two unsuccessful City Challenge bids. And planning for seven further park-and-ride sites is now taking place (albeit on a fairly opportunistic basis as sites become available).

On both industrial and commercial developments the land use changes and the planning applications show that the road investments are more important than the tram investment. Both forms of investment here had a role however in unlocking sites which previously had poor access. This is particularly true close to junctions which required a major re-design. In this sense, the detail of the routing of both roads and tram has been very important. On householder planning applications there is a negative impact of both the tram and the road corridors, particularly close to the route. There is limited evidence of a pedestrian footfall effect on retailing close by a limited number of the 50 stations on the tram system. There is no direct evidence from the examination of planning applications and of land use changes of a positive impact of the tram on reviving retailing in the city centre. The city centre was hard-hit by recession but especially by the opening of the Meadowhall Shopping Centre in 1991. The tram and related road improvements have been seen as an element in an overall strategy of retail and commercial regeneration.

4. Business Operations

The two company surveys, in 1993 and 1995, do reveal before-and-after effects from both the road and the tram investments. This source of evidence confirms the land use change evidence: of a relatively greater significance of the road investments to the location decisions and to the operations of both commercial and manufacturing businesses.

There are two reasons emerging for this. In a city economy dominated (now, as compared with two decades ago) by smaller businesses, premises to purchase and to lease are more important than sites. Smaller firms frequently experiment with premises, and their perspectives on transport are dominated by road access and road congestion (even though they find it all but impossible to turn these perspectives into cost burdens or cost savings). Secondly, the pattern of new building on released vacant sites includes much development by developers, typically of smaller units to let on relatively short leases, for both industrial and commercial uses. Most units are taken up by relocating businesses from within the local region.

The telephone surveys confirm a further prior expectation: that employers of large numbers of skilled and semi-skilled workers particularly welcomed the new tram system, as widening their labour catchment areas. This was important for both firms in the inner and central city and for the newer suburban 'green field' firms at Mosborough, towards the end of one of the three tram routes. In terms of general operations, the Mosborough firms, however, were the ones to lay great stress on the significance of road improvements in general, and their access to the M1 motorway in particular. To the degree that this widening of labour catchment, and the reduction in road congestion, results in an enhanced competitiveness of Sheffield based enterprises, then the welfare of the Sheffield economy is increased.

5. Labour Market

The ten major employers in the central area of Sheffield who provided employee information recruited between 7 per cent and 8 per cent of their staff from within a 500 m corridor of the Supertram lines in 1994. Analysis of results from 1996 (with data now collected for 8 of the 10 organizations) will confirm whether this proportion has increased as the lines have opened. The percentages compare with an estimate of 14 per cent to 15 per cent of the total population of the city being served by the train corridors.

The initial studies of job-seekers show a clear impact of the Supertram on job search areas, for 10–11 per cent of the respondents, with a concentration of the expansion of the job search areas being along the tram corridors as may be expected.

CONCLUSION

The Sheffield study has demonstrated that in a general sense there are important indirect and non-transport benefits to major investments on transport infrastructure within cities. It has demonstrated that a general picture of these benefits may be built up from a variety of sources of information; and that there are clear linkages with aspects of local urban regeneration programmes. It also demonstrates that development impacts tend not to be well anticipated, either by private sector investors or by public sector agencies; that employment creation claims tend to be optimistic; and that the timing of the flow of related economic development activity is very much dependent upon the state of the national economy.

The Sheffield study also underlines the findings of the Tyne-Wear Metro study and the Manchester Metro-Link study: that quantification of the impacts in any precise way is extremely difficult. Urban road schemes are preconditions for industrial and commercial regeneration where the previous road system had grave inadequacies: they are not generators in their own right. And the non-user and indirect benefits from a tram-system are small, involving more local redistribution of welfare rather than its enhancement. Gains are dominated by benefits to users, facing an increasingly congested urban road system without extensive priority being granted to buses.

REFERENCES

Antwi, A. and Henneberry, J. (1995) The Impact of New Public Transport Infrastructure on House Prices: The Case of the South Yorkshire Supertram. RICS Cutting Edge Annual Conference, University of Aberdeen.

Bateman, I., Turner, R. K. and Bateman, S. (1993) Extending cost-benefit analysis of UK highway proposals: environmental evaluation and capacity. *Project Appraisal*, **8**(4), pp. 213–224.

Berechman, J. (1995) Transport infrastructure investment and economic development, in Banister, D. (ed.) *Transport and Urban Development*. London: E & FN Spon.

Cevero, R. and Landis, J. (1995) Development impacts of urban transport: a US perspective, in Banister, D. (ed.) *Transport and Urban Development*. London: E & FN Spon.

CURDS, TORG and DTCP (1990) The Longer Term Effects of the Tyne-Wear Metro. Report to the Transport and Road Research Laboratory by the Transport Operations Research Group, the Centre for Urban and Regional Development Studies, and the Department of Town and Country Planning, of the University of Newcastle upon Tyne.

Dabinett, G. and Lawless, P. (1994) Urban transport investment and regeneration: researching the impact of South Yorkshire Supertram. *Planning Practice and Research*, **9**(4), pp. 407–414.

Department of the Environment, Department of Transport (1994) *Planning Policy Guidance: Transport*, PPG13. London: HMSO.

Department of Transport (1993) *COBA 9 Manual*. Highways Economics and Traffic Appraisal Division. London: HMSO.

Forrest, D., Glen, J., Grime, K. and Ward, R. (1995) House Price Changes in Greater Manchester 1990–93 and the Impact of Metro Link, Working Paper 16, Department of Geography, University of Salford.

Hay, A. and Haywood, R. (1994) South Yorkshire's Supertram: construction problems of new urban infrastructure. *Local Government Policy Making*, **21**(3), pp. 42–46.

Hill, R. (1995) The Toulouse Metro and South Yorkshire Supertram: A cross-cultural comparison of light rail developments in France and England. *Transport Policy*, **2**(3), pp. 203–216.

Huddleston, J. R. and Pangostra, P. P. (1990) Regional and local economic impacts of transport investments. *Transportation Quarterly*, **44**(4), pp. 579–594.

Lawless, P. and Dabinett, G. (1995) Urban regeneration and transport investment: a research agenda. *Environment and Planning A*, **27**, pp. 1029–1048.

SACTRA (1992) *Assessing the Environmental Impact of Road Schemes*. Standing Advisory Committee on Trunk Road Assessment for the Department of Transport. London: HMSO.

SACTRA (1994) *Trunk Roads and the Generation of Traffic*. Standing Advisory Committee on Trunk Road Assessment for the Department of Transport. London: HMSO.

Townroe, P. M. (1995) The coming of Supertram: The impact of urban rail development in Sheffield, in Banister, D. (ed.) *Transport and Urban Development*. London: E & FN Spon.

Townroe, P. M. and Dabinett, G. (1995) The evaluation of public transport investment within cities. *Annals of Regional Science*, **29**, pp. 175–188.

CONCLUSION

Peter Hall

The challenge for policy is clear enough: like St Augustine, people pray to be made virtuous, but not yet. They increasingly accept the arguments of the environmentalists: that the present and projected levels of traffic will bring serious environmental impacts. But they believe that these arguments apply to everyone but them; and if to them, then not now. Thus they collectively produce a classic case of the medieval tragedy of the commons: acting each to maximize their own interests, they end by committing collective suicide.

The facts are stark. Traffic in the UK rose by 21 per cent in the six years 1985–91. Half this increase was due to more cars on the road, half due to people travelling further. There was a real increase in people's propensity to travel, far more than could be explained by movement out of cities into smaller towns and villages. People support positive improvements like better public transport and pedestrianization, but are opposed to curbs on the car; this spells 'bad news' for policy makers (Taylor and Brook, this volume). They will not act on their own; government will have to cajole them, and that will not be popular. British governments have not demonstrated a very impressive record on this point over the past thirty years; it could take some major event, such as a catastrophe, to goad them into action.

In this regard, the work by Sugden (this volume) is much more significant for policy makers than might at first sight appear. He shows that people's attitudes to restraints vary greatly, according to where they are starting from: the 'reference point', in the jargon. If they already drive a car in a rural area, they would need to be paid a lot of money to give it up. But if they do not yet drive a car, it would not take nearly as much to persuade them not to buy one. The significance is that people's expectations always ratchet upwards, not downwards: once they have access to a car, they will be loath to abandon it. So a principal objective of policy, crudely, is to find ways of persuading them that they do not need to take that critical step, at a time when most households have already taken the plunge.

All this suggests that the right policy would be to initiate a swingeing tax on purchases of new cars: tricky under EU law, unpopular everywhere, and politically disastrous in Sunderland, Burnaston (Derbyshire), Solihull and Swindon. It might also mean even faster increases in petrol duty, constituting one form of a carbon tax; equally difficult without EU agreement, and again highly unpopular. But without such a general basis, other policies – such as urban road pricing – might be less effectual.

Then there is a problem: that the experts themselves are not totally agreed. Most think that traffic should be curbed on the grounds of resource use and pollution. But it is quite possible that within a decade the industry will produce cars that are five times as economic, and (because they might be powered by liquid hydrogen or electricity) far less polluting to boot. What then would be the appropriate policy response? There would still be congestion, perhaps much more congestion, but in turn that might be remedied by the use of information technology to produce automated vehicles, as are now being tried in real-world conditions in California. And then the environmental imperative would be far less evident.

Again: take the question of sustainable urban form. For some of the experts, the only answer is to house many more people in dense urban environments, whether they like it or not. But Headicar and Curtis (this volume) suggest that the resulting reduction in travel would not be very significant: as people move from big dense cities to small less-dense towns they travel more by car, but their journeys are shorter. Within the range of densities that are practicable and realistic (neither Hong Kong, nor Texas), the variation in travel is quite small.

Again: some experts (like Headicar and Curtis in this volume) conclude that peripheral greenfield growth around medium-sized cities is most sustainable; and the recent research of Banister, Watson and Wood (1997) reaches very similar conclusions, particularly that settlements close to motorway interchanges may generate energy-intensive long car trips. But Breheny, Gent and Lock, in their study for the UK government (Breheny, Gent and Lock, 1993) reach a subtly different conclusion: true, urban infilling scores best on transport energy use, and urban extensions score next best; but on overall ranking, based on multiple criteria, urban infill and new communities emerge as the best solutions. There is an interesting qualification here: new communities should be located in quite remote places, distant from major urban centres, to minimize the potential for commuting and other journeys. And there is a qualification: both Headicar and Curtis, and Banister (this volume) also stress that every geographical location is unique, and it is difficult and dangerous to generalize; not much help there for the hapless policy maker.

Size also plays a part in this, as Banister (1997) demonstrates, quoting the Breheny, Gent and Lock study: large settlements have the lowest car dependence, small settlements the greatest, though in all size ranges dependence has grown. Because he believes that new settlements of the right size may prove difficult to build because of local opposition, he opts for additions to existing settlements – even though Breheny et al. found this solution to perform 'moderately'. All this, once again, seems to demonstrate the limitations and uncertainty of our present knowledge – as Banister, Watson and Wood (1997) underline.

What conclusion emerges from this welter of expert evidence, sometimes apparently contradictory? It is first that the planner needs to look at the specific geographical context, and especially at the long-distance motorway and trunk road system, which may provide an incentive to drive (or perhaps, more accurately, the removal of a disincentive). One might cynically conclude that a congested motorway, such as many stretches of the network are becoming, might also prove a disincentive: the free-flowing M40 in North Oxfordshire is rapidly becoming an anomaly in the UK system. Second, the right combination might well be urban infilling, where this proves economically feasible, plus fairly distant new communities, outside regular commuting range of major agglomerations (Hall, 1996; Hall and Ward, 1998). And this could be joined by selective expansion of medium-sized settlements.

But that brings us back to the question of acceptability. Breheny (1997) shows quite clearly that rural people show the highest levels of satisfaction with their area of residence (73 per cent 'very satisfied'), followed in order by rural resident/village centre (68 per cent), suburban/residential (51 per cent) and urban (36 per cent). The same ordering emerges when satisfaction with housing is the criterion, though here the differences are a little less extreme (rural 69 per cent, urban 46 per cent 'very satisfied'). Further, he quotes other work suggesting that most people markedly prefer houses to flats. Breheny concludes that 'the geographical areas and house types that the compaction argument promotes are the very least popular'; (Breheny, 1997, p. 215); people would have to be 'coerced' into living in compact communities. He also shows that employment is decentralizing from cities to rural areas, so that the argument based on shortening distances to urban jobs may be losing some of its force. And there is serious doubt as to whether urban infilling will be physically capable of accommodating as much as 50 per cent of the projected growth of households, the government's target announced in November 1997 (Breheny and Hall, 1996).

Breheny concludes that these arguments do not lead to the conclusion that the compact city is now outmoded; but he does suggest that there is need for a rigorous appraisal of the costs of benefits of different urban forms – including the Social City concept proposed by Breheny and Rookwood (1993). That is surely the only reasonable conclusion. The fact is that, despite a plethora of research in recent years – some of the most significant of which has been reported in this volume – some of the key questions remain open, mainly due to lack of data. Above all, we need more extensive comparison of the transport implications of alternative urban forms in terms of distance, size, access to work and service opportunities, and physical separation. Ideally this would be based on all travel for all purposes, but the data are not yet available at a sufficiently fine-grained scale for sufficiently wide areas. Lacking such complete data, a start can be made on analysing the journey to work, for which full data exist in the decennial Census of Population. And, wherever more comprehensive data exist (or could be collected) for reasonably large areas embracing different kinds of settlement, these too should be analysed. Because critical decisions will need to be taken at both national and local levels about the most sustainable ways to accommodate the 4.4 million additional households expected in England between 1991 and 2016, this research now represents an urgent priority.

REFERENCES

Banister, D. (1997) Reducing the need to travel. *Environment and Planning B,* **24**, pp. 437–449.

Banister, D., Watson, S. and Wood, C. (1997) Sustainable cities: Transport, energy, and urban form. *Environment and Planning B,* **24**, pp. 125–143.

Breheny, M. (1997) Urban compaction: Feasible and acceptable? *Cities,* **14**, pp. 209–218.

Breheny, M., Gent, T. and Lock, D. (1993) *Alternative Development Patterns: New Settlements.* London: HMSO.

Breheny, M. and Hall, P. (eds.) (1996) *The People – Where Will They Go? National Report of the TCPA Regional Inquiry into Housing Need and Provision in England.* London: Town and Country Planning Association.

Breheny, M. and Rookwood, R. (1993) Planning the sustainable city region, in Blowers, A. (ed.) *Planning for a Sustainable Environment.* London: Earthscan, pp. 150–189.

Hall, P. (1996) *The People – Where Will They Go?* (The Denman Lectures, 18). Cambridge: University of Cambridge, Department of Land Economy.

Hall, P. and Ward, C. (1998) *Sociable Cities: The Legacy of Ebenezer Howard.* Chichester: John Wiley.

INDEX